BIOGRAPHY AND SOCIAL EXCLUSION IN EUROPE

Experiences and life journeys

Edited by Prue Chamberlayne, Michael Rustin and Tom Wengraf

with Roswitha Breckner, William Hungerbühler, Elisabeth Ioannidi-Kapolou, Elizabeth Mestheneos, Numa Murard, Martin Peterson, Susanne Rupp, Antonella Spanò, Elisabet Tejero, Birgitta Thorsell and Laura Torrabadella

The POLICY
PRESS

First published in Great Britain in November 2002 by

The Policy Press
34 Tyndall's Park Road
Bristol BS8 1PY
UK

Tel +44 (0)117 954 6800
Fax +44 (0)117 973 7308
e-mail tpp-info@bristol.ac.uk
www.policypress.org.uk

© The Policy Press 2002

British Library Cataloguing in Publication Data

A catalogue record for this book is available from the British Library

ISBN 1 86134 309 4 paperback
A hardcover version of this book is also available

Prue Chamberlayne is Senior Research Fellow in the School of Health and Social Welfare at the Open University, **Michael Rustin** is Professor of Sociology at the University of East London and a Visiting Professor at the Tavistock Clinic and **Tom Wengraf** is Visiting Senior Lecturer in Sociology and Social Research Methods at Middlesex University.

Cover design by Qube Design Associates, Bristol.

Front cover: photograph kindly supplied by www.third-avenue.co.uk

Printed and bound in Great Britain by Bell & Bain Ltd, Glasgow.

Contents

Appendices on method

Abbreviations

BNIM   The Biographical-Narrative Interpretive Method used by Sostris researchers for generating (auto)biographic narratives and then for interpreting the interview material you will find in this book.

In the chapters that follow this common method is variously referred to as 'socioboiographical', biographic-narrative' and sometimes as 'biographic-interpretive'. The names and emphasis may differ; the method is the same.

Sostris   The seven country 'Social strategies in risk society' research projects from which the case material and case discussion embodied in the chapters of this book was taken.

We gratefully acknowledge the funding that enabled this research, under the European Union Targeted Socio-Economic Research Programme 4 on social exclusion – SOE2-CT96-3010. For her lively involvement and ready support, we also thank Fadila Boughanemi at the European Commission.

Acknowledgements

For important and often taxing language editing and translation, the editors wish to thank those who helped them: Jude Bloomfield, Katie Costello, Pierre Marteau, Becky Hall and Jo Lovett, as well as staff at The Policy Press and their freelance copy-editors and proof readers, Stuart Gallagher and Hilary Brown.

Notes on contributors

Roswitha Breckner (roswitha.breckner@wu-wien.ac.at) is a lecturer and researcher at the Institute of General Sociology, Vienna University of Economics and Business Administration. During 1996/97, she was methods consultant for Sostris. Following a biographical approach, her work is based on interpretive sociology and methodology. Her research has focused on East–West migration processes in the context of divided Europe, and on the biographical impact of the Nazi past in Germany and Austria. She is currently working on picture analysis. Her main publication in English to date is *Biographies and the division of Europe. Experience, action and change on the 'Eastern Side'* (co-edited with Devorah Kalekin-Fishman and Ingrid Miethe; Leske & Budrich, 2000).

Prue Chamberlayne (p.m.chamberlayne@open.ac.uk) became interested in biographical methods in the course of a study of caring in East and West Germany and as a means of extending comparative social policy to the informal sphere. She taught for many years at the University of East London, where she was director of the Centre for Biography in Social Policy, and was project coordinator of Sostris. She is now a Senior Research Fellow in the School of Health and Social Welfare at the Open University. Her current research focuses on the use of biographical materials in professional training and evaluation work. She is co-editor of *Welfare and culture in Europe* (Jessica Kingsley, 1999) and *The turn to biographical methods in social science* (Routledge, 2000), and co-author of *Cultures of care: Biographies of carers in Britain and the two Germanies* (Policy Press, 2000). She is co-editor of *Biographical methods and professional practice: An international perspective* (Policy Press, forthcoming).

William Hungerbühler began his academic career in Spain and has also worked as a sociologist for the Science Centre in Berlin (WZB), the Free University, Berlin and the Martin Luther University, Halle-Wittenberg. He has extensive experience in international comparative research with biographical methods. His interests are cultural modernisation, the changing transition to adulthood and Luhmann's systems theory. After working as a project coordinator for a social services company in Berlin, he is now training in communication skills for private organisations. He regularly undertakes reinsertion training for unemployed graduates for the German Labour Office.

Elisabeth Ioannidi-Kapolou (ioanel@otenet.gr) is a sociologist and researcher at the Department of Sociology, National School of Public Health in Athens. She is a member of the SEXTANT research group, and undertook the Greek Sostris research. Her research focuses on sexual behaviour and HIV risk in a cross-national perspective, social exclusion, and migrant and refugee integration. Her most recent publication in English is 'Attitudes towards people with HIV/

AIDS' in N. Bajos, M. Hubert and T. Sandford (eds) *Behaviour and HIV/AIDS in Europe* (with M. Haeder; Taylor and Francis, 1998).

Elizabeth Mestheneos (liz.mestheneos@mail.sextant.gr) studied at the London School of Economics, and Brunel and Kent universities in the UK, and taught sociology at North East London Polytechnic before it became the University of East London. She left England to live in Greece in 1983, working briefly in television production and then as a freelance social researcher and consultant and a member of the SEXTANT research group (www.sextant.gr), now associated with the National School of Public Health. She headed the Greek research team for Sostris. Her research is concerned with social exclusion, older people and family care, and refugee integration in Europe. Her most recent publication is the Greek chapter in I. Philp (ed) *Family care of older people in Europe – COPE*, (with J. Triantafillou; *Biomedical and Health Research*, vol 46, IOS Press, 2001).

Numa Murard (murard@paris7.jussieu.fr) is Professeur de sociologie in Denis Diderot University, Paris. His field of research is social policy with a special interest toward life experienced in poverty, as well as ethics, and the moral, social and political history of popular classes. His main publications include *L'argent des pauvres* (with J.-F. Laé; Le Seuil, 1985), *Citoyenneté et politiques sociales* (with A. Madec; Flammarion, 1995), *La protection sociale* (4th edition, La Découverte, 2002) and 'From welfare to workfare. Ordinary scenes of public policy in a French province', *Ethnography*, vol 3, no 3.

Martin Peterson is an historian with a background in social anthropology and cultural studies. He worked on a Swedish state committee for a new industrial policy in the 1980s and has contributed to the state committee on democracy at the end of the 1990s. During the 1990s he developed a faculty programme on Europe at the University of Gothenburg and worked on a Swedish Research Council committee on European and global affairs. He has participated in four EU projects.

Susanne Rupp (susannerupp@web.de) currently manages a project funded by the EU Social Fund on tackling discrimination and inequality in labour markets in South Hesse (Germany). Her academic specialisation is biographical research with an emphasis on the influence of historical events on biographies. From 1996 to 1998 she joined the British Sostris project as a researcher and as a specialist for questions of method.

Michael Rustin is Professor of Sociology at the University of East London, and a Visiting Professor at the Tavistock Clinic. He was project coordinator of Sostris, with Prue Chamberlayne. His work on clinical and observational methods in psychoanalysis, and on the study of literature from psychoanalytic and sociological perspectives, have informed his interest in socio-biographical methods. He is co-editor of *Welfare and culture in Europe* (Jessica Kingsley, 1999), and a contributor to *The turn to biographical methods in social science* (edited by Chamberlayne et al, Routledge, 2000). His books include *The good society and the inner world: Psychoanalysis, society and culture* (Verso, 1991), *Reason and unreason: Psychoanalysis, science and politics* (Contimuum, 2001), *Narratives of love and loss: Studies in modern children's fiction* (with Margaret Rustin; 2nd edition, Karnac, 2001) and *Mirror to nature: Drama, psychoanalysis and society* (Karnac, 2002).

Antonella Spanò (spano@unina.it) is Professore Associato of Sociology at the Faculty of Sociology, Federico II, University of Naples. Following a biographical approach, she has explored social exclusion, poverty and unemployment in the context of the Italian dualism between the North and the South. Her research is now focused on the biographical effects of active politics for employment. Her published works include *La povertà nella società del rischio. Percorsi di impoverimento nella tarda modernità e approccio biografico* (Franco Angeli, 1999). She is editor of *Tra esclusione e inserimento. Giovani inoccupati a bassa scolatità e politiche del lavoro a Napoli* (Franco Angeli, 2001). Her main publications in English are 'Structural and cultural dimensions of poverty in Italy: the implications for social policies', in P. Chamberlayne, A. Cooper, R. Freeman and M. Rustin (eds) *Welfare and culture in Europe. Towards a new paradigm in social policy* (Jessica Kingsley, 1999) and 'Modernization as lived experience: contrasting case studies from Sostris project' in J. Bornat, P. Chamberlayne and T. Wengraf (eds) *The biographical turn in social science. Comparative issues and examples* (with P. Chamberlayne; Routledge, 2000).

Elisabet Tejero (etejero@eutsb.org) graduated from the Autonomous University of Barcelona with a Masters degree in sociology. Since 1998 she has been teaching 'Social movements' and 'Urbanism and housing' at the School of Social Work, University of Barcelona. Her research focuses on the social impact of urbanistic transformation processes in European and Latin American cities, and on biographical processes of social exclusion, within which she has participated as researcher in Sostris. Her main publications include *El poblenou: Un barri a les portes del segle XXI* (with R. Encinas; Associació de Veïns del Poblenou, 1997), 'Urbanismo: ¿dos disciplinas y un destino?' (with J. Costa; 1999, *Revista de Servicios Sociales y Política Social*, vol 47) and *Mujeres y lucha cotidiana por el bienestar* (with L. Torrabadella and L. Lemkow; Icària, 2001).

Birgitta Thorsell is a sociologist based in Sweden. At the end of the 1970s she led a research project on women and trade unionism, and has subsequently worked on women's issues in rural areas and in relation to unemployment. She has taught social psychology at the University of Gothenburg and elsewhere. She has participated in two EU projects.

Laura Torrabadella (lauratorrabadella@btlink.net) is a sociologist at the Autonomous University of Barcelona. Her academic and professional research focuses on gender, the family, and processes of social inequality from a qualitative approach. In addition to her Sostris activities, she has worked at the Institute of Childhood and the Urban World, Barcelona. She is currently preparing her doctoral thesis on the Spanish feminist movement and processes of memory recollection from a biographical perspective. Her published works include *Mujeres y lucha cotidiana por el bienestar* (with E. Tejero and L. Lemkow; Icària, 2001), 'Family and gender relationships in democratic Spain: cultural change from a biographical perspective', in R. Freeman, M. Rustin and A. Cooper (eds) *Welfare and culture in Europe* (with E. Tejero; Jessica Kingsley, 1999) and 'Familisme i exclusió a l'entorn urbà de Catalunya: una mirada biogràfica' in *Les desigualtats socials a Catalunya* (with E. Tejero; Mediterrània, 1999).

Tom Wengraf (tom.wengraf@cheerful.com) studied history at Oxford University, sociology at the London School of Economics and contemporary cultural studies at the University of Birmingham. Having earlier researched agrarian reform and socialism in independent Algeria, he worked at Middlesex University, researching student experiences – and suffering the staff experience – of higher education. Specialising in interview methodology, he worked on the Sostris project as methodology advisor between 1997 and 1999. He is co-editor of *The turn to biographical method in social science* (with P. Chamberlayne; Routledge, 2000) and this volume. He is currently working on the evaluation of a community development project (Bromley by Bow). In 2001, he published *Qualitative research interviewing: Biographic narrative and semi-structured method* (Sage Publications).

ONE

Introduction: from biography to social policy

Michael Rustin and Prue Chamberlayne

This book describes the life experiences of individuals in contemporary Europe whose lives have been marked by one or more forms of 'social exclusion', as this term has come to be used over the past decade or so (Askonas and Stewart, 2000; Levitas 1998). We try to make meaningful such experiences as being made redundant, being blocked in a career, leaving school without qualifications, finding a place as a migrant in a European country, or bringing up children as a 'single parent'. These were among the life contingencies that had originally led to individuals being selected for our study sample in the Social strategies in risk society (Sostris) research project, upon which this volume is based.

The project's research was undertaken between 1996 and 1999, and was funded by the EU Targeted Socio-Economic Research Programme 4 on Social Exclusion. Its aim was to investigate the experience of individuals who found themselves excluded, or at risk of exclusion, from important spheres of life in their societies. For, of the categories of risk that we chose – early retirement, loss of work for traditional industrial workers, unemployment among graduates, and unemployment among unqualified young adults – all were related to the labour market. This choice reflected widespread concern about unemployment in Europe during the 1990s. The other two categories – single parenthood, and migration or membership of an ethnic minority – highlighted dimensions of gender, race and civic status. Our research was conducted in seven European nations – Britain, France, Germany (in particular the former German Democratic Republic), Greece, Italy, Spain and Sweden. We studied samples of individuals in all of the categories in each nation. Our project team comprised small teams of researchers from each country. The biographical interviews and other data collection were undertaken by the separate national teams, on the basis of agreed protocols. However, analysis of the data, and reflection on its meanings, was guided by regular joint research conferences at which the contextual knowledge and theoretical understanding of the different teams were intensively shared. In the third year, a second phase of the research was devoted to studying examples of 'flagship social agencies' within each country. These were agencies that were developing new practices in working with individuals who were facing problems of social exclusion. The research project drew on other work with which its members were engaged: sociobiographical methods, welfare in contemporary Europe, and the theory of social risk. This book, and the other work associated with it[1], proposes a new approach to social research and social policy in Europe, which begins with the complexity of the individual's experience of change, and the need for policies and practices that are sensitive to this. Further information about Sostris and its methodology is given in Appendices A and B[2].

Biographical studies of individual citizens are a valuable means of exploring the conditions of life in rapidly changing societies. In particular, these studies can illuminate the experiences and problems of *transitions* from one social situation and milieu to another, transitions that are increasingly both expected and demanded of citizens. Our subtitle, 'Experiences and life journeys', signifies the central importance of transitions to our approach, and the view that it is experiences of these that the sociobiographical method is best adapted to describe and analyse. The onset of a 'globalised' economy and deregulated labour markets, substantial migration, and changes in the relations of genders and generations will continue to expose citizens to experiences of transition, which involve risks as well as opportunities. We argue that if adequate provision is to be made for facilitating and preparing citizens for such transitions, there needs to be considerable changes in social policy and practice.

Above all, social policies need to become increasingly sensitive to individual and cultural differences if they are to have a creative rather than a merely disciplinary role in conditions of risk. It is vital that both the complexity of experiences of individuals, and that of the particular cultures in which their lives are embedded, be 'brought back in' to the social sciences. The sociobiographical approach is one way to achieve this.

This chapter introduces Sostris, our research project. It provides a sociological context for the life journeys we later describe, and outlines our sociobiographical method. It explores the implications of our approach for social policy and practice, and proposes the use of biographical methods in social scientific and professional education.

Understanding life journeys

Although the focus of our research programme was on individual 'life journeys', our aim from the start was to explore the connections between these and their larger social contexts. As sociologists, we had in mind Mills' oft-quoted insistence on the public dimensions of private problems, and on the role of social science in exploring these:

> Know that many personal troubles cannot be solved merely as troubles, but must be understood in terms of public issues – and in terms of the problems of history making. Know that the human meaning of public issues must be revealed by relating them to personal troubles – and to the problems of the individual life. Know that the problems of social science, when adequately

formulated, must include both troubles and issues, both biography and history, and the range of their intricate relations. Within that range the life of the individual and the making of societies occur; and within that range the sociological imagination has its chance to make a difference in the quality of human life in our time. (Wright Mills, 1970, p 248)

The defining quality of a sociobiographical approach is, after all, that it is both biographical (concerned with individuals) and sociological (concerned with societies), and one of our first tasks was to establish how these links could be made and developed.

Our primary data consisted of narratives related by individuals, which were focused on life journeys such as those brought about by enforced redundancy or early retirement, by difficulty in entering the labour market after formal education, or by exile and migration. Considering these accounts, we had then to ask what was 'individual' and particular about these stories, and in what ways they represented a more common experience that could be generalised[3].

Two outcomes of our method surprised us. The first was how extraordinarily different from each other were the experiences of our subjects, and how strongly their particularities impressed themselves on our imaginations. The purpose of the sociobiographical approach is to avoid the overgeneralisation and abstraction of many other social research methods, which often reduce individuals to aggregates, averages, or bundles of variables, and which lose sight of the coherence of individual lives. Our method made us think about our subjects as individuals, and see the societies in which they lived from their point of view. The second compelling outcome was the power of the detail of the lives of individuals to generate insights into larger social structures and cultures. Our subjects' descriptions illuminated situations within their societies that were not specific to them alone. Their particular ways of describing their experience – what we call their 'told story' – was often as revealing as the literal facts they described – their 'lived life' – since the told stories made evident the ways of thinking and feeling that a society constructs and normalises for its members. These told stories also brought out areas of difficulty, conflict, inarticulacy and silence in our subjects' experience. Although our subjects were mostly resilient in the face of the hardships they had encountered, many of them had endured considerable pain and loss. We learned about societies not only through our subjects' factual descriptions, but also from the assumptions that framed their accounts, and from the stories of what had happened when their hopes had encountered painful external realities. A society is a shared subjective reality – a patchwork of beliefs, norms and ways of thinking – as well as a set of material facts, such as who owns what, or who exercises power over whom.

Our sociobiographical method sought to capture these dimensions of consciousness and subjectivity, as well as the objective constraints that shape individual lives. We wanted to know how our subjects interpreted their life situations, and what choices they had made in response to them. We aimed to show that our subjects' societies were not only external forces that shaped their lives, but were also in the process of being continually interpreted and made by them. Margaret Thatcher famously said "There is no such thing as society, only individuals and families". Our research shows that the opposite is true: there is no such thing as individuals, only individuals who are related to others, and to the larger social networks, structures and cultures that lie beyond them and function to co-constitute them.

It was only after much deliberation that we named our project 'Social strategies in risk societies'. We approached the life stories of our subjects with the idea that they were likely to be active, self-reflective agents in their own lives. Even though damaging life contingencies often imposed themselves with unexpected suddenness and force, we found that many of our subjects had actively negotiated threats to their wellbeing, and were rarely wholly passive in face of them. Other transitions, such as migration, had usually depended on substantial individual and family commitments. Refugees from war or extreme poverty often have to make desperate decisions and careful plans to escape from them. Those subjects who seemed to have difficulty in finding the words to describe their lives seemed to have been additionally deprived by their inarticulacy. Young people without school qualifications were found to be particularly vulnerable in this respect.

By ascribing 'agency' and 'strategy' to our individual subjects, we were not implying that they should be regarded as 'rational actors' according to the assumptions of economic theory. The concept that individuals can or should calculate the benefits and costs to themselves of every course of action and every decision underpins the rewards-and-punishments model that increasingly dominates post-modern economic and welfare systems. On the contrary, we believe that individuals make life choices in multidimensional ways. They choose courses of action for emotional and moral reasons, as well as for material ones. Our biographical subjects were concerned, in different instances, with questions of dignity and recognition (especially when they were denied respect by the treatment they received); with meaning and satisfaction (for example in their work); and with sustaining relationships. Changes in a work situation often impacted seriously on families, and few decisions could be made that did not have implications for others. We came to see that it was more accurate to describe some individuals' adaptations to their circumstances as 'tactical' rather than 'strategic'[4], where they were highly vulnerable and struggling to live 'one day at a time'.

Transitions can only be made well, and with lessened risk of human damage, where there is social and mental space to think about their implications. 'Reflexivity' is resource-intensive, whether the human resources come from informal networks (family members, friends and colleagues) or from 'formal' resources (teachers, supervisors and managers, counsellors and professional advisers of many kinds). Individuals and institutions will be exposed in future to transitions of greater severity, not least as a consequence of more exposed and 'flexible' market conditions. Furthermore, 'transition-facilitating' policies and practices are going to be increasingly necessary[5]. These require high investment in human resources, since to ensure that adequate reflection takes place during episodes of crisis requires the engagement of mentors or counsellors, formal or informal, with the capacity to engage with experiences emotionally as well as practically. Sociobiographical study should be of value in providing the education and training necessary to develop these human skills (Chamberlayne et al, 2003: forthcoming).

Social theory and social change

Our project's design was influenced by theoretical debates that had been taking place in the preceding years about the development of modern capitalist societies. The 'risks' and experiences of social transition and exclusion studied by Sostris are the outcomes of processes of globalisation and 'marketisation', theorised by social scientists such as Castells, Harvey, Beck and Giddens. Although we are more critical of the market domination of contemporary globalised society than some of the theorists we draw many of our ideas from, our own approach to social policy and practice shares Beck's and Giddens' view that creating greater space for greater 'reflexivity' – rational reflection and informed participation by citizens – is a necessity in this climate of change, both for individuals and for social institutions. We later describe social agencies that attempt to embody such a conception in their everyday practices.

The social context of the experiences of risk and exclusion is the marketisation of societies in the 1980s and 1990s, and the weakening of the earlier institutions and compromises of the postwar welfare state that had earlier provided citizens with substantial measures of social protection. Our case studies reflect these changes, as individuals were placed under pressure to yield higher productivity, experienced the collapse of entire industries or the loss of secure employment, or discovered that the secure and interesting jobs that they had expected to be available when they finished their studies had disappeared, and that they had to return to dependence on their families.

Relevant literature for understanding this transition came from many sources. These included theories describing the transition from 'Fordism' to 'post-Fordism' (Aglietta, 1979; Amin, 1994) and 'the end of organised capitalism' (Lash and Urry, 1987), which analysed how structures of industrial production, class organisation and welfare were being challenged, and displaced by more consumer-oriented and individualised patterns. Also important were Beck's theory of 'risk society' and Giddens' accounts of the development of a globalised and 'individualised' world. There are links between some of the political prescriptions that were advanced by these writers, and our own view of social policy, but there are differences also.

Connected to the idea of globalisation is the theory of 'individualisation', elaborated by Giddens and Beck, which explores the consequences for individual 'life worlds' of such factors as the lessening of social embeddedness, the weakening of boundaries of space and time, and enhanced flows of information. Giddens and Beck both assert the emergence of new possibilities for 'reflexiveness' in these conditions. They argue that reflexivity is more possible and necessary for the social actor as structures and boundaries become weaker. Enhanced and speeded-up communication flows are important catalysts of this new space for reflection and choice.

These concepts of societal transition proved relevant to our study of individual life journeys. Many of our older subjects' working lives had taken shape within the earlier 'Fordist' regime of industrial production and welfare bureaucracies. Some of them were victims of the intensified competition, the decline of industrial work, even the disappearance of entire industries, which marked this transformation. Some discovered that the welfare entitlements they had hoped to count on had become smaller in the tougher welfare regime of the deregulated service economy, and certainly more conditional in nature than they had expected. Husbands or fathers could not adjust to emerging norms of gender equality that their wives or daughters desired. Host societies threw many obstacles in the path of migrants and their children as they sought to build the new lives they or their parents had hoped for. This broad conception of social transition provided a useful frame within which to think about the many individual transitions our subjects described to us[6].

Mobilities and liquidities

Recent work by Urry (2000) and Bauman (2000) has further developed these perspectives. Urry argues for a drastic recasting of the object of sociological study to take account of the processes of globalisation and time–space compression. Instead of taking persisting structures (or societies) as their key object of inquiry, he argues that sociologists should instead study the flows and mobilities of persons, information, symbolic forms, commodities and capitals. Whereas sociological descriptions have until now given greatest prominence to 'social structures', while giving more peripheral attention to the flows and movements between them, Urry argues that the main task in this new environment is to understand flows and movements.

Bauman developed a parallel argument in a subtle way. Whereas early 'modernity' sought with some success to impose new rationalised structures, such as bureaucracies and 'Fordist' modes of production, on societies regulated by tradition and custom, late – or as he prefers to call it, *liquid* – modernity is eroding all settled structures, especially those that depend on the face-to-face engagements of place, and the enclosures of a shared lived time. Bauman argues that, while in early modernity the vagabond, the person of no fixed above, was cast as the enemy of progress (in fact this goes on in the contemporary treatment of refugees and asylum seekers; see Chapter Twelve of this volume), in the present era nomadic identity is becoming the norm.

> The era of unconditional superiority of sedentarism over nomadism, and of the settled over the nomad, is on the whole grinding to a halt. We are witnessing the revenge of nomadism over the principle of territoriality and settlement.

> In the fluid stage of modernity, the settled majority is ruled by the nomadic and extraterritorial elite. (Bauman, 2000, p 13)

In a brilliant insight, he adds that the contemporary global elite is shaped in the pattern of the old-style 'absentee landlords'. These rulers do not feel much need to actively involve themselves in the survival and improvement of their subjects. Sennett (1998) has made a similar point about the fragility and impermanence of modern employment relations compared with a generation ago[7]. Modern employers hold power without responsibility, Sennett says, imposing ever more stringent demands to achieve constantly raised 'outputs', while no longer offering the security and recognition that had become part of earlier relations of production. "Travelling light, rather than holding tightly to things deemed attractive for their reliability and solidity – that is, for their heavy weight, substantiality and unyielding power of resistance – is now the asset of power" (Bauman, 2000, p 3).

Invisible structures of power

It is a mistake, however, to assume that persisting social structures are fading away, simply because networks, flows and mobilities have greater salience. The erosion of spatial and temporal boundedness has negative consequences for many kinds of structure and system, but the global circulation of capital, commodities and information creates new forms of 'invisible structure', deriving from powers whose distinctiveness lies in their transcendence of earlier constraints of time and space. If citizens or states cannot move, but money, capital and information can and do, it is citizens and states who become weaker, and those who control these flows of power and energy who become stronger. The argument of neo-Weberians such as Mann (1986, 1993) and Giddens (1981) that power is increasingly exercised through different modalities, in different frames of time and space, and no longer within the single power container of the nation state, is an illuminating one. However, this does not mean that such powers within modern capitalism are becoming more widely diffused or shared.

Just as some versions of the globalisation theory fail to recognise the new structural constraints that have emerged in this new environment, so the theory of 'individualisation' and 'reflexivity' advanced by Giddens and Beck overstates and idealises the 'disembedding' of individuals from social and cultural settings. Our research shows that individuals usually remain deeply embedded within social networks and relationships, and that they depend on these for their wellbeing. Most changes imposed on individual lives will necessarily affect others close to them. Similarly, 'reflexivity' is rarely an individual accomplishment alone, but depends on the empathetic sharing of experience. Traditional forms of social solidarity, whether based on family, community, or class, have their restrictive limitations to be sure. But our biographical studies often show them to be providing crucial resources for action. New forms of social solidarity need to be evolved in response to more flexible and individualised societies, but this is not to say that social solidarity itself has become obsolete or dispensable. One positive aspect of the concept of 'social exclusion', in contrast to the more individualised and demeaning British concept of 'poverty', is that it recognises disadvantage as a multidimensional social condition, and not merely one of material deprivation. As Turnbull's (1973) frightening study of the Ik showed, the 'fully individualised' person is fully excluded from sources of support, solidarity and social action, entirely on his or her own, fighting the Hobbesian war of all against all. This is a warning image of desocialised individualisation.

Mapping mobile societies with biographical research methods

The sociobiographical method of Sostris is well adapted to the study of mobile and liquid societies. This method (which we developed from Rosenthal and Fischer-Rosenthal's model, see Appendix A) invites subjects to describe their life stories in their own words[8]. In our approach, categorisation and interpretation of subjects' experiences and their social contexts *proceeds from* the production and collection of their own accounts; it does not precede or prestructure them. The methods of data analysis employed are rigorous and multidimensional. Our analysis of a life story gives attention to the chronology of events, the sequence and emphasis given to events by their tellers (each of these two stories – the 'lived' and 'told' life – rarely coincide), and to the 'performative style' in which different events are narrated. We consider narrative texts through line-by-line micro-analysis that enables us to generate and test hypotheses as the text unfolds. These are both conjectures about the meanings that might be implicit in a fragment of narrative, and hypotheses about 'what happened next' in a life story, which the later events in the told story resolve. In this way, we aim to ground our understandings in the evidence given to us, and to move from biographical particulars to their larger sociological context. We search for resemblances and differences between life journeys, as we move between what seems specific to an individual, and what seems to represent a social pattern.

The analysis of biographical life histories is a development of the 'grounded theory' approach (Glaser and Strauss, 1967), which is an inductive process of developing theoretical constructs from qualitative empirical data, then returning interactively to the data to see how much explanatory work these emerging concepts can do. This contrasts with hypothetico-deductive research methods in which hypotheses are first formulated on theoretical grounds and are then tested empirically. The leading practitioners of grounded theory have thrown light on different kinds of social role and process, for example through the idea of status passage applied to such events as divorce and dying. The main weakness of this tradition has been its theoretical 'thinness', a reluctance to make reference in interpretation to the wider context of social structure[9]. In the American symbolic interactionist tradition, Glaser and Strauss (1967) were more sensitive to their subjects' own capacity to generate social meaning than to the structures and cultures that usually constrain this process for most actors. What we try to do is to follow the methodology of inductive inference from particulars established within the grounded theory protocols, but with reference to more 'European' assumptions of structural and cultural constraints.

Taking such constraints into account required us to think about the interactions between subjects and their own contexts of activity, decision making and social survival, as well as in the relations between theory and evidence so firmly grounded within the Glaser and Strauss paradigm. To think about the relations between subjects and their social milieus, we turned to Giddens' structuration theory (Giddens, 1984). The essential idea of structuration theory is that social structures and cultures are continually reproduced through the social action of subjects, and are subject to modification and evolution through the reflexive dimensions of this process. Our biographical method makes it possible for us to study the interaction of subjects, structures and cultures at a detailed micro-level, from the perspective of individuals and their immediate networks. A 'biographical strategy' is constructed from social and cultural 'materials' encountered within the biography. As we witness a biography undergoing elaboration, we are able to take note of its 'external' reference points – the 'elements of the social' that have to be negotiated, internalised, or opposed by individuals – as they make their adjustments to their social environment.

The advantage of our life-history method from this point of view is that it enables us to track the process of 'structuration' as it takes place within an individual's life. One interpretative problem involves discerning the relevant segments of social structure and culture from the life-history narrative that are 'in play' in a given case. That is, both the specific context that is shaping a life, and the social spaces being remade, or reinvented, by an individual in their life career. One might also add the problem of discerning *when* a segment of 'structure' is encountered and engaged with by an individual[10].

In short, then, we brought to our biographical narratives all the theoretical and contextual knowledge we could call to mind, in an interactive process of interpretation. We found that our understanding of apparently unfamiliar societies was greater than we had anticipated. Even 'unknown countries' were suddenly illuminated in the minds of investigators, when a pattern emerged linking apparently contingent facts. Comparison of cases was often the catalyst for identifying differences of context, both in discussion and in writing up. It was very important to the analytic process that investigators from each national team came together in the periodic cross-Europe workshops to debate these interpretations. Indeed, it was often the result of dysjunctions between the 'taken for granted' social phenomena and the national assumptions of different participants that these moments of insight occurred.

The biographical interpretative method is like other life-history methods: it is primarily interested in processes of change in individual lives over sequences of time. However, it complements the interest in personal narratives of other life-history methods with a commitment to locate individual biographies in contexts defined in sociological terms. It seeks above all to identify the 'representative' features in an individual's life trajectory, the respects in which a life situation, or a pattern of action, are similar to or different from others of their kind. This method moves continually between the individual life world and the social configuration that both produces it, and is reproduced by it. This method provides a means of studying the processes that Giddens has called 'structuration', as it has happened in the recollection of subjects. This method recognises the relevance of both the point of view of the subject, in constructing descriptions and models of social life, and of the point of view of the researcher. It seeks to bring both of these together, interpreting the details of individual life narratives through the lens of sociological conceptualisation, and rethinking these conceptualisations through their capacity to grasp and make sense of these narratives.

We contend that social biographies of individual subjects provide a valuable means of investigating and mapping the social contexts in which they have lived, and through which they have moved in societies of mobility. Individual life journeys can be viewed as luminous 'traces' of the social elements through which they pass. These are rendered visible through the subjects they have formed. Segments of narrative produced by subjects can be interpreted within broader patterns of thinking on which they draw. In this way the larger social discourses that have given meaning to different phases of a life journey can be identified and described by researchers. Memories of a transition between life in one time and space and a new life in another can illuminate both these settings, and what it means to make a life journey between them[12]. Our project has used the sociobiographical method to study experiences of social exclusion in modern Europe. We are convinced that this method could have many other fertile applications.

Social policy and practice in risk societies

Some social theorists of globalisation and individualisation, as well as the transition to 'risk society', (Beck 1992, 1997), have also become advisers to those who are trying to manage this process politically. Foremost among these is Anthony Giddens, leading academic theorist of New Labour's 'Third Way' in Britain. This programme argues that the collectivism and statism of the industrial era are now both obsolete and irrelevant. Instead, the role of the state must change to enable citizens to adapt to the demands of flexible markets, and to instil the reflexive and autonomous capacities that they will need in this new context. Although this 'Third Way' originated in the US with Clinton's 'New Democrats', and in Britain with New Labour, its ideas and approaches have been influential throughout Europe. More important, perhaps, is that the situation it responds to and promotes – one of greater competitive pressures and the enforcement by markets of greater 'flexibility' – is presented as an inescapable reality. Margaret Thatcher's conviction that 'there is no alternative' has been quite persuasive, and her Labour successors have followed many of her examples.

Therefore, 'capacity building' replaces 'welfare' as the object of social policy. Social assistance becomes more conditional on flexibility; that is, the acceptance of worsening conditions for labour – and individual self-development. An ethos of self-help, of Samuel Smiles, is combined with energetic programmes of counselling and retraining, to help 'prostrated' individuals get back on their own feet. Focus groups, which are an instrumental approach to the involvement of citizens in policy making, have been adopted as an alternative to the traditional forms of deliberation in party meetings. Governments have abandoned 'social guarantees' because they are convinced that they cannot be afforded, or that they are disincentives, or that they will drive away foreign investment. This is why these new approaches to social policy are so pervasive in Europe and elsewhere, though resistance to them remains significant in some countries[13].

The theory of 'risk society' suggests that enhanced 'reflexivity' is a necessary concomitant of the social environment that faces individuals in risk society, since it offers a better survival strategy than collective identification and affiliation. As individuals become more exposed to changes in their lives, with the disappearance of 'jobs for life', the insistence on flexibility, and the demand for repeated retraining, reflexive self-monitoring and individualised life strategies become necessities for survival. This has become a guiding norm of the new social order, a new kind of 'governmentality' in Foucauldian terms[14]. In education, the demand for curricula that result in greater employability, and for student development of a portfolio of certified competencies, has become influential. Unemployment benefits are made conditional on counselling, job searching and retraining.

Several of the social agencies we investigated reflect in their practices these increasingly individualised and self-active conceptions of welfare. Some are innovative and idealistic, a reaction against the demeaning aspects of bureaucratic forms of welfare, and are seeking to empower both individuals and communities. Others are more compromised by the minimalist and punitive aspects of government agendas. Many of them function in a semi-independent relation to the state, usually supported by one or other of its branches, but outside its statutory and bureaucratic domains. Agencies such as these are the means by which the postmodern state tries out its new forms of social intervention and regulation, though they can also enable new social movements to explore counter-possibilities. Governments have sought, therefore, to respond to the societal transition that we have described, and changes in policy and practice are taking place that respond to these new contingencies and risks.

Such changes are, of course, far from total. Rather, through them we see existing welfare and cultural structures being reinvented – perhaps we can speak of restructuring at the institutional level. Unlike much comparative social policy, our book does not use welfare regimes as its principal organising categories. Nor do the case studies provide many examples of direct negotiations with welfare personnel. The argument that welfare structures are therefore unimportant is refuted at every turn, however, through constant references to the ways in which lives have been assisted or blighted by the presence or absence of adequate support systems. The biographical case studies that form the core of this book demonstrate that the scope of social policy needs to be expanded in at least three directions. They indicate a need for greater 'depth', by pointing to the social and personal energy involved in daily individual accommodations to processes of social transformation. They suggest a greater 'breadth' in the approach by pointing to the wealth of human and civic resources that could be more fully used by an enabling state. They also point vividly upwards to the absence of supportive political scripts amid ruthless, market-driven processes of global social change.

Debates on 'Social Europe' and key actions within EU Targeted Socio-Economic Research programmes abound with references to active citizenship and moral agency, to social capital and cultural difference, and to governance and new political forms. Participating projects span the levels of subjective experience, informal cultural resources and global pressures (see, for example, Castles, 2001). Yet policy-making channels and service and insurance institutions remain structured around labour market assumptions and concerns, which impede holistic views of social change. Furthermore, global financial legislation, rarely glimpsed in social policy, is rapidly prescribing more stringent market conditions on social welfare. It is such that privatisation is sweeping across Europe in the domain of public services as the World Trade Organisation programme gathers force, especially in the form of the General Agreement on Trade in Services, a rolling programme for commodifying the public sphere. The gap between the values of the European 'social' model of welfare and its underlying economic structures is widening by the day. The danger is that even research on the scale of the EU's Framework 4 and 5 programmes is reduced to a fig-leaf for neoliberalism and global deregulation.

While our case studies amply convey the social catastrophes wreaked and threatened by neoliberalism, they also point towards increasingly positive possibilities, based on more dialogical forms of solidarity, in which individuality is enhanced by mutuality.

Again and again our case studies highlight the extraordinary pace and extent of social change, and the amount of biographical work necessary to accommodate the (apparently) individualised circumstances of risk society. The less support and direction that public institutions provide, the more individuals are thrown on their own resources. The paradox is that the individually experienced situation is not at all 'individual', but collectively produced, and it is this more holistic view which is missing from both politics and social policy.

The strikingly devastating absence of collective forms of social integration emerges from comparing the life journeys of older workers and younger age groups. Earlier generations of men achieved their rites of passage to adulthood through workplace forms of discipline and solidarity. As Spanò says (in Chapter Four of this volume), the fact that the labour movement struggled so bravely to reduce hours of work should not detract from the recognition that the same generation also built its identity on self-realisation through work. Older workers' narratives are testimony to the ways in which even the most isolated individuals with backgrounds of neglect or violence achieved a sense of social belonging and attachment through intergenerational and peer relationships at work. While many such formative experiences emerged from peer camaraderie and union structures, they also involved dependable, though often antagonistic, relationships with management. In manual occupations, work relationships often entailed close physicality as well as emotional and moral challenge. The global and local intensification of unemployment leads to a loss of these structures. Such a loss is devastating for older workers, but the consequences of their total absence for present-day youths are more serious still[15].

The family is no longer a reliable mechanism of social integration. Our Spanish case studies highlight the disastrous effects on a younger generation, which, growing up with expectations of early independence and upward mobility, is suddenly finding itself thrown back on family dependencies. The chapter on transculturalism shows second-generation immigrants having to devise flexible strategies that clash with their parents' strategies of protective closure. In the case of lone parents, we found many young women struggling to achieve new skills of partnership negotiation against multigenerational patterns of gender segregation, whether for cultural reasons, war, death or separation. The area in which we felt lone parents wanted most help was working out partnership issues. This area is one that is largely absent from the design of welfare services, which therefore do little to lessen the isolation they claim to deplore.

Members of all six of our social categories had to flexibly adjust their aspirations and resources to find new footholds and opportunities, in ways that needed both public and private resources. Constant innovation was not a skill in great demand in traditional industrial society. Previously, an underground train driver with a broken family life and low educational levels might enjoy his job precisely because it required few social skills. Furthermore, he might still derive a sense of public esteem and belonging from working for a public service. For such a person, being thrown back by redundancy onto the private sphere can be disastrous.

Defending and rebrokering the private sphere, and identifying new opportunities and resources, require an immense amount of emotional and reflexive energy, and usually a moratorium during which adjustments can be worked through. Partnership difficulties are commonly involved. In older age groups this crisis often takes the form of illness, which might occur before, during or after the point of severance from work. In the younger age groups it took the form of opting out of school or training and 'messing about', taking an extra year at university or taking a considerable time after graduation to find a viable way forward, or to adjust to disappointed hopes.

The moratorium that characterises the life journeys of so many of our cases suggests that the capacity to be reflexive and the heightened adaptability to the labour market that reflexivity can promote are not 'natural' at all, but are slowly and painfully acquired. In nearly all cases, achieving a satisfactory solution in terms of meaningful activities and relationships requires a major improvement in social skills, which is something that can be aided by mentoring. Mentoring implies advice and example from an older or more experienced person, offered in a context of personal attentiveness and friendship. It presupposes openness on the part of the recipient – a quality that requires a capacity for trust. Mentoring inspires and spreads social confidence. It is therefore a springboard for networking, which can support the 'horizontal' relationships of civil society to which Putnam (2000) attributes civic competence.

The transitions from school to university and from each to work are predictable life passages in our society. However, the biographies of the unemployed graduates in our sample revealed that few of them seem to have received much support in thinking about their prospective transition from university to employment. Courses are often designed with little regard to their relevance to work. The idea that students should be encouraged to reflect while they are students on this crucial transition still seems foreign to much of the higher education system. If education–work transitions are so little attended to by professionals in institutions whose task it is to prepare young people for adult life, what can be expected of transitions where adults are conventionally expected to take responsibility entirely for themselves?

And what about outside the schools? In her review of six youth development projects in the US, Rauner (2000) gives a moving account of the long-running struggles to establish attentive and responsive relationships between staff and 'kind of scary' youths, and of the successful forms of social engagement that are achieved by doing so. She argues that many youths could benefit from more proactive efforts to connect them with caring adults (Rauner, 2000, p 77)[16].

It is a moot point whether statutory services can generate these kinds of relationships, or whether they require a wider change in societal values and social processes. Rauner reaches the depressing conclusion that quality personal relationships are not compatible with statutory services. Young people respond to staff for *how* they are rather than for their professional personae – *who* they are. The voluntary dimension of the agencies she studies is positive from this point of view. Statutory services are often associated with legal compulsion rather than personal choice, their insistence on measurable outcomes clashes with uncertain and 'messy' processes, and their specialised briefs preclude a holistic view. However, the work of professional staff in many agencies providing human services, for example, schools, colleges and health centres, suggests that Rauner's gloom about the public sphere may be excessive.

The agencies that were considered by Sostris to be innovative in tackling social exclusion shared many of the features of these radical American projects. Invariably, they centred on quality mentoring and/or networking relationships, and did not lend themselves to audit measures. Instead of treating individuals as static cases, a focus on collective experience allows a dynamic notion of trajectory, of evolution. Projects such as these provide residents with relational, emotional, even political space, which goes beyond material and psychological needs, and occupies a different terrain from the individualising benefit approach within mainstream social services. They break with the ethic of voluntarism, prioritising instead social reciprocity and instrumentality. Chapter Fourteen on agencies takes this further.

It is clear that quality relational work and networking demand generous and flexible amounts of time. In a keynote speech at the British Sostris policy meeting (Institute for Public Policy Research, February 2000), Andrew Cooper defined the role of government as "not to provide programmes, or solutions, but conditions in which creative and disruptive activity directed at positive change can be stimulated and guided". He sees the audit and regulation explosion as a hopeless and desperate move by administrators, managers and politicians to retain control over complex and accelerating processes of social change. Lower-level organisations need to be given space to take risks and act on their own initiatives.

Political scripts

In *Liquid modernity* (2000), Bauman argues that the public *agora* of debate and negotiation between the individual and common, private and public good, has become empty, and urgently needs rebuilding. Biographical methods have a role to play in closing this gap, which is often also a time lag, between social theory and social policy. They also offer the means to explore the discrepancies that he points to between the de jure and de facto status of individual lives – the supposed scope for self-determination as against the very 'unfree' quality of actual lives. He says that the key to human emancipation lies in relearning forgotten citizenship skills and reappropriating lost citizenship tools, though this must be done in new and more generous ways than before (Bauman, 2000, p 41). He is surely suggesting a new kind of politics, one in which people would be recognised as *who* they are rather than *what* they are. Cavarero (2000, p 21) points to the similarity between such personal recognition and Arendt's idea of politics as an interactive scene or scenes in which human beings appear to each other not as objects, but as subjects *acting* with words and deeds.

Many of our case studies showed individuals struggling personally, without any sense of social support, in what were actually collective situations. We have spoken of individual and network mentoring, but political discourse also plays a vital levering role in social change – think of the vociferous and creative political thinking, writing and speaking that took place during the period of postwar reconstruction, in the national independence movements, in the new social movements, or in the early stages of industrialisation. One reason for the silence, as Norman Geras put it in a speech at the conference 'The politics of welfare' (Tavistock Clinic, March 2000), is that we have lost our utopian nerve, even though good enough utopias might do very well.

In this situation, researchers have the opportunity and responsibility to become mediators. In *Pedagogy of the oppressed*, Freire writes of the "true words, with which men transform the world. To exist, humanly, is to *name* the world, to change it" (1970, p 76, quoted in Rauner, 2000, p 4). As Rauner comments, 'naming' helps to bring about deliberate action in coordination with others.

Biographical material provides for the possibility of this kind of mediation. Our presentation of such material in this book, and its 'naming' (through description and theorisation), is a contribution towards such shared projects.

Biographical case studies are a new kind of research output that could play a useful role in social policy and political developments, and that suggests a different relationship between social science and society. However, it is not always easy to find an appropriate social policy and political language. Biographies, the analysis of narrated lives, can reconcile the depth and complexity of individual experience with social and political situatedness. This corresponds with our argument that social policy needs to expand into the realm of emotion and personal meaning (the inner dynamics of inclusion and exclusion), out to networks and wider social resources, and upwards to the policy-making process.

Case studies in teaching and learning

The core of this book lies in its case studies, both of individuals in their various life journeys, as we describe them, and of innovative social agencies that are working with individuals in situations of risk and transition. In some fields, such as social work, and in management education, case studies have long been used as the basis of problem- and enquiry-based learning (Savin-Baden, 2000). In this book we demonstrate their use as a learning resource. We seek to show how they can engage our imaginations, enabling us to appreciate the complexity of social experience through the comparative analysis of life stories. By starting at the level of everyday lives, case studies evoke emotional identification and enlist every individual's own personal experiences as relevant comparative data. Case studies allow us to bring our own social knowledge to bear on our reading and interpretation, so that from the start we are engaged in a dialogue. As the case studies and comparisons between them develop, we can be led on to appreciate the need for comparative concepts and institutional descriptors, which come to life through the case-study examples. For students, case-study methods enable them to enter into active dialogue with the material, with each other, and with their teachers[17].

Learning from detailed examples of complex situations has been especially important in the areas of professional education where reflexiveness and autonomy among practitioners is valued[18]. Since psychoanalytic psychotherapy depends on response by practitioners to unstructured and uncertain situations, their professional education also relies on case examples. Through the understanding of complex encounters involving aspects of the self as well as the client, trainees build a conceptual and emotional resourcefulness that can be deployed in new situations. These vocational disciplines take the complexity of individual experience seriously, and hold that good practice depends on a capacity to engage with individuals' states of mind and feeling. Learning to observe, listen and think is critical in working in complex human environments.

The evidence of our study is that we are all now living in such environments. We propose a way of understanding contemporary society through study of the experiences of individuals within it. Without this dimension, sociological knowledge will be abstract and empty of meaning, and social policy will be inadequate or even destructive. We argue for a social policy and practice that are responsive to individuals' situations and enable them to mobilise their own aspirations and resources for change. We suggest that sociobiographical methods are relevant not only for developing the knowledge base necessary for appropriate social action, but also in educating and training social actors and citizens. Education in sociology and social policy in contemporary societies requires giving more attention to individuals, enabling students to see the ways in which they are both made by, and make, the societies and social networks they inhabit.

By focusing on individual case studies and detailing our process of interpretation, we hope to generate in the reader the process of creative emotional and imaginative identification that, as we have already described, contributes so importantly to thinking. Learning from the book will be enriched if this helps students to become aware of, and reflect on, their own emotional responses to the life journeys we present, and to the interpretations we have made. We hope to promote in the reader an interactive process comparable to that played out in the interviews and in our interpretative process, moving to and fro between reflection on individuals and on the structures and cultures that frame their lives, and leading also to increasing engagement with concepts within social theory and approaches to social policy.

Notes

[1] See, for example, Chamberlayne, Bornat and Wengraf (2000); Chamberlayne, Cooper, Freeman and Rustin (1999); Wengraf (2001); Chamberlayne and King (2000).

[2] The Sostris Project published nine working papers and a final report, available from the School of Social Sciences, University of East London (www.uel.ac.uk/bisp).

[3] Wengraf's appendix on research methods discusses problems of generalising from single cases.

[4] This distinction is made by Murard in Chapter Three of this volume.

[5] This concept of 'transition-facilitating' practice had been adapted from a different context, namely the observation of nursing practice in a neonatal ward, where in the critical condition in which the premature babies live, attention to the everyday transitions of their lives is of great importance in ensuring adequate containing care. This idea has a suggestive application to much larger social settings. For the original concept, see Sorensen (2000).

[6] The EU's research programme into social exclusion reflected the concern of the European Commission, during Jacques Delors' presidency, for the consequences of these transitions. This was, of course, the context of our project.

[7] One of his research subjects was the successful, mobile and rootless son of one of the subjects of his earlier book, *The hidden injuries of class* (1972), who had lived a life of bounded endurance, sacrifice and meaning.

[8] See Appendix B on methods and Wengraf (2001) on method for further discussion. Layder's (1998) observations on the unduly 'micro-social' focus of Glaser's and Strauss's approach are useful.

[9] Our approach to grounded theory is discussed further in Appendix B.

[10] Appendix B discusses Archer's (1995) recasting of structuration theory within a temporal dimension, which is important for sociobiographical studies. She points out that structures change in response to actions upon them, in a complex process of interaction situated in time. Sociobiographical methods provide a resource for exploring such interactions, since they report individuals' engagement with their social contexts, and their own adaptive or transformative strategies in interaction with them, over periods of time, sometimes prolonged.

[11] On the methods of part–whole analysis, see Scheff (1997).

[12] Some leading practitioners of biographical methods in sociology – such as Bertaux and Thompson (1997) – have argued that such methods are most illuminating when used to investigate the life histories of more than one generation in a family. This extension from the isolated individual case study is valuable because the similarities and contrasts between the experiences of members of different generations of a family are inherently likely to illuminate changes over time. This is both because of differences evident in the investigating social sciences, and differences of experience that will be articulated by subjects themselves. Such biographies of more than one member of the same family also allow a measure of triangulation, thereby avoiding some of the problems of the unknowable representation of small samples of individuals.

[13] Hutton (2002) recently published a powerful polemic, *The world we are in* (2002), in defence of the 'European model' of social capitalism, as opposed to the Anglo-Saxon one.

[14] One effect of this is that individuals are encouraged to blame themselves and their limitations for their problems, and seek individual solutions to them, rather than finding collective explanations and remedies.

[15] The only substitute seems to be in sport, but that quickly evaporates, however, through deselection at professional level.

[16] A longitudinal study, conducted among the Kauai in North America, associated resilience to adverse circumstances with a wide network of adult connections outside the family, continuity in the life course, and 'school-connectedness' (Werner, 1992). These 'protective factors' compensated for the vulnerabilities arising from invidious family circumstances.

[17] All too often, traditional teaching delays the point at which students can enter into such dialogue, because it takes time for philosophical and historical concepts to acquire meaning and familiarity. By that stage, disempowering learning hierarchies have become established.

[18] Schön's 'reflective practitioner' concept (Schön, 1983, 1987) is one influential formulation. See also Flecha (2000) on dialogic learning.

References

Aglietta, M. (1979) *A theory of capitalist regulation: The US experience*, London: Verso.

Amin, A. (ed) (1994) *Post-Fordism: A reader*, Oxford: Blackwell.

Archer, M.S. (1995) *Realist social theory: The morphogenetic approach*, Cambridge: Cambridge University Press.

Askonas, P. and Stewart, A. (eds) (2000) *Social exclusion: Possibilities and tensions*, Basingstoke: Macmillan.

Bauman, Z. (2000) *Liquid modernity*, Cambridge: Polity Press.

Beck, U. (1992) *Risk society*, London: Sage Publications.

Beck, U. (1997) *The reinvention of politics*, Cambridge: Polity Press.

Bertaux, D. and Thompson, P. (eds) (1998) *Pathways to social mobility*, Cambridge: Cambridge University Press.

Castles, F., Rogers, A., Vasta, E. and Vertovec, S. (2001) *Assessment of research reports carried out under the European Commission Targeted Socio-Economic Research (TSER) Programme*, Oxford: Centre for Migration and Policy Research, University of Oxford.

Castells, M. (1996) *The Information Age: Economy, society and culture*, 3 vols (Vol 1: *The rise of the network society*, Vol 2: *The power of identity*, Vol 3: *The end of millennium*), Oxford: Blackwell.

Cavarero, A. (2000) *Relating narratives: Storytelling and selfhood*, Routledge: London.

Chamberlayne, P. and King, A. (2000) *Cultures of care: Biographies of carers in Britain and the two Germanies*, Bristol: Policy Press.

Chamberlayne, P. and Rustin, M. (1999) *Sostris Working Paper 9: Sostris final report – From biography to social policy*, London: Centre for Biography in Social Policy, University of East London.

Chamberlayne, P., Apitzsch, U. and Bornat, J. (2003: forthcoming) *Biographical methods and professional practice: An international perspective*, Bristol: The Policy Press.

Chamberlayne, P., Bornat, J. and Wengraf, T. (2000) *The turn to biographical methods in social science*, London: Taylor Francis/Routledge.

Chamberlayne, P., Cooper, A., Freeman, R. and Rustin, M. (eds) (1999) *Welfare and culture in Europe: Towards a new paradigm in social policy*, London: Jessica Kingsley.

Flecha, R. (2000) *Sharing words: Theory and practice of dialogic learning*, Lanham: Rowman and Littlefield.

Freire, P. (1970) *Pedagogy of the oppressed*, New York, NY: Seabury Press.

Giddens, A. (1998) *The Third Way: The renewal of social democracy*, Cambridge: Polity Press.

Giddens, A. (1994) *Beyond Left and Right: The future of radical politics*, Cambridge: Polity Press.

Giddens, A. (1984) *The constitution of society*, Cambridge: Polity Press.

Giddens, A. (1981) *A contemporary critique of historical materialism*, Basingstoke: Macmillan.

Glaser, B.G. and Strauss, A. (1967) *The discovery of grounded theory*, Chicago, IL: Aldine.

Hutton, W. (2002) *The world we are in*, London: Little, Brown.

Lash, S. and Urry, J. (1987) *The end of organised capitalism*, Cambridge: Polity Press.

Layder, D. (1998) *Sociological practice: Linking theory and social research*, London: Sage Publications.

Levitas, R. (1998) *The inclusive society? Social exclusion and New Labour*, Basingstoke: Macmillan.

Mann, M. (1986) *The sources of social power. Vol 1: History of power from the beginning to AD 1760*, Cambridge: Cambridge University Press.

Mann, M. (1993) *The sources of social power. Vol 2: The rise of classes and nation states 1760-1914*, Cambridge: Cambridge University Press.

Mills, C.W. (1970) *The sociological imagination*, Harmondsworth: Penguin.

Morgan, H. (1998) 'Looking for the crevices: consultation in the mental health service', *Soundings*, no 8 (Spring), pp 171-83.

Piore, M.J. and Sabel, C.F. (1984) *The second industrial divide*, New York, NY: Basic Books.

Putnam, R.D. (2000) *Bowling alone*, New York, NY: Simon and Schuster.

Rauner, D.M. (2000) *'They still pick me up when I fall'. The role of caring in youth development and community life*, New York, NY: Columbia University Press.

Savin-Baden, M. (2000) *Problem-based learning in higher education: Untold stories*, Buckingham: Open University Press.

Scheff, T.S. (1997) *Emotions, the social bond, and human reality*, Cambridge: Cambridge University Press.

Schön, D. (1987) *Educating the reflective practitioner*, London: Jossey-Bass.

Schön, D. (1983) *The reflective practitioner: How professionals think in action*, New York: Basic Books.

Sennett, R. (1998) *The Corrosion of character*, New York, NY: Norton.

Sennett, R. and Cobb, J. (1972) *The hidden injuries of class*, Cambridge: Cambridge University Press.

Sorensen, P.B. (2000) 'Observations of transition-seeking behaviour – developmental and theoretical implications', *International Journal of Infant Observation*, vol 3, no 2.

Turnbull, C.M. (1973) *The mountain people*, London: Cape.

Urry, J. (2000) *Sociology beyond societies: Mobilities for the twenty-first century*, London: Routledge.

Wengraf, T. (2001) *Qualitative research interviewing: Biographic narrative and semi-structured method*, London: Sage Publications.

Werner, E. and Smith, R. (1992) *Overcoming the odds: High risk children from birth to adulthood*, Ithaca, NY: Cornell University.

TWO

Suffering the fall of the Berlin Wall: blocked journeys in Spain and Germany

William Hungerbühler, Elisabet Tejero and Laura Torrabadella

Introduction

The research work carried out by Sostris was based on the shared assumption that our subjects were active and resourceful individuals dealing with all kinds of challenges. This chapter puts this basic assumption to the test. Nicolás from Catalonia and Heike from eastern Germany, two well-educated young adults who, geographically speaking, happen to live at opposite ends of the EU, have both come to a dead end in their life journeys – a 'biographical blockage'. Although we found it demanding enough to try to understand the processes that brought these two young people to this point, we also wanted to find out how they have coped and where they might go from here. Finally, we were also intrigued to find out whether the profound and rapid social changes that both their (otherwise very different) home countries – Spain and Germany – have experienced in the recent past had any tangible bearing on their personal situation.

We belong to our interviewees' generation, and have shared similar educational paths. For us, Heike's and Nicolás' trajectories are disconcerting: potentially, they mirror and contrast with our own biographical paths. We trust that this 'subjective involvement' has not distorted the outcomes of our inquiry but has served an indispensable role in the exploration of the social (Ibañez, 1994).

'Biographical blockage', and peoples' experience of it

We contend that the exploration of the interrelation of historical, social and personal dynamics can best be achieved by listening to the voices of the individuals involved. Here, these are people who, in spite of their youth, or indeed because of it, seem to be immobilised or stuck in their current situation without a future that appears accessible or meaningful to them – a situation that we have called 'biographical blockage'. We understand that 'biographical blockage' cannot primarily be defined by objective criteria; for example, both our subjects work full time. Rather, it is constituted by subjective experience. Since these experiences are woven into a wider social context, their analysis yields insights that have a far wider relevance than the individual cases studied.

This chapter aims to raise the profile of the relatively invisible phenomenon of 'biographical blockage' and to contribute to a better understanding of it. Above all, this requires elucidating the experiences that give rise to it, and highlighting the social contexts in which it emerges. Each of our cases are projected against a background of recent, far-reaching and rapid social transformation. We ask whether this has contributed to their current situation of 'biographical blockage' and, if so, how?

Nicolás

'I have neither great ambitions nor dreams'

Nicolás was 32 years old when we interviewed him. He was born into a family of working-class origin. His grandparents had migrated to Barcelona during the Spanish Civil War. His father, who was about to retire, was a white-collar worker in a steel factory; his mother was a housewife. With his parents and his elder sister, Nicolás has always lived in a working-class suburb near Barcelona. While studying economics, Nicolás became an active member of the Communist Party, which he left in 1990, some time after graduating. Within or outside the party, he has never ceased attending church with his parents. As a student, he took temporary employment in various firms, and continued to do so after graduating. That was still his situation when the interview took place. Nicolás has a girlfriend whom he has been dating for four years.

Nicolás' biographical trajectory is quite common among young graduates in Catalonia. He belongs to a vast second generation of internal migrants who, in contrast to their parents, have had access to higher education, but who are now experiencing the precariousness of the labour market. His years as a politically active member of the Communist Party set him apart, and that is what attracted our attention. On the one hand, his life journey may not be as exceptional as it seems, if we take into account his working-class origins. However, given that there is no tradition of active political involvement in his family, it is, in fact, quite exceptional. The general lack of political activism among young people during the 1980s only adds to making this a surprising course of action. What motivated this course of action?

A second issue – one that will not surprise anybody familiar with the Spanish context – is that Nicolás is still living with his parents, at the age of 30, despite a relationship with his girlfriend that has been going on for years. From a comparative perspective, this may be worth looking into more closely.

Other than these exceptions, Nicolás' biographical journey corresponded, up to that point, with the social script laid down for people of his background and generation. He had reproduced the social and familial aspirations for upward mobility through higher education. His decision to study economics might appear to be perfectly in line with the interests of a rather idealistic person, adhering to Marxist ideology. However, it may just as easily point to a rather instrumental, career-minded strategy, corresponding to his own, or to his parents', desire to secure a good start for himself in the labour market. Fortunately, Nicolás' own assessment is unambiguous:

> Economics was the most pragmatic option I had. I thought I would have more professional opportunities this way, and prestige. I've now realised this was a silly thing to think.... It is also a rather easy-going career; everybody can make it. There were other studies, such as journalism for example, that I was more interested in, that I would have liked better. In hindsight, I regret this now.

We have, therefore, reached a point where we can safely expect friction to occur sooner or later between Nicolás' 'praxis' – an utterly pragmatic choice to study economics – and his idealistic ideas. It will be interesting to see whether he chose to revise his half-hearted professional choice or to adapt his ideas, or whether he found some other solution. It was only in his third year at university that these frictions manifested themselves. Nicolás was about to abandon his career:

> I was about to leave during the third year, but, since, with a lot of effort, I had gone half of the way, I didn't feel like abandoning it.

He solved this problem by further affirming his pragmatic side and his life journey – he did not want to lose the time and effort invested, albeit clearly recognising, by that time, that he did not like what he was doing. He even managed to reconcile this most pragmatic, utilitarian 'strategy' of his with his 'idealistic self'. Finding a normative justification for it, he transformed it once again into an act of higher value: "I didn't feel like abandoning it. For me finishing something you don't like is important".

The effect of this sophisticated manoeuvre, and the price he has paid for it, has been even deeper confusion about who he really is and what he really wants. On the other hand, he has achieved a reconciliation of intellectual opposites. What he *experiences*, however, is different. He has 'condemned' himself to a future that does not hold any promise for him, and one that he is not really looking forward to. His political utopia has vanished, as have his energy and motivation to act for his future. Furthermore, he has not been able to construct another personal utopia for himself, be it with regard to his private or his professional life.

> Yes, of course, I have a girlfriend. It is now four years that we have been together … and I find thinking about things like marriage, children and so on pretty horrifying. Marrying, for example, well, I don't know, I don't much

> like it, but well, maybe one day I might do it. But kids … no, I think I will
> never have kids. She doesn't think likewise, of course and that is a big
> problem…. So, therefore, I don't like thinking about the future.

The only 'utopia' left to him, it appears, is to perpetuate his present state of
immobility, although he perceives that, for some reason, this is not right:

> My life, the way I live right now, is fine. Comparatively, I am fine and I'd go
> on like this many years. But … I am already in my thirties, and I don't know.

This is Nicolás' life so far, as he presents it. We describe this present state as
'biographical blockage' – a temporary dead end in an individual's biographical
development. In other words, the absence of a meaningful future horizon. It is
here that our questions about the case begin. What sort of biographical dynamics
have led him to this dead end? Are there broader social issues looming behind
the problematic aspects of Nicolás' individual trajectory?

In order to tackle the question of what led Nicolás gradually to trap himself
in a situation that does not seem to lead anywhere or leave any options that he
can see, we have to try to reconstruct the biographical dynamics at work. We
need to pay great attention to the sequential development of Nicolás' narrative,
the words he uses, the people he introduces, and the themes he develops.

Memories of a happy childhood

When Nicolás agreed to be interviewed, we initially expected to be told in
detail about the vicissitudes of his career and the transition to working life. In
fact, we witnessed something rather different – the story of a 'demythologisation'.
That is how Nicolás presented his life. Demythologisation of a world sustained
by his communist ideology. This was related to a demythologisation of 'the
university', of human beings in general, and of himself. Seen from his present
perspective, there was a life *before* and another *after* the shattering of his illusions.
Constant references to the moral dichotomy of 'good' and 'bad' show that he is
evaluating his 'two lives' also from a moral standpoint; that is, the temporal
divide in his biography is paralleled by a moral divide. In the very first sentence
of his account, this form is already present: "Well, I don't know…. I've always
had the reputation of being a good student. But this was not always the case.
Well, it was, in elementary school and so on". The general idea he introduces
here, which, as a 'leitmotiv', dominates his entire account, can be paraphrased
as follows: *Things, including myself, are not what they seem to be.* More concretely,
there is a gap between things 'said' and things 'believed' (discourse and ideology)
on the one hand, and things 'as they really are' (reality) on the other. His
reputation is that of a good student, but 'in reality' this is not true. It was true
in the beginning, though. Later on, according to him, things must have changed;
he was no longer a good student.

Several of the aspects already present in this fragment can be followed through the development of his narrative and turn out to be key elements of his present perspective on life, primarily the temporal divide. First things are one way, and then they are another; he perceives this as a decline from good to worse. Finally, this reveals his perception of a wide gap between ideology and reality. As we hope to establish, this is in fact quite a lucid representation of the situation he has manoeuvred himself into.

Thematically, in this first fragment, he introduces the domain of education with a focus on his performance that others thought was highly satisfactory, but which he knew better. He continues:

> Well, I was a very obedient child, very disciplined, and, well I had a childhood, a relatively, well not relatively, I had a quite happy childhood. I can't complain. As far as the family is concerned I didn't lack for anything, I scarcely had a problem.

Nicolás states he had a happy childhood, and that in his family he did not miss out on anything. However, the way he conveys this manifest message is anything but convincing and raises serious doubts as to whether he indeed experienced his childhood that way. Instead, it points to a latent and very different meaning that is barely concealed. In fact, he utters an impressive series of fragments. He is trying to say he was a happy child, but fails in every one of his attempts to do so: "relatively, well not relatively ... quite happy ... can't complain ... barely had a problem". So, we have to suppose a disciplined, obedient child who has experienced childhood problems. Possibly, Nicolás is still the obedient child, insofar as he does not say what his childhood was really like for him but is trying to maintain a proper image. It may or may not be his intention but one effect of this is to protect his parents.

After he finished his account, we asked for memories of his 'happy' childhood:

> Yes, I remember, well, a very pleasant life at home. My parents ... well, that's the main thing: they've always behaved very well, I've always received their support, they've behaved as they should. This gives you stability, above all when you are a child, and you have the support of your loved ones.

He connects happiness in his childhood with being supported and loved by parents and 'loved ones'. The traditional imagery of the family comes to mind, as a taken-for-granted reality, a sphere far from conflict, a natural shelter in which generosity, stability and solidarity are found. In other words, he seems to adhere to ideas and images one would expect to be held by the parents in a conservative, Catholic family such as his. After this rather general statement, he mentions for the first time an actual event that he remembers from his childhood:

> I also remember my grandparents and I felt very sad when they died.... Everybody loves their grandparents very much, because their love for you is the most disinterested love there is, isn't it, the love grandparents have for their

grandchildren? The other way round it is not the same, it is more interested. Over time, you realise all the things they do for you, and with no self-interest whatsoever. And, yes, that was a hard time for me, when all of them died.

Nicolás is introducing a new and surprising theme here: love – disinterested versus interested. The good/bad divide he has already used is taking on here a new shape. The disinterested love of his grandparents contrasts with other forms of love that are more interested; that is, love that is conditional or demanding something in return. This distinction emerges in his account just at the moment when he talks for the first time about real people and an actual event in his life, in other words, when he is beginning to delve into his recollections. We must assume, therefore, that the distinction of interested versus disinterested love is important, and that it corresponds to biographical experiences of his. Though his statement is vague enough to suggest other possibilities, he insinuates that it was he who loved in a more interested way: "The other way round", he states, was not the same.

In the light of this new theme of interested love, we can assume that the loved ones he refers to were probably his grandparents. His message therefore suggests the following polarity: Nicolás experienced disinterested love from his grandparents and more interested love from his parents. His above-mentioned indication that interested love referred to himself (with respect to his grandparents) is another instance of him protecting his parents. Certainly, his feelings towards his parents are a trifle more complicated than the way he tries to present them.

At the point that very intimate and detailed knowledge about the interaction within the family is apparently called for, data of a kind that could be expected to emerge in a therapeutic setting rather than on the occasion of a single biographical interview, we might expect to have to stop. Yet, there is another methodological option. Instead of delving deeper into the specifics and idiosyncrasies of our case, exploring its 'inner' context, we will do the opposite and explore the 'outer' social context of the case[1]. Therefore, we will leave Nicolás for the moment, and open the windows on the outer world, taking into account the background information we need to tackle our question of his parents' 'interested love'.

Background: the Spanish welfare process and the promise of higher education

One of the most prominent issues on the political agenda of the Socialist Party, as well as one of the major achievements during the 15 years of socialist government (1982-96), was to reintroduce republican educational values and make them universal through institutional implementation[2]. Over the past two decades, secondary and higher education have become available to wide sectors of the Spanish population[3]. It is fair to say that, after Franco's demise in 1975, aspirations of upward social mobility through children's access to higher education became a 'leitmotiv' in the strategies of parents whose children attended secondary school at the time. Especially when, as in Nicolás' family, only one child could possibly fulfil that goal, this often became the unconscious, dominant mission in a child's life. The parents' unfulfilled life plans, their hopes and expectations, were then delegated to the child, whose prime responsibility was to fulfil these expectations[4]. In other words, whereas access to higher education represented a privilege for the generation of Nicolás' parents, it became a widely shared and normal expectation of Nicolás' own generation.

What happened from the late 1980s on, however, after these young people graduated? The massive enrolments in higher education institutions led to an inflation of academic degrees and certificates and to their subsequent devaluation in the labour market (Martín, 1998). The impact of the economic crisis in the 1990s and the decline of skilled job opportunities added their share to the already difficult transition from education to working life for Nicolás' generation. Although undoubtedly the Spanish economy was itself undergoing a far-reaching modernising process, it was by no means prepared to absorb the numbers of graduates that left Spanish universities from the mid-1980s onwards. Therefore, the widely taken-for-granted correlation between higher studies and a stable position in the labour market in Spain and, what is more important, the biographical stability associated with it, was a reality only during the early 1980s, when the growth of the state generated employment. In other words, the increased precariousness of the graduate labour market radically brought into question the biographical mission that Nicolás' generation had been prepared for, as well as the transmitted knowledge and experience about the transition from education to working life.

Biographical education–to–work transitions of young people are not merely a shift from inactive to active work life, but form part of a complex process towards the comprehensive emancipation of the individual. It includes becoming an autonomous subject, exercising the practice of citizenship and becoming an adult (Casal, 1997). The authoritarian Franco-era model of 'becoming an adult' undoubtedly left its imprint on the present understanding of the emancipation of young people in Spain. Yet experts prefer to speak of a more general 'Mediterranean model of emancipation' in order to refer to the cultural understanding and social timetable for reaching adulthood in Spain. This involves a normatively much stronger social script than in other, northern European countries. According to this script, young people live with their parents until they marry. Before they marry, they have to find a stable job and to own a place in which to live. Only then are they supposed to leave the parental nest (Flaquer, 1995).

Undoubtedly, the transition to adulthood in Spain has become an intricate and difficult process for Nicolás' generation and that of his parents, putting considerable strain on both of them.

Returning from our outside excursion to Nicolás' world, we have now a fairly good picture of what is clouding the relationship between him and his parents. We can endorse his experience of an interest that he cannot name but perceives as inseparably linked to his parents' love for him. It is their aspiration to achieve through him the mission they have invested in him. As their only son, he has to prove himself worthy of their hopes and sacrifices. As the parents' delegate to the outside world, the mission he is entrusted (or burdened) with is to fulfil their expectations, unaccomplished wishes and hopes: a successful career through educational achievement, and subsequent professional reputation. He is to salvage the family, be their pride and joy, and secure a high social status for them. He faces a choice between loyalty towards his parents and the mission they have laid on him and loyalty to himself, and to his own life. They are incompatible – and betrayal seems unbearable but inevitable. In what way could this dilemma possibly be resolved?

His way of coping is, literally speaking, fantastic. He resolves the conflict by turning it inside out. He ignores the original conflict and finds an adequate surrogate terrain in ideological battles that he wages in the outside world. In this terrain, his deeds – or words for the most part – remain virtually without consequences. Hence he is eager to take sides; he joins the Communist Party, for example. He performs, more specifically, a radical split: revolutionary thinking on the one hand, and conventional, pragmatic, behaviour on the other.

Let us have a look at how he talks about these aspects. We have already seen that he talks about his childhood as a peaceful and happy period. In contrast, Nicolás introduces the existence of emerging negative feelings during his adolescence. More specifically, these conflicting feelings appear manifestly linked to the construction of his identity and with the consequences of his ideological and moral choices. The following sequence is remarkable:

> I had internal conflicts, above all … nothing to do with family.

It is right there before our eyes, his great deception: his conflicts are internal, yes, but they have *everything* to do with family. Far from acknowledging this, the family is again rapidly taken out of the field of conflict – problems have to do with himself, not with his family.

> [A]part from the normal health problems of my father and grandparents, everything progressed well, but the problems had to do with myself, I'm a very shy person, I had problems relating to others…. I hated going to discos, I had very clear principles according to which discotheques were a distraction from the important things. I was very much imbued with political ideals and my only worries revolved around this.

Certainly, the only worries he seemed aware of did revolve around politics. However, it is his personal conflicts that were projected onto that outside world in which he perceives himself as a fighter for justice.

> I considered myself very leftist and then I met a friend at school whose father belonged to the 'Comisiones Obreras' trade union, and he was one of those

real fighters, and his son too, and we became close friends. We used to listen to Radio Tirana, which was clandestine in those times because it was Stalinist, anti-Soviet, anti-Cuban – it was too much.... I was very sensitive to all kinds of injustice, and I didn't like the society in which I lived.

The final sentence can be read in terms of his genuine conflict: the primordial injustice that he has sensitively registered is the one that he suffers from: not being allowed to live his own life.

We have seen the kind of internal dynamics that led Nicolás into a dead end and the external conditions that contributed to it. And yet we have not reached the core of his problem, the elements constituting his blockage. We need to take another detour in order to find alternatives. It brings us to the former East Germany, or German Democratic Republic (GDR), where Heike is facing serious trouble.

Heike

Stations in a good girl's life

Heike stands for a type of biography that could hardly be found elsewhere within the current confines of the EU. With her particular biography, she was one of many women who were designated as female 'losers' in the transformation (*Wendeverliererinnen*) soon after the fall of the Berlin Wall. In hindsight we may be tempted to see the biographical turnarounds Heike experienced as unsurprising – perhaps justified, even – given that hers is a biography marked by closeness to the former GDR political system. At the time, however, she did not need to consider her moves in the light of a new world order that was to come about later, in her early adulthood. It is part of the nature of life-course decisions that they involve considerable risk, but are nevertheless unavoidable. Let us consider what those decisions were in Heike's case, what their consequences were and whether we can identify an underlying pattern.

From the beginning, Heike's life was designed to follow an elite trajectory. Her well-off parents were both members of the former GDR ruling party. Her father, with a doctorate in history from a cadre university in East Berlin, was a party official of high standing[5]. Heike had always been a good girl. An inconspicuous kid, she took an interest in school and readily followed her parents' suggestions in all aspects of life, occasionally taking some liberties. Parallel to her successful educational career went her involvement in party politics. She actively participated in the official youth organisations at school and always held prominent posts in them. When, at the age of 13, she suddenly took up playing electric guitar in a combo, after passing her final piano exam at the state conservatory, her parents would look at this, too, with benevolent eyes.

Only once did their agendas diverge, only once did they have a serious difference. Against her parents' advice, Heike finally rejected the opportunity to study in Moscow, not feeling comfortable with having to go abroad for five years. Although she liked journalism and was contributing to a youth journal, she took up history, graduated ahead of time and was promised a grant for her doctoral studies. As was usual in the GDR she married early, at 21, and moved with her husband into a small room in a students' dormitory. He had a sporty type of proletarian background, and was going to be a teacher of Marxism–Leninism after graduating. A good match – much less complicated than her previous romantic affair with a boy from the Portuguese Communist Party. Politically, this was very correct and no threat to her own professional future. In 1988, aged 23, Heike sealed her political allegiances by joining the ruling Socialist Unity Party. The following summer, while working on her doctorate and tutoring at the university, she got pregnant. Therefore her pregnancy fell exactly in the period of highest political disorder that ultimately led to the demise of the GDR and the integration of its territory into the Federal Republic of Germany. After her daughter was born in the spring of 1990, she took the one-year maternity leave typical of the GDR, with the aim of resuming her job in 1991.

However, she was not to return. When she was ready to resume work on her thesis in 1991, everything had changed. The archive material she had been working on was confiscated by the state prosecutor. Her former thesis supervisor, like hundreds of other GDR university teachers, had been ousted on political grounds. Finally, her grant was due to end soon, and when efforts to get additional funding from other institutions failed, she began to look for work. Getting a job in those times of all-out transformation, which began by producing unemployment on an unprecedented scale, was anything but easy. However, her social contacts were still good enough for her to be placed in a university library doing administrative work on a temporary contract. At least she remained in an academic environment and could hope to move to better jobs from there.

However, the social turmoil did not spare her marriage either. As expected, her husband's educational credits were utterly devalued and he was lucky to get work as a travelling insurance salesman, often returning home very late. When she found out he had been gambling and had lost all their savings, she was about to leave him but reconsidered, following her parents' advice. Instead, she opened a separate bank account and took control of the payment of essential bills.

At the time of our interview Heike was 31. She still held the same menial job. Her contract had been prolonged once, but her situation was still insecure. Her doctoral thesis remained unfinished – she had found herself unable to combine working on her thesis with maintaining the full-time, though temporary, job and her childcare duties. This notwithstanding, she was looking forward to taking driving lessons.

An initial summary of Heike's trajectory is quickly completed: we have a projected, and partially initiated, trajectory that is clearly linked to the regime. In a sort of historic catastrophe, the regime gets blown away – and with it,

Heike's anticipated career. Her efforts at rescuing it do not yield the desired results. Indeed, she must know that her career as anticipated is over. She is sensitive and realistic enough to perceive that, without the goodwill she enjoyed before, she will hardly prosper academically in the new circumstances. So she adapts, rapidly and well – as she has always done, we would add. Indeed, is there such a big difference between adapting to her parents' (particularly, her father's) wishes and adapting to the force of other imposed circumstances as an adult?

Professionally, she may have adapted; but what about the private sphere? Her marriage is severely affected, and seems beyond salvage. In an otherwise very similar case in our sample, where the couple involved felt more intimately linked, the family, and the partner in particular, was a strong resource that helped deal with the strain of these transformations. In Heike's case, the relationship is more of symbolic and possibly practical importance, and it breaks up when it becomes clear that the couple face different individual challenges. Their love and solidarity has not been tested before and it fails in the face of a very harsh reality.

Evidently, Heike's blockage is of a different nature to that of Nicolás. Here, what is blocked terminally is a project, an anticipated journey, that is taken out of this young woman's hands without her having a chance to fight for it. Her life thereafter goes on, but on a different and very modest path.

Background: the East German transformation as biographical challenge

A specificity of the transformation type of social change that East European countries have been experiencing in the past years, and one that is especially prominent in East Germany, is the gap between biographically acquired orientations and the newly established social and political system. In our view, this 'orientation gap' has become a structural feature of the process of social transformation.

While the former context of institutions and networks in the GDR providing support and biographical stability for a vast majority of its citizens has vanished, orientations guiding present activities remain linked to biographical expectations and strategies developed in the former social context, often unrecognised by the social actors themselves. Individuals brought up in that society, and who had been living in that society, were suddenly confronted with a deeply altered social environment. Experiences and knowledge gathered in years of living in the 'old' society were suddenly of little use, strongly challenged in many respects and from different perspectives. Social networks dissolved and everyday life lost much of its 'taken-for-granted' quality. Yet, in the absence of other orientations, citizens of the former GDR at first had no other choice than to rely on those they had already acquired. Gathering new experiences and developing new orientations is a slow process. So it is with the transformation of knowledge, values and emotional structures. Furthermore, since there was hardly any continuity on the institutional level, a sense of continuity in daily life had to be based on the routines that had been biographically acquired and established under the previous social system.

Carrying mental baggage unsuited to present circumstance can lead individuals to engage in forms and lines of action that are utterly unsuccessful in a newly established context. However, an established set of basic orientations and certain biographical strategies may also turn out to be very helpful resources for getting by and regaining control under the new and unexpected circumstances (see Weihrich, 1996).

Transformation – in the sense of reshaping institutions according to an existing model – may have worked fairly well as a top-down strategy for political, administrative or legal institutions for example. However, it is not applicable in the case of personal orientations and guidelines for everyday life. These could not be updated or matched by simply replacing them with West German ones. Apart from the question of how such a feat should be accomplished, such models do not necessarily work and, worse still, there may not even be any models available. There were – and are – hardly any reliable, undisputed and secure orientation models left that citizens of the former GDR could adhere to, in order to become oriented to 'what to do and what to expect'. In short, while old orientations have become obsolete, new ones are not readily available but have to be found or constructed anew. To a greater or lesser extent, an individual biography is affected by this process of reconstruction.

Choose what you must

Heike's biography is marked by closeness to a defeated political system. Her involvement with 'the Party' and the political establishment of the former GDR make abandonment of her old biographical project objectively inevitable. This is the 'blocked journey' in her case: the life that her father had prepared her for, that she has been trained for and for which she had made all the necessary arrangements, including marriage, to make it prosper, is suddenly and quite irretrievably lost. An imagined life, but one taken for granted; not an option among others but the one prospective trajectory she had embarked on – life that she had already heavily invested in and spent years preparing for. Not much of her training, her achievements and her experiences is suitable for transfer to the new social framework. Not much of it will withstand scrutiny in the mechanisms of 'social trading', for example the labour market, that determine her position in the new German society. She has no choice but to start all over again, in the quest for social recognition and the pursuit of a good life.

Surprisingly perhaps, at first glance, she is well equipped for this task. The biographical strategy that she has developed over the years and that has remained unaffected by the turmoil of German unification will serve her as a reliable resource. This dominant, albeit latent – that is, not necessarily conscious – strategy can be described as a pattern of guided autonomy: a pattern of voluntary adaptation to pressures and necessities. She does not just follow guidelines, she agrees to do so, accepts them and makes them her own. In other words, with some reluctance at times, but predominantly with a view to what is in it for her, she embraces what seems to be inevitable anyway. What is necessary, inevitable or expected of her, therefore, becomes inseparably linked to and identified with what she wants. She chooses, in short, what she must. This is certainly a paradoxical modus operandi, but a fruitful one, and eminently practical[6]. It made Heike happily follow the pre-established career path that her parents had laid out for her, and it then enabled her to avoid a serious crash when the political system that supported her imploded.

In the sphere of work, she quickly adapted by reducing her expectations and adopting a pragmatic course of action. The social network that had put her on a career track in the GDR was still capable of providing her with the modest employment that she still holds, but aspires to improve. Similarly, in the domain of private and family life, her husband had added coherence and symbolic gains to her GDR life arrangement. Under the new circumstances, however, he is much less able to cope. Having to accept jobs of low prestige, and displaying new personal traits that trouble her, she does not now find him attractive as a partner, but respects him as the father of her child. She has suggested that he move to another flat in the same multistorey building, and is actively pursuing a new partnership. There is little doubt, in the end, that this strategy will enable her to regain control over her life and establish a satisfactory future for her and her daughter in unified Germany.

No way out and disenchantment

We have identified Heike's basic biographical strategy as 'choosing what she must'. How does this relate to Nicolás' strategy? For Nicolás, there is no such purely external element that his troubles could be be attributed to. Therefore, in his case, internal factors must be crucial in the genesis of the biographical blockage. This makes for another difference. Nicolás' internal struggle, the clash of conflicting loyalties and the translation to the 'surrogate field' of the outside world are a terrible strain on him. They drain his energy, reduce his resources and constantly occupy his thoughts.

What is the core of those internal factors that provoke and sustain Nicolás' blockage? We have established the conflict of loyalties between the interests of his parents, forcefully embodied in the mission they have bestowed on him and his own interests, needs and preferences as an individual. This is certainly a severe conflict but, per se, not yet an extremely unconventional one. A conflict of interests is manageable – it can be decided one way or another. Nicolás, however, faced with this crucial question, is unable to decide. His adopted solution is a strategy of 'neither–nor' and it is this solution that is ultimately cementing his road to nowhere.

Disenchantment ultimately has come to be the core of Nicolás' strategy. He establishes a parallel between the disenchantment that the end of 'real' socialism signified to adherents of leftist political ideas worldwide and his own disenchantment that invades him and his immediate world.

> I had utopias, a very firm political consciousness. I considered myself a pure Stalinist. I joined the Communist Party and that also was a disillusion. Then followed the crisis of the USSR, the fall of the Wall … the end of real socialism …. And, well, to have a life plan full of hopes regarding the project of a socialist society and to see all of it shattered to pieces – it was disheartening. With religion, it was just the same. Nothing special happened, it is only that what you see makes you lose your faith. It wasn't as drastic as in the political side of my life, but little by little you begin to lose your pillars, your moral and ideological pillars.

Nicolás has found in the fall of the Berlin Wall an apt metaphor that symbolises the irremediable cracking up of his self-enchanted world. The demythologisation of society, politics and religion, the shattering of the beliefs and utopias of his childhood and youth merge for him with a disillusionment in himself. He is no longer able to attribute all the misery, hypocrisy and mediocrity to others, society, and the outside world alone. He is part of the misery. The world he constructed, that shielded him for so long from very uncomfortable decisions and enabled him to avoid a necessary confrontation between himself and his parents, has evaporated. The new reality is beginning to sink in.

> Now, well, as I tell you, we get worse and worse [he smiles], we become more aware of how we are. Because I don't think that I am such a nice person as I once thought I was…. You realise that you're not any better than the others, rather you are as miserable as any human being … and, well, right now, none of my projects have succeeded but that doesn't really bother me … I am not really an ambitious person and I settle, for the moment, I settle for the basics, a normal living for instance. I do not have strong ambitions or dreams.

We have seen that Nicolás, contrary to Heike, does what he must – but does not choose it.

Discussion: the significance of the fall of the Berlin Wall

We want to conclude by briefly highlighting two interesting aspects that the cases have brought to our attention. Nicolás and Heike draw upon elements of contemporary social imagery and put them to private use for their individual goals. They use public social *topoi* as resources to construct and present their biographies. Such *topoi* seem to facilitate communication since they are known to everybody. However, they are rather empty formulas, enabling individuals to put them to the most diverse uses by investing them with personal meaning.

Both our young adults use the paradigmatic political earthquake of the end of the 20th century, condensed in the popular metaphor of the fall of the

Berlin Wall, as a core element in their biographical accounts. However different their biographical backgrounds, personal circumstances and their actual experiences linked to this political macro-event can be seen to be, they both have in common a particular view on the fall of the Wall. What is predominantly seen in the West as a symbol for the advancement of freedom and enhancement of individual options has acquired a different personal significance for them, where the connotation of 'breakdown', of something coming to an end, prevails. For Heike it represents the end of a projected life; for Nicolás it symbolises the disenchantment of his world.

Heike, additionally, could be warranted in claiming added legitimacy to her biographical construction of herself as a victim of the circumstances through the social *topos* of female 'losers' in the transformation (*Wendeverliererinnen*). It is not even necessary for her to mention this topical label in order to trigger the process of recognition and to embed her individual experience in this particular framework of interpretation. Her own active political involvement – and that of her family – and the educational privileges that she enjoyed, in short, her privileged position in the defunct society, shift out of focus. Her entire biography is smoothly 'normalised' in this way, transformed into one of a million who just happened to have bad luck. Nicolás has no such resource.

The pace of social change and biographical requirements of the future

Nicolás' blocked journey highlights the profound contradiction between two sets of expectations that are typical of our late modern societies but are especially relevant for societies that have undergone rapid social and cultural transformation, such as Spain. The first set of expectations could be described as 'family missions'. Young people, especially from a Mediterranean and working-class background, are expected to fulfil a very rigid biographical script in order to reach adulthood and 'emancipation'. This takes place under the umbrella of the social imagery of a meritocratic, full-employment society. In practical terms, it means getting a stable job through educational performance, buying a flat, marrying, and raising a family. The second set of expectations has to do with the more general climate of individualism and the cultural expectations related to it: the need to be an autonomous subject, a distinctive or singular individual, behaving freely and therefore, at a given point in time, breaking the links with the family of origin.

Nicolás' journey shows that his blockage is related to being trapped in a particular family constellation, to the difficulties of becoming an adult, and to the fact of belonging to a specific generation that has been the recipient of collective aspirations for upward mobility through higher education in a rapidly changing society. Those constellations of values and strategies that were useful for a specific generation within a specific political and cultural context have been anything but effective for the next generation, which grew up in a society that has undergone unexpected transformations in the meantime. So much so, that well-assumed biographical resources can even become handicaps – just as was the case, in a more radical way, in the GDR.

What then were the social conditions that were of prime importance for the emergence of the two cases of blocked journeys that we have presented? The fact that both are living in societies governed until very recently by very authoritarian regimes? The accelerated pace of unexpected social transformations that both societies are, or have been, experiencing?

We have come to no conclusions about the first question, but the answer to the second one must be affirmative. While, in Nicolás' case, transformation opens up a gap in experience, orientations and expectations between the generations of parents and children, the transformation in Heike's case is even more profound, affecting an entire population in an extremely short period of time. In both cases, biographical challenges for our interviewees – frictions, disorders, discrepancies in guiding expectations, a need for reorientation – are closely related to these social changes or transformations. Since the dawn of modernity, constant change has probably become the one stable feature of western or modern societies. Responsiveness and variability of biographical plans, goals and strategies seem to be required to an extent so far unprecedented in peacetime.

Notes

[1] The notions of 'inner' and 'outer' context as employed here were developed by Oevermann in his structural hermeneutics (see, for example, Oevermann et al, 1979, p 414).

[2] The republican government (defeated by Franco in 1936) launched a radical reform in various fields of action, within which education had a clear strategic value. The philosophy behind the republican education policy was the defence of education as an emancipatory and liberating tool of social progress.

[3] Even though objective data demonstrate that the impressive growth of the Spanish university population cannot be directly attributed to the increased access of the lower classes, but rather to the growth of female middle and upper classes (Martín, 1998), it is indeed so, at the level of social perception.

[4] The concepts of 'mission' and 'delegation' as employed here, were developed in the fields of family theory and therapy (see, for example, Stierlin, 1982). The main difference from the sociologically more familiar concept of (latent) roles lies in the added dimension of personal trust and loyalty of the 'delegate' towards the 'giver' of the mission, typically a parent, and the psychic exploitation that this strong and durable bond may imply.

[5] The ruling Socialist Unitary Party in the GDR claimed the primacy of its views even in the field of scientific theory and methods. Historical science was particularly important in this sense as an ideological spearhead of the regime (see, for example, Malycha, 2001).

[6] It may also be somewhat subversive for social scientist observers, as it collapses the opposition of autonomy to heteronomy. Epistemological and systems-oriented strands of theory have long recognised the potentials of paradoxes. See Esposito (1991) for the Luhmanian perspective.

References

Beck, U. (1992) *Risk society. Towards a new modernity*, London: Sage Publications.

Beck, U. and Beck-Gernsheim, E. (1993) 'Nicht Autonomie, sondern Bastelbiographie', *Zeitschrift für Soziologie*, vol 22, no 3, pp 178-87.

Breckner, R. (1998) 'The biographical-interpretative method – principles and procedures', *Sostris Working Paper 2: Case study materials – the early retired*, London: Centre for Biography in Social Policy, University of East London, pp 91-104.

Bourdieu, P. (1993) *La misère du monde*, Paris: Seuil.

Casal, J. (1997) 'Modalidades de transición profesional, mercado de trabajo y condiciones de empleo', *Cuadernos de relaciones laborales*, no 11, pp 19-54.

Castells, M. (1997) *The power of identity in the Information Age. Vol 2: Economy, society and culture*, Oxford: Blackwell.

CEDEFOP (European Centre for the Development of Vocational Training/ Eurostat) (2001) *The transition from education to working life. Key data on vocational training in the European Union*, Luxembourg: Office for Official Publications of the European Communities.

Esposito, E. (1991) 'Paradoxien als Unterscheidungen von Unterscheidungen', in H.U. Gumbrecht and K.L. Pfeiffer (eds) *Paradoxien, Dissonanzen, Zusammenbrüche. Situationen offener Epistemologie*, Frankfurt-am-Main: Suhrkamp, pp 35-57.

Flaquer, L. (1995) 'El modelo de familia española en el contexto europeo', in S. Sarasa and L. Moreno (eds) *El Estado del Bienestar en la Europa del Sud*, Madrid: CSIC, pp 289-311.

Freysson, L. (2001) *Educational attainment levels in Europe in the 1990s – Some key figures*, Statistics in Focus, Theme 3: Population and Social Conditions, no 7, Luxembourg: Eurostat.

Giddens, A., Bauman, Z., Luhmann, N., Beck, U. and Beriain, J. (1996) *Las consecuencias perversas de la modernidad*, Barcelona: Anthropos.

Ibáñez, J. (1994) *El regreso del sujeto. La investigación social de segundo orden*, Madrid: Siglo Veintiuno de España.

Kohli, M. (1985) 'Die Institutionalisierung des Lebenslaufs', *Kölner Zeitschrift für Soziologie und Sozialpsychologie*, vol 37, no 1, pp 1-29.

Kohli, M. (1986) 'Gesellschaftszeit und Lebenszeit. Der Lebenslauf im Strukturwandel der Moderne', in J. Berger (ed) *Die Moderne – Kontinuitäten und Zäsuren*, Soziale Welt Sonderband, no 4, Göttingen: Schwartz, pp 183-208.

Luhmann, N. (1992) 'Kontingenz als Eigenwert der modernen Gesellschaft', in N. Luhmann (ed) *Beobachtungen der Moderne*, Opladen: Westdeutscher Verlag, pp 93-128.

Malycha, A. (2001) 'Das Verhältnis zwischen Wissenschaft und Politik in der SBZ/DDR von 1945 bis 1961', *Aus Politik und Zeitgeschichte*, vol 30-31, pp 14-21.

Martín, E. (1998) *Producir la juventud*, Madrid: Itsmo.

Oevermann, U., Tilman, A., Konau, E. and Kranbeck, J. (1979) 'Die Methodologie einer objektiven Hermeneutik und ihre allgemeine forschungslogische Bedeutung in den Sozialwissenschaften', in H.-G. Soeffner (ed) *Interpretative Verfahren in den Sozial- und Textwissenschaften*, Stuttgart: Metzler, pp 352-434.

Stierlin, H. (1982) *Delegation und Familie. Beiträge zum Heidelberger Familiendynamischen Konzept* (revised edn), Frankfurt-am-Main: Suhrkamp.

Weihrich, M. (ed) (1996) *Alltag im Umbruch? Alltägliche Lebensführung und berufliche Veränderung in Ostdeutschland. Zwischenbilanz der Wiedervereinigung. Strukturwandel und Mobilität im Transformationsprozess*, Opladen: Leske & Budrich.

THREE

Guilty victims: social exclusion in contemporary France[1]

Numa Murard

And now they have invented this little placebo word, 'exclusion'.... As society becomes more and more insane, language is given the task of concealing this insanity within a respectable vocabulary. (Pennac, 1995, my translation)

Let's delve into this insanity instead of believing – or pretending to believe – that a placebo is the way to cure it.

A short story about an empty box[2]

'Exclusion' is not a concept rooted in the social sciences, but an empty box given by the French state to the social sciences in the late 1980s as a subject to study. It was exported to Brussels at the same time, and acknowledged by the EU in 1994 (the poverty programme being renamed Programme Against Exclusion). It was then re-exported to all the European countries. The empty box has since been filled with a huge number of pages, treatises and pictures, in varying degrees academic, popular, original and valuable.

Why has France been the centre of this invention? Because this country is at the centre of Europe, a transitional space between northern and southern countries. It suffers both types of social problems identified in the other countries. First, the weakening of primary social ties (family, neighbourhood, and so on), which have remained stronger in southern countries. Second, the weakening of secondary social networks (unions, volunteer organisations, and so on), which are stronger in northern countries (Ion, 1996).

Does this mean that the empty box is not in fact empty? It has to be admitted that it has been filled with so many things that it is impossible to turn back. And back to what? Before 'exclusion', the word 'poverty' was also a very weak notion, filled with very different things to denote *la question sociale* – the social question. That is, the issue of misfortune, the inability to survive, the inability to be autonomous, and also the political consequences of inability, the political risk of social disorder.

If 'exclusion' is a modern word for a very old issue, what is new (and insane) about it? In the French version, exclusion means, in latent or explicit terms, that several turning points have occurred in the management and thinking of social policies:

1. It means that the welfare state is no longer understood by local and central government as a way of reducing inequalities and promoting individuals. Rather, it is a way of compensating for only the most flagrant disparities, while reducing the cost of welfare in general, in order to meet international economic challenges.
2. It locates on the margins of society what is actually happening at the heart of society: the destruction of the wage-earning society and of the welfare system based on it (Castel, 1995)[3], the fact that "the economy is destroying society" (Perret and Roustang, 1993). It can therefore be argued that exclusion is a political attempt to respond to and depoliticise problems like unemployment which the government does not know how to solve and does not want its political opponents to aggravate (Chevalier, 1996).
3. In short, it has become a respectable word that expresses the uncertainty of citizens about themselves and their families, the inability of the state to solve *la question sociale*, and the loss of control over the nation's fate which has been handed over to the hazards of the world economy.

Here is the insanity: exclusion is a word to denote a small number of excluded people, when the issues raised by the word are in fact a source of anxiety for a very large part of society, especially in the working class and lower middle class.

Fear, pity and guilt

Structural changes have their counterpart in emotions and feelings. The building of the welfare state has been the work of politicians, civil servants and the upper classes motivated by very strong feelings of fear and pity. They fear riots and revolutions that have punctuated recent French history (1789, 1830, 1848, 1871, 1936 and 1968) and pity the innocent victims of misfortune and destiny (mainly of the Catholic type).

However, the welfare state itself has had a very strong effect on subjectivity, especially at its peak in the early 1970s, just before it began to weaken. Life's accidents – sickness, unemployment, poverty, the inability to survive by oneself – were no longer faults, or a matter of luck or fate, but risks. What is a risk in the context of the welfare state? It is something collective (it happens within a group, class or category), foreseeable (it can be said – more or less precisely by statistical means – how many will be involved) and insurable (it can be calculated, by actuarial means, how much everybody must contribute to insure against future accidents; see Ewald, 1986). Consequently, when the risk occurs, there is no point in identifying the cause; it is just a matter of evaluating the need.

Subjectively, this mutually supportive organisation was a powerful means of reducing the feeling of guilt that naturally accompanies the question 'why is it happening to me?'. This feeling has by no means completely disappeared. In particular, the stigma of poverty remains a constant feature of social policy and of common sense. Suspicion of those who are entitled to various benefits designed for small categories of deprived people has always been stronger than suspicion of the general categories of the social security system (such as sickness, old age or family allowances). Within the social security system, suspicion of the unemployed has also been stronger than of the other categories. And everybody and anyone could be suspected of cheating, making a profit out of this mutually supportive organisation. However, until recently the legal framework of welfare, founded on this concept of risk, and above all the continuous improvement of welfare, have not only received strong support, but have been seen as dedicated to the eradication of poverty and bound to succeed in this in the long run.

This line of improvement was interrupted in the mid–1970s and has given way to discussions about the cost of welfare; calls for a new, individual, responsibility; injunctions to autonomy; and the identification of a 'dependency culture' – that is, the idea that deprived people have settled into the welfare system, happy to live on welfare benefits and unwilling to work or look after others at home. In France, this talk came at first mainly from right-wing politicians and the mass media, but it was quickly picked up and slightly rearranged by the socialist party. Related to this discussion about welfare, there has been new talk about delinquency and the social order, mostly juvenile delinquency, which was interpreted as the result of parental neglect, and in all these discussions the target was deprived people, migrants and deprived areas.

This explains why the main outcome of our biographical research is the discovery, through the narratives, of a strong feeling of guilt associated with situations in which people experience difficulties in managing their lives by themselves. Guilt and not shame: the 'culture of shame' (Benedict, 1946; Dodds, 1965) has slowly vanished to be replaced by a 'culture of guilt'. As Paul Ricoeur puts it, "The human being asks: since I am unsuccessful and ill, what is my sin?" (Ricoeur, 1960, p 46). The shame culture belongs to societies with a high level of social control, control by the group, while the guilt culture implies a high level of self-control, and belongs to modern individualised societies. This guilt culture is not something new. Previously, for instance, Cobb and Sennett stressed "the hidden injuries of class" (Cobb and Sennett, 1972). Furthermore, Dejours has recently shown the devastating effect of guilt in companies and at work in France (Dejours, 1998). We can now picture a mass feeling of guilt, permeating the *whole* of society. Although there is evidence that these people are victims of the structural changes that occurred in the 1970s, 1980s and 1990s, their narratives reveal that this guilt is a feeling that structures their narration and their life strategy. Before giving examples and the contents of this report, we ought to explain the concept of subjectivity and the way it is structured by guilt.

Subjectivity without a subject?

Social workers, magistrates, physicians and a raft of other agents who are familiar with the life stories, or sections of life stories, told by deprived people stress the opposite: the fact that their clients are always trying to deny their responsibility. They keep saying: it is not me, it's not my fault, I could not have done anything else, I couldn't stop myself, and so on. Some of these agents smile at such talk, interpreting it as denial and the effect of defence mechanisms. Others are irritated: they claim the clients are lying and cheating, and even blame the victim. In both interpretations, however, something is concealed. It is the sense of blame.

If the same person can at one and the same time be victim and offender, this implies that his/her reflexivity is affected by different and opposite forces, sources or interpretations. Psychoanalysis has given a brilliant version of this theoretical problem, locating the struggle inside the subject, a divided subject. For our purpose, however, it is better to stand on theoretical grounds that can be firmly demonstrated. The only subject whose existence is not in doubt is the linguistic one, the subject of the verb, of the sentence (Agamben, 1978). If this subject can claim to be a victim and feel like an offender, the sources of this division can be found, from a sociological point of view, *outside* of the subject. It is the law that requires the linguistic subject to associate its name with its actions in order to create a responsible person, a person required to give an account of himself (Douglas, 1986). And it is in court that blame and misfortune are weighed in order to declare the subject victim or offender (Benjamin, 1996 [1919]).

This is exactly what is reflected in the narratives of our interviewees: a constant trial of their own lives, in which they act as their own advocate and their own accuser, in which they acknowledge that they are the authors of their lives and define themselves as being acted on by circumstances. In fact, not one of our interviewees has been brought to court. They are pleading guilty to a vague or indefinite crime, so indefinite sometimes that their burden could be likened to Kafka's desperate search for an object of his feeling of guilt[4]. Even the sociologist, from his external vantage point, cannot give a very precise content to this feeling. Its content can, however, be approximately defined: it is a feeling of not having succeeded in life. It is therefore strongly related to society and social theory. What does it mean, 'to succeed in life'? The narratives provide an answer – to succeed in life is to fulfil normative requests that originate in the family, the environment and society as a whole. In the first presentation of the self, in answer to the question, "Can you tell your life story?", one can hear the defence speech of a person pleading that she has not committed this or that crime against the norms, that she is not responsible for the crime she may have committed against the norm, and so on. In the case of Irène, for instance, her main aim (in the interview) is to demonstrate that she is, and always has been, a good mother, caring for her three children in spite of the great difficulties created by family neglect and unfaithful men. She underlines the plea against herself as a mother, the very strong feeling of guilt for not having been, and not being, a good mother.

The case of Irène[5]

Born in 1948 in a rural area surrounding Paris, Irène is the daughter of a waterman and a domestic helper, who eventually became a nurse's assistant. She has no qualifications; she starts working at age 12 as a printing industry worker, unregistered first (the legal age for work is 14), then regularly registered. She works continuously from 1960 to 1991; her longest single job is that of concierge for eight years. Her last job is as a cleaning lady in a private hospital. She had hoped to become (as her mother did) a nurse's assistant, but she says it was too late, she was too old. Dismissed from a number of jobs, she has since been mostly unemployed, except for six months spent in a psychiatric hospital. With no interest in trying to find a job, she is now home with the Revenu Minimum d'Insertion (RMI) – minimum income.

Policemen, physicians, judges, lawyers, social workers: these are the main characters of her life story. Violence is omnipresent, with beaten wives (her own sister) and even a murdered one (the daughter of a first marriage of a grandfather). Her children have been battered by her partners and she has a history of several suicide attempts. Irène's story does not always fit the facts of her life. Why? Irène has been ashamed during her whole life: shame of being deserted by her mother, shame of being an unmarried mother (people looked down on her in the village), shame of having attempted suicide while still having a young baby (she became an unworthy mother, known to the police and social service), shame of being beaten by her husband in the presence of her children, shame of being 'known to the school authorities', shame of her son's homosexuality.

Yet none of this will give any insight into the risk strategy undertaken by Irène if we do not recall that, from the point of view of her 'strategy', everything she tells is true. Deserted by her mother, she deserted her, losing therefore a possible source of support, relying instead on the grandmother of whom she says, "she is my mother; when my grandmother died, it was my mother who had died". This feature of family transmission will be duplicated for the next generation when Irène's children will desert her in turn, relying on their own grandmother, that is, Irène's mother. So the family network is cut at both ends. Irène is deserted by the first violent and jealous partner, and by her second partner, after having contributed to his social success. With the third partner, *she* is the support, as she declares, the mother as well as the partner for a young man and his younger sister whose mother is absent and whose father is ill. With the fourth (and last significant) partner, she again tried to do something constructive. He was handicapped, following an accident at work, but, together they bought a piece of land in the village she was born in, in order to grow fruit and vegetables, make some money and improve their material life as well as build something new. This relationship also failed.

Therefore, the only reliable support is welfare, but Irène wants to avoid welfare support. She will first ask for support only when quitting the first partner, and again when quitting the second partner, both times out of concern for her children. Again, with her ill son, she has to ask that his handicap be recognised. This does not happen until after he has died. She does receive help from volunteer organisations and later a sickness pension from social security, with some shame: "It was a big sum, really enormous". Unemployed for the first time in 1991, she feels bad at being forced to register for unemployment benefit: "It's shaming". Little by little, she will change her mind, first because she cannot pay back loans: "I don't like credits, but when you are forced to, you are forced to". Later on she will look on welfare support in a more positive way, as a right "for people like us".

Her sense of shame becomes mitigated by a sense of having some rights to sufficient support. She has accepted that she belongs to the most deprived group in society. Therefore she fights to have her housing debt reduced. She accepts herself as somebody who is mentally ill, she fits the situation of somebody making a living on RMI. In other terms, her welfare strategy is exactly within the limits of the objective constraints of her life.

Irène's life exhibits a pattern of a 'struggle against exclusionary probabilities', well documented, for example, in Bourdieu et al (1999). Her life is one of a complete lack of support from family (except her grandmother), husbands, children and society. Her 'family stories' are full of pain and shame, and some degree of misrepresentation (when checked against accounts given by her children). However, both in their truth and their untruths they bear witness to the transmission of violence and emotional 'wildness' both in the family she found herself in and the unsuccessful families she made, and in the authorities by whom her case was processed formally and informally. Her history illustrates, as many do, the transmission of emotional trauma through generations, and suggests the poor treatment of herself as a mother by the authorities in respect of their slowness in processing claims, and their occasional economic generosity but emotional blindness. Her strategy of becoming temporarily mentally ill has at least brought her some measure of emotional–psychiatric help, but only *after* the disasters have happened. Preventative emotional work is not the forte of most welfare systems.

We did not choose this example at random. When reviewing the collection of French interviews, the gender dimension stood out. It has already been demonstrated, in the case of divorces, that male and female narratives are shaped in opposite ways (Théry, 1993): as tragedies by the women (narratives of inevitability), and as drama by the men (narratives of a sudden, unexpected event). Even the contents of the life stories are different. Male stories are mainly concentrated on work, even where family and private life is obviously decisive. Career forms the backbone of the narrative. Childhood is often recalled as a time of preparing for work. The play is mainly acted by male characters. Mother, wife, female characters, positive or negative, appear as secondary characters in the background. Female stories are concentrated on family, even where there is an intense life of work. Husbands, male partners and children appear in the foreground, to the point that the narrator, Ego, may disappear almost entirely. Emotions and feelings are also mentioned and spoken of more frequently. Childhood is often recalled as a time of preparing to build a family, and the new life (with a partner) is a natural progression from the old one (with parent). Male characters in female stories are essential and ambivalent: their ability to harm, their childishness, their alcoholism and violence, are counterbalanced by the hope that they could bring emotional and material security.

The gender division of the narratives is one of the main factors that shapes subjectivity; another is class. Usually (but not always), our interviewees belong to a working-class environment. It has long demonstrated that social exclusion is a selective process, a process selecting from among those who lack various kinds of resources[6]. What does it mean, to succeed in life, when you belong to a working-class environment? Working-class ethics and culture have been changed dramatically in recent decades. The class has been split, with many manual workers becoming technicians or white-collar workers while the rest are engaged in precarious and tedious jobs. The result is that the working-class condition is something to be avoided (Beaud and Pialoux, 1995), and to succeed in life means to escape one's parents' condition. Social exclusion is often the objective and subjective situation of people trapped in a stigmatised social status, not having been able to fulfil their own or their parents' expectations of escaping the working-class condition. However, escaping this condition can also be a source of guilt feeling for working-class people imbued with a strong sense of solidarity from an early age. They experience their improved condition as a loss of sense of solidarity, a form of betrayal.

Is there something especially French in the forms taken by social exclusion? Work ethics, family ethics, working-class ethics are shared in different proportions by all Europeans countries and are difficult to weigh in quantitative terms. French features, especially the class struggle, but also the Catholic culture, are rooted in history. The combination of these two features could lead to powerful aspirations for upward mobility and a strong sense of guilt when this aim is not reached[7]. The power of these normative requirements in French society is revealed by underlining the feeling of guilt despite the apparently liberal way of life. And this feature is also a good criterion of what social exclusion means. Socially excluded people do not, as in previous forms of poverty, now share a "common fate" (Pétonnet, 1982) and its consequence, "a compulsory sociability" (Laé and Murard, 1985), but rather share this debate and this struggle with themselves and against themselves.

The experienced world of vulnerability

Presenting the life experienced by our interviewees with the aim of shedding light on social strategies means opening a door on their private life. It is not by chance that this issue arises because social exclusion today (and poverty yesterday) can be defined precisely as a lack of power – an inability – to protect one's private life. Poor people are required to tell their life story in order to obtain various services and benefits, and various experts evaluate these lives in order to locate the origin of the problem and the exact target for their intervention. Sociologists are no different, just worse. They only have corresponding symbolic rewards to offer.

I will give three different and short samples of the guilty-victim process, raising the issues of love and family, work, and adulthood. These samples do not draw a picture of people in extreme social exclusion, like homeless people, by *désaffiliation* (disaffiliation) in the sense of Castel (1995), but rather a picture of the experience of a world of precariousness, or, in Castel's term, of *vulnérabilité* (vulnerability). The vulnerability zone can be located in the neighbourhood of social exclusion. It signifies fragility either in the area of employment status, activity and resources, or in the area of family and network status, daily life and resources. We therefore add, on the basis of our interviews, that this fragility is reflected in the feeling of guilt.

1. Love inequalities

Mercia's story is a good starting point for understanding the price of love. It is a life devoted to professional and social success, whose cost is the renouncing of ambitions for a romantic love partnership and a feeling of guilt towards the children for not having been a good mother or given enough love. The professional and social success story is aimed at escaping a poor and violent childhood environment, which involved migration (from Spain) and constant hard work. Mercia did not marry the only man she fell in love with, but another man, more of a partner with whom to build a company and a family at the same time. Constant hard work also meant that both of the children, and especially the first one, a girl, were not given as much love as they deserved. Both of these assessments were formulated by Mercia herself at the age of 48, in a period of intense introspection brought on by a crisis in her work career. Looking back at her life, Mercia recalls the impossible love story with the man she met only twice, first when she was 16, in Spain, then, second, when she was already married with children. An impossible love story made of whispered confidences and tender glances, a love story that remained private throughout her life like "a secret garden", "a secret love". Mercia does not denigrate the man she married; she is still building and rebuilding a stable family life with him. However, she was never in love with him. Regarding the children, Mercia recalls both a failure to care for them adequately because of the demands of work, and a lack of love for the eldest. Her husband's parents wanted Mercia to have a boy. When the baby was born, in hospital, the husband's parents put the baby on Mercia's abdomen, the umbilical cord not yet cut. Mercia realised the baby was a girl, closed her eyes, and refused to care for her. Later on, she told the story to her daughter, who urged her not to worry about it, but Mercia is sure the baby did not receive the love she deserved from her mother.

Mercia's introspection goes far back into her life story, allowing us to link the story of her marriage and motherhood to her own experience as a child, fascinated by her violent father and not getting enough care and love from her mother.

Among several life stories that stress the core impact of love, Mercia's gives an insight on both dimensions of love – sexual partnership and parenthood. In each dimension, the romantic revolution ended in a sort of schizophrenia between subjectivism and rationalism (Taylor, 1989). A strong pattern of thinking and doing dictates that the sphere of love (passions, feelings and emotions) should be strictly separated from the sphere of money (interests and social status). As the saying goes, "He who loves doesn't count", implying that he who counts does not love (de Singly, 1996). Consequently, love is a luxury. In the romantic version, it is an inexhaustible spring, whose source is located in the heart. In biographies, however, in the experienced world of vulnerability, it is a scarce resource. It is inherited or earned, like other resources. Love, given and received, is the outcome of labour, rumination and fermentation. It is therefore affected by the amount of all the other resources that can be dedicated to this work: time, intelligence, money, and so on. In vulnerability or precariousness, the feeling and willingness to love is no less than in stability. On the contrary, the lack of other resources may increase the manifestation of love. However, the lack of material, financial and social resources continuously interacts with the emotional life. The norm of romantic love in conjugal life, with a satisfying sexual relationship, and the norm of parental care, with a devotion to children, is often not achieved. The result is a feeling of guilt[8].

It can be demonstrated that family stability is a recent phenomenon in French history, something won in parallel with the improvement in wage-earning conditions, which reached a peak in the 1970s (Verret, 1995). Since then, not only have working-class families been weakened by mass unemployment and precariousness but the traditional patterns of sexual roles and education have been challenged by new, liberal patterns (Neyrand, 2000). Consequently, a division has occurred within the working class in this sphere as well as in others. Some have had the resources to cope with change and have taken up the new patterns (Hurstel, 1996). Others, more vulnerable and often unemployed, have withdrawn to the domestic sphere, hanging on to former patterns but unable to implement them, in a sort of exile from the new standards (Schwartz, 1990). Between these two poles stands Mercia, a figure of vulnerability, that is, she is required to cope with unsatisfying life conditions, to choose an improvement in one aspect of life to the detriment of the other, to relegate aspirations for other improvements in a subjectivity closed in on itself, a secret garden, and to sublimate her desires[9].

2. Class culture

In the process of deindustrialisation in the 1980s and 1990s, hundreds of thousands of industrial workers, with varying levels of training, were faced with unemployment unless they were ready and able to change jobs, to leave the former industrial areas where mass unemployment was rampant, and often, in the case of stable older workers, to sell at a low price the house they had bought on credit and paid for with additional hard work. Why did some of them succeed in changing jobs, location and life, while others remained trapped in the past? The case of François[10] sheds light on the role of class culture in life strategies. Aged 40, the son of a miner, and working as an unskilled steelworker in Longey (an area deserted by industry in the 1980s), François chose to train in computing. Two years later, he took a job in Paris; he sold the house in Longey and moved to the Paris region with his family. He finds fault with fellow workers who are not ready to change, and criticises unions that do not encourage workers to commit themselves to the long-term interests of the firm.

In his narrative, François recalls the move to Paris as a turning point in life, and associates it with feelings of suffering, linked firstly to difficulties in the new location, difficulties in coping with the new life, and secondly to the distance from his original environment in Longey. Moving was "like an abandonment". Who is abandoning and who is being abandoned? In recalling the traditional working-class culture and environment in Longey, François expresses nostalgia for the past and for the rich social life in Longey. At the beginning of their new life in Paris, the family used to return to Longey every weekend, then less often, then not at all. To account for this progressive distancing, François gives a curious explanation:

> You cannot be fully integrated in this very close-knit family and community
> life if you are not working and living with the people on a daily basis.

He is quite right; but the distance created by the departure of the family can also be interpreted in sociological terms as a social distance, as a departure from and out of the working-class culture and condition. François' family had not long been integrated in working-class culture. His father had indeed been a miner, but that was as a result of his failure at school and something of a source of shame in the family. François' position was also the result of his own failure at school – his three sisters did not belong to the working class – and he had not married a working-class woman but rather the daughter of a peasant. The strategy of leaving Longey was therefore also a strategy of leaving the working class, and this strategy was possible because working-class culture was not deeply rooted in François' history[11]. The defence speech in François' narrative is aimed at showing firstly that it was not easy to leave and, secondly, that François is not the one who did the abandoning. However, the facts run against this speech. François made use of the opportunity of deindustrialisation to leave the area and the environment.

This case illustrates a very pronounced feature of social strategies in a risk society; that is, the influence of class structure and class culture in society. Indeed, the process of class reproduction has been disrupted by several changes.

The condition and the meanings of being a worker have changed, and have confused the boundaries and identities of the working classes. Features of ethnicity, sex, age and residence have become more important and more visible, but this process is precisely what exclusion is about. 'Exclusion' is the name given to the process of splitting up and reconstructing the working classes, a process in which a section of the former workers abandons the working-class condition. Another section is condemned to continuous precariousness or exclusion, a process whose culmination, not yet reached, is the weakening of the political power of the working class. Meanwhile, the fear of the upper classes is no longer that of revolution but rather of delinquency, crime, individual degeneration and urban insecurity (Wacquant, 1999).

3. Adulthood as a duty[12]

Young people's social strategies require a specific interpretation because for them the risk of social exclusion means not the risk of being *désaffilié* (excluded), but the risk of not being *affilié* (included). When looking, for instance, at the social trajectories of young adults on the streets (Laé and Murard, 1996), one can see that being on the streets, being without a family, is the outcome of a failure in the process of inclusion. In other words, that is the process of becoming an adult by obtaining a stable job and creating a new family. The injunction to become an adult can be said to be hypocritical, or even insane, first on account of the high rate of youth unemployment and, second, because adults urge the young to become adults as quickly as possible while they themselves are assiduously copying youth style and desperately trying to remain young for as long as possible.

Being urged towards inclusion, the young are like someone standing in front of a hurdle, which is the labour market. The material and emotional experience of childhood, family history and environment and the parents' plans for their children can be seen as resources that enable them to jump over the hurdle but also as greater or lesser handicaps that prevent them from jumping. Indeed, to become an adult involves a moratorium period, a time devoted to deciphering oneself and the world around, and this is more and more often turning into a precondition for finding a place on the labour market. In every case, young people think of work as a duty, accompanied by a feeling of guilt at not being able to achieve it. In many cases, however, the duty to enter the labour market may be less important than finding a good reason, an incentive, the commitment to become an adult as well as the search for freedom from family demands and expectations, in emotional and normative terms.

Pacing back and forth in front of the hurdle, waiting for something to happen, for the motivation to jump, vulnerable young people – especially when they have no qualifications – are faced with three different risks and opportunities. First, they can join a youth scheme, training scheme or job scheme, organised or funded by the state. This can be an opportunity to jump over the hurdle, but it also means the risk of being trapped in the situation of someone incapable of autonomy, and remaining in the situation of someone waiting for the solution to be provided by social workers. Second, they can join the black economy – petty illegal business and/or illegal work. This can be an opportunity to learn about themselves, their strengths and weaknesses, and about the world, its competition and rules. And it is obviously a risk, whose consequences can turn out to be very serious and prevent them returning to normal life in the future. Third, they can stay in the care of their family and wait for their parents to provide the solution. The state uses this as an opportunity to deny young people their right to various benefits (for instance, RMI is not available to young people under 25). Parents can also use this as a way of keeping their children at home. And the risk is not only dependency but also in many cases the risk of violence against themselves or others, when there is clearly a lack of love in the family. In other words, becoming an adult requires a connection, a spark between the close environment and the outside world.

Karim's case shows how the motivation towards autonomy is affected by the local environment and experiences in different areas. Born in 1976, Karim had a low vocational qualification in electronics and was still living with his mother (divorced) and siblings. His mother was working as a cleaning lady, supporting all the family on her low income. Karim discovered that his qualification did not entitle him to a job, that to get onto shortlists you needed skills not taught at school – you needed to demonstrate your motivation and also your submission to the employer. He started to work illegally, selling magazines and books in the street, learning how "to charm people into buying things". Then, when the boss refused to employ him on an official basis, Karim began a two-year moratorium period during which he claimed assistance from the state while at the same time working for an illegal small business. He did not make much money with the business and felt ashamed when he stayed in bed in the morning, seeing his mother going out to work while he, as the eldest boy, should have been able to support her after her divorce. He joined a training scheme, which he did not experience as useful (they did not provide jobs) or realistic (they spent days "finding out who you are"). However, he discovered that he had more abilities and resources than most of the young people attending the training. He rejected the stigma of being like them. It is likely that the confidence and love his mother continuously provided were the origin of his desire to prove that he was able to support her and the family. In the last months of this moratorium, he got involved in his community neighbourhood centre and became a youth leader. He then once more faced the ordinary labour market, jumping over the hurdle in one easy step. His first application got him onto the shortlist, he succeeded in acquiring professional training, obtained a qualification, and was given a stable and reasonably paid job.

When studying youth trajectories over a long period, one discovers that almost all of the young people eventually find their route into adulthood. Among a cohort of more than 1,000 unemployed young people, all aged 20, fewer than 10% were still unemployed after a period of 10 years (Nicole-Drancourt, 1991). These unemployed young people manifest not only a serious shortage of social and educational resources, but also stigma (associated with colour, language or culture), and these stem from a combination of negative biographical events and economic circumstances. Consequently, it can be said that social exclusion among the young is highly selective in the sense that it selects the most deprived young people, the group that remains after the others have been selected by the labour market. The issue of becoming an adult is a difficult one for almost all young people, and social exclusion of a minority is the outcome of a process that affects them all. Because of this process of competition, young people are likely to incline to an individualistic ethos. However, many young people try to find their route to adulthood and citizenship through commitment to volunteer groups, social work or political action (Madec, 1999).

From biography to social policy

Most amazing, in my opinion, is the fact that the interviewees scarcely make any spontaneous mention of financial or material difficulties, or speak of the role of welfare agencies in their life story. Of course, if the interviewer raises these issues, he can get interesting material. Several conclusions about welfare can be inferred from this fact. First, it is a distinctive feature of autobiographic narratives that neither material and financial problems nor the supporting role of welfare are mentioned, because, as the authors of their own life, the interviewees emphasise their actions and feeling rather than the material and financial constraints and supports they experience. Life stories are therefore very different from case histories constructed by social workers and social agencies, case histories being focused on needs, agencies, success and failure in being integrated into society. Second, this disparity reflects the inability of welfare agencies and welfare agents to understand the emotional and experiential sources of social exclusion or vulnerability. Third, this disparity may be different in different European countries and it is especially wide in France because the welfare state there has been set up and implemented mainly on a financial basis, as a means of compensating for the financial consequences of risks. The disparity therefore reflects the social division of welfare work, since welfare agencies are able to support people financially but unable to grasp their life experience. Private, volunteer agencies, on the other hand, although funded or supported by the state, may be able to gain people's confidence but are unable to support them properly at a material or financial level.

By focusing on face-to-face interactions in welfare agencies, however, this research has enabled us to bring out the significance for vulnerable and poor people of the relationship with welfare agents and welfare agencies (Moulière and Murard, 1998). The stigma of being poor, of being obliged to ask for support, even though this support is provided within the framework of the law, can be reinforced or reduced, depending on the attitude of welfare agents, by their verbal and body language. Interviews with welfare agents reveal a diversity of attitudes: from *empathy* (ability to feel with the client and to encourage him) to *pity*, at once sincerely trying to help and looking down on the client, judging who is deserving and who is not (apparently 'giving' support, rather than implementing the law, and so requesting a symbolic reward in the form of gratitude and humility) to *fear*, the wish to escape from the relationship as quickly as possible, identification with the agency and its norms, sheltering behind the law and regulations.

Interviews with welfare agents reveal that these different attitudes are strategies that allow them to cope with the stigma of social exclusion, to avoid being contaminated by this stigma of their clients. When we interviewed the agents about their vocational career as well as about their current work, we kept the door open for pieces of biographical narration. We discovered that agents with a capacity for empathy with their clients were also likely to give spontaneous accounts of large chunks of their own biography. We also discovered among these agents an objective and subjective closeness to the life their clients were experiencing. To use a medical metaphor, they do not fear the stigma because they were vaccinated at an early age. This is not to say that all agents who have experienced poverty are able to show empathy and remain professional at the same time. Empathy associated with closeness to the experience of social exclusion is an outcome of a trajectory experienced as positive: "I got out of it, I am lucky to have this position of agent". It includes the idea of a reward for the clients. Amazingly, this is the deep meaning of social citizenship as used by the French Revolution and later by the Fourth (1946) and Fifth (1958) Republics. Empathy includes the use of humour, and a distancing between the agent as person and the agent as representative of the agency. Conversely, the greatest distance between agents and clients occurs when the position of agent (representing a low level of qualification and wage) is experienced as downward mobility compared to the environment of origin and/or expectation. To interact with clients means to experience the danger of loss of purity (Douglas, 1967).

Welfare agents and welfare agencies can be thoughtful and innovative, as is shown by the following research in a local *Caisse d'allocations familiales* (family allowances agency). Several executives of the national body, the *Caisse nationale d'allocations familiales*, were very interested in the results of this research, because in recent years local agencies had been finding it difficult to get their agents to do desk work, the face-to-face work with clients, particularly since the implementation of the minimum wage. They called us in as experts, to tell them what needed to be done in terms of training. This was an opportunity to try the top-down method. "You have called us in as experts", we said, "and of course we think that we know better than you what is going on in the agencies. But that's not true. *You* are the experts, you know much better than we do what is going on in the agencies, because you are there every day and we have been there only for a short time." This idea was new to them, and we were able to continue: "Your position towards your agents is the same as our position towards you. You think you know what the agents do and think but that's not true. *They* are the experts." This idea was also new to them. And eventually we said: "The agents are in the same position towards the users as you are towards the agents. The agents think they know everything about the clients but that's not true. The users are the experts."

A process of learning from each other could now begin. The national body decided to launch a national call for research in eight different local agencies to check that the results of our research could be generalised and validated at national level. They asked us to make a scientific assessment of this research. In parallel, a working group in these agencies undertook a consultation exercise to mobilise the agents in the process, including the research but also including the elaboration of a project to change the organisation of work in order to facilitate the front-line work with the users. When the group comes to an agency, the group's executive members are asked to explain their project clearly in order to mobilise the agents. Their reply, however, is to say that the agents are the experts – support them and explain the importance and value of their work on the front line[13].

So far, the results from the experiment are:

- From a scientific point of view, the researchers have underlined not only the significance of the agent's biography but also of the agency's biography; that is, the weight of local history, outside and inside the agency. A local culture of welfare is implemented day after day, is included into the organisation of work and internalised as an ethos, notably through the words and attitudes of the executives, at the highest and intermediary levels. Fear, pity and empathy are not only features of individuals but also a construct formed by groups in their daily interactions.
- With regard to the agents, it became clear that attitudes towards clients were varied because the content of desk work – the work with clients – had not been defined by the agency but was left to the judgement of each agent. This was an occupation without a defined content, without a defined code of ethics, and without acknowledgement from the local and national body.
- With regard to the local executives, there emerged a clear duty to change work organisation, in order to give value to face-to-face work, and a duty to reinforce the training, support and supervision of the agents in face-to-face work, whether specialised or not.
- With regard to the national body, there emerged the need to elaborate a code of ethics for face-to-face work, and to rethink the division of labour (notably the separation between social workers and welfare agents) in the context of social exclusion.

Destiny and nature

It was under this title that Walter Benjamin advocated the idea that misfortune and fault, the constituents of destiny, are not mainly the domains of religion but of law:

> But an order whose sole intrinsic concepts are misfortune and guilt, and within which there is no conceivable path of liberation (for insofar as something is fate, it is misfortune and guilt) – such an order cannot be religious, no matter how the misunderstood concept of guilt appears to suggest the contrary. Another sphere must therefore be sought in which misfortune and guilt alone carry weight, a balance on which bliss and innocence are found too light and float upwards. This balance is the scale of law. The laws of fate – misfortune and guilt – are elevated by law to measures of the person. (Benjamin 1996 [1919], p 203).

This idea allows us to understand why the narratives of vulnerability are presented as speeches for the defence. It also suggests to the sociologist that he should ask himself about the relationship between 'sociological laws' on the one hand, which supposedly deal with ideas and actions, and, on the other, laws or norms to which witnesses refer themselves in their narratives in an explicit or implicit manner. In other words, the relationship between guides chosen by individuals for their action and the causal determinants held by the social sciences to be responsible for these actions; between auto-constraints and hetero-constraints, in Norbert Elias' terms. This issue is crucial in biographical approaches, because the constraints the witnesses give to themselves can add to the constraints attributed by sociologists to the point of impeding any kind of liberation. The promise of liberation included in the philosophy of enlightenment would be broken if science limited itself to the determinism already privately experienced.

Two different sorts of solution have been experienced in recent decades, and are still being experienced by our interviewees to fulfil the promise of liberation. The first one, roughly Marxist, is the political struggle experienced by one of our witnesses, Gérard[14]. The fact that he says he is happy, his humour and biographical voluntarism are a good indication of the validity of this choice at an individual level, but collectively he does not have much impact. The second one, roughly Freudian, is the work of introspection and is well illustrated by the case of Irène (Murard, 1998a, pp 35-8), even though she has by no means reached the end of it. However, Freudian introspection is only a solution for an individual and it can be argued, even in the language of those who advocate it, that Freudianism reinforces the social order, that it conspires with the law in weighing misfortune and fault and is therefore not an opening for change (Legendre, 1989). Consequently, in social sciences, the use of biographies could turn out to be more satisfying if, instead of producing categories, and instead of filling the empty boxes provided by governments and the authorities, and instead of looking for typical cases and the inevitable, we concentrated on singularity, the nature of each witness and the value of each single life.

Regarding risk society and social strategies, however, we must come to a conclusion on this guilt-centred approach and assess its value in the analysis of social exclusion. Adorno (1951) provides the key, in this respect, of the relationship between exclusion and inclusion, outside and inside, margin and centre of society:

––––

Between the upper classes' solidarity and their attempts to get closer to representatives of the lower classes, there is a mediator: the feeling of guilt – legitimate enough – of the rich towards the poor. (Adorno, 1951, p 71, my translation).

While waiting for the liberation, we can base ourselves on the feeling of guilt – that is, advocate welfare. Better still, we can take action in order to transfer the feeling of guilt from the poor to the rich, to push it bottom-up instead of top-down. Historically speaking, fear has been a powerful incentive for the implementation of welfare. The upper classes are no longer afraid enough – they just play at urban insecurity as an election argument. The feeling of guilt can be an incentive for welfare and, with the aim of implementing innovative and good practice in the field of welfare, it can be more than a concept. It can also, for the reasons given above, be an experience shared, for different and opposite reasons, by the included as well as by vulnerable, disaffiliated people. Social exclusion may no longer be an empty box – it may not even be an appropriate concept – but it can be an illusory idea which the state uses to seduce the supporters of welfare onto its side, like bees around a poisoned honey pot.

Notes

[1] I would like to acknowledge the help of all the participants of the French Sostris research team (Nathalie Busiaux, Karima Guenfoud and Vanessa Stettinger) and the interviewees for giving of their time and of themselves.

[2] For a more detailed picture, see Murard (1997).

[3] This is also why the continental models of welfare, mainly funded by employers' contributions, have been directly weakened by mass unemployment (see Friot, 1998).

[4] In the field of psychoanalysis, this feeling of guilt has been especially studied by Rank (1936). Hesnard (1949), who introduced the translated works of Freud to France, was strongly concerned by the issue of remorse of innocent people. In this book, he acknowledges his debt to Rank.

[5] The case is developed at greater length by Murard (1998a, pp 35-8).

[6] For instance, in the most recent statistical report about homelessness in Paris, more than 80% of the homeless are of working-class origin. See Marpsat (1999) and Marpsat and Firdion (1999).

[7] Statistical evidence shows no increase in upward or downward mobility in France since the Second World War, despite the changes in the nature and distribution of jobs

(fewer manual workers, more white-collar workers and technicians; see Merllié, 2000). The social reproduction process (Bourdieu and Passeron, 1970) is still efficient.

[8] A more extended treatment of Mercia's case can be found in Murard (1998a, pp 32-4). Another, shorter, view is Chapter Eight of this volume.

[9] The issue of homosexuality should be raised here as an unbearable solution and a deep desire. Between the husband and Prince Charming stands, in Mercia's life story, a charming man, fashion designer, homosexual – a man from whom she has nothing to fear and receives a lot.

[10] This case is discussed in greater detail by Murard (1999).

[11] For an example of the very opposite, the reader might look at the case of Bernard quoted in Chapter Seven of this volume.

[12] For a complete discussion about concepts and experiences of the transition from youth to adulthood, please see our composite report 'Unqualified youth', and the report about youth in France, 'Change into a transition', both in *Sostris Working Paper 5* (Murard, 1999b).

[13] This process, called action-research, is seldom found in France where there is a strong separation between 'pure' (mainly university-based) and 'applied' research (in agencies), the latter normally belittled by academics for being supposedly 'unscientific'.

[14] Quoted in Chapter Six of this volume.

References

Adorno, T.W. (1951) *Minima Moralia*, Paris: Payot (French translation *Réflexions sur la vie mutilée* [1980]).

Agamben, G. (1978) *Enfance et histoire*, Paris: Payot.

Beaud, S and Pialoux, M. (1999) *Retour sur la condition ouvrière: Enquête aux usines Peugeot*, Paris: Fayard.

Benedict, R. (1946) *The chrysanthemum and the sword*, 1989 edn, Boston, MA: Houghton Mifflin.

Benjamin, W. (1996 [1919]) 'Fate and character'; reprinted in his *Selected writings*, vol 1, Cambridge: Harvard University Press, pp 201-6.

Bourdieu, P. (ed) (1993) *The weight of the world: Social suffering in contemporary society*, Cambridge: Polity Press.

Bourdieu, P. and Passeron J.-C. (1970) *La reproduction*, Paris: Minuit.

Castel, R. (1995) *Les métamorphoses de la question sociale. Chronique du salariat*, Paris: Fayard.

Chevalier, G. (1996) 'Volontarisme et rationalité d'Etat. L'exemple de la politique de la ville', *Revue française de sociologie*, vol 37.

Cobb, J. and Sennett, R. (1972) *The hidden injuries of class*, Cambridge: Cambridge University Press.

Dejours, C. (1998) *Souffrance en France: La banalisation de l'injustice sociale*, Paris: Seuil.

De Singly, F. (1996) *Le soi, le couple et la famille*, Paris: Nathan.

Dodds, E.R. (1965) *Les Grecs et l'irrationnel*, Paris: Aubier-Montaigne.

Douglas, M. (1999 [1986]) 'La connaissance de soi', in *Comment pensent les institutions*, Paris: La Découverte, new French translation, pp 153-62.

Douglas, M. (1967) *Purity and danger*, London: Routledge/Kegan Paul Ltd.

Elias, N. (1974) *La société de cous*, Paris: Calmann-Lévy.

Ewald, F. (1986) *L'Etat providence*, Paris: Grasset.

Friot, B. (1998) *Puissances du salariat*, Paris: La Dispute.

Hesnard, A. (1949) *L'univers morbide de la faute*, Paris: Bibliothèque de psychanalyse et de psychologie clinique, Presses Universitaires de France.

Hurstel, F. (1996) *La déchirure paternelle*, Paris: Presses Universitaires de France.

Ion, J. (1996) 'L'exclusion, une problématique française, *Lien social et politique*, vol 34.

Laé, J.-F. and Murard, N. (1985) *L'argent des pauvres. La vie quotidienne en cité de transit*, Paris: Seuil.

Laé, J.-F. and Murard, N. (1996) 'Célibataire à la rue', *Actes de la recherche en sciences sociales*, vol 113, pp 31-40.

Legendre, P. (1989) *Le crime du caporal Lortie, traité sur le père*, Champs, Paris: Flammarion.

Madec, A. (1998) *Le quartier, c'est dans la tête*, Paris: Flammarion.

Marpsat, M. (1999) 'Les sans-domicile à Paris et aux USA', *Données sociales*, Paris: Insee, pp 480-9.

Marpsat, M. and Firdion, J.M. (1999) 'Sans domicile et mal logés. Bilan des travaux de l'Ined', *Travaux et documents*, no 144, p 414.

Merllié, D. (2000) *La mobilité sociale*, 'Repères', Paris: La découverte.

Moulière, M. and Murard, N. (1998) 'Le travail des uns et le souci des autres. Approche biographique des agents et usagers de la CAF', *Recherches et prévisions*, vol 54, pp 7-24.

Murard, N. (1998a) 'French national report on lone parents', in *Sostris Working Paper 3: Case study materials – lone parents*, London: Centre for Biography in Social Policy, University of East London, pp 30-42.

Murard, N. (1998b) 'The economy is destroying society: social exclusion in France', in *Sostris Working Paper 1: Case study materials – social exclusion in comparative perspective*, London: Centre for Biography in Social Policy, University of East London.

Murard, N. (1999a) 'Unqualified young people: the injunction and aspirations to become an adult. Composite Report', *Sostris Working Paper 6: Case study materials – unqualified youth*, London: Centre for Biography in Social Policy, University of East London, pp 1-6.

Murard, N. (1999b) 'Unqualified young people: change into a transition', *Sostris Working Papers 6: Case study materials – unqualified youth*, London: Centre for Biography in Social Policy, University of East London, pp 76-82.

Murard, N. (1999c) 'Qualified and unqualified workers: across changing times', *Sostris Working Paper 6: Case study materials – ex-traditional workers*, London: Centre for Biography in Social Policy, University of East London, pp 8-16.

Neyrand, G. (2000) *L'enfant, la mère et la question du père*, Paris: Presses Universitaires de France.

Nicole-Drancourt, C. (1991) *Le labyrinthe de l'insertion*, Paris: La documentation française.

Pennac, D. (1995) 'Interview', *Lire*, 2 May.

Perret, B. and Roustang, G. (1993) *L'économie contre la société,* Paris: Seuil.

Pétonnet, C. (1982) *Espaces habités*, Paris: Galilée.

Rank, O. (1936) *Truth and reality: A life-history of the human will*, New York, NY: Knopf.

Ricoeur, P. (1960) *Philosophie de l'esprit. Vol 2: Finitude et culpabilité*, Paris: Aubier-Montaigne.

Schwartz, O. (1990) *Le monde privé des ouvriers*, Paris: Presses Universitaires de France.

Taylor, C. (1989) *Sources of the self*, Cambridge, MA: Harvard University Press.

Théry, I. (1993) *Le démariage. Justice et vie privée*, Paris: O. Jacob.

Verret, M. (1995) *Chevilles ouvrières*, Paris: L'Atelier.

Wacquant, L. (1999) *Les prisons de la misère*, Paris: Raisons d'agir.

FOUR

Premodernity and postmodernity in Southern Italy

Antonella Spanò

Is Southern Italy (il Mezzogiorno[1]) the most economically underdeveloped and culturally traditional part of the country, in the throes of the processes of 'detraditionalisation' and individualisation? Is there a waning of the influence of tradition, which, although 'freeing' the individual from the bonds of the past, brings with it the eradication of frames of reference and exposure to uncertainty?

Does the dismantling of life trajectories associated with the demise of the 'job for life' model make it impossible to plan the future according to a shared social calendar?

Does the collapse of collective allegiances and solidarity give rise in turn to a process of individualisation, and leave responsibility for decision making entirely to the individual? If so, how do these processes manifest themselves, and what effects do they have on individual life stories?

And, ultimately, what implications do such issues have for social policy?

This chapter seeks answers to these questions.

It may seem strange to pose the question of whether a reality such as Southern Italy can remain wholly intact in the face of such overarching phenomena. Their connection to the globalisation process alone seems to suggest its pervasiveness. To suggest that intractable backwardness/tradition might act as a form of antibody, or antidote, rendering this part of the country impervious to change, may even seem misleading. Nevertheless, the view presented here is that this is a legitimate question, and one that deserves attention. The combination of the common conceptualisation of globalised, flexible, post-industrial, late-modern society – or however else one wishes to define it – as the society of the future, and the equally deep-seated tendency to view the South as the *locus* of the past and of premodernity, can easily generate misunderstanding. For example, consider the way that Southerners, experts in the art of 'making do' by doing a myriad of jobs in the underground economy, are seen as being at an advantage when it comes to withstanding the conditions of 'fluidity' imposed by the new social and economic order, and which has flexibility as its cornerstone.

As with any field of enquiry, it is possible to address the issue at hand in a variety of ways. The approach adopted here takes the form of a comparison between the biographies of two Neapolitans, Filippo and Franco[2]. Filippo is a 'victim' of the shattering of the *société salariale* – the waged society (Castel, 1995) – more specifically of company restructuring following the introduction of a new system of production. He is, in other words, 'newly excluded' (Wolf, 1995). Conversely, Franco, is 'hitherto excluded' (Wolf, 1995). He has not, in fact, 'lost' his position in society; rather, he has simply never had one. Franco's story exemplifies the typical lot of the young, unemployed, unqualified Neapolitan, who has grown up amid social deprivation and marginalisation. As will be seen, despite the overwhelming differences that distinguish them, Filippo and Franco have many common characteristics, particularly that of being deprived of certainties.

Filippo

Filippo is born in 1950 into a highly traditional, middle-class family. His father, a journalist, has devoted his life entirely to his work; his mother, a housewife, has dedicated hers to the family.

Throughout his childhood and youth, Filippo's life seems to follow a normal course: he keeps up with his studies, leaves school with qualifications in classics and obtains a degree. His choice of faculty, though, deserves comment. Filippo opts to study law, the discipline best able to equip him for taking part in state competitions that will lead to a 'permanent and stable work', rather than literature or political science, disciplines more suited to a career in journalism. Job 'exchanges' between father and son are commonplace at the regional paper where his father works – apart from the fact that several of his older relatives have got into journalism in this way (it is something of a family tradition). However, Filippo chooses not to follow in his father's footsteps. The 'full-blown modernism' of the 1970s has taken hold, the ties of inheritance have been severed, a climate of conflict pervades intergenerational relations, and therefore Filippo prepares to fulfil himself in his own right rather than as someone else's son. However, the difficulties he faces in achieving this will condition his life for years to come, as we shall see.

Not long after his father retires, when it becomes clear that it would no longer be possible for Filippo to take over his job at the newspaper even if he had changed his mind about it, Filippo becomes active in the Communist Party. This is a completely alien area of politics to his family. At the time (1973), left-wing activism was certainly no exception among university students. Nevertheless, the way Filippo describes his choice clearly indicates that, for him, political militancy is dictated more by the desire to belong than by ideological motives. It is a substitute for the career guidance he has been deprived of by his father. Significantly, Filippo never recounts his story in the first person; rather, he speaks from the point of view of a 'we', initially constituted by the dyad 'my father and I': "After I graduated, *we* set out to find an occupation, *we* started to do some state competitions" (emphasis added). Later, it comprises the political group he joins during his university years: "*We* also founded a subdivision .... *We* were involved in political activism". The only time he uses the first person is when he describes his change in affiliation from the family to the party: "As a young man *I* joined the Communist Party". Moreover, after completing his studies, Filippo's strategies for entering the job market clearly indicate how he uses political militancy as a substitute for paternal support for his entry into the workplace. Thanks to contacts made through the party, he starts work as a proofreader for a communist journal. Therefore, it seems as though Filippo is pursuing his own personal compromise with tradition. On the one hand, he seeks to escape the 'social reproduction' strategy of the good bourgeois, namely the intergenerational transmission of professional and social capital, while on the other hand, he follows in his father's footsteps, entering the world of the printed page thanks to the party he supports.

Only his steadfast determination to become a journalist without the help of his family can explain why, even before intellectual unemployment reaches grave proportions, and despite having a good degree and a reasonable network of family and party relationships, Filippo should remain so attached to such a precarious occupation. Certainly, his field of work does not meet all of his aspirations. Nonetheless, the possibility of working for a newspaper is an acceptable compromise: as a proofreader, he is still able to be among journalists: "When I used to do the proofreading they would come and fetch me with a car, with another journalist, and we would both go – me and the journalist". Also, at this point, he has still not lost hope of writing for a paper: "Some of those intellectuals urged me to write, and I began to write, in fact I wrote an entire article, which I still have. They wanted to help me get started".

When, in 1976, he is offered a job as secretary on the editorial staff of a new Neapolitan daily connected to the party, Filippo has no doubts; he accepts, even though it means sacrificing his ambitions. For him, joining the paper is equivalent to becoming part of a new family. His commitment goes well beyond the call of duty. He carries out tasks outside the bounds of his remit: "Before we opened for business, I even had to take care of getting the desks and chairs and sending the first faxes". He spends the majority of his time at the paper, but it does not bother him because, as he sees it, his secretarial job is his key to accessing that world, and the paper is the hub of his network of relations:

> I used to do the 'Entertainments' page. I would have to call 60 or 70 cinemas and ask, "What films are you showing today? And tomorrow? And the day after tomorrow?" There was this direct communication with the box office ... organising the diary, appointments, conferences and debates, that was a job in itself. Then we would get the 'Film' page ready, 'Art and Current Affairs', and then we had to deal with the public; that was a whole area of work that was interesting because then you got to know people.

In addition, for the first time Filippo has a regular income and the security that goes hand in hand with becoming a permanent employee.

The way he deals with the conversion required when the paper moves over to typesetting (1978) shows that, at that time, Filippo is fully able to readjust. Just as before he managed to withstand the frustration of his journalistic aspirations thanks to the personal and relational components of his job, this time he overcomes the radical transformation of his profession through the support provided by membership of the paper/party. Now deprived of these relations, he is made to work for hours on end in front of a computer. Filippo reorients himself, and makes his technical–professional capabilities a point of pride:

> We were one of the first newspapers to get rid of old technology and introduce computer-aided design and composition. Well, then you have no need for secretaries – a quick typing course, and then a course in Rome, you stay at a hotel, eat, travel up to Rome, all expenses paid, spend a day and a night in Rome.

This allows him to compete with university professors and journalists, and to retain his job, even when in 1982 a number of employees are made redundant when the newspaper is taken over by different management:

> I wasn't directly affected by redundancy or dismissal. Why? Because I worked with computers. Computers were still a new thing in the 1980s; hardly anyone knew how to use them, journalists wouldn't go near them, so the cutbacks affected other unskilled people, not me.

Subsequently, buttressed by the backing of his colleagues/comrades, Filippo even manages to cope with the bankruptcy of the company that owns the newspaper. In fact, the employees form a cooperative and take it over and, albeit with great sacrifices, manage to stave off its closure. Despite such difficulties, Filippo enjoys a period of stability during these years. Never having had a girlfriend, he gets engaged, then marries (1981) and later becomes a father (1985).

Work, then, constitutes the driving force in Filippo's life. Indeed, his autobiographical reconstruction focuses almost exclusively on his professional trajectory, from graduation, "my life ... from 1975, the year I graduated in law", up until his redundancy, which represents the 'end', not only of his story, but of his life:

> I am 46 years old. I have 13 years of contributions to my name, when the minimum needed for the basic rate of 650,000 lire is 20. The pensionable age has been raised to 65 whereas here, by the time you are 45 or 46 you are already finished.

In Filippo's own reconstruction of his life, 1989 is the year that marks his decline:

The POLICY P~P PRESS

The Policy Press
University of Bristol
34 Tyndall's Park Road
Bristol BS8 1PY • UK

Tel: +44 (0)117 954 6800
Fax: +44 (0)117 973 7308
E-mail: tpp@bristol.ac.uk

Direct: +44 (0)117 954 ———

with compliments

Date as postmark

Dear Andrew

**Biography and social exclusion in Europe**

We would like to take this opportunity to thank you for your input in the refereeing process for this title, be it in providing comments or a testimonial endorsing the book.

The book is priced at £19.99 and further copies can be purchased directly from our distributors, Marston Book Services (PO Box 269, Abingdon, Oxon OX14 4YN, tel: +44 (0)1235 465500).

We may contact you in the future for the possibility of refereeing other titles – please could you let us know if you would not be interested in being approached.

If you would like further information on The Policy Press, or would be interested in submitting a proposal yourself, please do not hesitate to contact myself or Alison Shaw, the Director.

With all best wishes, _**Dawn Rushen**_ (Editorial and Production Manager) www.policypress.org.uk

> The cooperative lasted until 1989, then in 1989 the Wall came down, the Soviet Wall, the Communist Party almost ceased to exist.... The cooperative had a few debts, and then in November the newspaper closed for good, even in the form of a cooperative. How is one to reinvent oneself? It's easier said than done! It's easier said than done! How was one supposed to reinvent oneself in 1989?!

As a result of the shifts that follow the fall of the Berlin Wall, the communist newspaper suffers financial losses. It is forced to close down and the cooperative is disbanded. Undoubtedly, this event indirectly has a deep impact on Filippo's life. After 13 years of stable employment, at the age of 40 and a father, he finds himself with no a job, and no form of welfare. Nevertheless, from his description of his lived life, there is no sign of crisis during that year. On the contrary, once again Filippo shows himself to be highly resourceful. Immediately after the closure of the newspaper, thanks to some contacts, he manages to get a position at a sports news agency, working as a secretary. Then, six months later, thanks to union pressure, he is hired as a keyboard operator on the staff of a new regional daily paper, this time unconnected to the party (in fact, tending more towards the right).

For all its problems, then, the year that marks Filippo's professional decline is not 1989, but 1993, when he finds himself under renewed threat of losing his job. His boss at the paper becomes implicated in judicial proceedings. Then, all the employees are laid off, and later given redundancy. The purchase of the paper by a new company, which does not rehire the old employees, marks Filippo's definitive exit from the editorial world. Unlike in the past, now Filippo must deal with his problems alone, his new colleagues being strangers to him:

> I always had a close relationship with my old colleagues, we were very, very close, and there was also respect. At the new place, the pay was better, but the environment ... I didn't like it, it wasn't good, there wasn't that sense of fraternity. There just wasn't.

Moreover, Filippo is forced to accept that the era of struggle is over. Even his old comrades at the cooperative, probably aware of the changing landscape, have adopted individualistic strategies, and taken up other activities, rather than mobilising collectively.

It is at this point that Filippo begins to reinterpret his life story as one of a victim of external causes. Above all, his failure is due to his father who, failing to 'elect' him as his heir, pushed him towards finding a permanent job:

> We were always a family that worked in the newspaper business. My father was a celebrated journalist, one of his cousins was an editor-in-chief. My father was a journalist for 30 years.... Instead, my father urged me to do state

competitions, he didn't push me to go into his field, he pushed me to do entrance competitions.

Secondly, his ruin has been caused by transformations that have affected society as a whole, over which he has no control, such as technological innovation:

Life changed when they brought in those computers ... always sitting in front of a computer ... it was, it was, it was mortifying. And the fall of the Berlin Wall: the catastrophe of the Wall, the Wall collapsed and the whole paper, the whole party, collapsed with it.

Filippo is aware that his biographical trajectory has been hampered by his inability to act as an individual once his time with the party is over. This is why he associates 1989, the year of the collapse of communism, with his own demise. However, incapable of self-honesty − an obligatory step towards self-reflexivity, as Giddens affirms (because in order to reinvent oneself one must come to terms with one's mistakes) − and unable to analyse the causes of his weakness, Filippo is consumed by self-justification, and constructs a narrative that serves purely to keep his sense of personal failure at bay.

Unable to reorient himself, or to discern any conceivable future, Filippo begins to get back on his feet by taking on some casual work. Approaching his fifties, and with a law degree, he is compelled to type graduation dissertations on the computer or distribute flyers in order to survive, and gives up all hope of reinstatement. Furthermore, just as before, when stability at work went hand in hand with stability in his personal life, so losing his job is accompanied by a collapse in his family relations. Following a path that mirrors that described by Paugam (1991), though continuing to live with his wife and son, Filippo now lives on the fringes of his family. It is no coincidence that he refers to his wife and son as 'they' rather than 'we'. He feels ashamed towards his son because he is without a concrete professional role:

Sometimes they ask him, "What does your father do for a living?" And he says, "He works in newspapers." "Which newspapers?" "He does bits and pieces for different ones, he moves around", my son says. One day he might well turn round and ask me, "What do you actually do?"

He feels excluded from family activities: "I can't go away with them, *they* go on holiday with the relatives, my wife's relatives" (emphasis added). He feels unable to compete with his wife's family: "She has four brothers who have all settled down, they are in good health, they have good friends, one is a university professor, another an engineer". They are, in fact, 'taking away' his wife and son from him:

> *They* are always going round there, Saturdays and Sundays, they are always there for the holidays. *My* son is brought up by his uncles. *I* feel alone, alone, all alone, I have no involvement, no incentive, nothing.

Unable to look to the future, Filippo seeks an unlikely solution in an equally unlikely return to the past – he thinks the unions might help. He even gets in contact with his old school friends, now successful professionals, in the hope that they might be able to assist him. Even his endless free time allows him to immerse himself in the past. He reminisces about his days on the 'Entertainments' page. He goes regularly to exhibitions; he takes part, alone, in every type of cultural event publicised in the newspapers, of which he is now merely an avid reader. He wanders the cinemas and theatres, whose owners he known for years on a professional level, in search of free tickets.

The loss of his job and the disintegration of the sense of belonging which previously constituted his main source of affiliation and identity, namely the party, have undermined Filippo's biographical integrity. He is part of a generation who trusted without a second thought in the guarantee of job security, and was an industrial worker; that is, he felt himself sticking entirely to a standard biography based on the full-time, 'job for life' work model. He has, therefore, been bitterly disappointed. Sadly, not only has he been unable to reinvent himself as a good father and husband (it is impossible for him to do so without being a breadwinner), he has also been unable to redefine himself as an 'endless worker'. Having grown up in a middle-class milieu, the art of 'making do' is completely foreign to him. Moreover, the comparison with his wife's relatives, who embody such an environment, reinforces his image of his failure.

Franco

Franco, the youngest of six children, is a 19-year-old unemployed Neapolitan whose father is a driver for a public transport operator and is approaching retirement. He lives in a city suburb, once the seat of many industrial enterprises that have since closed down. Unlike his father, who never went to school, Franco, being the son of a regular if humble worker, does not avoid compulsory education and is enrolled in school as normal. His experience of secondary school, though, is not easy. Effectively, Franco has learned little at primary school. He manages to avoid failing purely because teachers tend not to reject anyone during the first phase of school in order to avoid drop-outs, particularly in lower-class areas. At secondary school, however, everything comes to a head – Franco starts to get low grades, there is no one at home able to help him with his homework, and his parents cannot pay for private lessons. What is more, Franco completely lacks the social skills necessary to take school discipline on board. When he is given a 10-day suspension by the head for an aggressive reaction to a teacher's telling-off, he decides to leave school for good. After all, the value of education is entirely absent from his family's culture. Indeed, it is his mother who presents him with the option of dropping out of school:

> When they suspended me for 10 days, I went home and my mother said,
> "Either you go to school or you go to work", and I chose work.

At just 12 years of age, then, Franco initiates a course of exploitation and instability comparable to many of his peers. He does one job after another, always looking for something better, that pays more or takes fewer hours. He leaves his job as an assistant mechanic because he finds it unbearable to have grease on his hands at the end of the day when all he wants is to be like the other boys in the neighbourhood. Even though they might carry out some bag snatching and such like, they are always well dressed and have designer clothes. Working as a flower seller at the market seems infinitely more attractive – but he then realises "it wasn't much money, only 20,000 lire a week. I couldn't even buy a pair of shoes because they cost 100,000 or 200,000 lire". Next a bar job seems preferable, as he can make more money with the tips. But then this, too, becomes unsustainable because, "I was a bit older then and I was embarrassed going back and forth with the tray serving coffee, with my friends all watching and taking the mickey". Finally, he thinks he has found the right job working as a painter for a construction firm. After a few months, however, he discovers that having an irregular job has its risks: "They were meant to be giving me 80,000 lire a day, but after 15 days' work they gave me 300,000 and said they'd give me the rest later. And I've not seen them since." And so the years go by, with one job following another. Nothing really happens – nothing, that is, until fear of the future starts to set in.

There is still another route to be taken, one that is always available to boys in deprived areas: crime. As Franco relates, at 16, "I started doing some silly things, like selling a bit of hash, little things like that". However, even this cannot last – he comes from an honest, hardworking family who have instilled in him the value of honesty. Consequently, deviance is a path that:

> I cannot follow because my mother isn't one to tell me to go out and steal, or
> get up to mischief and bring home the money, like some of my friends' parents
> do. If my mother knew of anything like that she would suffer terribly. My
> mother and father are decent people, they're good people who work, not like
> some, who give their kids drugs and tell them to go out and sell them.

So, on reaching adulthood – that is, when he is old enough to risk prison for petty offences – he gives up this activity too. All the while, his fear of the future is growing, as is his sense of loneliness. He used to have a girlfriend, of whom he was very fond, but has now lost her:

> She said to me, "You don't work, how can you have the front to present
> yourself to my father? Get a job first and then show your face". And she's
> already found another boyfriend who works. They're engaged, the family
> approves, she's settled down and that's where it ended.

Finding another girlfriend is not easy: who will have you if you do not have a job and the money for a pizza? On the other hand, asking for money from his parents, from a mother who has grown old and has still never treated herself to having her hair done, or a father who has become ill from working hard to support his family, inspires deep shame:

> I can't say to my dad "Give me 5,000 lire, or 10,000 lire". I can't ask my mother – then she'll go without.... That's all the money they have, and we have to buy food with it, pay the bills. My mother already deprives herself to give me money.

Sometimes, however, he has to ask for money, and is racked with guilt:

> If only I had listened to my father when he told me not to leave each of those jobs I had.... If I had continued with my studies, I wouldn't be in this position. I mean, I can't even write, I've forgotten everything. When I was seven or eight I was good at it, I've still got my books at home where the teacher wrote 'Good, excellent' by my work, but now, with a pen in my hand, I can't write.... It's a shame because writing is important. I can read, I'm not stupid, but I'm not clever either, because I didn't go to school. In the end school is what really counts.

What is there in Franco's mind? Not much hope, of course. Friends and acquaintances he supposed he could count on have served little purpose, except for helping him get some job that he left at the earliest opportunity. The 'permanent job' his father managed to find after years of uncertainty now seems like a mirage – you would have to be mad to still want that. Everyone agrees that the era of mass hiring in local/state administrations, used as a social cushion against unemployment, has come to a definite end. The days of the 'movement of organised unemployed'[3], which once allowed many Neapolitans to find a stable work, are long gone. The possibility of learning a job is also lost forever: who would ever dream of taking him on as an apprentice? No one, since employers prefer to take on 14- or 15-year-olds, who are satisfied with only 50,000 lire a week.

What could he do, then, in this state of an empty future and an equally amorphous present? Dreaming, for example, that a pools coupon might change his life, or that sooner or later a job in one of the cities in the north of Italy will magically materialise ("There are four or five of us who talk about getting on a train, heading for Parma and staying two or three days to see if a job comes up"). Or travelling, with his mind at least, since geographical as much as social mobility is denied him ("smoking a joint from time to time"). Or taking time, waiting for military service, which hopefully will fill his tragically empty days, each the same as the one before:

I wake up at midday, then I go down to the café. You always do the same things. Then it's 2.30 and I have lunch, then I have a lie down. I go down to the café again at six, then back home for dinner at eight and then out again at nine or nine-thirty. I hang around outside the café, go for a stroll with some of my friends, by then it's 11.30 or midnight so I go home again, and the next day it's the same thing all over again – get up, go down to the café.... I'm fed up of just getting by. If I worked, things would be better ....

Comparing cases

How does this connect to Filippo? What can a decent, 50-year-old, middle-class husband and father, with a degree, a history of political participation and a clearly defined (if disrupted) working life, possibly have in common with a young Neapolitan who is practically illiterate, has a history of instability and virtual poverty, is unemployed, has no girlfriend and can only enumerate the failures in his life? If one were merely to compare their economic, social and cultural resources, the sociocultural contexts they live in, the roles they fulfil, or, above all, the risks they run of falling prey to poverty and exclusion, the answer would be nothing. But if one were to go beyond and set aside their differences, looking, instead, for similarities, it would become clear that striking analogies can be drawn between them. These all derive from the fact that they are both products of a society that has said 'there is no long-term' (Sennett, 1999), and of an epoch deeply marked by risk, uncertainty and the absence of ready-made scripts.

These traits, then, are characteristic of both men. Clearly, Filippo and Franco come up against the reality of their historical context at different stages of life: one is already an adult, so his life is 'cut short', whereas the other is a young man, and therefore his is 'impeded'. Nevertheless, the crucial elements of late modernity, such as uncertainty (Bauman, 1999) and the lack of the frames of reference needed to orient one's life course (Giddens, 1991), are evident in both. Moreover, both are victims of a further cardinal feature of post-Fordist society (Beck, 1992; Castel, 1995), namely the collapse of the great collective fraternity. When facing redundancy, Filippo is unable to rely on the solidarity of his comrades because the era of collective struggle has passed. Similarly, faced with unemployment, Franco cannot depend upon the practical or psychological support that membership of a movement would have provided, whereas in the past, the unemployed movement would provided a source of identity, as well as assistance in finding work. In other words, both are *alone*, unable to conceive of themselves in terms of a collective 'we', and forced to be solely responsible for themselves and their decisions, thanks to the process of intensifying individualisation (Beck, 1992).

Above all, both have been deprived of the linearity of time, and therefore of the chance to foresee not only what circumstances might create in the future, but when and under what conditions. Both have been prevented from following a career, a term which, whether the objective was an elevated, average or menial type of occupation, indicated exactly where individual energies needed to be directed, a direction that had to be maintained for life (Sennett, 1999). Both are denied a foreseeable future: Filippo, of the image of his old age (where will he live when he is older?), of playing with his grandchildren (will he have any?) and enjoying his son's educational and professional achievements (what will become of him, given that his father has nothing to pass on to him?), and Franco, of the expectations that were certainties for his predecessors (eventually getting a state position, learning a job through a long apprenticeship that enables survival, marriage, fatherhood, and so on).

As a background to this, macro-processes have undoubtedly occurred, transforming systems of production and regulation. Examples of these include the globalisation of markets, the intensification of competition, the acceleration of restructuring processes, the relocation of mass production, more widespread flexible employment, the new burden of information technologies, the withdrawal of welfare and the increasingly precarious nature of career paths. However, as Sennett (1999) rightly affirms, it is more the temporal dimension of the new capitalism than advanced technological data transmission – the global shareholders' market or the free market – that directly influence people's emotional lives. It is that crucial principle of flexible society, 'down with the long term', which has not only affected people's life stories in concrete terms, forcing them to deal with instability, uncertainty and disorientation, but also how they experience the world. This has occurred at a worldwide level, not only in the wealthy America described by Sennett, but even in the deepest Italian south. And it has happened within all sectors of society, among undereducated, unemployed youth as well as blue-collar workers. Indeed, in the light of the two cases presented here, it seems fair to conclude that the 'reflexivity losers' (Beck, Giddens and Lash, 1994, p 120) also count among their numbers the victims – or better, the excluded – of industrial society, not just the victims of its decline.

If those who agree with the foregoing should encounter the proposition that it is easier for Southern Italy to deal with conditions of flux because the 'art of making do' is already a part of southern genetic heritage, they should try to convince its exponents to reflect. It should not be overlooked that in certain micro-contexts, such as poorer neighbourhoods with a marked sense of *Gemeinschaft* (belonging to the community), or among specific categories of people, for instance, those who, through social and/or generational extraction, have networks connoting strong solidarity, the endurance of premodern characteristics can be advantageous[4]. To suggest that this occurs in less developed areas by default, however, would be misguided.

Rethinking policy

The reflections presented in this chapter should help us think about the lines along which social policy should be oriented. The question of policy is fundamental, not only because one must pose the question of 'What can be done?' when studying phenomena that cause hardship and suffering, but also because policy is never an impartial bystander, disconnected from the processes that are unfolding. Rather, it can be seen as contributing substantially to the social construction of the process of change. One need look no further than the widespread ideological repudiation of welfarism, nowadays totally discredited, and the end of mass employment, on the one hand, and the growth of flexible forms of work, such as irregular contracts, fixed-term employment, interim work and so on, on the other, to see how policies determine the ways our lives are structured. A further example is the withdrawal of welfare, and the ensuing collapse of a system of social cushioning that, particularly in Southern Italy, constituted an enduring and powerful means of redistribution. In other words, policy is not subject to, but actively involved in, the changes occurring around us.

One initial reflection offered here is directly connected to the debate about so-called reflexive modernity. This debate (and the two biographies presented here) has clearly exposed how, in a context where the detraditionalisation and destandardisation of life trajectories 'liberate' individuals from the constraints of social structures, the ability to choose, define and reinvent oneself – that is, the capacity to act self-reflexively (Lash and Urry, 1994; Beck, Giddens and Lash, 1994) – assumes ever greater importance. Indeed, under such conditions, identity itself can be defined in multiple ways. As Melucci (1991) argues, our condition is such that we are continually seeking to answer the question 'Who am I?', a question that the collapse of certainty and the rise of instability make it increasingly hard to answer. In this new scenario, exclusion can be seen as the result of a 'deficit of reflexivity', that is, the lack of a 'fundamental asset', which enables individuals to maintain their 'narrative course' (Giddens, 1991).

Under conditions of this nature, reflexivity – namely the individual's ability to reflect upon the course of his/her life and gain a sense of the dynamics that drive it, to formulate solutions to difficulties and exploit one's resources, especially when they become depleted – becomes a critical resource, as does the ability to continue to maintain a particular narrative (Giddens, 1991).

Reflexivity, however, is not an individual resource. It is a collective one, which, paradoxically, becomes scarce at the very time when, in a society no longer able to offer frames of reference, it becomes indispensable. If this is so, facilitating the 'generative processes of reflexivity' (Balbo, 1997, p 105) is not only a priority for late modernity, but also an essential task for policies, which must ascertain how best to stimulate the self-reflexive capacities of their beneficiaries. One thing, then, is clear: unless interventions are conceived of in terms of promoting greater reflexivity, understood as the capacity of the individual to stay the course of their existence, they will be ineffective.

From an operational perspective, it signals the urgent need to develop integrated intervention strategies based on the concept of 'taking things in hand' (*prise en charge*). Far from implying a passive conception of the policy beneficiary, taking things in hand involves drawing up a long-lasting programme in the form of an adequate counselling system that actively supports the subject through the array of transitions that are crucial in contemporary society. In the realm of employment, for instance, to address solely the problem of young people's entry into the job market is clearly reductive, compared to the real objective of promoting permanence and/or re-entry. Considering such increasing biographical fragmentation and instability, it might also be suggested that episodic initiatives simply do not work.

Closely connected to this is another priority: supporting subjects in building up a solid and sufficiently large social network. With regards to relationships, the family – particularly in Southern Italy – represents the main resource in material as well as in immaterial terms. Actually, the family effectively controls both the risk of '*disaffiliation*' (disaffiliation) (Castel, 1995) and the processes of '*disqualification sociale*' (social disqualification) (Paugam, 1991). Yet, as Filippo's story clearly shows, not every family 'holds'; besides, it is not that everybody has a family. Moreover, strong ties do not always work as a resource for the individuals (Granovetter, 1974). On the contrary – and Franco's case is proof of this – networks based on kinship as well as on friendship can easily become a constraint. In fact, by enclosing the subject in a limited social space, they can preclude his possibility of having new opportunities, of working out new projects, of maturing new aspirations. However, what is sure is that personal relationships constitute an extraordinary source in developing self-identity, self-confidence, and so on. Therefore, it seems that any intervention addressed to an 'atomised' beneficiary – that is, disembedded from the context of his social networks – will be unsuccessful.

A further observation of the Sostris project relates to the profound need for decategorisation, or rather for the personalisation of policy. The contrast between the cases of Rita[5] and Filippo (both Neapolitans, aged 50 and rejected by the job market) clearly demonstrates how the sheer range of family and social contexts and their associated psychological resources, both relational and cultural, necessitates highly individualised policies that take account of difference. In other words, policies able to deal with the specifics of their subjects and get away from a fetishism of policy[6]; that is, considering policies as themselves capable of producing positive effects. Clearly, this involves the need to address the individual, not so much in relation to their status (long-term unemployed, young unemployed without qualifications, mobile worker, in receipt of benefits, and so on), but rather on the basis of their manifest needs, the restrictions imposed upon them by social structures, and their own transferable resources (cognitive, psychological and relational), by way of an accurate system of *profiling*. Therefore, it can be argued that in addressing the abstract individual, rigid standardisation must be avoided for any such intervention to be effective.

From the point of view of intervention philosophies, all this entails a decisive move towards a truly *active* system of policies. Actually, it is the nature of risk itself, as a crucial feature of contemporary society, that calls for a radical change. Risk, in fact, does not imply a zero sum game, but a positive sum game. Unlike danger, risk gives new opportunities to those who want to run it. As Giddens (1994) argues, risk has an active feature, for it concerns those dangers we decide to face in order to achieve some results. Consequently, the aim of 'positive welfare' is not neutralising the risk, but rather supporting the people who face it, thereby turning threats into challenges.

It is worthwhile underlining that such a renewal of welfare philosophy can be obtained only through affirming 'responsibility ethics' (Giddens, 1998), that is, establishing a contractual optics between welfare and beneficiaries. Actually, obligation (asking something as a counterbalance of giving) is the only way to have a real citizenship, since it is the possibility of taking part in increasing collective wellbeing that guarantees the right of insertion (Rosanvallon, 1995). What is really important for individuals is not simply achieving results that objectively improve their condition of life, but the role they feel they have played in achieving them (Sen, 1992).

Intervention strategies must be thoroughly reconsidered, then, in this new climate. In a society characterised by risk and fluidity, the ability to incorporate new elements derived from experience (Giddens, 1991), the capacity to adapt to change – or, in other words, reflexivity – is required not only of individuals, but also of institutions.

Notes

[1] This area includes eight regions: Abruzzo, Campania, Molise, Basilicata, Puglia, Calabria, Sicilia and Sardegna.

[2] Filippo was interviewed as part of a group categorised as 'early retired', and Franco as part of 'unqualified youth'.

[3] This movement is a Neapolitan phenomenon, which had its origin in the huge unemployment rate in the city. Originating in the 1970s, it represented precariously employed people on the more or less unofficial local labour market, unqualified young people looking for their first job, released convicts, and so on. The aim was to obtain the creation of new jobs. Those committed in the movement, registered in the so-called 'lists of protestors', were considered the most needy of work. The political objective consisted in getting these 'lists' accepted officially by the local government, and hence in being given priority in the waiting lists for jobs. These objectives were, in fact, achieved.

[4] The case of Rita is an example of this. See Chapter Nine of this volume.

[5] See Chapter Nine of this volume.

[6] Similarly, Sen (1991), in his discussion of different concepts of wellbeing, argues that, in order to assess standards of living, it is necessary to overcome the 'fetishism of goods'. It is not useful, in fact, to ask what one has but, rather, what one is capable of doing with it. Indeed, it could be argued that it is high time to realise it is not so much a question of ensuring that individuals can have access to some sort of assistance, but of asking what these policies do for them, and, above all, what they are able to do through these policies.

References

Balbo, L. (1997) 'Una modernità a riflessività limitata', *Pluriverso*, no 3, p 105.

Bauman, Z. (1999) *La società dell'incertezza*, Bologna: Il Mulino.

Beck, U. (1992) *Risk society. Towards a new modernity*, London: Sage Publications.

Beck, U., Giddens, A. and Lash, S. (1994) *Reflexive modernization*, Cambridge: Polity Press.

Castel, R. (1995) *Les métamorphoses de la question sociale*, Paris: Fayard.

Giddens, A. (1991) *Modernity and self-identity*, Cambridge: Polity Press.

Giddens, A. (1994) *Beyond Left and Right. The future of radical politics*, Cambridge: Polity Press.

Giddens, A. (1998) *The Third Way. The renewal of social democracy*, Cambridge; Polity Press.

Granovetter, M. (1973) 'The strength of weak ties', *American Journal of Sociology*, vol 78, pp 1360–80.

Lash, S. and Urry, J. (1994) *Economies of signs and space*, London: Sage Publications.

Melucci, A. (1991) *Il gioco dell'Io. Il cambiamento di sé in una società globale*, Milano: Feltrinelli.

Paugam, S. (1991) *La disqualification sociale. Essai sur la nouvelle pauvreté*, Paris: Presses Universitaires de France.

Rosanvallon, P. (1995) *La nouvelle question sociale. Repenser l'état providence*, Paris: Edition du Seuil.

Sen, A. (1991) *Capability and well-being*, New York, NY: United Nations University Press.

Sen, A. (1992) *Inequality re-examined*, Oxford: Oxford University Press.

Sennett, R. (1999) *The corrosion of character: The personal consequences of work in the new capitalism,* New York: Norton.

Wolf, M. (1995) 'Globalization and social exclusion: some paradoxes', in G. Rodgers, C. Gore and J.B. Figueiredo (eds) *Social exclusion: Rhetoric, reality, responses*, Geneva: ILO Publications, pp 81-101.

FIVE

A tale of class differences in contemporary Britain

Michael Rustin

The chapter demonstrates how the life experiences of a small number of individuals can illuminate an important dimension of British social structure. Its particular focus is an ever-present aspect of British society – class[1]. The meaning and effects of class are seen through the prism of four people's experience of enforced redundancy or early retirement during the early 1990s. Two of our subjects belonged to what would normally be described as industrial working-class occupations – both were coal miners. One had worked on the coalface, the other was a craftsman engineer, engaged in maintenance work underground. Their stories show that apparently small differences of position within a social class are associated with substantial differences of experience and outlook, differences we believe are representative[2]. Our two other subjects were middle class. One of them had been educated at 'Oxbridge', and had worked in an overseas service of the British government. His experience reveals that anxieties about class and status can loom as large for the relatively privileged as for mineworkers. The lives of the first three of these subjects had all been shaped by strong 'class cultures', and even in personal crises the influence of these cultures remained strong. Our fourth subject was a woman who had been a personnel manager. Her experience was like that of our other three subjects: it showed the pervasive pressures of the 'marketising' reforms of Thatcherism throughout British working life in this period. She might well have been an agent of those pressures on account of her job; she seems also to have been a victim of them. It seems that no occupation escaped the reach of these ideological forces. In this woman's case study, we can glimpse gender as an additional source of vulnerability. We can also note her lesser preoccupation with the values and cultures of class. We also found this smaller salience of class in the experience of subjects from ethnic minorities (for example, Djamilah and Steven in Chapter Thirteen of this volume), suggesting that consciousness of class may have a less significant role in some emergent groups in British society than it did for those formed in the pre-Thatcherite period. What is remarkable about these narratives is how much is revealed about a larger social process and its history by considering and comparing just four individuals' experiences. These life stories illuminate a particular moment in British society, when the class settlement of the postwar period came under serious pressure, and when individuals were forced to look to themselves and those close to them if they were to adapt and survive.

One of the strengths of the life-history method is that it captures experiences of events that take place over periods of time, and is not confined, as survey methodologies often are, to a snapshot taken at one moment. In our study, we selected many of our subjects for life-history interviews by the criteria of current unemployment or early retirement. Our research design included four such categories of the non-working – unemployed graduates, unemployed young persons without qualifications, the 'early retired', and unemployed manual workers[3]. The experiences of these were very different from one another, as one might expect. What was striking, however, was the importance in the narratives of our older subjects concerning their experience of the specific economic climate of the 1980s, as pressure was placed on private sector firms or public sector enterprises to become more competitive, to obtain higher output from their employees, and, where necessary, to reduce their workforces by one means or another. Our unemployed subjects generally spoke more about their experience of this pressure, and the strain this had imposed on them, than about their present lives, either without work or in the new work that some of them had found after their redundancy or retirement. Our study therefore provides a window into the experience of the labour market in Britain in the 1980s.

A second strength of our methodology is the attention it gives to the specific experiences of individual subjects, who are encouraged to tell the story of their lives in their own ways, with as little prompting from the researchers as possible. This method does not invite its subjects to locate themselves in predefined categories, or invite them to select values or preferences from a set predetermined by the researchers. The data come in a relatively raw form, structured largely by the subjects' own conceptions of themselves and what is significant to them. Underlying this research is the assumption, or implicit ontology, that the relation of subjects to their social experience is invariably complex and differentiated. This is true of individuals, since particular biographical histories are shown to influence the ways in which people respond to the stresses and opportunities in their lives. However, it is also true sociologically, since sociobiographical analysis captures the distinctive micro-structures and micro-cultures by which individual lives are shaped by larger social forces.

We argue later in this book that social policy and practice need to take more account of subjective dimensions of social experience, in both their individual and more socially typical forms, than they currently do. Social policies need to recognise the complexity of individuals' interface with institutions and their rules and practices, and ensure that these are mediated to them through person-sensitive interactions. There is a need to develop methods of training those who work with clients that ensures understanding of individual particularity. We also recommend our biographical research method for the way in which it permits researchers to elaborate the properties of social structures, and their typical roles and relationships, from the starting point of an individual's life.

While the social sciences (sociology included) normally relegate individual experience to a residual item – what appears to be left when all the social factors have been taken into account – the biographical–interpretative method begins its inquiries with the experience of individuals, and then elaborates the social world as it impinges on their lives in the past, present, and, through subjects' expectations, the future. From the point of view of social policy, this chapter pays attention to the particularity of the experience of its subjects, and the ways in which this complicates any a priori notions one might have about what is typical. In order to devise social policies and practices that are sensitive to individual needs, practitioners need to be sensitive to the individual and social differences revealed by methods of study such as this.

The experience of occupational risk in the working class

We discovered from our research on unemployed or 'early retired' subjects in the UK that unemployment had usually been preceded by an experience of increased occupational pressure and strain. This was usually the background, and often the precipitating factor (through illness, for example), for the eventual loss of work. We also found that the experience of these pressures were markedly differentiated, not only by reference to individuals' resilience and by the existence or absence of broader support systems such as intact families, but also by the location of individuals within a system of class differences, structured by principles of both hierarchy and antagonism. It is striking that, in a period when class has been supposed to be withering away as an organising principle of British society, its shaping influence was so pervasively felt by the typical victims of processes of marketisation and downsizing which were supposed to be sweeping class structures away.

One theatre in which these social facts were most clearly displayed was the coal mining industry, which had virtually disappeared by the time of our study. Our two autobiographical narratives from this industry bring back into mind the antagonisms – heroic from some points of view, misguided and tragic from another – that had characterised the past two decades of large-scale British mining[4]. They also reveal the far-reaching consequences that apparently small differences in biographical and personal location within the workforce can have for individuals' experiences.

Harold

Harold was originally a worker on the coalface. Later, after an industrial injury, he was transferred to the surface, where he worked as a crane driver. Having been made redundant, he worked in the private sector, also as a crane driver, before finding a new field of work. After taking a college course, he took a job in the social care sector. Harold fully identified with the miners' struggles against their employers, and remained loyal to Arthur Scargill's leadership of the National Union of Mineworkers (NUM) throughout the period of conflict, indeed up to the point we met him. The year-long miners' strike of 1984–85 formed the centre of his autobiographical narrative – the strike ended, as he pointed out, on his birthday. He saw it as a heroic struggle. He proudly recounted that his friend and mentor was a leading local militant, whose success in speaking to hundreds of miners in one moderate pit persuaded them to join the strike. He was himself a member of a group of activists, 'The Magnificent Thirteen'. The strike was defeated in his view in part as a consequence of the defection of renegade miners, notably in the Nottinghamshire coalfield, but also in his own mining area. The Nottinghamshire miners from the start only wanted their redundancy money, he said. The NUM had not been left-wing enough, and there had been too many intellectuals in it – he named one (then a university lecturer, now a MP for a local constituency), who had attacked Scargill's leadership and in Harold's view undermined the strike.

The threat of pit closures and redundancies had hung over the coalfield for many years. Harold described the strike as a disillusioning experience that changed his view of his fellow miners in a way he could not have anticipated.

> I couldn't imagine how I would have such dislike for some people because of the deeds that they did.

The legacy of antagonism he reports was a lasting one – years of abuse and ostracism of former 'scabs' followed the miners' eventual defeat and unwilling return to work. It is clear that hostilities were mutual:

> Colleagues that I admired so much changed their attitude towards me and even now I see them in the street, you know, we won't pass the time of day, we won't even get eye contact.... That's the only way I can deal with it, I don't wish to engage in any form of conversation.... To me they're just another person that walks across the street as you may walk in London. (Or New York, he added, referring to a visit to New York he had made as young man.)

Although he retained considerable bitterness from the strike days, there was another, much more positive, side to Harold's narrative. He talked with affection, but also with sadness, of his large family. His mother had died when he was 11, and he thought this was the reason why he had not done well at school and had followed his father into the pit, as was common in the area. He had loved mining in many ways:

> I always found that fascinating working in the mines. There was never a dull moment. There was always something, there was always an interesting day, and I can only relate it perhaps like being a fireman or an ambulance driver ... you get the call, you don't know what it's going to be like.

He had got to know the colliery manager, having been to ask him to provide a reference for his passport application when he first arrived in the pit at the age of 16, and discovered to his surprise that he could talk with him, even have an argument with him. Thereafter they had a bantering relationship – a love–hate relationship, he called it – which we refer to again later. (It seems that this manager might have had rather a protective attitude towards Harold, feelings that he seems also to have evoked in others.) Harold spoke of the humour and joshing at the coalface, but he remembered also the concern his workmates showed for him when he was hurt by a machine. The NUM arranged for him to sue for industrial injury compensation – an indication of the collective support that miners could then count on. With the aid of expert medical advice paid for by the NUM, he won an award of £4,000.

There were also resources in the community he could depend on and learn from. He went on a rugby trip to Canada, and followed this by visiting New York the following year with a friend – a psychiatric nurse who had never been abroad before. "I needed to go," he said, "I wanted to go to other places, I wanted to meet other people". They had stayed with friends he had met on the previous visit, and he described a youthful adventure, getting on a bus to Niagara Falls, it seemingly taking too long, and Harold trying to reassure his friend that it was just like "a detour round the valleys". They soon discovered that they were indeed on the wrong bus and were eventually put on to the right one, without any extra charge. These were happy memories of his youth.

He talked at length of his admiration for a politically active friend who was a carpenter in the mines, and of the latter's own mentor, his uncle, who was a militant in the 1926 General Strike and who had for that reason been barred from work throughout the 1930s. This uncle then refused his military call-up in 1939. There was no direct acquaintance between Harold and this man, who was dead by this time, although his friend tried to imagine one, thinking perhaps that he had delivered newspapers to him when he was a boy. Given the death of Harold's mother when he was 11, and his father's subsequent difficulties and remarriage, Harold had perhaps been seeking a substitute family that had more to offer him than his own could at that moment. What was also being created here was a kind of 'political parentage' going through two generations, which gave a larger meaning to the sacrifices and struggles of the last years of the mining industry. This community seemed full of human characters in Harold's memory: his workmates, his friends, his colliery manager, and even a larger-than-life publican who, on one memorable occasion, insisted on serving him only with beer even when he was under-age and had asked for a soft drink. This was the textured human aspect of a narrative that also contained a good deal of rambling and embattled political argument.

Harold's sense of belonging to a world of relationships also saved him, perhaps even in his own view, from the more corrosive effects of the bitterness of defeat and his ultimate redundancy. He moved from crane driving for the Coal Board – the job he performed after his injury at the coalface – to crane driving for the private sector, after the pits closed. "Arthur Scargill was absolutely right when he said we're gonna become industrial gypsies within 12 months," he said, and this was his experience, with many job changes. He said he had been "used to company, working in teams", and he found the unpredictability and insecurity of working on your own, all around the country, a great strain. "It had a profound effect on me physically and psychologically," he said, "huge, huge. I'd be sitting in that chair where you are now and breaking down crying."

Harold described how he would refuse to see or speak to scabs after the strike, but that he did not harass them as others did, such as by putting offensive material in their lockers. One of the most moving moments of the interview was when Harold described how in his new role as a community care official he had to assess for benefit one of his redundant fellow miners, an individual whom he regarded as having scabbed. He had told him he would ask another assessing officer to come, if he preferred that, but Harold said he would be professional, "I will deal with it as I would deal with any other client". His ex-colleague's reaction was, "Just do your bloody job", and he made his assessment, it seems, without bias. Harold said he had subsequently received a 'phone call from the man's wife, to thank him for what he had done. Harold, who remained deeply partisan in his identification with the collective struggle of the strikers, nevertheless had kept hold of a sense of fairness and professional self-respect.

He had a second mentor, who was very important in the next, post-mining, phase of his life. This was a friend of 20 years who had studied forestry at Oxford University, and who still lived and worked in the local area. They had played rugby together, and had been companions on their memorable rugby tour to Canada. Harold had recently been seriously injured, playing rugby, and his friend now encouraged him to take a course. "Why bother with BTEC[5]?", his friend had said, "You should be doing a degree." This support seems to have been important to Harold in making a radical change of career that led to his becoming a community care worker. The considerable informal resources of the South Wales mining community – its politics, its support for education, its rugby – are fully evident in this life history, and in the survival by Harold of events that had the potential to be extremely destructive for him.

Donald

Donald was another ex-miner from the same area[6]. He had worked in the mining industry for 36 years, and also had a father and brother who had been miners. His position in the pit had been a different one from Harold's, however. Whereas Harold had started out as a coalface worker, finishing his mining life as a crane driver on the surface, Donald had been a maintenance fitter, at first working underground, and later above ground. Harold's narrative was reflective and composed – even his antagonisms were somewhat muted and contained; Donald's narrative, on the other hand, was at times rendered chaotic by his rage and despair at what had happened to him. Donald was now ill, both with serious back problems and a psychiatric diagnosis of depression. He was reluctantly and angrily housebound. He saw no prospect of being able to resume work, and at the point of the interview he scarcely knew what to do with himself. Shopping at the supermarket could bring on panic attacks – he was trying to fulfil the role of house husband while his wife continued with her interesting and enjoyable job. What he liked to do most – travel with his wife – was now physically very difficult because of the acute pains in his back.

As a maintenance fitter, he had been located between the main body of the mining workforce, and the professionally qualified mining engineers under whose authority he worked. When he was young, he had chosen the short-term benefits of high earnings over the longer-term advantages of obtaining formal qualifications as a mining engineer. He now regretted this decision, feeling that it had harmed him:

> I always, always earned good money ... money became my goal instead of education. You know, I dropped college because I was working so much overtime, I couldn't cope with education then, and working, so I dropped the education side of it then which was a little bit damaging to me then because I could have been an engineer – a shift charge engineer in charge of shifts.... Then in the latter days because I wasn't qualified I could only be acting and it affected my pension and that, you know.

In Donald's view, craftsmen like him were caught in the middle, treated without respect by the managers and engineers, but also resented by the unions:

> I always thought craftsmen were underpaid, never had the respect they should have had, and a lot to do with that was the union, because the unions never liked craftsmen because they knew we were powerful, powerful enough to shut a pit like that [he clicks his fingers], we could do it, but they always supported the face workers, the unions did, that's in the early part of my working life, and that's basically why I became so union-orientated..."

He described how he became craftsmen's rep on the lodge committee, "a very controversial figure in work because I would always believe in speaking".

It had been difficult for him since he had a speech impediment: "It was nervy for me, basically, but I had to, I had to do it, I had to push myself, had to suffer the indignity of stammering". He said he "never agreed totally with what the union were doing then", so "he was a bit of a thorn in the side". (He referred to some of those he met on the committee as "nodding donkeys".) He was supportive, he said, but also controversial. "I always believe in speaking in meetings because that's the place to attack anybody, in a meeting. I'm not saying it outside the meeting, or in a closed room, I'm saying it publicly, basically, and I was very, very outspoken."

This must often have placed Donald in an exposed and isolated position, perhaps one that is recurrent among craftsmen and technicians who find themselves placed between collectivised workforce and its management, belonging fully to neither group. This was associated in Donald's case with an extreme independence in his engagement with the wider politics of the industry.

He thought nationalisation "had been one of the worst things that had ever happened to the industry", and he thought the miners' affiliation to the Labour Party was "very damaging to miners". It was "too much of the cloth cap and muffler image I used to call it". Whereas Harold was an admirer of Scargill, Donald was very critical of him, holding that his political agenda had taken precedence over his responsibility to speak for the miners. He could see the revenge coming for the victorious strikes of the 1970s, and thought Scargill had provoked Thatcher into crushing the miners.

Donald's greatest anger, however, was directed at the management of the industry. On account of his years as a maintenance fitter on the coalface – a long period of his working life that he remembered with great warmth – he had defended miners against what he thought was their abusive treatment by overmen. He had also once roundly and publicly denounced the pit managers for their complicity with the Coal Board's strategy, as he saw it, for closing down their pit. His report of this episode is dramatic:

> I said, "Look, [addressing the manager by name], it's evident in this meeting this morning that you don't want to be saying this, you've been instructed to say it, you are the generals, we are the soldiers.... Now you as a general want to get up to Hobart House and tell them your soldiers are in revolt. We are not shutting the colliery". I was furious, I was mad.

Donald thought their colliery was a profitable one, but that it was deliberately being thrown into loss by stopping production, leaving the miners to 'play games' for two or three days a week. He felt he had been punished for his outspokenness by being summarily sacked, when craftsmen were still needed to keep the pit going on a care and maintenance basis after it ceased production, one reason being to prevent flooding. The day of his dismissal was a terrible one for him – the traumatic memory of it repeatedly breaks into his life story:

> But that day was an awful day for me because I had to empty my cupboard on the same day that I was told I wasn't wanted and I just couldn't understand, although I was outspoken, I was loyal. Very, you know, I was very loyal.

At this point, Donald recalls how he would be called upon, sometimes at three or four in the morning, to go to the pit to deal with some crisis.

Although the personnel manager shook him by the hand, and he had one colleague who was very helpful to him (he describes photos being taken of him and his colleagues undressing after work for the last time), he has special bitterness for the engineer who "never even said to me, 'All the best, Donald', you know", even though it was maintenance men like him who had made their well-paid jobs possible.

There is a significant contrast here with Harold, who also reported moments of great outspokenness towards his pit manager, but who felt he had an understanding with him that protected him from being punished for his defiance of authority. Harold described how he had got to know this manager when he first arrived as a very young man in the pit, and by his sense of being seen by him as "one of the lads". Harold seems to have kept hold of a sense of how far he would safely go in his arguments with him, though he had been worried more than once about overstepping these limits. One of the rows he recalled brought out the occupational group rivalries in which an individual worker could find himself situated. Harold was by this time a crane driver on the surface. The pit manager noticed some cable lying around, at risk of being run over and damaged, and demanded that Harold remove it. Harold insisted that it was the electricians' responsibility to clear up their equipment, and not to expect others to do it for them. This seemed a familiar accusation against the electricians' claims to superior craftsman status, and their expectation that others should have to clear up after them. To Harold's relief, the manager's wrath was diverted in the direction of the electricians. It looked as if, when push came to shove, this particular pit manager would identify with the miners against the claims to special privilege of the craftsmen. But this episode may also throw some indirect light on Donald's feeling of isolation.

Donald had taken part in the miners' buy-out of their colliery, no doubt investing some of his redundancy compensation money to do so, and he remained an active shareholder, even though he was not now a miner. He described his role as a shareholder in the buy-out company, attending meetings and speaking out, but also feeling anomalous now that he was no longer working in the mine. It seemed from his report that he remained as controversial and outspoken in his shareholder role as he had been in the union. This also indicated, however, that his relationship with his work was a more 'privatised' one than Harold's, whose experience of the private sector had by contrast been short-lived and hostile. Harold eventually found new work in the social sector, once again in a more protected and negotiated sphere of public employment.

Donald had, however, also loved the challenge and responsibility of his work, and he spoke of it with immense pride. He was an enthusiast for the technology of the mine, and for all the activity involved in keeping it going. It seems that the day-to-day work of the pit depended on the maintenance crews. Machinery could and did frequently break down, and needed repairing at speed, in the most difficult conditions. There is a heroic quality in Donald's stories of having to wade waist-deep in water to repair pumping gear, and of needing to rush around to respond to emergencies as they arose. Even the danger was, at least in retrospect, a source of excitement for him:

> I worked underground for 28 years, in lots of different areas, long wall faces, heading faces, extraction faces, which I don't suppose you could ever imagine. Extraction faces were, they would drive two roadways inside for 500 or 600 metres, parallel, they would install a conveyor, two or three daleks [famous talking exterminator robots from the television series 'Dr Who'] we used to call them, which were hydraulic supports, with hydraulic systems then, hydraulic props, and then again metre bars…. It would be the retreat system,

> it was a very dangerous practice, how it was ever allowed I will never know in
> a million years.... It was horrendous, oh it was dangerous, yes an extremely
> dangerous method of mining.

It seems that his long period of working as a maintenance fitter on the coalface
had been very satisfying for Donald. He worked all hours, had enjoyed being
needed, and felt a good deal of comradeship with his fellow workers. He
describes moments of wrestling underground, and being sat on someone's knee
like a ventriloquist's dummy, showing the physical intimacy of these conditions.
When he came up to the surface it was a different matter, as it had been for
Harold, since there the total commitment was lacking, people tended to "watch
the clock and skive", as he put it. It seems that the pressure and danger of the
work underground bonded the maintenance crews and the face-workers
together, despite their differences, and this explains Donald's continuing
identification with them when he was working on the surface, in more troubled
times.

Whereas Harold talked primarily of people and activities that linked him to
the public sphere – via politics, rugby, football, or going to a local college, each
of these involving significant personal friendships – Donald's life, apart from
his work, seems to have been mainly oriented towards his wife and daughter,
and to the pleasures becoming available in the consumption and leisure spheres.
He and his wife had bought a camper, a boat and water skis, and he had loved
going on family trips with their daughter, including one memorable visit to
Florida. Here his enthusiasm for technology of all kinds was expressed in his
memory of a visit to the Saturn rocket site:

> They've got the Saturn rocket there, and the capsule. Oh, I was in awe of it,
> I was, I loved it, it was fabulous ... because we were on holidays in America,
> we were a couple of hundred metres from it, from the shuttle.

He spoke about his wife with tenderness and appreciation – he described
himself as having known nothing about women when they met, and how
much she had taught him. His life history seemed to reflect a new focus on the
conjugal family[6], and opportunities for quite an adventurous leisure time together.
His wife was a librarian, and so clearly this partnership included recognition
that she had a role in the public world at least the equal of his own. However,
he was now also feeling torn apart by his jealousy and resentment of the fact
that his wife was still able to enjoy her work, while he had to stay at home
every day.

Despite the family resources available to him, Donald was both unwell and
very unhappy when we interviewed him. He had serious back trouble, which
at times immobilised him completely; but he also seemed to have little
conception of what to do with himself now that he was unemployed. He
described doing the housework, and doing a bit of cooking, but that in reality
he found himself just killing time, waiting till his wife came home from work.

He had become a house husband, in fact, while being quite unprepared to be physically inactive after a working life and recreational activities that had been emphatically physical. He described a family visit to a motorcycle show, and wistfully described his desire to buy a large BMW motorcycle, even though by this time he was incapable of riding it, as became clear to all when he had a trial ride on one of the bikes. Reflected in this story was his wife and daughter's affection for him, as they tried to help him to recognise what was realistically possible and what was not, while still allowing him to enjoy these moments of pleasure with the spectacular motorcycle that he would love to have owned and ridden.

One might say that Donald had some of the attributes of 'new Thatcherite man', in his independence, individualism, family-centredness and disengagement from the collective solidarity of the mining communities. However, this outlook was in the wrong place and at the wrong time, since the employment framework that might have sustained this new kind of individualism had collapsed around him, as the mines were abandoned. Donald experienced the end of his career as a terrible trauma – it could be a textbook example for employers and public policy alike of how not to manage this process. He seems to have been handicapped by his inarticulacy, which is evident in his narrative, in which he also describes how good he is with his hands and how limited in his literacy. Nor do his psychiatrists, with their suggestions of different antidepressant drugs, seem to have realised that what Donald needed most was to work through in his mind all that had happened to him. It seems possible that his difficulties in doing this were contributing to his paralysing illnesses, which seemed likely, in part, to be the physical expression of intolerable states of mind. There seems to have been little support for Donald from outside his family in coping with his difficult post-redundancy situation, though his own sense of independence may have made it difficult for him to seek this out.

By contrast, the sense of solidarity and membership that came from a more traditional working-class identity seems to have left Harold with greater internal and external resources to cope with change, so that he was able to start afresh when it became necessary to do so. Some of the social and cultural capital that had been generated within the politically conscious mining community seems to have been available to be transformed into a new form in this particular life history. The experience of two miners suffering enforced redundancy could hardly have been more different.

Middle-class experiences of occupational stress

It is sometimes assumed that it is only the working class or persons entirely marginal to the labour market who suffer from occupational stress, including those brought about by demands for increased productivity, reduced costs and downsizing. This, of course, cannot be the case, since the effects of these pressures are felt throughout the occupational structure, and not exclusively at one end of it. The experience of two of our middle-class subjects shows how occupational stresses can be experienced from relatively more privileged positions. One of these life histories, of a semi-retired man in the civil service, shows the relatively privileged and protected position of civil servants, even when the civil service was actively seeking to reduce its staff costs by early retirement. Retirement, in this instance, was followed by his re-engagement on a half-time basis, and although the unwelcome event of full retirement at 60 loomed large ahead, it was not certain that this would then be enforced. This particular life history shows how experiences of relative deprivation or inadequacy can be felt at virtually any level of the occupational and educational system.

The other middle-class life history is that of a woman who had worked as a personnel manager in a newly privatised industry, probably administering the kinds of downsizing that some of our working-class subjects had experienced through enforced redundancy. This case shows how stress and injury can be experienced by those who administer downsizing pressures as well as by those who are its most obvious victims.

Peter

At the time of our interview, Peter was a semi-retired civil servant, who, since retirement, was still working half time for the civil service. He had worked for most of his career for an overseas agency of the government, "the cultural arm of the diplomatic service", as he put it, which we will refer to in this chapter as the Agency. Like his two siblings, he had gone to a grammar school, and then to one of the Oxbridge universities. His parents were well-educated, middle-class people, whose careers had been in teaching – his father held a senior position in the school system. He described a "fairly cultured and intellectual background", and mentioned some degree of economic difficulty in the family, though by the time his father retired he had been "fairly well off". Peter seemed to be following a well-trodden family path. Especially in the decade when he graduated, an Oxbridge degree seemed a safe passport to many kinds of rewarding professional work. Quite a lot, however, had gone wrong after his graduation.

According to his life story, he had done little work at university, and had disappointed himself and everyone else with his lower second-class degree. He had wanted to stay at university to do research, and then go on to become a university teacher, "but with that class of degree there was no real way I was going to do that and so I went into schoolteaching, which had also always been something which I wanted to do". It seemed that high personal and family expectations had not been fulfilled, and that Peter had been living with a sense of failure ever since.

He had studied science at university, and initially he became a science teacher[8]. He described the abundance of job opportunities that were available when he graduated. "I applied for about five jobs and was offered every single one of them and it was very much more not did they want me but did I want them."

After a quarrel with his first headmaster in a public school, he had the good luck to become a head of department in a grammar school, at the age of 22. He then had what he described as six good years, building up "quite a successful department". At the same time, he studied part time for a Masters degree, and on the strength of the quality of his work he had been offered the opportunity to take up a post in the college as a postgraduate researcher. However, by then he had a wife and small child, and the drop in salary was too great a risk. He now viewed this decision as a mistake in his life, since if he had continued with research work and studied for his doctorate, he would have established a much more secure basis for a career in science. His later remarks about his being better at communicating the ideas of other scientists than at having original ideas of his own suggest that lack of intellectual self-confidence may also have been a factor leading him to turn down this research opportunity.

> It would have been taking a risk. I might have turned out to be no good at research, you know. I was very good at passing examinations and studying other people's work but unable to contribute anything myself. So put the two together and probably it was the right decision not to take the studentship.

However, he decided that he did not want to be a schoolteacher all his life. This may have been one outcome of his return to university and his discovery that he could do well in his studies after all. With encouragement from his wife, who wanted to spend some time living abroad, he applied to join the staff of the Agency, and was appointed to a first posting that made use of his qualifications in science. (It is possible that his Oxbridge background was also helpful to his selection.) He had several postings – in all, he worked abroad for 18 years.

This Agency experience seems to have been a continuation, in post-colonial Britain, of an option not unlike those available in the former British Empire, in which the less capable and less successful sons of the middle class went overseas to make their careers. These postings, however, provided scope for Peter to exercise considerable initiative, more than might have been available to him at home, where he would have found himself in more crowded institutional environments, having to compete with people as well or better qualified than himself. Far from London, as the best-qualified person around, one could find the opportunity to do things one's own way.

In the first of these postings, his work was to advise on primary science education in an African commonwealth country. As a result of arguments with an awkward headmaster, he had been sacked from his first job. However, he soon moved rapidly to a position where he was able to shape the primary science curriculum for a new nation, and more, though on his own admission he had no experience of primary education. "This was a country in the 1960s," he said of his posting, "where, if you had a talent to offer, it was used."

In a third posting, this time in Asia, he became responsible for the coordination of scientific aid programmes on quite a large scale, and he was given recognition for this. He described this work as a new and successful departure for the service. There was, however, a marked colonial tone to his account of the local situation:

> And in particular you have to bear in mind that one of the main reasons why poor countries are poor is not because they lack talent; it is because they lack administrative skills ... and therefore you had to be extremely careful not to become impatient with the incompetences and foul-ups and messes and failures to do things that you know, inability to comprehend that certain things have to do be done by a certain time.... You have simultaneously got to be, you know, very firm and at the same time very good-natured and, eh, good-tempered about it all.

At the same time, he was aware of the complications of the situation, because of anti-colonial sensitivities.

> Any foreigner finds it difficult.... A British foreigner is likely to find it in some ways particularly difficult because of the suspicions and resentments.

That was one end of it. The other, he went on to say, was interpreting the wishes of the British government, "which ... is a very peculiar animal". Peter described himself as a mediator between the "dry and precise" civil servants in London, and the realities of a poor country, "between one government which is one of the most efficient in the world and one which is one of the least efficient". During this posting, however, he became an alcoholic and, as a result, his marriage broke down. He describes alcoholism as an occupational risk of the diplomatic service, but gave no other explanation of why it had afflicted him, except to say that the responsibility for it, and subsequently for the breakdown of his marriage, was his and not that of his former wife.

His final posting was to Latin America. According to his own account, he revived a moribund Agency, manipulating and even defying "express instructions" from the London head office to do so. He changed the mission of the Agency from a focus on the poor and needy elements of the population, to serving its elite, setting up an expensive but profitable language school as part of this project. He made use of a subterfuge – the imagined danger of a terrorist bomb – to move the Agency's offices out of "this ghastly area" to the modern part of the city where there would be more scope to attract people into the building. He argued that the Agency should be concentrating on commercial opportunities in the country. He took the programme "right away from any interest in helping poor people, and said 'No, we aimed at the top levels of ... society, the wealthy, influential, powerful, successful'". He had spoken of his sympathy for "African socialism" in the context of his first posting; this one seemed to represent a move away from social idealism. This was the early 1980s, and here may be another example of the influence of the emerging Thatcherite ethos on an individual's career path.

Peter talked about the many opportunities his overseas postings had given him: "Every one of my jobs in the Agency has been quite different from previous jobs". Of his final Latin American posting, he said: "Once you become head of a service, you're almost a totally free agent, you know, you were the captain of a ship.... It's one of the most independent jobs in the world, I would think". At this point, however, having been recounting what he saw as the most successful period of his overseas career, the self-confidence of his narrative broke down: "Or it was", he added, "it probably isn't any longer.... I think I did a good job, emm, and my employers didn't because I really was becoming quite a severe alcoholic". Later he says more about his difficulties:

> Yes, in the latter part of my time it was affecting my work, and in particular I was beginning to have rows with people and, you know, beginning to behave badly.... I was becoming known as a difficult, irritable person ... and I think if I'd stayed longer I would probably have done the service considerable damage.

It seems that Peter was in some difficulties even when he began his Latin American posting, and that he was in a very poor state by the time it had ended. He described himself as having been saved by his second marriage, to a younger woman he had met at the end of his posting in that country, and had married shortly after his return, with her, to England. This story of exceptional freedom, and its concomitant risks, has echoes of Joseph Conrad's classic narratives of seafaring and empire, written a hundred or so years earlier.

It seems that being a peripheral member of the foreign service made for a rather lonely life. Successive postings meant that that Peter made few lasting friendships. Family life was also impoverished by the fact that his two children by his first marriage were sent home to boarding school in England. (Peter said that he did not want his third child by his second marriage to go to boarding school.) The payment of public school fees by his government employers seems to have been one of the significant rewards of the work, and the custody arrangements when his first marriage ended were made in such a way as to retain this benefit. This benefit of private schooling supports the reproduction of social status in the next generation, which may be particularly significant to individuals whose endangered social status may have led them into government employment overseas in the first place.

After the Latin American posting, it seems that a period in London was a mandatory career move, and Peter was repatriated. Once back home, he became seriously ill, with a variety of complaints that did not appear to be connected with his alcoholism. His physical state ruled out another overseas posting. In any case, his second wife had no wish to live abroad. Faced with the prospect of purely administrative work in the Agency, which he found boring compared with the freedom of action of foreign postings, Peter decided to accept first a secondment and later to apply for permanent transfer to the main civil service. Although he passed the necessary "ferocious" examinations for this, the transition reawakened earlier anxieties about his own intellectual ability. He described the "excitement and glamour of the civil service" as its political dimension, such as "when a minister says I want this problem solved and I want it solved by half past one this afternoon". The other side of this, however, was the great strain he found adjusting to this work. He found the necessary procedures (consulting all relevant parties in a very short space of time, providing factual evidence to support every argument, and then preparing a "concise brief" to the minister) difficult to manage. Where his "senior colleagues can run off very quickly a very clear summary of an argument of really quite considerable complexity", he might spend "two days agonising over how to separate the essentials from the inessentials".

The feeling that he was finding the pace too hard contributed to Peter's decision to take early retirement. The intimidating culture of the "first-class mind" makes itself felt in this life story, probably re-evoking for our subject his earlier experiences of comparative failure at university when he failed to achieve the class of degree he and his family had wanted.

Peter's narrative reports that 'early retirement' was being sought from staff both in the Agency and in the civil service during the 1980s and 1990s. The occupational pressures experienced by our working-class subjects were therefore also present for the more privileged. However, there is a significant difference in how this process was managed at these two poles of the occupational spectrum. Peter had after all remained in a senior post during two important overseas postings, despite having severe problems with alcoholism. He was reabsorbed into the central administration of his organisation, although the routine character of his post suggests that he had been sidelined. The decision not to give him another overseas posting – on health grounds – seems, in fact, to be what he and his new wife preferred. Reacting to this, he secured a transfer to the permanent civil service, despite his earlier difficulties, and although on his account he struggled to meet its standards of work. When early retirement became available (at a relatively early age, because he had 10 years' postings in countries with "difficult climates"), he was able to take his pension. He was nevertheless immediately re-employed half time, because of a scarcity of remaining officials in his grade. He described his feeling of guilt at "strolling into his office'" for his six hours' work, three days a week, while his colleagues were working at full stretch on a full-time basis. There was a price to pay for this settlement – he feels his status is less, and his work is now relatively routine and dull, where his full-time colleagues' work is more interesting. However, since he wanted to spend time with his young child in any case, and in particular needed the income to pay for private schooling for him, the compromise was worthwhile[9].

One way in which Peter evaluated the outcome of his career was in terms of what it had made possible for his children[10]. It seemed that in their lives some of his own anxieties about living up to high cultural and educational aspirations were being reproduced. A grown-up daughter had chosen to do what she wanted, which was to work in the performing arts, but had uncertain prospects of paid employment. She was close to her father, but still depended on financial support from him, which he was worried he might not be able to keep up in the future. The other grown-up child, a son, Peter had once feared "was headed for a cardbox box at Waterloo", following a disappointing education at a new university. Although he now had work, neither he nor Peter were satisfied with it, and their relationship was not a close one. Social anxieties about the future of his young son were focused on the question of how his son's schooling was to be afforded in Peter's retirement.

Despite the pain and difficulties that Peter's life journey has involved, what is most noteworthy is how well he has been supported through his difficulties. Supported not so much in personal terms (there was little warmth in his references to his colleagues and superiors), but in what it was assumed – contractually, almost – that a person in his position was entitled to expect from his employer.

Pat

Pat is our second example of middle-class occupational stress. She was born in 1951, took a degree, and rose rapidly from a first-line junior management post in the early 1970s to a senior executive position in personnel services in a newly privatised public utility. In 1992 she started to suffer from gastritis. In the following year her health condition worsened and eventually she had to undergo surgery, followed by a long rehabilitation period at home. After one year off work, she was counselled to take early retirement. She had been living in a close relationship for a few years, and her partner and her child were very supportive during this period. Nevertheless, staying at home had brought a crisis in which Pat felt unable to do anything except "watch TV".

Eventually, in 1995, with strong encouragement from friends and family, and using her professional skills of contacting people, organising and negotiating her ideas, Pat became involved in voluntary work – "doing something worthwhile again", as she put it. She was then able to take up paid work again, in the administration of the National Health Service. She evaluated this, in combination with her earlier voluntary work, as a new experience that allowed her "social conscience" to return. With a recent offer of promotion, she faces a conflict between her new and old strategies and commitments. Does she follow up these new opportunities in management? If so, what might the risks of this be, in terms of the balance to be maintained between her work and her personal life with family and friends?

It is a curious feature of Pat's narrative that, despite her recent reflection on her life choices and the social values inherent in the new ones she has made, an underlying split persists between the public and the private aspects of her life. She insisted on being interviewed at work, and her narrative account focused on her professional career only. She divided her presentation in two parts: before and after the illness. After her illness she was preoccupied with being able to run again, and that was an image that pervaded the interview, as a metaphor for power, freedom, control and action. She found it difficult to talk about the help and support she received – possibly because her strong personality found it difficult to accept such 'weakness'. She diverted attention away from her personal perspective, and preferred to speak about how she had helped others, even when referring to a time when she had herself needed support, and had received a great deal in finding her way back to life.

Her's is a narrative of increased competitive pressures, which were experienced by someone who saw herself initially as benefiting from them, rather than as their victim. Her self-image as a proactive, effective and upwardly mobile manager seems to have been emblematic of the time in the 1980s in which labour processes were being transformed throughout British industry, especially in the context of privatisation in which Pat's career had been formed. Although we don't know what the specific stresses of the work that brought her to the point of breakdown were, she was a personnel manager, and may therefore have been called on to make decisions that adversely affected the livelihoods of other employees. There is a suggestion in her later explicit rediscovery of a social conscience in the voluntary work she undertook as part of her recuperation, that she did not feel altogether good about what she had been doing in her paid management role. The choice of NHS management when she returned to work also suggests that she is striking a compromise between her professional ambitions and the issues of social value, of which she became aware during her reflections in her period of illness.

There is, however, a driven quality in Pat's narrative, about which there may be a specifically gendered element. She seems to have developed an 'ultra-professional' identity, making few concessions in her wish to run again to the needs of her personal life, or perhaps to 'softer' claims of human entitlement for those people she was responsible for within the workplace. She was fortunate in having a family life – a loyal partner and their child – to fall back on when she needed it, as other successful women in her position at that time might not have done. It remained uncertain at the time of the interview how deep her self-reflections and self-evaluations had gone as she emerged from her crisis. The preferred form of her interview, more than her narrative, suggested that her earlier professional identity remained uppermost, though we were left in doubt about this. There were reasons to see Pat as an example of someone who had first favoured, but was then nearly devoured by, the Thatcherite revolution. Fortunately, she survived to tell the tale, and embarked on a fresh life journey after she had recovered from her nearly catastrophic setback.

Through these four narratives, insights can be gained into the structuring of individual lives by structures and cultures of class, though, as was usual in our research, this dimension of class seemed more salient for male than for female subjects. We were guided by our subjects' own words to see these patterns of hierarchy and antagonism as they were encountered by them. And there is already a sense of a 'time almost past' perceptible in these narratives. One can see in them the sharp impinging of a more stringent economic climate, and also some of the new opportunities it made available. Mrs Thatcher famously said "there is no such thing as society, only individuals, and their families".

These biographical studies, however, show how society, and the changes that the Thatcher governments brought to it during this period, deeply affected the lives of these four individuals and their families.

Notes

[1] For an overview of class cultures in post-war Britain, see Klein (1965a, 1965b).

[2] These differences go back to the earlier history of differences between 'the labour aristocracy' of skilled craftsmen and the unqualified labourers who formed the majority of the workforce. There is a classic essay on the labour aristocracy in Hobsbawm (1964).

[3] With hindsight, a less employment-focused approach would have given a more balanced picture of social exclusion.

[4] The context of the mining industry is further explored by Dennis (1968).

[5] BTEC national certificates and diplomas are awarded in many vocational subjects, providing an alternative educational route to traditional academic qualifications.

[6] Wengraf (2000) discusses the cases of these two miners in his chapter in Andrews et al (2000), but with more emphasis on their narrative structures.

[7] This narrative recalls Bott's (1957) classic analysis of the gender segregation of traditional working-class families, in which the strongest social ties are between workmates for the men, and among family for the women, in contrast to the stronger conjugal social ties of middle-class families. Harold's family was a large and close one, despite the complications of his father's remarriage and the membership in the family of children from his stepmother's two previous marriages. Harold described his sister as having taken the role of matriarch after his mother's death. It seems that a strong pattern of family solidarity was re-established despite two serious disruptions due to premature deaths. According to this model, Donald's family represents an emergent kind of smaller middle-class family, in which conjugal relations are given greater emphasis, encouraged by the new opportunities for leisure activities that the family took up with enthusiasm.

[8] The fact that Peter had chosen teaching as an occupation of second choice made his dissatisfactions with his experiences of it more likely. The insistence by governments on the importance of education has not led them to accord full professional respect to teachers, and this situation often generates anxiety and resentment.

[9] In the end Peter's choice to stay or leave his work is his own. On the other hand, Harold and Donald, the two miners, were compelled to leave.

[10] Daniel Bertaux and Paul Thompson (1997) analyse a number of biographies within family contexts from the perspective of social mobility, and the reproduction of life chances from generation to generation.

References

Andrews, M., Day Sclater, S., Squire, C. and Treacher A. (eds) (2000) *Lines of narrative: Psychosocial perspectives*, London: Routledge.

Bott, E. (1957) *Family and social network: Roles, norms, and external relationships in ordinary urban families*, London: Tavistock Publications, (2nd edition, 1971).

Dennis, N. (1968) *Coal is our life: An analysis of a Yorkshire mining community*, London: Tavistock Publications (2nd edition).

Bertaux, D. and Thompson, P. (1997) *Pathways to social class: A qualitative approach to social mobility*, Cambridge: Cambridge University Press.

Hobsbawm, E. (1964) *Labouring men: Studies in the history of labour*, London: Weidenfeld and Nicolson.

Klein, J. (1965a) *Samples from English cultures. Vol 1*, London: Routledge.

Klein, J. (1965b) *Samples from English cultures. Vol 2*, London: Routledge.

Wengraf, T. (2000) 'Betrayals, trauma and self-redemption? The meanings of the "closing of the mines" in two ex-miners' narratives', in M. Andrews, S. Day Sclater, C. Squire and A. Treacher (eds) *Lines of narrative: Psychosocial perspectives*, London: Routledge, pp 117-27.

SIX

The shortest way out of work

Numa Murard

Readers of Robert Roberts' famous book, *The classic slum*, will remember a photograph showing men standing at the doorstep of a pub, with the legend: "The shortest way out of Manchester". What these men wish to escape by drinking is not work in itself, the book relates, but the combination of low wages, exhaustion and awful working conditions, together with miseries in everyday life, such as terrible housing, shortage of food, illness, and all the outcomes of these at the levels of public and private life, privacy and intimacy. These men want to escape from their life as a whole, including themselves.

Certainly fantastic changes have occurred since then, dramatically improving living conditions, not only in the UK but also in Europe, and not only among the working class but in society as a whole. The working poor became less and less numerous until a shift in the 1970s, when new forms of working poverty started to arise. In parallel, the meaning of work has changed. Being fully employed in a stable job became the guarantee of a good level of security and integration in the democratic society. Moreover, despite the fact that alienated work among manual workers and low-level employees remained massively the norm, the meaning of work gained a hugely enhanced value, being less and less associated with suffering, and more and more with self-realisation. It is amazing how deeply this ideology has penetrated society, to the point of receiving support among unqualified or low-qualified workers, not only at the ideological level, but also at the experiential level. Currently, and as things stand at the doorstep of the pub, we should rewrite the legend to read: "The shortest way out of unemployment".

To provide evidence of the new meaning of work, and its outcomes, I will relate the journey out of work experienced by two early-retired persons in England and in France. Early retirement experience is an acute form of retirement. It is an intense experience because it occurs *before* it should. The bells are ringing earlier than anticipated. Whatever the meaning given to the work experience, it is amazing to see that among working class people who have worked hard and are able to criticise their past working conditions, who see retirement as their reward for a working life, and who are obviously happy to be retired and are capable of inventing a life in retirement, there are many nevertheless who cannot put their worklife behind them: like an enormous rock it still stands in the landscape of their life story. By its weight or shadow, this rock creates an emptiness in the present. Something is gone but yet is still there. A sort of Moby Dick. Certainly this experience is not absolutely new; it ensues 'automatically' from the experience itself, from the time and energy devoted to work, independently of its meaning. It is also rooted in working-class culture, as a work ethic and enthusiasm for work, despite, or even because of, the hardness of that work (Ranciere, 1981). What is remarkable, however, is its persistence in current times, despite the fact that the work ethic and strategies of lifelong commitment to work that were often rewarded with improved living conditions in the decades of economic growth has, in recent decades, brought fewer rewards and less security, especially to low-qualified workers. As a consequence, a change may have occurred within this continuing work ethic: is it now motivated less by aspirations and hope for better conditions than by the fear of destitution and the desire for protection against it?

I have deliberately chosen, from our materials, the cases of two male workers. The reason for my choice is that, in the past decades, the burden of employment has weighed heaviest on male shoulders. However, this is not to say that, from northern to southern Europe, the same burden is not currently becoming normal for women as well, the change being a core issue of "modernisation". We shall return to this point after the story of our two men.

It is not by chance either that I have chosen workers who have retired, because the prospect of a 'third age' – of a long period of life after work finishes – is new to modern history. It has not yet been shaped into firm patterns of thinking and acting. It remains, in part at least, a mode of life to be invented. My choice of recently unemployed subjects does not, however, imply that experiencing a journey out of work is not also an issue for younger, sometimes very young, persons in Europe. This issue is considered later in this chapter.

Further, it is not by chance that we shall examine first a British then a French case. Indeed, the UK and France are always in each other's horizons; furthermore, the future of work in Europe – its meaning and reality – will in part be an outcome of the confrontation of these two work cultures. However, this is not to say that other European countries are not involved in this future. Obviously, if I have chosen the British case of a London Transport railway worker (en)forced to take voluntary severance – note the words 'forced to take voluntary severance', and think about how nonsensical they are – it is because the British way of 'rolling back the welfare state' has had a strong impact, not only in Great Britain but also in France and all over Europe. It has made many people aware of what was going on, so they are now determined to prevent it ever happening to themselves. The French case, originally a manual worker in the automobile sector who ended up as a manager, has been chosen to clarify the conditions and the costs of upward mobility, despite the context of an obviously more generous welfare state. Enough gossiping, let us attend to our heroes. Everybody should be treated as a hero.

Tony

"It's almost like leaving home, isn't it?"

This morning Tony is packing up work. 'The guv'nor' allowed him out at 12 o'clock, and Tony is walking down to the pub in order to check out the details of the ceremony. It is a bright day, happily; it would be too sad to leave under a sky pouring with rain. With the collection given by the colleagues, Tony and his wife Margaret have bought a clock. They have wanted it for a long time. It will be a long time before Tony forgets this day. Every time he looks at the clock, he recalls this day vividly. He recalls the tear in his eye when he was given a kiss on the cheek by a young and pretty female colleague who had arrived in the job a few weeks before, and who had been very supportive during this time. Maybe, thinks Tony, this was because she had remembered her own father taking early retirement and how at the time she had wondered whether or not he would cope. In the end, however, he got on all right.

First comes the tear: "It's almost like leaving home, isn't it?", and then Tony laughs. Life is made of contradictions. "That was a memorable day, a sad one but in a way it was enjoyable." Thanks to the weather, positive feelings take precedence over negative ones.

> It was a fine day, actually, it was a lovely day, it was a nice, bright day. I'd hate to have left in the winter when it was pouring down with rain. It would have been a drab day, a miserable day. But no, it was a good day.

How flimsy is Tony's final assessment of the event! Shall I, from a scientific point of view, give you the final toll of Tony's life? Certainly not, because it is not finished, and also because the joy and pain of a single individual are only subjective indicators. What I will tell you, though, is how these balance out in Tony's subjective experience, in his reflexive and his unreflexive consciousness. It is not by chance, in my opinion, that Tony uses the metaphor of 'leaving home' a few minutes into the interview, having referred to the situation of people living in the streets, unable to get a job because they do not have a home, and who are unable to get a home because they do not have a job. This is not to say that Tony is experiencing his journey out of work as an experience of being slung out of home. Certainly not, because Tony points out that the people on the streets have the privilege of being liberated from the burden of responsibility:

> Is life worth living? Is it worth the trouble, is it worth the problem? I am sure there's a lot of people out on the streets because, if you have nothing, you haven't got to worry, that's the end.

Tony is not on the streets and he does have to worry. He has been enormously worried at work, worried to the point of being sick, and he is still worrying a great deal after his retirement, still to the point of being sick. Leaving work more or less as freely as one leaves home, he could not leave his burden at work; he packed up the burden and took it home, it is hidden in the clock: "It is still in my system". Would he have been better if he had gone onto the streets? Of course, I am kidding. But one should not joke about these things and Tony certainly is not. He has been thinking about it. Humankind can be divided into two sorts: those who have not thought seriously about being on the streets, and those who have, who have seen themselves on the streets, who have started in their imagination to live there, who have previewed how they would start, how they would cope, and how they would finish. Tony already knows what he would answer if an MP was interviewing him with a TV camera in the background: "I could cope with your lifestyle, but you couldn't cope with mine".

Let us go back to Tony's wedding day, 28 years ago. Everybody is there, family and mates from East London. Margaret's family too, farmers, although they are not overjoyed by her marrying a 'townie'. Eventually, they will accept Tony as a reliable person, which he certainly is. Before he got married, he was making a living in the City, doing odd jobs that might eventually have led into white-collar work. After the wedding, however, he will quickly leave these jobs and will do as his father did, as his brother does: he will work locally for London Transport. It is time to get a stable position in order to become a reliable male breadwinner for Margaret, who quits work when the children are born and will not return to work. And he has to pay for the house, bought with a mortgage. Tony starts as a cleaner and does not hesitate to work overtime. He goes from day work to night work, amounting to up to 26 days or nights every four weeks, leaving not more than two days for leisure. Look at the clock, every minute is money. However, his recollection is rosy. Tony's enthusiasm for work is endless; it is still evident today. London Transport means 'a job for life' – stability, and solidarity between colleagues, including colleagues in positions of command. A postwar spirit, a spirit of openness and camaraderie, very British in a sense, because of the war experience, but distinctive of the public services too, in France as well as in other countries.

From the bottom of the ladder, Tony works his way up, moves into maintenance work, and then starts to slow down. After 12 years, he shifts to day work: "The enthusiasm's there, but, as they say, although the mind is willing the flesh is weak". Tony does not yet know how weak. He becomes an administrator, a time keeper, and is able to remain on good terms with his colleagues despite the fact that time keeping is often a source of conflict. Tony is the master of the clock. It is the culminating point of his life. And it does not last long: in the quiet landscape of London Transport, computers arrive. Tony's job is computerised: "The job went and the computer took over". Tony is back to the tools. In his recollection, it was not a problem. But maybe in reality it was. Over these years he suffers periodic gastritis. The second invasion will be murderous: here come the Chicago boys, the American consultants who are paid £7,000 a week to offer London Transport what Tony calls, with bitter irony, "their infinite wisdom". The murderers have a smile on their faces and offer better wages to the staff: "Any fool could have turned round and said well if you get rid of 10 staff from 20 you are saving yourself half your costs; all you have to do is just increase the wages of the staff you have left by a little bit and get them do the work of 20 men instead of 10. Which is basically what they did".

Tony should be happy: he earns £20,000 a year. Money, however, does not buy happiness. "Worry, don't be happy", the song *should* say. From the beginning of the 1990s up until now, Tony's life has been a burden. First, he loses his work security. London Transport workers are obliged to sign a new three-year contract. The old contract "was not worth the piece of paper it was written on. I still don't understand how they were allowed to do that". Nor do I. In my eyes such a murder of the word given, of the promise made, is not only a fact of London Transport; it is akin to a society lying to its members, like a breakdown of the social contract. I would probably see things differently if I were British. I would think that London Transport management was so negligent and its workers so lackadaisical that it was necessary to break with this insured stability, to expose workers to risk – in order (of course) to improve the quality of the service. In Tony's recollection, however, it is *after* the breakdown in trust that workers became lackadaisical, either trying to escape the heavier burden of work or, just like the consultants and London Transport executives themselves, "not giving two monkeys".

The fear of being blamed, fired, or privatised settled into London Transport. People felt "their backs to the wall". At first, the unions said "don't sign" the contract, then said "sign it". Tony cannot recall the day he signed this new contract: "Everybody was so disgusted, they just didn't want to remember". Tony has never been politically active, even if his bitterness feeds a more critical view on society as a whole: "I never used to think that the world was so bad". The new contract forces him back to shift work, including night work, which is associated with sleeping problems for Tony, who is now aged 50 and has worked on day shifts for 14 years. Intensive training sessions are delivered in order to implement the extra workload that includes a large number of new tasks. Tony is snowed under: "It was a struggle.... More often than not you couldn't remember back that far (how to do a task for which you might have been trained 18 months before)".

How can the problem be solved? Tony's world is falling apart: "A whole spectrum of life just seemed to collapse". London Transport does not reward him any more : "I am doing my best and I give my best at my job.... I was always reliable, conscientious and I felt they were not reciprocating". A wall has been built between the executives and the staff: "The consultants encouraged the company not to get emotionally involved with the staff". Tony is conscious that it is a collective problem: "It was a very sad time, not just for myself but for the majority". However, he cannot accept the idea, nor does he make the choice to give up his work ethic: "'Just don't care because nobody cares'. But I couldn't bring myself to be like that cause it's not in my nature". What is

Tony's nature? "Grin and bear it." But the cost, and at the same time the true solution to the problem, is sickness: "So I ended up, it just made me ill". Tony is always linking his sickness to the changes in London Transport. But it is very difficult to put a name on this evil. Tony hesitates to define it as a mental illness, but knows that his feeling of exhaustion is not enough to justify not working: "I ended up having five months off with a severe exhaustion, which probably culminated with not only physical exhaustion but nervous exhaustion as well which was a combination".

This is not to say only that Tony is afraid, as all of us are, of the stigma of mental illness: "I am not depressed, I am suffering from exhaustion again", he will retort to his doctor later. Obviously he *is* depressed, and he takes pills for his depression, with some success. More important, however, is the fact that his illness is not acknowledged by the new company – London Underground Limited (catch the subtle scope of the difference, it means you should limit your demands) – as an illness resulting from the change in work. Tony's boss shows empathy towards him: "He recognised that I was genuine, that I wasn't trying to skive off work". However, the company's doctor cannot identify anything physically wrong and concludes: "If you are not happy with your job, if you can't cope with it, then the only thing you can do is to get another job".

Tony doesn't blame the doctor; instead he blames impersonal bodies, the company, the government. Tony's own doctor, independent of the company, will recognise his inability to work, and send him home for five months. But Tony is not happy with that. In fact, he asks for compensation. During the winter, Tony goes back to work against the advice of his doctor. The following spring, he takes voluntary severance with a lump sum of about one year's wages: "That was the first time in months I had a smile on my face". Tony thinks he will get rid of his burden, and the lump sum is a form of compensation – but it is far from enough. Although he does not complain, Tony is still thinking about all the vain promises the company made. It was supposed to help him find a new job with some counselling, but it did not; nor did it give him a long-service certificate and the gift he was entitled to. Look at the clock and wait.

The trial is not finished. It will come back like a nightmare. With a very small pension, Tony is forced to work. He goes for a part-time job and, in the meanwhile, registers for unemployment benefit, not very happy with the idea of being 'on the dole', because it does not suit his ethics. Following a misunderstanding with an official at the employment office, he is sent for a full-time job, six days a week, which he refuses to take. Consequently, he is denied benefit. "I just blew me top." Tony, the good worker, accused of skiving! "What have I done?" Tony is humiliated again because, when he protests against the injustice, he is so angry that they do not want to listen to him: "I had to sort of calm myself down, I said, well, I apologise". He eventually gets support for a proper hearing; the question of whether he should have taken the job will be discussed soon in a tribunal. He will probably win the case; but it is not the real case. Tony is sick again, of the same sickness that made him leave the railway.

London Transport Limited can be blamed not only for Tony's sickness, but also for having changed his attitudes, his state of mind, in a way unfavourable for society as a whole. Tony realised in his painful journey that doing the right thing was not an efficient strategy: "I can understand why people don't do what's the right thing.... The only thing I have learned is that it just doesn't pay you really to be honest and to do the right thing". Tony has started to do the wrong thing and he is feeling better. Doing the wrong thing allowed him to take a holiday, although he was in a situation where it was not permitted, and he liked it. Tony has a part-time job now. Tony feels supported by Margaret's love and their common feeling of being well together, even in cloudy weather. Can Margaret be a substitute for the loss of a sense of life and self-esteem experienced by Tony? Only the future will tell.

Gérard

"I definitely closed the curtain."

Unlike Tony, Gérard says very little about his feelings. He is not reflexive; he only wants to tell the success story of a self-made man, self-taught, a scrapper and adventurer. Facts and emotions that do not fit the scheme of the success story are mentioned as little as possible. He starts by making the following statement: "My name is X". And it shall remain X, we must understand. It is very difficult to peer behind the curtain. When you do, Gérard is not there. Concerning the period of retirement, he declares:

> According to my wife and my children, there has been a period of withdrawal. During a certain number of months, apparently, I was turned in on myself and didn't want to go out. I would only care about my dogs. For some months, I had the life of a hermit, I don't know why.

If not behind the curtain, where is Gérard? Maybe in the comics he is drawing and writing to recall the different stages of his life story. Or maybe in one of the foreign countries where the story takes place. We shall therefore try to find him in every page and everywhere.

As a matter of fact, Gérard's career is brilliant. Having started at the age of 14 in a Renault garage, without qualifications, he will end his career as an executive in the Renault company (in France, the term 'executive' is a distinctive marker of a position occupied in the hierarchy of posts):

> One must know what I am. I became an executive at Renault in 1974. I don't have any diploma, I passed the apprenticeship certificate in mechanics and that's it. I learned by myself, self-taught, on the field. No one could do that nowadays.

What underlines this success is the mention of an unfavourable family background: "As a result of family problems, I gave up studying, my mother ended up lacking money herself, so I entered a Renault garage as an apprentice". It is a sociological rule that people who succeed at the social level are keen to emphasise the length of the journey that they have made. Describing his family background, Gérard explains that his father was a truck driver and that his mother was well educated. She had gained a schoolteaching diploma, although she did not teach. His father died when Gérard was four years old, and his mother started working, not as a schoolteacher but as a clerk in the town council of a small village in Normandy. His less than clear recollection of his mother's good education ("Moreover, I think she was a schoolteacher for a short time, but she didn't work"), and her closeness to knowledge and culture, is probably important for Gérard because, when talking about his meeting with his future wife, he will immediately mention that she was a schoolteacher.

However that may be, there is something valuable in Gérard's family background, a sort of social capital. Mentioning his mother's second marriage, he deplores not only the age gap (mother is "20 or 15 years younger") but also the low status of the new husband ("He was a baker, a workman. Not a boss"). At an objective level, it means he was an employee, not an employer; at a subjective one, it means he belonged to the working class. This, therefore, implies that Gérard feels his milieu of origin was not merely working class. The social capital is located somewhere on his mother's side. She had a brother in the navy in Cherbourg, and Gérard recalls with pleasure visiting his uncle there. His aunt owned a food shop. The cousins were in the army, and told Gérard of their adventures in Vietnam ("Indochine", then, until 1954). It is not by chance that Gérard, wondering where to go for retirement, is thinking about Cherbourg, although he does not have contact with family there any more. He is thinking about an 18th century house he saw in a catalogue. To settle eventually in an appropriate place, *appropriate* in the sense that it would fit the social milieu glimpsed in his childhood, and then gained by for himself by his hard work: "Not in the place where I was living, because I don't have good memories of it. A difficult childhood, the family milieu. I could have become a hooligan. My mother did not find the time to care about me". Gérard did not get along well with his mother's second husband; he was violent towards him, and planned ridiculous futures for Gérard: "My stepfather was a fully practising Catholic and he wanted me to become a missionary. Then he wanted me to be a shoemaker. You see the type". Moreover, the new husband was not able to give his family a good status: "Even when my stepfather was here, we were poor".

The story then continues. The stepfather leaves Gerard's mother when Gérard is 14. As noted earlier, Gérard leaves school and starts working. In the boarding school, near Paris, where he was studying mechanics, Gérard also learns that it is shameful to be a peasant, to speak with an accent, to be a 'country bumpkin'. Back in Normandy, he does not remain in his mother's small village, but takes up his apprenticeship in a town where his grandmother lives. He can live with her during the week. His grandmother's house was bombed during the war and she lives in a house constructed from wood by the American army. Gérard discovers comfort: hot and cold water, central heating: "It was America" (an idiomatic expression, meaning "it was fantastic, it was 'the tops'"). In the garage Gérard does not learn much, only about washing cars, doing small repairs, putting in petrol. But he still dreams about cars. It could be said that at this moment of a concluding childhood, the landscape of his future life is completely settled: the army (because of the cousins), cars and America. In fact, it is also the landscape at the end of his working life, and the theme of the comics Gérard draws day after day. Of course, nobody could have known that at the time.

Having completed his apprenticeship, Gérard joins the army before he is called up, and is sent to Algeria as a paratrooper. He realises that most of the soldiers are 'country bumpkins' like him and understands that travelling is a trump card for social mobility. He will travel a lot in Algeria, participate in the military putsch of 1961, but, as an ordinary soldier, he escapes punishment. In the army, he really learns about how to maintain and repair all kinds of engines and vehicles. He meets his wife, Georgette, marries a few weeks before Algeria's Independence Day in 1962, and, out of the army, decides to remain in Algeria, where he works in the oil sector, as team leader in charge of the vehicles. Georgette is working as a schoolteacher. Two girls and one boy will be born. In 1966, life in Algeria becomes difficult for French people, and those of French origin. Symbolically, their village church becomes a mosque. The remaining troops of the French army are leaving. Gérard and his family are in France for a few weeks; he then learns that Renault is seeking staff for its operations in Canada. The family flies to Montreal and settles there for 13 years. At this time, Renault is trying to enter the American market. Gérard climbs the ladder in the commercial branch, driving from one garage to the next all week long, across all of Canada, then remaining in Montreal where he eventually becomes an executive. It is a sort of a fulfilment in life: "I was the Maharajah". Georgette graduates from university as a teacher of French and qualifies to work in a high school.

It is likely, after this fulfilment, that Gérard is not ready to take any further risks, but this will reveal itself to be very costly. In 1979, Renault and American Motors intend to merge. The new Renault office is to be based in Toronto. Why not move there, having moved before so many times? Against Georgette's will, Gérard decides to move back to France, despite the fact that they have already made unsuccessful attempts to do this for six months in 1972. He admits: "Georgette didn't want to go back, it was not her country. It took a long time before she got accustomed to it. And I, if you want, I wanted to go back only for my career". Back in France, Georgette realises that her Canadian diploma is useless, she is forced back to primary school; that is to say "down to hell", in a deprived area. Moreover, an area of total decay. Poverty looks close, again. As soon as possible – in 1984 – she will take early retirement and open a workshop where she makes and sells jewellery. Gérard's career does not improve any further. He remains an executive in the commercial branch, responsible for American sales. He has problems with colleagues: he feels he has taken somebody else's job. He also feels like a foreigner: "I, from French origin, Gaulish, descendant of the Vikings, I realised I was in an unknown country. I felt a foreigner, at work as well as out of work". His Quebec accent is mocked, just like the accent of a 'country bumpkin'. Georgette is also feeling like a foreigner; the children have problems at school.

After Renault's withdrawal from the American market in 1990, and a new, unsuccessful attempt by the family to settle back in Canada, Gérard is appointed to manage a technical team of 40 staff, including manual workers as well as technicians and engineers. He becomes ill. Stress, insomnia, diarrhoea, headaches. Gérard admits to having difficulties in managing staff. He attributes the problem to the fact that there are many foreigners or persons of foreign origin in this staff: "It is not easy to manage staff. It is almost like the UN: Portuguese, Moroccan, Algerian, a Serbian, a Croatian, a Montenegrin, a few Gauls, as well. It got to me. I had sickness problems". Gérard is therefore telling us about something difficult, if not impossible, to bear: "I, the Frenchman, am everywhere a foreigner, even in my own country, and having problems with all foreigners, except in Quebec, where I was a Maharajah". The sickness will last for five years before Gérard, at the age of 56, is allowed, in the frame of a collective agreement between Renault and the state, to take early retirement. Allowed to or forced to? The ambivalence is visible: "It lasted five years [the sickness] … until I left the company". The ambivalence is reinforced by the fact that, in formal terms, this retirement is a redundancy. Gérard insists that this redundancy is a formal procedure that applied to all members of staff: "It is the same procedure for all executives". It is "redundancy because of failure to adjust to the new process of work in the company". Gérard insists that being made redundant is an improvement financially, because the lump sum (one-and-a-half years' wages, in his case) is not subject to tax. Actually, Gérard's income after early retirement is not very different from his income in work (the difference is Fr3,000 per month – about £300, excluding the lump sum). However, Gérard must admit that he was in fact, and not only formally, maladjusted to the new process of work: "I had somebody to look after the computers, because I never wanted to deal with the computers. I followed a training session during one day and then I left. Too old to learn computing. I am not interested in it". However, since it is a procedure of redundancy, Gérard is also requested to register as unemployed and is supposed to look for another job until he is 57-and-a-half and therefore exempt from job seeking. Gérard insists that it is just a formal requirement and this was confirmed to him by the counsellor in the unemployment office. However, he admits that he was feeling "upset", "traumatised", when he returned home from the unemployment office.

Some people leave Renault, and then they go back every week to meet their mates. For me, the curtain is closed. Finished. It's enough. No, I don't feel any nostalgia. I definitely closed the curtain, I closed the curtain.

After his hermit period, Gérard started to do odd jobs in the house. He also started to classify his stamp collection: "I don't have problems finding something to do. I care about my dogs, I care about my stamps, and, if we buy a new house, no problem, I'll fix it. Early retirement has not been a problem. During the few months I have had the life of an idle king, but *keep cool, slow down*" (these last words are spoken in English). This shaping of the future, all centred on himself and the domestic sphere, coheres with Gérard's story, in which very few significant others are mentioned, with the exception of Georgette, the children and the dogs. Our hero concentrated totally on fulfilment at work. Following this, "I turned the page", says Gérard. On this page, there is only the domestic sphere.

Social death and the injuries to the self

One can learn a lot from the stories of Tony and Gérard. As we can see, the outline of work is not significant in itself. It becomes significant only if we can map the biographical line before work (how Gérard and Tony entered into work) and during the working life (the stages of their career). In both Tony's and Gérard's lives, the line is broken *before* early retirement. Early retirement occurs as an outcome of a previous event: difficulty in managing a team of 40 staff in the case of Gérard, difficulty in coping with the new system of work in the case of Tony[1]. Likewise, the biographical line in retirement continues straight ahead in the direction given before retirement. The map is not only oriented horizontally, from past to future, but also vertically, according to the positions on a social scale in which lives have been lived. For Tony, this line has been almost flat, until a decline; for Gérard, it has been rising, then flat, then declining. The purpose of a social security system (and more precisely of a pension scheme) is to limit the impact of this decline at the financial level, which is partly achieved in both cases even if the burden of earning an income is likely to be heavier on British shoulders than on French ones. However, financial support cannot prevent the way out of work being experienced as a 'social death' (Guillemard, 1971, 1986). It is the feeling and experience of being useless – not only unnecessary, but also insignificant. Obviously, the meaning one can give to life without work is related to the meaning one has been giving to life during work. If Tony still cannot understand why 'they' (the decision makers in London Transport) were allowed to do what they did (in other words, to destroy his world), and if Gérard does not know why he had a 'hermit period', it obviously impedes or diminishes their ability to give a meaning to their current life[2]. At the same time, however, this limited reflexivity gives its current meaning to their retirement: the meaning of retirement for Tony is *bitterness* towards London Transport; the meaning of retirement for Gérard is a *closed curtain* between himself and the past. In other terms, it is only from the normative and unrealistic point of view, according to which a 'pure' and complete reflexivity is possible and desirable, that a limited reflexivity is a handicap.

However the question 'What does life mean without work?' is far from being a problem for Tony and Gérard only. Rather, it is a general one. Early retirement is an acute version of this issue because the risk of social death occurs, although the persons concerned are still 'young' in their biological lives. However, the issue is currently shared by almost all retired persons, in contrast to the past, when the social and the biological calendars were more closely matched (Gaullier, 1988). Then, working stopped only when one was physically unable to continue, and one would die a short period after this (Bourdelais, 1993). Being ill, and having health problems at the moment of retirement, can be interpreted as an outcome of this cognitive dissonance: to be retired although still young (Spanò, 1999; but see also Beck, 1992). As evidence grows that social death is experienced at an individual level despite the fact that it is a collective issue, it is a concern for whole generations of people who started to work after the Second World War and who were threatened by the transformations of capitalism in the 1970s and the 1980s. These people walked, ran, or were pushed out of work with a pattern of thinking forged in the previous decades: that retirement was a well-deserved rest following a long period of hard work, which preceded the inevitable biological decay and death, the actual timing of which cannot be predicted. It meant odd jobs, gardening, leisure and hobbies. It is a working-class pattern[3], supported in actuality by social networks linked to past working lives (and sometimes often supported by the companies themselves), to the neighbourhood (like bowling groups in France), or to past events shared by a whole generation (such as war veterans' associations).

This pattern is still alive[4]. It has been challenged, however, not only by the transformations of work, the shortening of work time, the lengthening of biological life, and the weakening of traditional networks, but also by the welfare states themselves, promoting in Europe a new, middle-class pattern of thinking about life out of work. It is the concept of a 'third age'. This pattern is oriented toward 'activity', as a substitute for work, often including volunteer work and a social life among the retired persons. In France, local authorities have created thousands of 'third age' clubs to promote and support this pattern. Its ideological impact is visible in the told stories of the retired or early-retired people. They know that they are expected to justify themselves by describing their active lives in the 'third age'. In other words, it is a new form of compensation for not working. The guilt of being paid without working is compensated by the 'activity', the social life fitted to the pattern of the 'third age'. Consequently, the guilt or the burden is heavier in countries where the pension scheme is likely to offer incomes equivalent to work incomes. In countries such as the UK, or for persons where the gap is too big, retired people experience instead the burden of having to work to compensate for the loss of income.

Which is precisely what is at stake in the issue of going out of work. Do you want biological death, because you worked too long, too much, too hard? Or do you want social death because you do not work although you are still young?

This issue is not only a concern for those early-retired and retired. It is shared by unemployed people, notably male manual workers (miners and steel workers, for instance) having been sent back home in large groups in their forties and fifties with very few opportunities and resources to re-enter the labour market. They occupy the domestic sphere, become a sort of 'house husband', at the extreme opposite of their male pattern (Schwartz, 1990).

What about the wives? It is not untrue that, by virtue of tradition, the burden of wage earning used to be lighter for women (Jahoda, Lazarsfeld and Zaisel, 1971), and this is why women raised in this traditional pattern may have an easier way out of work[5]. However, the burden grows heavier in proportion to the growing participation of women in the labour market. Young women, even those who seem to have found a 'solution' in caring for husband and child (or children), are still looking at the labour market and getting back into it as soon as possible (Nicole-Drancourt, 1991). Among older women, retired, pre-retired or unemployed, the way out of work is frequently a painful experience, somehow more painful than for men, because as women get older, they are also losing their aesthetic capital, that is, their value in the eyes of men (Pitaud, 1983; Cribier and Dufau, 1977).

The strongest out-of-work experience is probably that of unqualified young people who are outside the labour market, unable to enter it. When studying their life experience, one discovers that inability to work is often due to problems located elsewhere, notably in the family and community spheres[6]. But this fact does not mean that being out of work is not a problem for them. Rather, the opposite is true: the obligation to work stands in front of them like an enormous rock, obstructing them from reflecting on, and dealing with, the problems they would need to solve in order to enter the labour market.

Whenever gods want to drive us crazy, they offer a gift. In Pandora's box, Epithemeus, the brother of Prometheus (the first work hero) found the want and the hunger that forced him to work. In the box of the welfare state, human beings found a certain freedom from want (as Lord Beveridge used to put it), but instead had to cope with more sophisticated needs, such as the need for human relationship (love), for activity (work for fulfilment, not for money), and for usefulness. As Godbout (1987) puts it, "a class that cannot think of itself as useful disappears". Instead of the gods wanting to drive people crazy, one could think of capitalism and analyse in that sense 'The new spirit of capitalism' (Boltanski and Chapiello, 1999). The most outstanding emblem of this new spirit that I have come across was a young man, who was required to work as part of a team of unemployed people in order to remain entitled to the minimum income. He was given the work of dismantling the tiles of an old brickyard. He found that, as part of *his* professional training, he was 'unbuilding' the very plant where his father had been working all his life – and the plant where he had expected to spend his life as well. This figure tells us what workfare is about: one tile after the other, we have to destroy our past and an expected future (Murard, 2002; see also Friot, 1998).

How do people cope with this new, post-welfare, form of want? According to their resources, obviously. All kinds of resources are required in order to find a safe way out of work. And strategies, as Bourdieu (1997) says, are derived from these resources[7]. Traditional strategies of withdrawal into the domestic sphere are still available, but are becoming less and less rewarding, spreading depression, sickness and high dependency on the family network and/or the state. New strategies, including a high level of activity and social networking, are much better rewarded, shaping the 'life without work' on the same pattern as 'the life within work', with a pension instead of wages, and also with less pressure on time and less responsibility. In other words, in life there is no other meaning than work – except if you can find meaning, as many young people do, in culture, art and music, whether they are in work or not (Roulleau-Berger, 1999). The future of these young persons, and of the retired persons they will eventually become, depends partly on whether and how European welfare states will support those kinds of cultural activities, for instance whether or not they will be included in minimum income schemes (which is not currently the case, in France at least).

Inevitably, each one of us will die, and death will remain the horizon of the way out of work. Not only do resources shape the life out of work, but they also shape the way out of life. The injuries to the self (Sennett and Cobb, 1993), which begin and end with life itself, draw the main line on the map of life, becoming increasingly visible as life goes on, remaining the only visible ones when life vanishes. In a seminar in Paris about 'the knowledge of oneself', the anthropologist Mary Douglas (1999) pointed out that when the speaker is blaming somebody (or something), the statements in the told life are different from when he is defending himself. The blaming self (the judge) is monolithic; it is an 'I'. The defending self (the advocate) is divided, in a trial with herself or himself[8]. To go out of work means to face both of these courts, inside and outside of the self. The more injuries you already have had, the quicker you will die. For what fault? Not the original sin, nor the oedipal one – both of them being 'against the father' (whatever his name) – but the fault against the rule of usefulness, capitalism inside and outside of the self. People "unuseful for the world" (Castel, 1995) are allowed to survive on the streets, free of responsibility, as Tony would say[9], in order to remind us of the cost of freedom. How long will this last? Until we make a reality of a world with much less work, a less concentrated worklife, and a less alienated work organisation. This is still a long way from reality. Looking for the shortest way out of work? Try the next pub. You might eventually find your Moby Dick.

Notes

[1] In that sense, it can be argued that exclusion from work – as well as other forms of social exclusion – is a selective process. The selection is not blind; it sorts out the weakest among a group of persons liable to be excluded.

[2] When I wrote that, I, like Tony, could not understand how they were allowed to do that, it was a political statement. Of course, I can understand it; and Tony too. But he refuses to admit it, although not for political reasons. To admit it would mean they were right to do it. It would mean there was no injustice in his exclusion from work. It would mean giving up the idea of being a victim. It remains, however, the only meaning for him after his redundancy.

[3] It is also why Gérard's case is emblematic. He has moved upward, therefore abandoning his milieu of origin, and has devoted himself to work, but without creating a social network in his new milieu. For these cases, showing the cost of upward mobility, see Gaullier (1988).

[4] In *Sostris Working Paper 2* (Spanò, 1999) one can see the strength of this pattern, not only in France but also in the cases of Greece, Spain and the former German Democratic Republic. The pain previously experienced at work compensates for the later guilt of being paid without working.

[5] See notably the Italian case in *Sostris Working Paper 2* (Spanò, 1999).

[6] See *Sostris Working Paper 5* on unqualified youth, notably the Italian case of a young man from Naples, who is almost retired at the age of 18, having worked in the informal as well as the formal sector (Spanò and Caniglia, 1999).

[7] "Against both ... theories (mechanism, ie the theory of action as the mechanical effect of external causes, and finalism, ie the theory of an agent acting freely and consciously, 'with full understanding'), it is necessary to stress the fact that agents are endowed with habits, internalised from past experiences: these systems of perception, evaluation and action schemes, allow the operation of actions and practical knowledge, based on the location and the recognition of conventional and conditional stimuli to which they are prepared to respond, and to generate, without any explicit expression of aims or rational calculation of means, adapted and continuously renewed strategies, but within the limits of the structural constraints by which they are produced and which define them" (Bourdieu, 1997, p 166; author's translation). This quotation gives a good idea of the difference between Bourdieu and Giddens concerning the concept of strategy.

[8] This is why he is irritating the listener, to the point that the listener starts "blaming the victim".

[9] Whether prisoners of want, or of guilt, Tony does not say.

References

Beck, U. (1992) *Risk society: Towards a new modernity*, London: Sage Publications.

Boltanski, L. and Chapiello, E. (1999) *Le nouvel esprit du capitalisme*, Paris: Gallimard.

Bourdelais, P. (1993) *L'âge de la vieillesse*, Paris: Odile Jacob.

Bourdieu, P. (1997) *Méditations pascaliennes*, Paris: Seuil.

Castel, R. (1995) *Les métamorphoses de la question sociale*, Paris: Fayard.

Cribier, F. and Dufau, M.L. (1977) *La mobilité professionnelle des parisiens à l'heure de la retraite*, Paris: CNRS, Laboratoire de géographie humaine.

Douglas, M. (1999) 'The knowledge of oneself', in *Comment pensent les institutions*, Paris: La Découverte, pp 153-62 (trans. *How institutions think*, New York, NY: Syracuse University Press, 1986).

Friot, B. (1998) *Puissances du salariat*, Paris: La Dispute.

Gaullier, X. (1988) *La deuxième carrière*, Paris: Seuil.

Godbout, J. (1987) *La démocratie des usagers*, Montreal: Boréal.

Guillemard, A.M. (1971) *La retraite: Une mort sociale*, Paris: Mouton.

Guillemard, A.M. (1986) *Le déclin du social*, Paris: Presses Universitaires de France.

Jahoda, M., Lazarsfeld, P.F. and Zaisel, H. (1971) *Marienthal. Sociography of an unemployed community*, London: Tavistock.

Murard, N. (2002) 'From welfare to workfare. Ordinary scenes of a public policy in a French province', *Ethnography*, vol 3, no 3, pp 299-315.

Nicole-Drancourt, C. (1991) *Le labyrinthe de l'insertion,* Paris: La documentation française.

Pitaud, P. (1983) *La retraite au féminin*, Doctoral Thesis, Université d'Aix en Provence.

Ranciere, J. (1981) *La nuit des prolétaires,* Paris: Fayard.

Roberts, R. (1973) *The classic slum*, London: Penguin Books.

Roulleau-Berger, C. (1999) *Le travail en friche*, Marseille: L'Aube.

Schwartz, O. (1990) *Le monde privé des ouvriers*, Paris: Presses Universitaires de France.

Sennett, R. and Cobb, J. (1993) *The hidden injuries of class*, New York, NY: Norton.

Spanò, A. (1999) 'Personal and social effects of de-institutionalisation of life courses. The case of the early retired', in *Sostris Working Paper 2: Case study materials – the early retired*, London: Centre for Biography in Social Policy, University of East London.

Spanò, A. and Caniglia, P. (1999) 'Unqualified and unemployed youth: blaming the victims', in *Sostris Working Paper 5: Case study materials – unqualified youth*, London: Centre for Biography in Social Policy, University of East London.

SEVEN

Male journeys into uncertainty

Elisabeth Ioannidi-Kapolou and Elizabeth Mestheneos

When you start off for Ithaki your wish should be that the road be long, full of adventures, full of knowledge.... You should always have in your mind Ithaki; to arrive there is your target but don't hurry on the journey. It is better if it lasts long and you arrive in old age at the island, rich in what you gained throughout the journey. Don't expect Ithaki to offer you anything; Ithaki offered you the wonderful journey and without Ithaki you would not have started out on your journey. (C.P. Kavafy, 'Ithaki', *Poetry 1905-1915*)

The notion of Ithaki for most men and women has been historically and socially differentiated, the result of socially determined gender expectations and personal and social constraints. Men's journeys in this century have typically been associated with their lives outside the home and at work (Seccombe, 1986). However, the social and economic changes of the past three decades have made many men feel that the journey to the island is no longer a well-charted one. Journeys in modern capitalist states have become increasingly uncertain. They depend on the ability of the individual to negotiate the Scylla and Charybdis[1] of unemployment, socioeconomic change, increasing stress and competitiveness, ambivalent gender relationships and the storms of insecurity that undermine the helmsman and make him wonder about his final destination.

This chapter aims to present aspects of two life journeys in contemporary Europe, dealing in distinctive ways with a changing social world in contrasting social, cultural and personal contexts. The first man, Dionysios, remains all his life within an apparently stable, traditional setting despite living in Greece, a country marked by rapid socioeconomic changes. The second, Bernard, has spent his life in constantly altering circumstances and work environments in France, from industrial to post-industrial and finally to postmodern. In France, during the 1960s when Bernard began working, industry and industrial employment constituted the essential structure for the formation of its class and socioeconomic system and marked the political and trades union relationships during this period. The late 1970s onwards saw the start in France (but not in Greece) of a radical restructuring of industry, the rapid growth of the service sector and a crisis in employment[2]. Retraining and welfare support helped to restructure the labour market and assist those most affected. In contrast, in Greece where Dionysios was growing up, the 1960s were marked by poverty and the exodus of the rural population to the cities, where rapid economic development and urbanisation was occurring. Welfare state support was very limited and highly discretionary, often through clientelistic policies such as employment recruitment into the wider public sector and the distribution of licenses (Tsoukalas, 1981, 1985). Dionysios lives in a specific social setting at a historical time characterised by the coexistence of traditional, modern and postmodern aspects in Greek society (Kataki, 1984). Although not unique life histories, they do make explicit ways in which men may confront and adapt to unavoidable changes in their lives. These men are both middle-aged and, since they have already charted a significant part of their life course, have a fuller story to tell about their lives and experiences.

The majority of men over 45 years of age in Europe grew up in an era where male identity was defined in terms of work. Whether as an industrial or non-industrial worker, an unskilled worker or a manager, men were brought up to see themselves as the main breadwinner, the person who had to provide for a family but received respect and had authority in the private sphere and local community. New technologies and industries, the decline of the old forms of production, the emergence of new forms of family where the male is no longer the "pillar of the house" (an old Greek saying), has led to a greater male reflexivity in some social contexts. Reflexivity may be reactionary, if men seek to assert supposed lost powers, or modern where there is a genuine effort to reconstruct or provide alternative male identities (Beck, 1992, pp 112-13). While sections of the male population still dominate and exercise power in the major political and economic arenas of their countries, the feeling of being the dominant force is no longer secure. In the past two decades, many middle-aged men have been forced into early retirement or redundancy, and for some the subsequent loss of a work-related identity made for a difficult turning point in their lives. In so far as men have restricted their social relations mainly to work-related contacts, the loss of work also leads to a loss of social networks and social status. The pillar is wobbling.

The two cases presented here, Dionysios and Bernard, are not part of the ruling male group in their societies, just working-class men from the dominant ethnic group, but without significant access to power. They share common experiences of poverty, the early deaths of their fathers, and working mothers who play a critical role in their development. As suggested, the distinctive nature of their life courses can partly be explained by the wider socioeconomic context of their lives, Dionysios in semi-rural Greece and Bernard in urban, industrial Paris. At the same time, each man starts out on his journey with different social and psychological personal resources, and subsequently reacts to structural changes by creating different strategies. While neither man's life is exceptional and similar life stories could be identified in almost any EU member state and social context, their life courses illustrate the way that gender roles are changing and the development of new forms of masculinity. The use of the biographical–interpretative method enables us to explore the complex interplay between public structures and changes, and personal life courses and choices, in men's lives.

Dionysios: a traditional male?

Dionysios is from a rural background, a village that has gradually become a suburb of a major seaside city and port in central Greece, where his family came to live a generation before[3]. Reading his story, one is struck by the degree of social reproduction (Bourdieu, 1973; Petmesidou, 1987), namely the extent to which he has almost exactly followed in the path of his parents. Dionysios' life can be summed up briefly.

He was born in 1948 in a fishing village near the large port town of Volos, in central Greece. His father initially worked as a fisherman and, as a disabled war veteran in 1952, obtained a licence to open a kiosk[4] that he was entitled to pass on to his wife but not his children. Dionysios has a younger brother. From the age of 12 Dionysios begins to help his mother with the kiosk as their father becomes progressively ill and disabled. He completes secondary school, studies at a technical college for plumbers, and completes his military service. When Dionysios is 24, his father dies, and Dionysios obtains work as a technician in a new local factory making ceramics. Two years later, he is fired from the factory as part of the industry's restructuring and for two years works exclusively in the family kiosk. At this point, he obtains a job as a general factotum in the local agricultural cooperative through the intervention of an uncle. He marries a local girl who is studying at the University of Athens. A year later, his first son is born and his wife ends her studies. Three years later, his second son is born. He continues working in the kiosk in the early mornings and evenings for the next 20 years in addition to his work in the cooperative. After the second child starts kindergarten, his wife begins work in a private company and subsequently with the Municipality of Volos. Ten years later, his wife gets her university degree. Dionysios is 44 when his mother dies and he loses the right to the kiosk licence. Two years later the cooperative[5] goes bankrupt and is sold to a private company. Having lost his job, Dionysios is offered an early retirement pension[6]. He currently stays at home but does odd jobs for friends and neighbours, although he continues to look for work in running a kiosk, the work he feel he knows best.

The life journey taken by Dionysios could, at a simplistic level, be described as traditional. Such a journey offers Dionysios a strong measure of psychological security supported by family, community and the social replication of roles learned from his family of birth. Such a characterisation of traditional implies the notion of patriarchy, the dominance in public and social life of the male figure. However, in traditional societies or groups there is a continuing tension between this conventional set of roles, including gender roles, and the reality of how individuals live and develop them. This is part of an inherent dynamic of change that such societies and groups may contain. Therefore, historical and cultural factors influence the configuration between traditionalism and patriarchy in Western industrial societies.

In Dionysios' current life, the problematic nature of patriarchy is revealed when he starts his narration saying: "We are two children of a disabled father". In the childhood and circumstance of the small community in which Dionysios grew up, disablement carried a very negative connotation since it was associated with poverty and an inability to fulfil traditional roles. A disabled breadwinner could not ensure a good income for his family and there were virtually no social security benefits. Even though his father's disablement was 'honourable', arising from war injuries, and gave him the benefit of the state-allocated right to run a kiosk, the image of the family would have remained disadvantaged and stigmatised. In this setting, Dionysios' expectations are restricted by economic necessity and the weight of responsibility transferred to him as the eldest son.

Although his choices in life exhibit strong patterns of social reproduction associated with traditional life journeys, in Dionysios' life, gender roles have not been strictly defined by patriarchy. The central role of his mother is evident throughout his narration, particularly her role in organising the home, kiosk, family finances and education, as a result of the physical dependency and serious illness of the father. He himself chooses to marry another strong woman who not only has two children but also then completes her degree and finds full-time, responsible work. Therefore, women are strong, central figures, to be relied on and looked up to. They are critical, even determining resources in his life.

> My whole life was a struggle for survival. The good thing was that I had my mother at home and at the kiosk because after I got married she helped with the children and also in overcoming my financial difficulties.

He tells us that his family currently manages on his wife's salary, his pension and good household management.

There are generational differences in the roles of the two women. The situation of his mother, uneducated and forced into taking on the duties of her sick husband, contrasts with that of her daughter-in-law. Dionysios' wife, though choosing to marry and temporarily leaving her studies, then makes the non-traditional choice to complete her degree and enter the labour force in the services sector as an employee. She is more qualified than her husband, and is economically dominant, and Dionysios reacts to this in a 'modern' way, accepting her as an equal partner. This gender relationship is a modernising force in his life.

Gender relationships have also trapped Dionysios. He lived all his life with his mother until her death; she shared his married life as part of an extended family[7] and they often shared the same work in the kiosk. At a symbolic level, the kiosk is so closely identified with her as to be a substitute for the womb, the nurturing place that allowed him to survive. It can also be said to be a prison, a place from which he was never free, trapped by his mother's financial and emotional needs for her eldest son's support. His mother had no vision of alternative routes available either to her or her son that would allow Dionysios independence and security for his family. He is 'forced' to reproduce his father's disabled role. Therefore, even after the death of his mother and in receipt of an early retirement pension, he continues to seek work in a kiosk to perpetuate his familiar familial context. This is part of the almost exact pattern of social reproduction that marks his life: not only does he attempt to replace his mother and father in the kiosk, but also tries to ensure that his own sons train as plumbers, the trade *he* never took up. He even adopts his father's personality. Therefore, not only does he work all his life in the village kiosk and marry a strong woman, but also has the identical hobby of fishing and appears to be a rather sweet and amusing man, in the same way he describes his father. He tells his story as a traditional man within a rural society, emphasising that marriage and family are the most important elements in his life. Asked about his most pleasurable moments, he says: "Happy events were my marriage, my children … the birth of my first son, who was named after my father".

His family and the kiosk are the two central axes of his life, both of them supporting him emotionally and economically, but also trapping him into a certain pattern of life. As he says:

> I couldn't leave the kiosk not only because of the money but because it would hurt me to give it up…. Imagine, I started working in it since 1952…. It was not just that I rented it then, I'd got bored and left it…. But I really cared about it…. Such a long time…. And I liked the work with all the people around me, lots of comings and goings.

His life's tragedies are the pivotal points of his initial narration: deaths, being fired, the illness of his father, the social restrictions on his life as a result of his work. And yet all this without any overt expression of feelings.

> All these events were very distressing (the death of his parents) because we were a very united family…. You see, poverty either binds you together or separates you absolutely.

Yet there is also a strongly negative aspect to this family support: he is constrained for the rest of his life by the choices deriving from his original family circumstances.

> My father was ill and the expenses were substantial and I was forced to work at the kiosk because of financial pressures. This meant that I had to postpone all my dreams of working as a plumber or whatever else, and work in the kiosk.

The element of constraint emerges not only in terms of his life choices but also in his style of speech, which is laconic, not because he weighs each word but because he feels he can describe his life course in a few words. For example, he sums up his life for 20 years with a verbal picture in three lines: that of getting up and opening the kiosk at 5.30 am, then going to work in the cooperative until 3.00 pm and then returning to the kiosk until late at night. He adds that he was permanently tired, rarely went out, had no holidays and either attended the major social celebrations late or not at all.

He interprets both difficult and good moments in his life mainly as matters of fate. The idea that everything relates to fate and chance and that this cannot be changed but simply has to be confronted or endured, makes him, 20 years after his dismissal from a factory, still unable to explain the reason: "Everything in life is a matter of luck". Later, he says: "It's my fate to work in a kiosk".

For Dionysios, the fact that he has been affected by events that are relatively rare – his father's disablement and then his unusual illness, followed by his mother's unexpected death – can only be explained as the result of bad fate. At the time of the interview, he no longer believes in choices but in reacting and dealing with what life brings him. In presenting his life story, he frequently uses the Greek word for 'survival', which for him unites several elements with strong emotional meanings. These involve economic subsistence as well as the emotional and physical endurance of illness and death. The effects of his father's disability have repercussions for Dionysios' dreams, ambitions and development. Although Dionysios attempts to become modern in terms of his employment in a factory, in his second job in the cooperative, which he keeps for 20 years, he needs no modern skills. His skills and training as a plumber are never used, and the traditional skills of communication, personal contacts and loyalties, individual responsibility and autonomy, learned from the family kiosk, are the ones he uses in the cooperative.

> I had a job as a general factotum … if you like … running around … bank business … agreements … tax offices … everywhere outside the co-op I was responsible…. Generally I knew my job. Since these people saw me often they got to know me and assisted me quickly. If you have to wait in queues you're lost … you lose all the day. So I, who knew the clerks, got out of there quickly and we saved time, all of us.

Since he is not part of the modern world of work, early retirement did not mean the end of employment in a satisfying trade. Far more important for him was the loss of the social world of the kiosk that also represents, in the true sense, 'a living'.

> I've been inactive a long time…. It's 18 months now … and I have come to the point, to a limit, I've understood that I can't sit anymore…. It's nice not to have to do anything but it doesn't suit me … just to be a house cat….. I've learned…. And in the kiosk it would be all right because I know the job ….

I like to see people, not be enclosed in four walls. I hope it'll happen (the work in the kiosk) it would do me good.

The family in Greek society is not only a production and consumption unit, but also that which provides security and welfare. Dionysios' efforts to participate in the modernising of Greek society – as a plumber and as a worker – failed, and postmodernism affected him in the form of early retirement forced by technological changes in industrial production. Even his village is affected by postmodern economic restructuring, yet Dionysios finds himself relying on traditional forms of support and social capital, including his family and the dense social networks encouraged through mutual assistance and practical exchanges.

Bernard: reconstructing a male identity

The life story of Bernard contrasts strongly with that of Dionysios. He speaks from the perspective of a modern man, one who is part of the industrialised, developed, capitalist world (Murard, 1999b). The majority of the long, initial narrative concentrates on the working sphere of his life, making this an apparently typical example of a male life dominated by the work sphere, rather than the private. In his narration he describes in great detail all the jobs, conditions of labour, relationships with work mates and employers and his trades union activities with which he has been involved as a working man. This is the central core of an extensive interview that seems to restrict the personal in the narrative except to illustrate his current stance in life.

Bernard was born into the French industrial working class in 1948. His very hard and often traumatic early life marks his life course, though does not dictate it. At the age of two his young father dies and an alcoholic grandmother brings him up while his mother works. His mother impresses him with tales of the hardships the women suffer in the factory where she works. His mother had initially tried to improve his chances by trying to keep him off the streets, giving him books and puzzles to play with and finally, when he got too tough, sending him to a residential orphanage. Bernard's mother plays a critical role in this early stage of his life, since she makes him conscious of the negative aspects of belonging to the working class such as being at higher risk of suffering accidents and exploitation at work. Providing him with books and ways of expressing himself as a child stimulates him, even though he remains in a dangerous and limiting environment. Bernard develops a strong sense of himself as an individual in street and school contexts, and he becomes an independent character who cannot rely on those around him but is a support for others.

In the strict monastic school to which his mother sends him, he learns manual skills as well as a negative attitude to formal educational institutions, authority and religion.

> I was sent at a very early age, eight years old, as a boarder, to the Orphanage for Apprentices in […]. It was well known that place, eh – a foundation, it's with priests, and when one gets out of there one is a model worker, but what *they* call a model worker. That is to say, one works hard, you work manually, one doesn't talk back, one goes to church, one prays to the Lord for a rise.

During his childhood and youth he is forced into various forms of training, all leading to working-class occupations. He would appear to have had few initial choices concerning the kind of career/work available to him; he was apparently destined to be part of the working class. However, when telling his story, he describes a working life where he constantly confronts employers and changes jobs frequently. As he matures, his general opposition and negative stance to employers stops being highly personal and he begins to represent the interests of workers through the trades union. He has the skills and ability to perform a variety of jobs but his preference is for those in industrial sectors where the conditions of labour are better whether in terms of status, such as the print industry, or in terms of providing a higher income, such as car manufacture. While his identification with the working class is a loyalty that he is unwilling to betray, his life consists of trying to avoid some of the traps of his contemporaries and other family members and to develop his own strategy.

Bernard's masculine identity begins in the context of a difficult family life. Discussing the construction of his identity is not possible without understanding the working-class industrial male expectations that he has to negotiate during his life course, including physical strength, pride in manual industrial work and commitment to being the male breadwinner for a family. Bernard confronts and conforms to, but also goes beyond these male identities, initially pursuing what can be termed a partly expected projection of toughness and proving his masculinity. Therefore he is physically aggressive, has a band of tough mates, drinks and smokes: "I was quite a tough guy … I was already smoking at the age of 13, 14".

He has also to confront the two subsequent, violent, abusive and alcoholic partners of his mother, and this influences the development of his own manhood. His main stepfather over the longer period, who had seven children, abuses at least one of his daughters and Bernard stands up for her, helping her to marry and start a family of her own. He also confronts him over the matter of his wages, after being given a very small amount of pocket money back from the wages handed over to his stepfather. Bernard reports himself as saying: "Look, there's already somebody exploiting me at the factory; that's quite enough, not two of you".

As a young man, he accepts the hard physical conditions of work, but when the situation is appalling or the workload too high he makes a moral point by leaving the job. He perceived this as a clever answer to exploitative employers. Later, he reacts by seeking better protection and working conditions for himself and other workers through the trades unions – therefore his political activity can be construed as part of his way of fighting. His tough, working-class male identity is partly reconstructed as one based on solidarity and a political ideology.

Another way of avoiding conformity to the male class norms of his origins is his unwillingness to take on family commitments, since he chooses not to marry[8]. This contrasts with the behaviour of his siblings and half-siblings, as well as his co-workers. The industrial working classes were often in the situation of being forced to work under difficult conditions since they had to support their families. Remaining single, though involved with women, enables Bernard to have more labour market choices. His private life becomes an area for individualistic choices not available to his working-class mates. His avoidance of overtime is possible since he has no family to support: in this way he refuses to make further profits for the owner. This notion of having choices in his life is a critical element in Bernard's narrative. He chooses to spend his free time in working for the union and supporting working-class solidarity in his own way. This choice about the kind of life he wants to lead outside the factory makes Bernard, partly at least, a postmodern man in the sense that he adopts different non-working-class lifestyles.

> My personal life is absolutely different, really something else. I go to the cinema quite often, I go to the restaurant more frequently, I buy records and books more frequently, I travel, I can go further, for a longer period of time.

His experiences of the French industrial working class of his youth (Murard, 1999b) lead him to tell us of how he avoided becoming an alcoholic like his grandmother, stepfather and many co-workers in the factories. However, he understands that people in industry turn to alcoholism because of the difficult conditions of work. His refusal to blame such behaviour is part of his resistance to the class system. Initially, he rejects any form of responsibility and authority that might make him 'like the employers'. Later, his participation in trade union activities and his support of migrants and actions against racists in the factories represents one of the main indicators of his reflexive behaviour.

Bernard is less vulnerable than many of his contemporaries – he has many labour market skills, is an active member of a trades union, has friends in Paris's Latin Quarter and among people who do not belong to the working class, and has many other outside interests such as the arts. These resources save him from the limitations of many male working-class lives. Many of these resources are institutions developed within the working class itself, especially trade unionism and education, of which he takes full advantage, since he belongs within the same radical tradition in which they developed. In addition, he makes personal choices of friends and interests that enlarge his horizons and protect him in times of change and unemployment.

Discussion

Using the initial metaphor of Ithaki, some men fear the unknown in life, preferring the charted and secure route. Others may travel to new shores, yet once arriving choose to stay there. In contrast, there are men who prefer to explore, to take risks and brave the unknown in return for the excitement that comes from a potentially interesting and perhaps magnificent journey.

In the first choice, termed traditional, what is expected of men is well-defined: their status is assured, their relationships emotionally supporting and social networks meaningful and dense – nearer to the form of mechanical social relations discussed by Durkheim (1964). Men follow traditional journeys for a variety of reasons, some unaware of, or blindfolded from, other possibilities. A traditional life offers emotional security, but can also be tedious and repetitive, providing little stimulation. Many men could not afford the risk of taking a different route, while others could never perceive that they had a choice. However, one hazard in the modern world is that the charted routes are altering radically. Men who are unprepared to be flexible, unprepared to learn and update their knowledge, are likely to be destined to the backwaters of life. Dionysios is an example of this. Among those who follow the traditional journey are men who define themselves in terms of their masculinity and their male roles, confined to the small circle of their family and kin. As heads of a household, the breadwinner, the dominant figure in the house, such men have an assured status, despite its high cost in terms of their need to work and secure an income. When forced to reconsider and readjust to a new situation that may involve losing their male dominance, some men inevitably become paralysed and ill, effectively staying on the shore and moving nowhere (as was the case with Donald in Chapter Five of this volume).

Postmodern society pushes people towards more individualised lifestyles, to consumerism and potentially greater reflexivity. This framework provides greater varieties of choices and may also be more interesting, but it is far more risky for the individual. For those men who follow the postmodern journey, the ability to build up resources, even if they set off with few, is important in protecting them against the inevitable obstacles they meet. In some societies, the welfare state offers some such help in the form of training and retraining, financial security through periods of unemployment and opportunities to start new businesses and jobs. Both in France and Greece in the past decade governments have offered such support, though it has been a more recent and limited development in Greece[9]. Men's families and personal relationships may be a support; but they can also be a curse, representing a further burden and arena of conflict.

Men in middle age are already well into their life journey. Some have achieved what appears to be some kind of upward mobility and career, though this tends to be class-specific. Others continue in the same kind of work without necessarily experiencing major changes in work-related status, income, or the type of work performed. For many, the shock that accompanies being forced to leave their current employment, whether as a result of early retirement or redundancy, represents a major turning point in their lives. This is not an easy time: middle-aged men may find it difficult to get jobs again, if this is what they seek, or to adapt to the new situation of having no work-related identity. Additionally, in so far as men have restricted their social relations mainly to work-related contacts, the loss of employment leads to a loss of social networks as well as social status.

The specific way in which men leave the labour force depends on their class position generally. Those from the working class are more likely to leave because of unemployment, ill health, disability and redundancy, while middle-class men are far more likely to leave through offers of early retirement (Arber, 1989). In either case, a shock to their identity and status may accompany this change. The decline of heavy industry, of manual work requiring male physical strength, the rise of service industries, increasing single parenthood and the decline in reliance on the male breadwinner have also been factors in forcing a realignment in men's perceptions and expectations of their lives.

The two cases presented above are examples of middle-aged men, facing radical changes in the labour market and social structures around them, who have constructed their life courses in very different ways. Bernard is an active agent in a risky but interesting journey, supported by his use of working men's supportive institutions as well as his individual effort. He seeks the challenge of the unknown, new friends, new experiences; he wishes to alter the existing social order, to improve the conditions of work and life for working-class people. Yet, in seeking the new, he is buttressed by his loyal, if rather distant, relationship to his 'old' community and family, though refusing to make a new family. Dionysios, in contrast, is not a fighter or innovator, remaining on a life course that he understands and that offers him protection through the family and local community in which he spends his life. Loss of his father, dominant female figures in his life and non-challenging and non-solidaristic employment[10] contribute to his being more of an observer than an active player. Other men, who tie their male identity almost exclusively to their work, may be particularly vulnerable, since loss of work often means a loss of identity. However, Dionysios and Bernard still have social resources, social 'life jackets' that ensure that, whatever their labour market fate, they are not stranded away from a social life with meaning.

The relationship to women as sexual and life partners is also interesting in men's life journeys. Dionysios confirms his male identity by working hard, but is not the sole breadwinner, since he shares the load with his mother and wife. They are all rowers on the same ship and since they share the same goals they manage to row in the same direction without overt conflicts. Perhaps he is not the captain. Women are part of Dionysios' life-support system. Bernard, on the other hand, has decided to sail his ship alone, but taking on responsibilities for, and giving support to, those who flounder around him. Marriage and family can also limit the choices available and, for Bernard, the notion of choice in one's relationships and life is a core value. Therefore, women as wives are to be avoided in his personal life course, but there is a cost to this choice.

There is a strong interplay between social structural constraints such as rural or working-class origins, poverty, gender expectations and male identities. Despite some commonalties in the lives of both men, including their deprived childhood and their industrial employment experiences, their entirely different life courses can be explained only in part by structural factors. There are also individual biographic elements that explain why life courses vary. Therefore Bernard and Dionysios were strongly affected by their mothers' influence. In the Greek case, the stigma of disability and the necessity of relying on family support limited, and to some extent oppressed, Dionysios. In Bernard's case, the degrading experiences of belonging to the working class, of having as a child to survive in very different environments including those of his grandmother, his stepfather and an orphanage, suggest the development of a tremendously strong, resilient and angry character. The strategies available to individuals are also socially bounded and affected by government policies. Bernard, therefore, lives in a context where there is state financial support for the unemployed and has a clear identity associated with membership of a class. In contrast, Dionysios faces economic insecurity all his life and, with the exception of his family and neighbourhood, has no identification with an occupational group or social class.

What makes a journey 'good' inevitably relates to resources such as loving and supportive parents, money and education. Such travellers have more possibilities of developing effective strategies when confronting obstacles in their way. Too much security, however, may block an understanding of, let alone a readiness for, alternative choices.

Despite the absence of initial resources, Bernard nonetheless appears to have made the most of his journey and choices. He participates in the modern world, he is reflexive, belonging to the circle of people who contribute to changing their world, since he understands and chooses the circumstances and rules of his own life (Rustin, 2000). His political capacities are the enabling force in this, allowing him to escape from the normal expectations of many from his background, and making him reach out to form ever-wider networks of relationships that become an individual resource. Bernard's reflexivity turns him into an active agent of change in the modern world. In contrast, Dionysios, lacking reflexivity, is a more passive traveller, restricted to the intense but limited networks of family and local community.

In both cases, life events, such as family tragedies, violence, poverty and unemployment, may require support from others. Such help can be provided by the state or other agencies or citizens, since their social networks, as well as their other personal resources, can assist them in overcoming barriers and traumatic experiences. However, there will always be some men unable to develop personal and social strategies, who cannot easily be helped by the existing welfare structures of support and who will be vulnerable, marginalised and at risk of social exclusion.

Notes

[1] In Homer's *Iliad*, Odysseos spends 10 years trying to return to Ithaki, his home island, after the 10-year war with Troy. One adventure is the passage of his boat through narrow dangerous straits between Scylla and Charybdis.

[2] Technological changes as well as the oil crisis of 1979 were felt strongly, and much earlier, in France than in Greece, where industry always represented a limited sector of the economy and was dominated, as it still is, by small manufacturers and workshop production.

[3] His family came to mainland Greece from Asia Minor as young refugees in 1921-22.

[4] A kiosk is a small pavement stand and operates as an independent small business run by one person. Kiosks are found throughout Greece selling newspapers, tobacco and sweets, as well as other small items, depending on local demand. Kiosks provide an income that varies in terms of their location and the hours of operation but is adequate for a family. They are taxed as small businesses. There is a clear resemblance to the sweet and tobacconist shops run by many Asian families in the UK using family labour. In the 1940s and 1950s, kiosk licences in Greece were originally allocated to those who were disabled through war service.

[5] Many agricultural cooperatives were under political patronage and, despite many having bad management and being highly inefficient, were backed by central governments. During the 1980s and early 1990s, the PASOK socialist governments supported the inefficient agricultural sector for clientelistic reasons, despite the high cost it involved (Petmesidou, 1998). Eventually, some were sold to the private sector, while others were modernised and were managed properly.

[6] During the early 1990s, some Greek employers, as in many other European countries, offered early retirement for older workers to deal with industrial restructuring. The larger state-supported or protected employers were more able to offer such early pensions (Mestheneos and Ioannidi, 1995).

[7] This form of family was common in Greek rural areas until the early 1980s, when everyone aged 65 or 67 (or older) received a small rural pension.

[8] See also Chapter Ten of this volume, which shows that not marrying or being divorced can be part of an individualising strategy and a way of escaping the trap of tradition.

[9] The National Manpower and Employment Organisation has gone some way to modernising its employment services while (re)training opportunities have been extended through private and public training bodies.

[10] Although he was employed in a cooperative, it did not generate or support strong working-class or farmers' solidaristic relationships.

References

Arber, S. (1989) 'Class and the elderly', *Social Studies Review*, vol 4, no 3, pp 90-5.

Arber, S. and Ginn, J. (1991) *Gender and later life*, London: Sage Publications.

Beck, U. (1992) *Risk society*, London: Sage Publications.

Bourdieu, P. (1973) 'Cultural reproduction and social reproduction' in R. Brown (eds) *Knowledge, education and cultural change*, London: Tavistock.

Connell, R.W. (1995) *Masculinities*, California: University of California Press.

Durkheim, E. (1964) *The division of labour in society*, Glencoe: Free Press.

Kataki, H. (1984) *The three identities of the Greek family*, Athens: Kedros (in Greek).

Mestheneos, E. and Ioannidi, E. (1998) 'Early retired – Greek national report', in *Sostris Working Paper 2: Case study materials – the early retired*, London: Centre for Biography in Social Policy, University of East London, pp 22-7.

Mestheneos, E. and Ioannidi, E. (1999a) 'The social consequences for workers of industrial restructuring', in *Sostris Working Paper 6: Case study materials – ex-traditional workers*, London: Centre for Biography in Social Policy, University of East London, pp 28-41.

Mestheneos, E. and Ioannidi, E. (1999b) 'The impact of industrial transformation on European older workers – composite report on ex-industrial workers', in *Sostris Working Paper 6: Case study materials – ex-traditional workers*, London: Centre for Biography in Social Policy, University of East London, pp 1-7.

Mestheneos, E. and Ioannidi-Kapolou, E. (1995-96) *Greek National Report: Overcoming age barriers in employment in Greece*, Dublin: European Foundation for the Improvement of Living and Working Conditions.

Murard, N. (1999a) 'Unqualified youth: change into a transition. French national report', in *Sostris Working Paper 5: Case study materials – unqualified youth*, London: Centre for Biography in Social Policy, University of East London, pp 76-87.

Murard, N. (1999b) 'Qualified and unqualified workers across changing times' in *Sostris Working Paper 6: Case study materials – ex-traditional workers*, London: Centre for Biography in Social Policy, University of East London, pp 8-16.

Petmesidou, M. (1987) *Social class and processes of social reproduction*, Athens: Exantas (in Greek).

Petmesidou, M. (1998) 'Mass higher education and the social sciences in Greece', *International Sociology*, vol 13, no 3, pp 359-84.

Rustin, M. (2000) 'Reflections on the biographical turn in social science', in P. Chamberlayne, J. Bornat and T. Wengraf (eds) *The turn to biographical methods in social science*, London: Routledge.

Seccombe, W. (1986) 'Patriarchy stabilised: the construction of the male breadwinner wage norm in 19thC Britain', *Social History*, vol 2, pp 53-75.

Sostris (1999) *Sostris Working Paper 4: Case study materials – ethnic minorities and migrants*, London: Centre for Biography in Social Policy, University of East London.

Tsoukalas, K. (1981) *Social development and the state: The constitution of the public sphere in Greece*, Athens: Themelio (in Greek).

Tsoukalas, K. (1985) 'Some thoughts on the social role of public employment in Greece', in K. Vergopoulos (ed) *The state in peripheral capitalism*, Athens: Exantas.

EIGHT

Love and emancipation

Birgitta Thorsell

Introduction

In this chapter, women's identities are conceptualised in terms of two poles – love and emancipation. In the Sostris case studies of women from varied backgrounds, these polarities were frequently seen to interact in the women's lives, to the point of cross-fertilisation, leading to new orientations. We have chosen the cases of three women whose circumstances are in some respects strikingly similar and in others notably different. Together these cases indicate new patterns in contemporary European societies: the crossing of cultural, social and geographical borders, as well as the growing importance of emancipation for providing a sense of security relative to love.

Both love and emancipation have an inherent potential for change. In art, literature, film and music, love has demonstrated an ability to mould and remould characters and perspectives. We consider first our two polar concepts, and then the three cases.

Dimensions of love

Love is a state of being as well as a state of mind. It can be a dynamic process of transformation, from infatuation through passion and romantic love to true love. In the Sostris cases, it is not easy to detect either such a state or such a process. If the love element in these cases represents a forceful hidden drive, it is in spite of the palpable shortcomings of love these women experienced in their childhood. In short, these various forms of love leave deep and complex imprints on culture. In the words of psychologist Ethel Person (1991, p 22):

> It is my central contention that love fills an important function not only for the individual but also for culture. It is the red thread in novels as in our lives. Love determines our feeling for obligation and time and also contrives to transform these magnitudes. Romantic love offers not only momentary excitement but possibilities for a dramatic change of the I. Hence it is a powerful force for change.

In our Sostris case studies, a different but equally real transformation process was richly represented in the more directed love of work and love of one's children or other family members. These forms of love drove social processes. They were sometimes powerful enough to trigger change from negative relations and situations to more functional ones and, vice versa, from functional to disturbed ones.

The social dimension of love is manifested as a search for security and a view of love as being a safe haven that will protect the loved one against the indifference or hostility of the surrounding world. According to Person, this is a twofold error. First, love is not a safe haven but an inherently *unstable* state. Second, and more subtly, there is a danger of our acquiescing in a state of security that implies a process of no change. This means the deliberate avoidance of risk and denial of the accompanying adventure or transformation of discovering in ourselves the person whom we have not yet met. In a deeper sense, love is a journey with an unknown destination. It is also a project involving major risk taking without which we may never attain a sense of self-realisation (Person 1991, p 426).

The perception of love as spatially and temporally located has been amply covered in literature. Such shifts are more in degree than in kind. In the mid-20th century, Michel Butor embedded love as fulfilment in a landscape or a city. The protagonist of Butor's *La modification* (1957), travelling by train from Paris to Rome, ruminates on the image of his mistress in Rome as "*le visage de Rome*" (the face of Rome). She could not be imagined "*sans Rome et en dehors de Rome*" (without Rome and outside Rome).

There is a stereotyped perception of love as an historical product of the transition from the extended to the nuclear family, which has also to do with a liberation from patriarchal and commercial aspects of love. Stendhal, writing in early 19th-century France, conceived of love as a gradual process towards a state of fulfilment. In 19th-century Germanic and Slavic literature, love is portrayed as more 'existential' – meaning emotionally grounded in the personality of the individual, as compared with the sentimentally flavoured Anglo-Saxon tradition.

The sensibilities implied in literary treatments of love were primarily connected with 19th-century emancipatory processes in the bourgeoisie. Approaches to love among the aristocracy and the lower classes were respectively and accordingly portrayed as arrogant or crude. From this essentially middle-class conception of love as a transcendent expression of self-fulfilment, the political significance of the private sphere emerged as a new focus for feminist agendas. Since amorous affairs in the context of the private sphere allowed a certain control by women, the politics of love could become a tool for feminist purposes, and a route to social mobility. In the end, love would then assume a more classless character.

Beck and Beck-Gernsheim have analysed love as a social phenomenon. They identify in contemporary society a prototypical conflictual tendency to put the family on a pedestal and simultaneously to tear it down. They contend that love has become a secular religion, which forces us "to break with family ties in order not to betray our personal search for genuineness, for true love" (Beck and Beck-Gernsheim, 1995, p 174).

A recent tragic event in Uppsala, Sweden, in the form of a Kurdish father's 'honour killing' of his 26-year-old daughter, may serve as a pointed illustration of how love can operate as a force for breaking with tradition. For some time, the girl had a love relationship with a Swedish man. Being a resident and citizen of Sweden, she had stepped out into global modernity, leaving behind her family and her cultural attachment to religion. The father had made violent threats against her, but neither the political nor the legal authorities heeded the danger.

In January 2002 the father, supported by the girl's brother, shot her dead. Almost instantly, she became a symbol for a whole generation of young women who are striving for an end to their enslavement under archaic tradition. By giving her a state funeral in Uppsala cathedral, attended by the royal family, the government and the speaker of parliament, the Swedish authorities made amends for their neglect. In terms of social impact and attention, many a famous love affair pales in comparison.

Love as a secular religion reached a height in the 1960s and 1970s. The limits of love were then stretched in the search for a matching of personal and social authenticity, often in social experiments such as communal living. In the present day, love in a context of affluence tends to lack such social goals. It suffers from being unevenly distributed, from a lack of meaningful direction, and from postmodern fragmentation. This picture is doubtless over-generalised, however, since in some respects postmodernism has also facilitated the return of old romance and attempts to re-elevate the nuclear family to a public norm, as in communitarian thinking (Etzioni, 1995).

While love nowadays extends into new cultural spheres, it is also subjected to 'glitzy' commercialisation. On the one hand, there is a wave of multicultural literature, with its important intercultural purpose. In the works of Hanif Kureishi, for instance, and many of his postcolonial literary contemporaries, love is presented as an 'idea creation', that tears down barriers between races, ethnicities and genders. On the other hand, there is the crude and false sensuousness of the audio-visual pop music industry.

Another prototypical testimony of love as a peak 'idea creation' has appeared in recent film version of Jane Austen's novels, where love is treated in its most sacred guise and on female conditions. This manifests an understanding of love in an historical sense. This historical approach lends legitimacy to a yearning for authentic love – which is doomed as long as the manipulative Scarlett O'Hara remains an archetypal subject of female identity[1].

The quest for authentic love can lead to a search for oneself through the flow and intensity of physical and intellectual relations. In defiance of a world run on the basis of pragmatic solutions and convenient lies, this approach to love can even acquire a quasi-religious character. In some ways, this contains all the promises and expectations of a social movement in its prime (Alberoni,

1983). Yet it has neither the institutional framework of a religious order nor links to a political tradition. It is a utopia that derives its strength from disappointment with all other credos (Beck and Beck-Gernsheim, 1995, p 175).

Alberoni (1983) distinguishes between stronger and weaker ties of love. Strong ties emanate from childhood and are linked to the close family – the very source of formative emotions. The only analogous form of such unconditional acceptance is an infatuation that is followed by a deep sense of love for a person. At the same time, Alberoni sees the genuine love relation as inherently complex. It is not so much a dialogue as a symphony built on seemingly contradictory principles such as substitution and complementarity. Love can crumble at the first sound of a false note.

These observations by the Becks and Alberoni, among others, are all relevant to the Sostris case studies. At best, love inspires social hope. By contrast, the Becks point to pragmatism and fragmentation:

> It is no longer possible to pronounce in some binding way what family, marriage, parenthood, sexuality or love mean, what they should or could be; rather, these vary in substance, exceptions, norms and morality from individual to individual and from relationship to relationship. (Beck and Beck-Gernsheim, 1995, p 5)

The dimension of emancipation

Love has attracted many metaphors, such as slumbering lions or volcanoes. The 'love-and-culture' constellation contrasts with the 'emancipation-and-civilisation' one. The former harbours revolutionary, genial and Dionysian features, whereas the latter is controlled, bland and Apollonian[2].

The Enlightenment set modernity in motion and, with it, emancipatory forces. Kant hailed man's emancipation from fettered subordination to a mature and autonomous control of the self. Emancipation has since been associated with rationality, individual autonomy and mature citizenship in the spirit of the Enlightenment.

Emancipation may be formally expressed in terms of citizens' rights: political, legal, cultural, economic and social. However, none of these rights was acquired automatically. They all had to be won and still have to be fought for and protected. Emancipation in the modern sense is much more than Kantian progress towards maturity and freedom from the bonds of ignorance-based dependence. In addition to independent decision making, it now implies freedom of movement, access to all sorts of information and capital resources of one's own.

For women, emancipation took a different and more thorny route. Even once women had become citizens de jure, in most parts of Europe their rights remained limited, as they still are in the present day. During the 19th century, emancipation took place in the cultural field in certain countries, but that was restricted to educated upper and middle-class women. This led to the creation of a narrow stratum of women with a large domain of expression, where love was treated as an existential potential for a state of self-realisation.

The contemporary state of women as mirrored in the Sostris cases is better described by Ulrike Prokop (1976), when she dichotomises the life contexts of women as being torn between limited strategies and unlimited desires. Prokop's perspective implies that women's productive forces and resources are more oriented towards the cultural than the civilisational. However, women's great capacity for spontaneous, creative and imaginative perceptions was hampered by their adjustment, for political and strategic reasons, to the civilisational state of the patriarchy.

As long as the institution of the family mediated between the individual and society, it remained a tool of patriarchal civilisation and a mirror of society's political hierarchy (Prokop, 1976, pp 71, 73). The three Sostris cases analysed below will show the extent to which culture and civilisation have facilitated or put restraints on experiences of love and emancipation.

As already indicated, love and emancipation have on occasion enjoyed a fruitful interaction. But in the later postwar period, the lifelong project of identity and its acquisition has been strongly determined by the values of modernity. Therefore the progress of upwardly mobile women, as our cases suggest, is decidedly more a result of emancipation than of the vagaries of love, critical though those are. This is illustrated in our cases.

Love as an emancipatory force

GunBritt: torn between demons and hope[3]

GunBritt lived in a country (Sweden) and in an epoch where she could move from very modest working-class conditions to the top echelons of society with apparent ease and without using 'elbows'. It was therefore surprising when she prematurely used the opportunity to take out her guaranteed pension. She had not compromised her political ideals on the way to the top. However, the price of her 'class journey' (a Swedish term for moving upwards from the lowest rung) was that she lived with a constant fear of doing or saying the wrong things and the headlines that might result. In order to free herself of constant adjustments to the demands of a municipal political culture run by patriarchal apparatchiks, she opted for early retirement to realise other parts of herself. A working-class girl with a professional career normally did not allow herself the extravagancies of devoting herself to the realisation of cultural experiences.

There was not much love in GunBritt's working-class background. Her parents got divorced after many years of fighting when she was 18 and, as the only child, GunBritt used to hide when the fighting became too much for her.

Her paternal grandfather kept an eye on her and told her to go on with her studies, something she has been doing all of her life.

> When I went to grammar school, grandfather used to come and wanted to know what I was reading and wanted to know how it was and exhorted me to keep on and never give in and go on as long as I can, and yes, he was my inspiration.

At the age of 17, on the basis of her grammar school leaving certificate, she took up office work. Her parents' divorce increased her sense of self-reliance. She continued to live with her mother, who needed her support, but she inwardly sympathised more with her father.

> I think father craved an honesty, which probably rubbed off on me; I think there exists a double standard in working life because people refuse to see injustice when it is committed, directly or indirectly. Father always noted when injustice occurred, but that was in his own field and I took his perspicacious mind into my field of work.

These were her first steps towards emancipation. GunBritt made the class journey. Through study she advanced in the field of office work, becoming an administrator in the town hall. During this period, she married a man with the same social background, who was also studying to improve his situation. Both studied ambitiously in addition to their work — he to become an engineer and she first for her abitur[4] and then a university degree. They had no children. For a long period, they tried to adopt, but were sickened by all the scrutinising and insensitive investigations on the part of the authorities. So they gave it up.

GunBritt was strongly engaged in the women's section of the Social Democratic Party, where she had prominent positions over long stretches of time: "In the women's movement of the party they had the same questions and attitudes as I had, so I could be myself". In other words GunBritt was – and still is – well-adjusted to the whole emancipatory project of the Swedish labour movement. Her first marriage was entirely in line with the ideal love-and-emancipation model in the Swedish political and cultural context of the half century (mid-1930s to mid-1980s), when Social Democratic hegemony was a formative force.

She felt secure within both environments – the embrace of the women's section in the party and that of her fellow social-climber husband. He was unfaithful to her, but she did not mind very much, since her married situation and status provided a basis from which she could enjoy the women's organisation – her friends, and social circles from work, her studies, her upward mobility, as well as the profound friendship and comradeship within her marriage.

After 17 years of marriage, the couple divorced. Her husband left her for another woman. This took her by surprise, since she had thought that their friendship was strong enough to make them bound to pursue their ambitions together. She changed jobs every five years.

> I moved to new jobs out of curiosity and a craving for excitement, but I retained contact with some of my mates at work after each job.

Her love of moving ahead to face new situations and challenges was made secure by her circles of old and new friends. More often than not, these had a clear connection to the women's section of the Social Democratic Party, with which she strongly identified.

> That is where I met those who were interested in the same questions and in the same things as I was. Not as something you do as a job, it is rather something you work with in a group, you work together with friends you like. Yes, this is a different way to work politically with women.

Since its inception, the Social Democratic Party had had a strong vein of male values, and the local council where she made her ultimate career was run by extremely macho men. She feared they would strike back with a vengeance when an intelligent woman like herself assumed a leading public profile. Since then, her workplace, the local council, has been the subject of upheaval and a major public discussion about the open society and its present enemies, the town councillors. The head of the local administration was forced to resign after an anonymous letter from bullied and sexually harassed women (they feared the worst had they signed it) pointed him out as the chief culprit.

Only now (2002) is an open discussion on democracy, accountable leadership and abuse of employees taking place. An expert psychologist has been appointed to investigate the malfeasance and misdemeanours of the current power structure. A number of improper conditions have therefore been revealed, only a fraction of which have reached the attention of the public. These existed just as strongly while GunBritt was still active. Her dilemma was a double one. On the one hand, the power structure responsible for these ills was Social Democratic, and, on the other, she both felt, and was, powerless to react to the malpractice she witnessed.

At all her previous jobs, she had observed with indignation the blatant injustices women were subjected to. This experience had driven her deeper into activities and leading responsibilities on behalf of the women's section of the party. She believed in being quite outspoken in her questioning and criticism of the wrongs and shortcomings she came across. She made no distinction between private and public employers. In fact, she considered her private employers as more fun and interesting. This clearly represented another step towards emancipation from the values she had inherited from home, where her father tended to support the Communist Party.

Some years after her divorce, GunBritt met a new man on her walks to and from work. He was a civil servant in the same office as GunBritt and held a responsible and exposed executive position. Was this love at last? He came from a well-established, upper-class family in town. They began to talk and found many interests in common. They started to meet outside the office and go for walks, picking mushrooms in the autumn, listening to music in the concert hall and so on. He was recently divorced from a feminist politician and member of parliament with whom he had two daughters, then 11 and 13 years old.

> It is so fantastic, I have never had such a good time.... To find someone to share a lot with, to feel you have someone to talk to ... and the children have also taught me a lot.

When she was 47, they married, and started to plan their retirement. If this was love, a Cinderella story, would GunBritt become more emancipated in herself?

> Many opportunities have been on offer. Lots of people have believed in me, that I could do many things, but I didn't believe this myself, so it never came to happen.

In many ways, GunBritt models the development of the welfare state in Sweden. As she never had any children, she could continue to study, and make a career in the provincial government, where she had once started with simple office work. On the other hand, she had her demons, her fear of what she might do wrong:

> I was always terrified of what might be in the headlines in the newspaper the next day, about me doing something stupid.

And this continued into the last years of her career. It would appear, then, that in her retirement years GunBritt is finally an emancipated woman, with a family of her own to love.

To sum up, GunBritt's love has been a lifelong learning process in which emancipation and identity are intertwined. She interpreted every relationship and social setting that had advanced this life project as a confirmation of her growth into an identity that boosted her personal integrity and self-respect. She had achieved her emancipation interactively, through the challenges posed by frequently moving jobs, and by people believing in her more than she believed in herself, as she puts it. To use Hannah Arendt's language about Ulysses, by performing actions in a shared political space, GunBritt reveals *who* she is to her peers. GunBritt's life story, which is a result of these actions, corresponds with a specifically 'human' existence, which is public and political (Arendt, quoted in Cavarero, 2000, p 57). As GunBritt said, this kind of interaction arose from the 'different' way women work together politically. The sense of personal emancipation, which she gained through her second marriage, however, clearly outgrew the Social Democratic project.

GunBritt's story is very telling about the achievements of postwar Swedish social democracy and how this affected the trajectory of a prototypical adherent. Her risk resided in her ultimate dependence on this culture, which underwent profound change after three self-assured decades (mid-1950s to mid-1980s). In every formal sense, Swedish society had reached further in emancipating its citizens than any comparable society in Western Europe. With increasing complexities, multiculturalism and, not least, globalisation, new demands have arisen. This is requiring a new practice and a new learning process. Both are still very much unfinished. There is a growing gap between the old formal truths with moorings in the successful construction of the Swedish model and new realities, which are profoundly changing the character of Swedish political culture.

In the postwar Social Democratic Party, the political emancipation of women was highly legitimised and its formalisation in party practice positively sanctioned. This provided GunBritt with a social and political sanctuary where she could relax and feel adequate up to a point. Here, unlike at work, she could lose her 'demons', her fear of nemesis; that is, the fear of unwittingly committing a mistake in an acquired culture. This milieu did not, however, enable her to pursue wider cultural and expressive forms of self-fulfilment. Nor, despite its ongoing work against employment injustices, had it managed to change macho and abusive culture at the executive level. GunBritt's second marriage, which is the result of love as a mature learning process, is too much linked to public life to be shielded from this aggression. Hence, in order to experience love as a complete dimension, she retires. Mature love, attained on the basis of a confident identity achieved through emancipation, then required a shift out of work. GunBritt regards this as further emancipation, rather than as a forfeit for the new love relationship. It is 'emancipation' in the sense that she is now confident in a cross-class relationship and is allowing herself to go for the realisation of satisfying high cultural interests. This is a possibility that a working-class lass would never allow herself under normal circumstances. She is no longer 'hiding under the stairs' in the face of parental or class violence. She feels she has done her work of representation, and she is happy that both she and her new partner can afford to retire from wage labour. The Swedish guaranteed pension, together with the 'richness' of their sense of personal fulfilment, means they can retire from the public eye at no loss and no cost at all. Perhaps this, too, in the context of the Swedish work ethic, is an emancipated step.

The postwar Social Democratic Women's Party adopted no explicit feminist ideology or feminist form of expression. 'Feminism' remained associated with a utopian and political programme for something not sanctioned. Yet the party's limitations are clear from GunBritt's life story, however much it provided her with a congenial 'home'. Significantly, only in the context of the new challenges facing the Swedish model has the new Leftist Party[5] (in 2002) made feminism into an emblem of its programme, as a contrast to the patriarchalism of the prevailing political power structure.

Mercia: a fairy tale?

Romantic love also features in the story of Mercia's emancipation, but this time as a more transcendental 'red thread'. She was interviewed by the French team within the category on 'ethnic minorities and migrants' (Murard, 1999, pp 32-4; Sostris, 1999).

Mercia was the eldest in a family of 10 children from northern Spain. Her father was born on a farm but left to became a miner and later a policeman in Franco's police force. Her mother owned a café. Mercia lived with her maternal grandmother until she was eight years old. This was the happiest time of her childhood. Then she was taken away by her parents to do domestic work – "Removed from my own life", she says. Her father was already ill and an alcoholic, and her mother had very little money. She never said "I love you" to Mercia.

Mercia started working as a child domestic cleaner in the neighbourhood. She gave her wages to her father, who spent the money on drink and, while drunk, he would beat both children and wife. Yet she admired her father and thought she could influence him by this token of love, by giving him her wages. As the eldest, she was from earliest childhood harshly exploited in household work at home from early morning before school and then after school late into the night. At 12, she began domestic work for a neighbouring woman. This brought a degree of emancipation as it liberated her from the difficult family that she had in her own way strenuously and precociously (and unsuccessfully) tried to change.

At 15, she met a neighbourhood boy, and stayed with him for five years. While he was away on military service, Mercia's uncle on her father's side came to visit from Venezuela. He had visited once before, but this time he brought a friend, a married man who was a doctor. This man spoke to Mercia's father and asked if he could take her to Venezuela, to help her to qualify as a nursing auxiliary. Her father refused. Mercia still believes that they were made for each other. When they met several years later, he told her he would have married her if she had stayed in Spain. This fairy-tale experience stayed with her for life as her secret love affair.

A female friend who had emigrated to France had inspired Mercia to do the same. Mercia asked her boyfriend to follow, but he refused. She went to Paris to find work but also to study, "to learn things that one didn't have the opportunity to learn at home in Spain. Above all, it meant to learn about life itself" (Sostris, 1999, p 32). During her first years in Paris, she looked after babies in different families. She had to change one family situation when the man in the house made passes at her. She guarded her integrity against any semblance of abuse, just as in Spain she had carefully guarded her virginity. Later on, she worked as a cashier in a supermarket.

After three years, Mercia married another immigrant from Spain. He belonged to a group of young communists. He was a fair, educated and literate man. She did not like him at first, but after a visit to the family back in Spain she saw him in a new light. The same year they had their first child, a girl. Four years later, they had a boy. She worried a lot about being an inadequate mother, reflecting her deep insecurity regarding her relationship with her family in Spain, whose pattern and habits she had not managed to bend or even influence.

Mercia wanted to stay at home and look after her children, so she started sewing and altering clothes for customers. But it was when she made a traditional Spanish dress for her daughter that she acquired a reputation as a dressmaker and started her new career.

She wanted to make dresses, so she introduced herself to a shop belonging to a famous tailor in Paris. After a disaster with a muslin dress, she was ready to learn everything. She describes the beautiful dresses she made for the rich and famous in Paris and throughout the world. She decided to open her own firm to design and make dresses for other tailors. Her husband became one of her employees. Five years later, Mercia had to close the firm and she became extremely depressed. She went to a psychiatrist and began therapy sessions, which gave her the opportunity to reflect on her life as a whole. She realised she missed the love of her dream, the Venezuelan doctor. However, there was still hope that she might be able to build something up again, together with her husband.

Mercia, who is now over 50, was one of the few Sostris cases to speak openly about love, and about romantic love – longing for it, dreaming about it, never really forgetting about it. In her childhood at her grandparents' house, she was loved and cosseted. The contrast when she came to her parents' home – "removed from my own life" – was a strange experience. That her mother never told her she loved her could be the reason why Mercia was prepared to take risks, with men and through migration. Besides being a risky venture, migration could also be an emancipatory way forward.

There is no doubt that Mercia has taken risks, but does this mean that she is emancipated? While romantic love remained a source of inspiration in Mercia's life, it seems doubtful that she ever thought about emancipation as a political issue. Rather it could be seen as a by-product of her self-steered life journey. Yet she wants to write her own autobiography because there are "interesting things in it". She explains how difficult it is to succeed at the professional and social level when you are a woman, uneducated, a foreigner, somewhat naïve, sentimental and harmless. She also felt that going to Paris was "to learn about life", who others are and who she herself is. These are her 'unpolitical', yet socially aware, self-descriptions. Like GunBritt, she seeks out a wide range of social relationships as a source of learning.

She had been able to live on two levels of ambition, which seemed to sustain each other. One concerned the brittle family she herself had made into a cohesive unit with moments of success, but also of setbacks. She was willing to work hard and take risks to share instances of self-fulfilment with her own family in Paris. At the same time, such moments never provided her with the sense of security and self-appreciation of which her family in Spain had deprived her. Parallel to this brittle world, which became doubly brittle in the light of her emotionally fissured background in Spain – loving grandparents, fiery, loveless parents – she cultivated and was buoyed up by the imaginary, virtual world she had been so close to realising with the Venezuelan doctor.

Where GunBritt was a Swedish prototype, Mercia appeared as very much her Latin counterpart. While GunBritt's advance in life is steered by education, political backing and public service opportunities, Mercia's involves more spirited personal initiative, and skilful use of her feminine resources in an environment in which femininity is valued and respected as cultural capital. In the more backward conditions of Spain, and then as an immigrant, Mercia's trajectory involves repeated setbacks, followed by renewed efforts to begin again and move on. Rather than being supported by public institutions, Mercia achieved emancipation through her concrete life project, both in the sphere of employment and in the family arena.

These two cases suggest that it is harder to realise love as an ideal than it is to achieve emancipation, even though clear elements of love are present in their respective emancipatory trajectories. GunBritt only achieves true love in her mature years, whereas for Mercia love remains transcendent. Yet it is clear that her secret bond with the Venezuelan doctor gives her enormous inner confidence, which she uses in her relationships with employers and with sponsors who helped her to set up her businesses over the years.

Suzanne: between two worlds

Mercia makes opportunities for emancipation through the project of migration, and her life is marked by the transcending of several borders: physical, geographical, cultural and spiritual. A similar, but less positive, prototypical crossing of borders is present in our third case: Suzanne, of the former German Democratic Republic (GDR), who was interviewed as a lone parent (Breckner et al, 1998).

Suzanne was born an illegitimate child in the sinister year of 1953 when the East Berlin uprising on 17 June was crushed by Soviet forces, an event that sealed the integration of the GDR with the Soviet bloc through mass collectivisation of agricultural lands. The seventeenth of June then became both a future national day and the starting point of a mass migration from Eastern to Western Germany. Among the migrants were five of Suzanne's mother's six sisters. Her mother remained in the east until 1958, staying with her parents and earning her living by doing domestic and waitressing jobs. Suzanne's maternal grandparents lived under pressure and duress as small farmers who had refused to join the collectivisation process.

In 1958 Suzanne's mother went with two young daughters to the small West German town where her sisters had settled earlier. Several weeks later, the five-year-old Suzanne wanted to go back to the East to live with her maternal grandparents. She had made up her mind, got her way and, amazingly, travelled back alone at five years of age.

> I was born in the village of […]; my mother she was not married, that is, I was
> born, as I said, illegitimate, and I grew up more or less at my grandparents'
> home. They had such a small house here in […] and I had no special
> relationship with my mother. Actually my grandma was my mother and that
> never changed until now. I mean she died in the meantime but that didn't
> change anything.

The father's side was conspicuously absent. Her mother claimed the local
baker, a married man, was the father, but he denied paternity. Suzanne did not
learn about this until a schoolteacher intimated it to her when she was 13 years
old. Up to then, it had not been an issue for her.

She was a success at school and in the children-and-youth organisations, so
much so that she was invited to attend special youth camps, where she met
members of the party elite, the 'nomenclatura'. However, her grandparents
denied her further education because of financial constraints, and instead she
became an industrial systems mechanic in a chemical combine.

At the age of 18, she became pregnant while working in this industry. Her
son was born in 1972 in a small, noisy apartment belonging to her boyfriend,
who was away most of the time with his job. Physical, alcohol-related abuse
was the core of their relationship, which continued for 14 years, nine of them
in marriage. One year after marrying, Suzanne moved to a new apartment to
separate from her husband, but he followed her and stayed for another eight
years, until they eventually divorced in 1986.

In contrast to this dreadful family situation, Suzanne's career developed more
smoothly. She worked full time and joined a range of organisations, all of
which were marked by tightly prescribed social behaviour. Work and 'the
enterprise' had a high social value in the GDR. Meanwhile, her son went to a
daily nursery from the age of three months.

For Suzanne, this meant that she could balance her difficult family life with
a good working life. In the GDR, this was a common way of taking care of
emotional problems: through collective action rather than by discussion and
communication about personal lives. After the reunification of Germany in
1991, Suzanne married again. In 1992 she gave birth to a daughter, 20 years
after the birth of her first child. Her new husband, however, continued his
affair with a former lover. This *ménage à trois* led to divorce within five years.

She met her mother and tried to form a relationship with her, not least for
the sake of her daughter. However, her mother blamed her for not being able
to keep her second husband.

> That day my mother died for me, and even if she were mortally ill, I wouldn't
> go there, I said, I never needed her in my life, I grew up without her, she
> didn't bring me up. And that she blames me now for (the failed marriage),
> that doesn't disturb me, but that she refuses contact with the girl, who really is
> innocent and can't do anything about it…. She should be happy that I

managed to come through and that I have such a daughter, because she didn't help me in any way.

Reunification changed Suzanne's working conditions completely. With her ability to study, she could attend new courses, but the likelihood that she would find adequate new employment seemed slim. Her life in the workplace and in the public sphere had previously offered her a form of emancipation from her unsatisfactory and flawed love and family life. Now she was faced with the question of why she could not make lasting intimate relationships. Her fatherless life was not a good basis for forming strong relationships with men, and her mother's unstable and disrupted history always spilled over into Suzanne's relations with her.

Suzanne was grateful for her intuition and strength of character at the age of only five when she had taken the decision to leave her mother and half-sibling in West Germany and return to the East to stay with her poor but decent grandparents. In GDR, public associations and the workplace had become her life. She had become defined by this public space and she had embraced it as her family.

Socialist brigades were formed in 1959, modelled on a youth brigade at the Elektrochemisches Kombinat Bitterfeld. These brigades were not very successful at mobilising a sense of ideological unity or at encouraging zeal for the party (Ross, 2000, p 164). Yet they managed to provide employees with a sustained working-class identity. This identity gave Suzanne a sense of belonging and dignified emancipation from a disrupted and damaged family life, where attempts at love quickly moved to physical violence.

She did not need any overarching socialist or national identity in order to feel she had roots and self-respect. Moreover, the failure of the GDR to foster socialist and national fervour eventually brought the state to collapse. For Suzanne, however, the new reunified Germany was little short of a disaster. Her attempt in 1991 at a new life with a new husband and a new child in the new Germany once again failed. Now, however, she could not compensate by being diligent and successful in public and working life. Open market society confronted her with her need for personal emancipation, and the importance within this of love.

In my view, self-help or consciousness-raising groups, such as were common in the women's movement in the West, could have enabled Suzanne to speak up about her situation and encounter an empathy and understanding that would have made her realise that she was not alone. That in itself would have made her see herself in a new light, which is a prerequisite for acquiring new perspectives on one's own identity and conditions, even though it might not reach the deeper levels of the problem (Breckner et al, 1998, p 84). Part of Suzanne's problem lies in her tendency to blame outside factors (her mother, her husband, the new German state) and to neglect the building up of her own personal strengths and relational capacities. Once she has overcome her disenchantment with the new system, she might perceive the possibility of new, more personal roads to emancipation.

Conclusions and policy making

These three women rose from underprivileged backgrounds by using the emancipatory potentials of postwar Europe. These potentials are revealed in the case studies as both contextually diverse, contradictory, and perhaps only part of the process of 'personal emancipation'. A woman's personal emancipation follows by no means automatically from the public provisions that purport to promote equality and social progress. Emancipatory policies appear somewhat hollow when not infused in an individual's life with what is inevitably an intensely personal dimension of love. Moreover, the story of GunBritt gives a sober reminder of how far European societies have to go before they remove sexual abuse and bullying behaviour, even – and perhaps particularly – at executive level.

'Personal emancipation' is in any case only meaningful in the fuller context of an individual life project or biography. The more public 'civilisational' goals of promoting social mobility, achieving equality between women and men, or facilitating women's independence from men, need to be 'rounded out' with more cultural developments. These include the more personal attributes of acquiring confidence, a sense of one's own agency and fulfilment, and ability to see oneself in a new light. 'Love' may be threaded through both collective and individual facets of emancipation. Mercia and Suzanne are opposite cases at both levels. While Mercia's exclusion from public forms of support is largely overcome by her transcendent love, Suzanne's 'father state'[6] is unable to compensate in the long run for the lack of love in her life, and certainly not in the market conditions of the unified Germany.

Following her class journey, GunBritt had reached a stage where her emancipation from very humble circumstances became matched by mature love and widening of cultural pursuits, both of which she wanted to enjoy to the full. Yet there was more to the story than that. GunBritt, a pillar of the Social Democratic Women's Party, also feels she is saving herself from anguish and fear by taking her guaranteed pension at the peak of her professional career. People like GunBritt are offered career opportunities at the top of the party. GunBritt, who is a decent person, refused to play along with the power structures that inevitably would have compromised her conscience. Despite her background in the politics of emancipation, she was up against major institutional obstacles that made her feel powerless. It was bad enough that she felt compelled to play it safe by not speaking her mind, though that made her retirement all the easier.

Mercia moved from rural Spain to the far more advanced society of Paris. This doubtless raised her expectations, even though, as a migrant and domestic worker, she was not in a position to be 'carried along' by emancipatory measures. Mercia's realisation during the interview that she had a lot to tell, and her idea of writing her autobiography, showed that she was not only conscious of the vagaries in her own life, but also aware that her own story was representative of the experiences of other exiled women.

Mercia made her journey into a new country at the age of 21, an uneducated young woman, alone, without money or relatives. One element of risk in her action consisted in being an immigrant and being identified as such. From her own point of view, emancipation may have come easier far away from the environment where she grew up, but at the same time she was not convinced of her own capacities. She was still haunted by the self-doubt that originated in her inability to handle her own family back in Spain. In fact, Mercia always had the ingenuity and courage to make something of whatever came her way. She was helped in this by her image of living with a redeeming love somewhere else, probably in Latin America, a belief that good and supportive forces existed out there, across borders and social frontiers.

In her search for personal fulfilment and learning 'about life', Suzanne seems to be at an earlier stage than GunBritt or Mercia. Yet she comes from the former GDR, a society that had some of the most advanced provisions for women in the areas of childcare, abortion and divorce – measures that enabled a woman to participate fully in employment without being dependent on a partner. Paradoxically, the very 'supportiveness' of collectivism in GDR society allowed Suzanne to avoid the reflective biographical work she needed to do. In this process, intensive personal interaction – as GunBritt experienced in the Women's Party, and Mercia in her learning about 'life' in personal encounters – is likely to be helpful.

In many ways, it is true that the state has no place in the arena of 'love'. Yet schools and other services surely can work in the arena of emotions, most especially in the case of missing or violent parents. It seems possible that the notion of romantic love fostered a sense of adventure in Mercia, and her story demonstrates how much can be achieved by young woman, even by those less capable than herself. Whatever it is that drives young women to move away from home, support from the authorities must match their ambitions, whether on a European or a national basis. This needs to be done in biographically sensitive ways. In this way, the Mercias, Suzannes and GunBritts of the future may make a major contribution to the improvement of European civic society.

Notes

[1] In Margaret Mitchell's *Gone with the wind*, Scarlett O'Hara struggles for survival in the social upheavals of the American Civil War. She uses her sexuality to manipulate men, and becomes tragically confused in the emotional imbroglio.

[2] The Greek gods Dionysos and Apollo, one representing anarchic hedonism and creative energy, the other rule-bound decorum and rationality, are often used at the societal

level to symbolise 'culture' and 'civilisation', or, in more individual Freudian terms, the id and the ego/superego.

[3] GunBritt was interviewed within the category of 'early-retired' people.

[4] Roughly equivalent to A levels.

[5] The Leftist Party is based on the reformed Communist Party.

[6] The 'father state' was a term used in post-unification East Germany to refer to the paternalistic nature of the GDR regime.

References

Alberoni, F. (1979) *Innamoramento e amore*, Milan: Aldo Garzanti Editore, (Swedish edition, 1983).

Alberoni, F. (2000) *Jag älskar dig (Ti amo)*, Gothenburg: Korpen.

Beck, U. and Beck-Gernsheim, E. (1995) *The normal chaos of love*, Cambridge: Polity Press.

Benedict, R. (1934) *Patterns of culture*, New York, NY: Columbia UP.

Breckner, R., Hungerbühler, W. and Olk, T. (1998) 'German national report on lone parents', *Sostris Working Paper 3: Case study materials – lone parents*, London: Centre for Biography in Social Policy, University of East London, pp 78-89.

Burns, R. (ed) (1995) *German cultural studies*, Oxford: Oxford University Press.

Butler, J. (1990) *Gender trouble: Feminism and the subversion of identity*, New York, NY: Routledge.

Butor, M. (1957) *La modification*, Paris: Éditions de Minuit.

Cavarero, A. (2000) *Relating narratives*, London: Routledge.

Chodorow, N. (1978) *The reproduction of mothering. Psychoanalysis and the sociology of gender*, Los Angeles: California University Press.

De Beauvoir, S. (1949) *Le deuxième sexe*, Paris: Éditions Gallimard.

Dinnerstein, D. (1977) *The mermaid and the minotaur*, New York, NY: Harper & Row.

Etzioni, A. (1995) *The spirit of community*, London: Fontana.

Fèbvre, L. (1944) *Amour sacré, amour profane*, Paris: Éditions Gallimard.

Gavron, H. (1966) *The captive wife: Conflicts of housebound mothers*, London: Routledge & Kegan Paul.

Gilligan, C. (1982) *Psychological theory and women's development*, Cambridge (MA): Harvard University Press.

JÄMFO (Delegation for Equality Research) (1988) *Kvinnors identitetsutveckling* (The development of female identity), Rapport 13.

Kolinsky, E. and van der Will, W. (1998) *The Cambridge companion to modern German culture*, Cambridge: Cambridge University Press.

Luhmann, N. (1982) *Liebe als Passion. Zur Codierung von Intimität*, Frankfurt-am-Main: Suhrkamp.

Mackie, L. and Pattullo, P. (1977) *Women at work*, London: Tavistock.

Miller, J.B. (1976) *Toward a new psychology of women*, Boston, MA: Beach Press.

Mitchell, M. (1936) *Gone with the wind*, New York, NY: Macmillan.

Murard, N. (1999) 'Risks and opportunities in experiences of migration and ethnicity', in *Sostris Working Paper 4: Case study materials – ethnic minorities and migrants*, London: Centre for Biography in Social Policy, University of East London, pp 30-9.

Person, E. (1991) *Drömmen om kärlek och livsavgörande möten* (Dreams of love and fateful encounters. The power of romantic passion), Borås: Borås Forum.

Peterson, M. and Thorsell, B. (1998) 'Swedish national report – the early retired', in *Sostris Working Paper 4: Case study materials – the early retired*, London: Centre for Biography in Social Policy, University of East London, pp 67-77.

Pieterse, J.N. (ed) (1992) *Emancipation, modern and postmodern*, London: Sage Publications.

Prokop, U. (1976) *Weiblicher Lebenszusammenhang*, Frankfurt-am-Main: Suhrkamp.

Rohrlich, R. and Baruch E.H. (eds) (1984) *Women in search of utopia*, New York: Schocken Books.

Ross, C. (2000) 'Staging the East German "working class"' in M. Fulbrook and M. Swales (eds) *Representing the German nation*, Manchester: Manchester University Press.

Sarsby, J. (1983) *Romantic love and society. Its place in the modern world*, Harmondsworth: Penguin Books.

Schierse Leonard, L. (1989) *Vägen till det inre bröllopet. Att förändra kärleskrelationer* (On the Way to the Wedding. Transforming the Love Relationship), Stockholm: Natur & Kultur.

Sostris (1998a) *Sostris Working Paper 2: Case study materials – the early retired*, London: Centre for Biography in Social Policy, University of East London.

Sostris (1998b) *Sostris Working Paper 3: Case study materials – lone parents*, London: Centre for Biography in Social Policy, University of East London.

Sostris (1999) *Sostris Working Paper 4: Case study materials – ethnic minorities and migrants*, London: Centre for Biography in Social Policy, University of East London.

Sostris (1999) *Sostris Working Paper 4: Case study materials – unemployed graduates*, London: Centre for Biography in Social Policy, University of East London.

Stendahl (1822) *De l'amour*, Paris: Gallimard, (Henri Martineau édition 1957).

Strickland, G. (1974) *Stendahl. The education of a novelist*, Cambridge: Cambridge University Press.

NINE

Female identities in late modernity

Antonella Spanò[1]

The condition of women has undergone impressive changes since the late 1960s. A series of interconnected changes have made possible a new way of being a woman: the new consumer culture, television, the technological transformation of domestic activities, mass schooling, the new youth culture, the political and cultural environment around 1968, and the feminist struggle that brought abortion, contraception and divorce to the forefront of public debate.

Such processes have produced multiple consequences, from a tendency to more equal sharing of domestic commitments to a decline in the fertility rate. If we were to select the most innovative feature, however, we would argue that the increasing centrality of work in women's biographical paths has been of paramount importance. Women born in the 1940s, and who were in their 20s in 1968, were the first to experience the break with the idea of the woman as housewife, which was the central role model for their mothers. They were the first to consider work as a keystone in their lives. Initially, they followed the principle of 'communicating vessels' – salaried work is increased, decreased or eliminated in various phases of the lifecycle according to family needs, and continuity of work is determined by family necessities (Saraceno, 1986). They then followed the 'double-presence' model, where family and work become parallel paths, and working became a right/duty connected with being an adult woman, independently of the needs of the family (Balbo, 1978)[2].

This model was progressively internalised by later generations of women, although at different rates – firstly in more economically developed milieus by educated women of higher social status before it gained more general cultural acceptance. During the 1980s, even those women who chose not to marry and/or work did so by challenging – and thereby diverging from – a 'typical' path. This path implied reconciling marriage, motherhood and work, often with difficulty.

At present, the situation seems to be changing once again. Increasing family instability, more precarious working conditions and, more generally, the current process of modernisation, seem to be threatening the solidity of those models around which gender identities have been constructed.

It is well known that one of the founding features of reflexive modernity is an increasing demand for control by individuals who are no longer guided by tradition and fixed scripts. Many phenomena that characterise the sphere of intimacy today are in fact connected to this shift. The widespread demand for psychotherapy, the increasing attention to food and fitness, even forms of sexuality other than heterosexuality, can all be easily interpreted as aspects of a general aspiration to exert self-reflexivity over 'objects' that were beyond individual control until a short while ago (Giddens, 1992).

From this point of view, late modernity can be regarded – with reference to Parsons (1951) – as an era characterised by a complete and radical rupture with ascription. As Melucci (1991) argues, reality constantly invites us to ask who we are and to provide plausible answers to questions of status that would once have previously been considered 'ascriptive', and therefore beyond our control.

The consequences of this are significant for the construction of gender identity. The collapse of ascription that organised the sexual division of labour (Beck [1992] spoke of 'feudal gender fates') places gender roles among those over which individuals can exercise free will and make decisions: do I want to be a husband/wife, a father/mother, and if so, how? What part of me do I want to devote to work, marriage, parenthood, or anything else? Today it is difficult to avoid such questions, but it is also increasingly difficult to provide answers. The instability that affects both the private and public spheres, the risk condition that we feel as threatening, make all choices difficult and all solutions hazardous.

This paper focuses on the 'earthquake' that is shaking gender identity – especially female identity – within a framework in which the founding institutions of everyday life, family and work, are affected by processes of modernisation and individualisation. By analysing the stories of three women coming from different social contexts and belonging to different generations, we will show that the reconciling of family (marriage and motherhood) and work in a coherent, unified identity, which is both personally stable and socially legitimated, is often an uneasy task. In particular, we will see that it is no longer possible today to argue that women experience lack or loss of work as a minor problem because, as was assumed in the past, 'they have two jobs, one inside and one outside the home'.

We will consider the stories of three women, Rita, Marisa and Sonia, all from Naples. It is not coincidental that their age, social status, family and working situations are different from one another. The three case studies were in fact selected to delineate a path that leads from the predominance of tradition to the domain of risk, through a stage of illusory certainty.

Rita: working for the family

Born in 1950, Rita lived her childhood and adolescence in an atmosphere of social and economic ferment. She grew up in a working-class neighbourhood in the historic centre of Naples where the economic boom was bringing about a deep transformation, from artisans' workshops to thriving export firms specialising in the underground production of 'made in Italy' goods (especially bags, shoes and gloves). Due to the increasing development of this sector, many of the old artisans became successful entrepreneurs, albeit in the underground economy.

Following the typical path of girls from her milieu, Rita (the youngest of four children in her family) left school at 11 immediately after completing her compulsory education. Like many other girls of her age, she began working in one small factory after another that produced leather goods. The high level of integration existing in the area, both in spatial terms (the workshops are located in the basements or in apartments in the neighbourhood) and social terms (employers and workers live in the same area and are linked by acquaintance or even friendship), made working a 'normal' experience for these girls, a continuation of domestic life rather than a 'separate' experience.

For Rita too, her job was not separate from her domestic universe, but a continuation of it. When at work, she felt at home, perhaps more so than she felt with her family.

Rita was animated by the enthusiasm of youth and by the energy derived from being a child of the postwar boom. Indeed, she wanted to participate in the vitality of the situation, while her father, a house painter who had spent all his working life in the same neighbourhood workshop, reflected an image of immobility. It is understandable, then, that, when she began working more regularly in a shoe factory at the age of 16 that had shown greater dynamism than other firms, she opted for it as the site for her personal development[3]. The factory became a new family for her – the owner was like an adopted father, her workmates like friends, even sisters:

> The owner helped us a lot, he helped us, he was a very good person.... It was
> a fine time, yes, we worked, but those were wonderful days. We felt well, we
> joked, we sang, then we girls told each other our experiences – "What about
> your baby?" "My baby does this and this".

Therefore, work became the central axis of Rita's life. Her complete identification with 'her' factory, however, is not one that we should understand in the sense of the career woman who sacrifices family in the name of work. On the contrary, Rita was a traditional woman – she married early (significantly, her husband worked in the same factory) and soon after, her first child – a boy – was born, perfectly in line with the social expectations of her milieu.

This does not mean, however, that her condition as wife and mother distracted her from her world of the factory. She went back to work only one month after the birth (when she could have taken three months' maternity leave), and handed her child over to her mother. Only at weekends did the boy sleep at his parents' house. However, these choices were not meant against the family, in the name of Rita's professional self-fulfilment, but rather *for* the family. Actually, Rita did not see conflict in her role of working mother: the familial and affective nature of her work experience in fact precludes a precise psychological boundary between family and work. As a member of a family-like firm, she devoted herself, body and soul, to the factory, but the fruits of being a good worker (her economic condition improved progressively) were dedicated to the family (a house was bought in 1972, a second child was born in 1975). In other words, the *Gemeinschaft* nature of the firm meant that her personal involvement in the job was not in conflict with the traditional value of total devotion to the family.

The importance of work for Rita is confirmed in her autobiographical narration. Rita, whose self-presentation focuses on her experience of lay-offs[4] that culminated in the final loss of work in 1994, presents herself as a betrayed worker and, like her workmates, a victim of injustice:

> We have been working there for 28 years. You [the firm] grew rich at the expense of the workers, you've exploited us, and you have also got a lot of money, of support, from the government.

Yet Rita has difficulty in dating the betrayal by the firm. Later in the interview, she suddenly remembered – "Oh, I forgot!" – that many years before (in 1976) she had been temporarily laid off. Although this could be seen as a minor event, since, after a few months, the workers were taken on again (and then retained until 1990 without interruption), Rita then presents it as a highly dramatic episode. In her interpretation of her life, this episode justifies a noticeable and definitive change in her attitude to work:

> After that dreadful experience I changed somewhat, I must say, to be honest. I began to be a bit selfish. If my daughter got measles I wouldn't leave her with my mother any more, but would look after her myself.

However, although Rita presents the first temporary lay-off as the turning point that led to a considerable decline in her devotion to work, it is not this period that marks her transition from a factory-centred to a family-centred life. As a premodern woman, always acting according to tradition, Rita is not used to analysing her choices reflexively; the interpretation she provides of her change is only an attempt to justify her sudden disaffection with work. Therefore, she is not fully aware of what happened to her and is unable to point out the event that caused her reorientation.

A deeper analysis of the text suggests that the irremediable change in Rita's life came with the shift in management, four years later (1980). When the previous owner, "who was one of us", fell ill and left the running of the firm to his sons, "who studied in Switzerland", Rita, who once felt like an appreciated and irreplaceable daughter, felt like a stranger in her own house.

> Their father loved that factory, because he'd come up from nothing, he'd been a worker like us, and knew what it was to be a worker, while he was there we were alright.... He'd come by, crack a joke, he was human.... They, the sons, understand nothing about work.

What Rita experienced and still interprets as an unjust usurpation was, in reality, the rupture of the *Gemeinschaft* ties in the firm and the introduction of cold market relations. The new identity that was necessary for a good worker in a *Gesellschaft* context required a separation between family and work that Rita was unable to make. Without any awareness of the process, Rita responded to the new situation with a radical reorientation. She shifted her main axis from the factory to the family. In the same year that the new management was introduced, it was decided that Rita's son, then 12, would return to live with his parents. The family embarked on a new strategy. With the help of loans, a very expensive taxi driver's licence was acquired for Rita's husband, who two years later voluntarily left the firm, both in response to the insecurity of their work situation and as a means of improving their standard of living.

Rita's new situation allowed her to survive in changed conditions. For 10 years she continued to work in the same firm, able to sustain the now more anonymous and impersonal relations because the centre of her affection had already moved outside the factory. After 10 years, in 1990, when she again suffered a temporary lay-off, Rita was quite prepared to accept an interruption to her work, since both her 'I' and her 'we' were then within the private sphere:

> Perhaps it has not been the same for me, because my children were grown up … but my friends cried, they lived through such an awful experience…. It has been different for me, because I'd already overcome…. For me it has been a bit better.

Rita began selling knitwear from home, which also enabled her to combine family and work in a physical way. She acquired the goods from a factory at which her brother worked. Her clients were mostly friends and her earnings paid for her daughter's university education. They obtained a taxi licence for her son. Rita's final retirement in 1994 was a relatively insignificant event. Although she presents herself as a victim of a terrible betrayal by the firm, she is now a happy woman, wife, mother, grandmother and worker.

The very lack of a definite border between the private and public spheres (between family and work) that prevented Rita from fully accepting modernity became her main resource when she had to face early retirement.

Marisa: work as self-realisation

Rita's story shows that a lack of opposition between the public and private spheres can be an important resource for coping with a traumatic event like the loss of a job. Marisa's story, on the contrary, shows that expulsion from the job market has a seriously destabilising effect on women who have tried to overcome traditional gender roles by constructing their work identities in opposition to their identities as wives and mothers. Indeed, Marisa did not work for the family at all, but against the family or at least against the traditional idea of the family based on a strict division of roles. Marisa, in other words, worked for herself.

It is surprising how exactly Marisa's biography follows the life path of the so-called '50-year-old girls', as Marina Piazza (1999) recently described the generation of Italian women born between 1945 and 1953. These women were the first to experience different and alternative models from those of their mothers and believed that, besides being wives and mothers, education and work were their 'normal' fate (Saraceno, 1986).

Marisa was born into a white-collar, middle-class family and, unlike Rita, who is of the same age, she fully shared the transformation of women's condition and the social mobility that affected her class after the Second World War. Marisa was born in 1949, the eldest of five children, in a rather run-down suburb. When she was a young adolescent, the family moved to a typical, middle-class, residential neighbourhood (inhabited by the white-collar and commercial middle classes) erected in the boom years. Notwithstanding her modest origins (her father was a civil servant and her mother a housewife who had only completed primary school), Marisa, like many girls of her age, obtained her secondary-school diploma (although she belonged to a class that could not send its sons, not to speak of daughters, to university)[5]. Typically, she attended a technical school, not a grammar school – *liceo* – because "I primarily wanted a degree that would allow me to find work. Attending a *liceo* would have implied going to university and so, although I hated numbers because they made me panic, I chose a technical school".

After getting the diploma in 1967, Marisa began looking for a job. This was difficult in that period, because the increase in the supply of female labour and chronic lack of work in the cities of Southern Italy made it difficult, particularly for a woman without a university education, to find a job. After secondary school, therefore, many girls became housewives. Marisa, however, had firmly decided to work and refused to surrender, even though it took her three years to find secure employment.

As her memories of school show, her determination to find a job was deeply influenced by the ferment of the period. On the one hand, this derived from objective opportunities for upward social mobility for middle-class young people and, on the other, from mass schooling that facilitated mixing with classmates of a higher social class:

> If I look back, they were wonderful years, although we had some difficulties …. My family relied on a civil servant's salary which was insufficient at that time, with five children…. You had to cope with lots of difficulties and sometimes you went to school with a ladder in your tights, but you didn't care…. Today it would be tragic, you would feel a dramatic gap … not in those times. In my school, there were girls of higher social standing, including my best friend, whose father had a very good job. But the way in which the families brought up their children was the same, and we didn't feel the difference that much.

However, social mobility was not the only factor that led Marisa to find a job with such determination. Brought up in that particular social milieu and period, she was objectively involved in the process, but she also showed the will and determination to emancipate herself from traditional gender roles through a project that – unlike the former one – she pursued with intent and charged with emotional meaning. The idea of life as a housewife was unbearable to her, particularly when contrasted with the new opportunities that education and work could offer to women.

> I began working at 21 and I never thought I wouldn't work, because the life of a housewife is one of the most horrible things on earth.

Her mother's life, as well as those of women who entirely devoted themselves to the family, was the model she sought to oppose:

> My mother devoted herself to us children too much, too much.... She sacrificed herself for her children, she cancelled herself out, and I must say, although I love her, that she is the wrong model, she is the person who sacrificed herself for her children, etc, and therefore I did my best not to.

In her strong desire for emancipation, Marisa fully embodied the typical position of young women in the 1960s. The '50-year-old girls' did not escape marriage and motherhood. Almost all of them got married and had children, mostly at a very early age[6]. However, they did these things in a completely new way. For these women who studied and conceived themselves as potential workers, marriage did not mean accepting traditional roles. Rather, it had a 'revolutionary' significance – autonomy from the family of origin, negotiation of a more equal partnership, models of child rearing characterised by respect and lack of authoritarianism – distinct from, or even in opposition to, the preceding generation of women (Piazza, 1999). Typically, Marisa got engaged at 14 and married at 23. This choice, however, does not suggest that she was fundamentally interested in stabilising traditional roles or in interpreting them traditionally. On the contrary, she tried to build an equal relationship in her marriage:

> I struggled with my husband, we had a lot of quarrels when I told him, "Look at me, help me, give me a hand".

She tried to be a good mother in a different way:

> I've never been a domineering mother with my children, not even when they were very small. I've always respected the person, whether child or adult.... I respect a person, what the person expresses, and it is the same for me whether this person is 10 or 100, I hate every form of authoritarianism.

Above all, she tried to be different from her mother.

Let us return to the account of Marisa's life. After three years of job applications, many interviews and some unsatisfactory work experience, an important multinational firm in the photographic industry finally employed Marisa on a short-term, three-month contract. We can visualise her, excited and happy, as she was preparing for her first working day.

> It was beautiful, it was exciting. I had got my diploma three years earlier and I was beginning to worry about ... then, really, it was a wonderful experience because working for the first time ... you don't know anything about the world of labour, you don't know what to expect, and for me it was wonderful. I repeat, I was happy to go to work because I liked working.

Her enthusiasm was perhaps noticed by the firm, for, after the first three months, Marisa's position was confirmed.

> The firm used seasonal contracts, but after the summer, instead of laying me off, they decided to keep me, so I got a contract with no time limit and it was wonderful.

The firm made a good investment. In the work sphere, more than any other, Marisa proved to be a child of her times. As is the case with other educated young women who experienced equality at school, the 'communicating vessels' principle does not apply to Marisa's experience. She was sincere when she said:

> I had no intention of being a housewife. That is, my work wasn't intended to provide a second salary, to give me the money to get married or to buy a new dress. No, I had studied and I wanted to work. I didn't want to be dependent on my husband – I wanted to achieve something for myself.

Once in the company, Marisa soon proved to be a good worker, devoted to work and loyal to the firm. Notwithstanding her marriage two years after being employed, and the birth of two children within five years (whose care was handed over to a grandmother and babysitters), Marisa's investment in work was unaffected. She proceeded, without uncertainties, in her strategy of professional fulfilment and did not draw back, even when she had to travel to various Italian cities to attend training courses:

> Although I had two small children, I agreed to go to Milan to attend a course for several weeks. I left home, I came back by plane or train at weekends.... A stressful life, because my work often required me to stay away from home for two or three days, since we also had an office in Rome.

She did not stop even when she had to move to a new workplace. On the contrary, she voluntarily opted for the new place – although it meant staying away from home all day – to pursue better career prospects.

> A new factory also meant an opportunity for development for us workers, for our careers, for advancement, because if the firm developed, we also developed.

The firm rewarded Marisa's commitment to the work and, as she says, "the proof is that my career proceeded, my salary increased and my position advanced".

The virtuous circle between commitment and reward had clear effects on the construction of Marisa's identity. Actually, she completely identified with the firm (which, many years after being laid off, she continues to call "my firm") and fully accepted the logic of profit: "Firms are not charitable institutions. Firms act in a certain context in order to make profits". Her loyalty to the firm, which she perceives as an abstract entity rather than identifying it with the 'managers' or 'bosses', arises from the very awareness that, being based on the need to make profits, the firm is ready to reward those who produce. Marisa was, therefore, safeguarded by her feeling of being a modern model worker and, unlike Rita, was able to tolerate the deterioration in the working environment, following a change in the firm's management:

> Then the firm changed because the managers were replaced, somebody retired and somebody went away. The firm's philosophy changed and the atmosphere also gradually changed, but, I must say, it remained a major firm.

Marisa was also able to understand the reasons why the firm first closed a laboratory, and then the whole factory, for reorganisation. In the work sphere, she did not act as part of a 'we' (we, the workers, or women workers), but as a single individual who was linked to the firm by a proper relation of exchange, regulated by a contract.

Marisa, who orientated her adult life towards a 'double presence', experienced the lay-off as a betrayal. For Marisa, as well as for the authors who first used this term, 'double presence' means:

> ... double citizenship also as double responsibility and loyalty ... not only double workers or double sets of roles, but parts – citizens – of two complex social systems (work and family), mutually dependant and yet symbolically and institutionally separated, to which women are expected to be fully responsible. (Saraceno, 1986, p 168)

In laying her off, the firm undermined the confidence pact by which Marisa felt protected, but it also undermined her life-project and identity. Indeed, the lay-off showed her that the interests of the firm and of the workers were not the same.

> I don't think that our plant closed down because of a crisis. It is still a thriving firm.... When they decided to close down, the balance wasn't in the red — they had profits of billions.

Above all, the lay-off showed Marisa that good workers were not safeguarded.

> They had been speaking of that reorganisation for a year, but in the personnel department where I worked, we weren't worried because the firm had rewarded us, they had acknowledged our value, and we thought that a possible downsizing wouldn't involve us.

Out of the whole personnel department, only two employees were kept on: "They were two female colleagues who had only completed compulsory school. Another colleague and I, who held higher responsibilities, had to leave our jobs".

Suffering this injustice, Marisa felt "rage more than depression, a terrible, ferocious and devastating rage" that gave rise to the desire for revenge against the firm. Along with only one female and six male colleagues out of the 100 workers involved, she decided to reject the status of 'redundant and available for work' and obtained a temporary lay-off[7]. She then decided to sue the firm. Two years later, she was the last to give in, and only because the firm was threatening to withdraw the offer of a retirement bonus.

The rage that led Marisa to revenge was, however, more deeply rooted than the episode that caused her to feel betrayed. Her words shed light on this hidden aspect.

> I felt betrayed ... the firm retained people who had exploited the situation on numerous occasions, if they were pregnant they requested maternity leave and invented some health problem.... I had never been like them, and I was enraged.

The pathos and sincerity in her words reveal the gender element of her suffering, as well as the true content of what she felt as an injustice: in order to be a good worker, she ended up acting like a male, both at home and work. Marisa had even gone beyond her genetic make-up and changed her nature as 'mater mediterranea':

> I think work was also a salvation for my children, because I was obliged to make them independent, while my psychological nature would lead me to be the typical 'mater mediterranea', the mother who is always asking, "What do you want?", "What do you need?", "Wait, I'll do it", etc.

She rejected all the commitments she saw as normal in the past:

When I was a girl, some chores were commonly assigned to daughters, for example, sweeping the floor or making beds.... Even though I got very angry and often quarrelled with my brothers, it was quite normal for me to take the cloth and dust.

She grew to despise domestic chores: "I hate, hate, I hate housework, I hate looking after the house. It is aberrant because it is repetitive, it leads you nowhere, today you brush dust away and tomorrow, when you look at the furniture and see there is new dust, you cannot pretend not to notice". She also transformed the nature of her relationships at the office where, unlike her female colleagues, she stayed on her own:

They said I walked with my nose in the air, but I didn't like the way that colleagues stabbed each other in the back immediately after speaking in confidence. I was sick of that behaviour, I had a fair relationship with everybody, but I didn't like to get involved in that ... and they said I turned my nose up at them.

All this, however, proved insufficient to save Marisa.

In the light of the deeper meaning of the injustice she suffered, her perseverance in the lawsuit appears to have been driven by both her desire to take revenge on the firm, and her desperation. Since she had built her life and her identity entirely outside of the family, Marisa could not rely either on traditional roles or on a supportive network of relationships when she was forced to redefine herself after the loss of her job.

Although her husband has retired due to poor health and needs care, she cannot redefine herself as a devoted wife. She expected a great deal from her marriage, but it has collapsed under the weight of disillusionment. Marisa believed in a special relationship, thinking that her marriage could be different from traditional models, based on cooperation and mutual support. Retrospectively, she clearly perceives that her husband "offered little or no collaboration at all, because of his macho mentality that survived all the revolutions of 1968". Marisa has been forced to admit that her marriage "was normal, with its ups and downs, with its crises, but I remain a convinced opponent of marriage", and that her husband's presence is "heavy, very heavy".

Marisa cannot even redefine herself as a mother. In her project of self-realisation as an independent and emancipated woman, motherhood was a danger, both to herself ("I knew perfectly knew well what the risk was: to stop living"), and to her children. She therefore kept the danger at bay through strict self-discipline and the full acknowledgement of their autonomy. Marisa has always lived her life in a first-person perspective. She has never had a projective relationship with her children and today she cannot live through them – she needs her own life. She is aware that she has devoted more energy to her achievements than to her children, whom she has always considered "as autonomous individuals". She does not think it is fair that she should be credited with their success: "I've been lucky with my children. Above all I've been lucky". Although her children are "wonderful" people, they cannot help her to reorientate herself.

Marisa cannot even resort to her roles as daughter, sister and friend. Her family of origin, from which she detached at a very early age, is not a reference point for her. Her mother and sisters, "who speak every morning on the phone and exchange recipes", are like aliens and although she loves them, she shares little with them. She has no female friends because she has never had time to establish relationships.

Without any ties, without any 'we' to which she belongs, after 20 years of work and at the age of 43, Marisa is dangerously lacking in alternative roles:

> After six years I can't get used to living without ... that is, to being unemployed.... I tried not to die in the psychological and social sense.... I visited museums, looked around bookstalls, read books and magazines, I learnt to use a computer, at least for writing a letter and browsing through a CD-ROM.

These activities were only useful at the beginning, however, because "later it becomes a burden, you understand that you are doing it to spend time away, and then I didn't like it any more. I felt a sense of apathy even when I had to go shopping in the neighbourhood".

The feeling of being sentenced on the basis of her gender is, for Marisa, the key to interpreting herself, as well as the entire world. Her only certainty is that gender cannot be eluded, while her only comfort is that she has no daughters. She feels a victim of an ineluctable gender fate. This aspect can explain why, notwithstanding her passion for work and her young age (43), she remained paralysed after being laid off, and was unable to find a way of being reinstated.

> I am 49, nearly 50, I've been a redundant worker for more than five years, and I'm still unable to accept it, although I know I haven't many job prospects. For a woman the situation is still worse. When a man loses his job, it is a tragedy, but when a woman is laid off – it seems paradoxical – it is worse because there is a strong discrimination based on gender and age. When the two factors combine, that is female gender and maturity, everything is over. It means that all doors are closed, even if I think it is a nonsense.... Women are always discriminated against; if they are young the employers fear that they will get pregnant and miss a lot of working days, but if they are not so young and their children have grown up, they are still at a disadvantage.

Marisa had introduced her account with these words. They serve equally well as her final evaluation of her life.

Sonia: the risk of paralysis

Sonia's story is of a very different kind. The eldest of three children, she was born in Naples to a wealthy bourgeois family. At the age of 30, Sonia was still starting to take on her adult roles. She had received a university degree in electronic engineering some years previously, and yet she had not found a coherent career path. Moreover, despite her numerous love affairs, she had not established any stable relationships. At first sight, Sonia could be included in the so-called 'young adults' generation, a term used to describe the condition of prolonged youth that is common in Mediterranean countries. The origins of this phenomenon are usually traced to high unemployment and excessive family protection. Behind Sonia's delay in entering adulthood, however, are not only objective factors, but above all, an experience of risk that prevented her from making definite choices, especially with respect to her gender definition.

Neither Sonia's lived life nor her told life can be understood without considering her childhood experiences, in particular the difficult relationship between her parents that deeply affected her, although it did not end in divorce. Sonia grew up identifying herself completely with her mother who, after a series of painful experiences, got married, hoping to establish the family she never had (her own parents got divorced and she spent her childhood – between the ages of three and 18 – in a children's home. She then moved to her father's home in Argentina and had an affair with a violent man, after which she returned to Italy where she took a university degree). Sonia's mother, however, had become a victim of her husband's betrayals.

Sonia's childhood was a period of suffering both for her mother and herself which she cannot forget:

> I remember those years very well, perhaps I can't date single events exactly, but I remember that when I was seven or eight my parents quarrelled, my mother cried and my father humiliated and tormented her.... My mother was terrified, I think. She feared he would desert her. There is nothing to do, you can't get rid of that terror. Fearing that your children can suffer the same fate as you did. She didn't even oppose ... she was intelligent and had sufficient dialectical skills to answer back, but she lacked psychological strength, and therefore she put up with it.

Sonia cannot forget what her mother often told her: "You must work, you must achieve something, because if you make your own money, you can say what you think, and you won't be a slave, but if you depend on someone else, what can you ever say?".

The mother communicated to her eldest daughter that she regretted not being able to divorce because she could not provide an adequate standard of living for Sonia and her brothers. By listening to her mother's story, the young Sonia reached three closely interconnected certainties: firstly, that the family is an unstable institution; secondly, that men are not to be trusted; and thirdly, that the only thing women can do to safeguard themselves is to be economically independent. As a consequence, Sonia divided the world rigidly into two categories: women as good and men as bad. In this divided world, women are far better than men but they succumb because they are weaker; wives are victims and husbands are perpetrators:

> My mother cried and felt hopeless, she was the victim, and my father was the torturer.

Sonia's words suggest that in her worldview this reality not only applies to her parents, but to all men and women. She is aware that she has been deeply affected by her mother's fate. On the basis of this experience, Sonia "developed a great interest in the question of gender, and began reading books, newspapers and magazines, learning a lot about the subject". At the end of her adolescence, this interest led her to make a precise choice about her future – she wanted to live like a man. Recalling the period when she decided to attend the Faculty of Electronics, Sonia says:

> I want to have a male job, to achieve a man's social position. I want to be economically strong, to be my own master. I don't want to say thank you to anyone, I don't want to depend on my husband.

In Sonia's interpretation of her life, the decision to attend this faculty fits into a framework of general distrust of men that she internalised as a girl. The motivations she suggests throughout the interview refer to "good employment prospects", "earning a high salary", and a dislike of "typical female jobs". However, there is also a specific challenge to her father's authoritarianism:

> I decided to attend this faculty because my father is an engineer in the building industry. He thought that women were not cut out for engineering, and this convinced me even more. I chose electronic engineering because I didn't want to work for my father.

Clearly, Sonia could have pursued her aim of becoming a well-paid career woman in many other fields if she had chosen to. Rather, when she entered the Faculty of Electronics, her attitude was that of a young woman who was taking up arms against her father, the symbol of domination, authoritarianism and machismo. This weapon had immediate effects. In fact, by alleging a series of problems (the need to study at night, proximity to the university, and so on), Sonia achieved an unexpected result – being allowed to live with other female students in a house near the university. For Sonia it was a turning point. She felt free and independent, she met new people:

> In living outside the family house, my life began, and I found a balance.

However, something happened during her university years. In Sonia's memories, the first years were "wonderful" owing to her new-found feelings of freedom and autonomy, but they were followed by "a very difficult period". The "amusing, exciting and satisfying atmosphere" of the students' apartment vanished. Exams became "progressively harder". Sonia slackened her pace, took exams less frequently and received poor results. She got her degree after four years' delay and her final mark was poor. This result was so incongruous with her past as a model student ("I liked being the best pupil in the class") that it requires an explanation. Sonia feels that her detachment from study arose from her diminishing commitment and tries to identify the source of her transformation. The reasons she mentions are clear: overcrowded classes, anonymous and unsupportive relationships with teachers, the coldness of the subjects she studied, the competitive and macho environment:

> It was really sad, it was a male province where women were regarded with suspicion or pity, but never respected.

All of these aspects can be traced to a 'male' element as opposed to a 'female' climate made up of solidarity and affection. Therefore it appears that Sonia's detachment (the loss of determination to become an engineer) was caused by the impact of reality that revealed that it was not possible, or perhaps even desirable, to live 'like a man'.

Yet Sonia, whose conclusion is that "in the face of obstacles, it is quite normal to lose some enthusiasm", seems unable to understand that she changed her mind about her own project of constructing a gender identity. Later in the interview, she reveals that her delay in finishing university was due to her fear of going back to her parents' home:

> It was taken for granted that once I had finished university I would return to my parents'.... I knew it, and it was a nightmare.... This aspect also influenced my delay.

But she immediately admits, in all sincerity, "my parents expected me to go back home, at least temporarily, because they also thought that I would find a job out of town".

Sonia is still unable to understand that her nightmare was not about 'returning' to her parents' house, but about 'leaving' for her future as an adult woman. The strategy of delay that she began in the university years, and continued after her degree, clearly demonstrates this. After the degree, Sonia took it easy – she admits this herself. She left for one month's vacation and then flew to the US to learn English, after which she went to Milan to visit her boyfriend. She claims she sent many job applications, but she makes only a passing reference to entering labour market (one line in 30 pages of interview), which suggests the brevity of this period in her life. Three months after completing her degree, however, she accepted an offer to become a partner in a firm established by a childhood friend who only needed an engineer for legal reasons: "It's a fake job because I have little or nothing to do, in reality I am unemployed". Widespread unemployment was a perfect alibi: "I got my degree in the middle of the employment crisis, I had no illusions and I lost my motivation". The truth is that Sonia rejected three good job offers in the following two years.

At the time of our interview – three years after completing her degree – Sonia is still uncertain about her future. The only certain element to her work is that "I lost my ambition to have a career". Confusion reigns in her mind as Sonia says that she is going to send off "some applications somewhere, but I don't know whether I really want to". Then she is going to attend a course in plant engineering that could be useful for a career in the building industry. The only thing that she seems certain of – "I will do that, I'll surely do that" – is that she wants to train as a teacher. Significantly, this is like her mother rather than her father, who is an engineer.

Sonia's ideas about her affective life do not seem to be any clearer. Within two years, she got engaged and had "an important but highly conflicting affair". She then left her fiancé and experienced "a somewhat unfocused period" when she frequented night clubs and lived the life of a single person together with a male friend, "a mate I went out with at night on adventures". Finally, she fell in love again with "a wonderful man with whom I'm living an incredible relationship". For the first time, she thinks of getting married and having children but once again she hasn't made up her mind:

> When I began university I said I would never marry and have babies.... I
> can't say I have decided now, I remain reluctant, but I can take the thing into
> consideration and perhaps, one day or another, I will be ready.... I will have
> to make up my mind, anyway, I haven't made a final decision yet.

Sonia lives in a condition of paralysis. She is stalled by a deep uncertainty about her interpretation of gender roles. Having orientated her life according to her mother's orders ('Be independent!'), she realises, through participation in the male world of engineering, that she does not really want to live like a man. However, she does not understand what a woman is supposed to do and what kind of woman she wants to be[8]. Under such insecure conditions, Sonia feels that the safest path is to live a normal life, to work as a teacher, to have children and a love relationship. However, she also fears these things because she thinks "it is unthinkable that you rely on someone else, someone you marry and then ...". The fact is that, at the age of 30, when her mother was already a wife, mother and worker, Sonia is still struggling with doubt that is no longer 'to be or not to be', but rather 'who shall I be?' This doubt in some ways embodies the essence of contemporary life.

From tradition to uncertainty. Implications for gender identity and policies

Numerous comments can be made on the case studies of Rita, Marisa and Sonia. Some of them are general considerations on the feminine world; some concern the particular condition of the younger generations; others regard possible implications for gender policies.

The first relevant aspect is that the three stories confirm that the reality of women's lives is multifarious. Furthermore, the differences within gender are as significant as the differences of gender. The gap between Rita and Marisa on the one hand, and the younger Sonia on the other, clearly shows that when we speak of differences within gender, the age group is a crucial variable[9]. However, the difference between Rita and Marisa, who are both 50 and yet so far apart – Rita's identity is based on tradition, whereas Marisa is challenging traditional roles in the effort to create an emancipation-oriented model – clearly shows that the difference between age groups cannot compensate for other forms of inequality. In the cases of Marisa and Rita, for example, belonging to a certain class was fundamental both materially (since it gave different access to education and work resources) and culturally (in evaluating more or less modern cultural models). This means that:

> ... cohort differences and differences in social conditions and circumstances, as well as differences in individual biographies are intersected and combined so as to outline female life profiles that cannot be simply reduced either to generation gaps or to class or strata differences. (Saraceno, 1986, p 36)

The cases of Rita and Marisa, moreover, also show the relevance of geographical factors. Interestingly, all three women are from Naples. This fact allows us to verify that case analysis can grasp the social and cultural characteristics of the context (for example, husbands' and fathers' authoritarianism and machismo). It also shows that social change proceeds at different paces, not only in the different areas of the country (north and south), but also within the same geographical area – Naples[10].

These comments seem to indicate the complete abandonment of determinism and evolutionism in explaining development. They also show that it is impossible to consider women as a homogenous category[11]. However, it would be misleading to conclude that any generalising attempt is bound to fail, as if one life could only represent itself. On the contrary, an important result of this analysis is the individuation of some typical paths in the building of gender identity that appears to be linked with three different stages of the female condition: tradition, modernity and late modernity.

Of course, Rita is the woman who best embodies the idea of tradition. She does not regard herself as 'residue of the past'; on the contrary, she is proud of having been a passionate worker. If we compare her with the model of a housewife or of a woman who needs to work and for whom work is only a burden, we can see that her pride is well founded. However, belonging to a traditional context meant that she could escape the question "Who am I?" and was not compelled to face many challenges. Led by tradition, Rita was able to be a worker, a wife and a mother without conflict. Although she has a strong attachment to her work, she does not work either for her self-fulfilment or for emancipation from her husband, but rather for her family. Rita and her husband have autonomous projects, but they share a common prospect. In this sense, it can be said that although Rita feels that she is the leading character in her life story, her account has a choral flavour, since her 'I' is constantly part of a 'we' (inhabitants of that neighbourhood, workers, family members). She tells a story of a tiring and painful life (because of work and job loss) but with a happy ending. She did not internalise the career woman model and, therefore, has never had to reject the traditional roles of wife and mother. This significantly reduced the impact of the lay-off and today Rita is a balanced woman who can peacefully turn to the 'third age' model as her deserved resting time.

Marisa could not be more different. We can see her as an example of modernity, an individualised woman who could define herself as a person before being wife and mother. Historically, this opportunity corresponds to a period of important achievements by women: the possibility of education and the achievement of professional positions closer to those normally attained by men. This process has its pros and cons. The opportunity of advancing in the productive world requires total conformity to male models of market participation; think, for instance, of the lack of measures to facilitate the reconciling of domestic and paid work. This leads modern women to an often painful revision of gender roles, in particular, of the maternal role. Moreover, as a fundamental feature of conformity, modern women internalise the idea that nothing but work can make sense of life. As we have seen in the case of Marisa, the loss of a job becomes a destabilising event that leaves women in a condition similar to the marginal individual, described by Merton (1949). They do not belong to their original group of traditional women, nor to that group they aspired to be part of. Individualisation and conformity to a male model are the high costs that career women have had to pay. Professional achievements may hide these costs, but they are suddenly revealed with the loss of a job. For women like Marisa, the end of work is not the beginning of a new life; rather, as she says, it is social death. This is the sentence reserved for brave women who have committed the crime of hubris: like the heroes in Euripides' tragedy, they have tried to overcome their limits by challenging not the gods, but tradition.

On this basis, we argue that belonging to the female gender is not *automatically* an important resource for 'biographical reintegration'. Being a woman can be a resource, and it often is for women who do not experience a conflict between reproductive and productive roles. However, it cannot be a resource when self-realisation entails a rejection of traditional roles. Having said this, it would be a mistake to argue with a nostalgic or traditionalist approach that the cases of Rita and Marisa suggest that the key to happiness lies in tradition. We should not forget that the possibility of reconciling the private and public spheres without conflict has historically had its cost. It is a well-known fact that traditional women have always been less privileged, less educated and confined to employment at the lowest level.

The dilemma that is presented to the new generations is evident in the case of Sonia. The choice is between two models. Firstly, there is the model of their mothers, who found comfort in feeling part of a 'we', but had to give up the project of self-realisation and suffer the double burden of work inside and outside the home. Secondly, there is the model of their elder sisters, who developed as individuals and achieved self-fulfilment in work but had to pay for the cost of conformity. The choice is not an easy one, especially when instability and uncertainty mark the context. While the traditional model is safeguarded against the risks of the productive world, it leaves women unprotected from family instability. (What would happen to Rita if she had to cope with the collapse of her marriage, instead of a lay-off?) The emancipation model is a protection against the risks of dependency, but offers no safeguard against the risk of remaining alone in the face of external threats. (How many women found themselves jobless at 40, after sacrificing their marriage in the name of self-fulfilment and rejecting motherhood in the name of career?)

Such are the doubts of young women in late modernity. Not all of them remain paralysed like Sonia. Many women begin a period of experimentation – they marry, divorce, remain single, try cohabiting with a new partner, commit themselves to work, care for their children, find free time for themselves. Many others establish more stable situations. These adjustments, however, do not deny the fundamental character of the contemporary age; that is, the doubt about past and present choices, and about the duration of the (temporarily) achieved balance. Sonia is a woman less well suited to tackle a problem faced by all women today. Her first-person perspective in the account of her life is therefore quite different. She also centres the whole narrative on herself, but her individualisation has a Cartesian trait: *dubito, ergo sum*, Sonia seems to say.

It is impossible, of course, to make accurate predictions about the kind of female model that is going to emerge in the near future. We could say that individualisation will lead both women and men to find certainties in the sphere of intimacy (home, marriage, parenthood) and that the economic system will also contribute to a return to the family. (Should unemployment remain a widespread phenomenon, it is very likely to cause a revival of the ideology of the male breadwinner and to push women back to housework.) On the other hand, we could also think that the increase in family instability and the resultant lack of confidence in marriage would lead things in the opposite direction. Individualisation "no longer hesitates at the gates of the family, marriage, parenthood and housework" (Beck, 1992, p 106). The assertion of the Ego, the right to one's self-assertion as a person, freed individuals from the constraint of traditional roles but in so doing undermined the basis of marriage – that is, the separation between the productive and reproductive roles. So, if marriage is to return to being a stable institution, it will be necessary for one of the partners (the woman?) to relinquish his/her individuality. If this were the case – as Beck (1992) has wittily argued – history would have to turn backwards, women be expelled from the labour market and from schools, and perhaps also be deprived of the right to vote! Another possible scenario could be an equally problematic world of single people, who have survived more or less difficult experiences of cohabitation.

In the face of this future uncertainty, and above all, the difficult dilemma that women are required to solve today, there is much to be done. Policies can and must be effective, but they must also be differently directed. The concept of parity and equal opportunities embodied in gender policies so far needs to be entirely revised, and the ideas expressed here can be useful in establishing a new framework.

The starting point is to realise that what women have been offered until now is not integration but conformity. That is, participation in paid work like men, and with the obligation to act like men in relation to working hours and lifestyle. The case studies we have reported clearly show that women are reluctant to identify their entire lives with their careers, thereby relinquishing part of themselves and the possibility of establishing balanced and satisfying relations. They are experiencing a painful self-reflexive stage in which they are trying to define a new model of reconciling work and the private sphere. From this perspective, a first clear indication is that gender policies should not be conceived of as policies of equal opportunities but rather as policies to support the building of a new model of gender identity. These policies should not be limited to removing obstacles and discriminatory factors. They have to support women actively in their attempt to achieve autonomous life projects no longer based on the principles of productivity and accumulation[12].

The second step in defining policies is to realise that men are not safeguarded against the processes that are today threatening female identity. When men are threatened in the work sphere, they perceive that they are also victims of the strictly sexualised division of roles and of a social organisation in which work is the supreme value. Evidence of this is shown in the high number of requests for child custody made by separated fathers. Further evidence is the withdrawal into the household by men (in particular, unemployed and early retired men) who, having lost their jobs, turn to the domestic sphere in order to spend their time, but also to feel useful and preserve their self-esteem. Men are also beginning to feel a need to find a new balance between the public and private spheres.

At a policy level, and from a concrete point of view, this seems to indicate that caring work should be assigned more value, while every solution that can facilitate reconciling domestic work and work for the market should be promoted for both sexes. As far as the philosophy of intervention is concerned, however (and now this aspect seems crucial), a significant change in terminology is needed. It is necessary to speak more of policies for genders than of gender policies. This would be a major contribution to 'thinking' about the interventions in this field as tools to guide men and women in experiencing new forms of cohabitation, rather than as tools to help women to be like men, according to a lifestyle that is no longer suitable even for men themselves.

Notes

[1] The ideas and arguments put forward here have been deeply discussed with Paola Caniglia, with whom I shared every moment of the Sostris project. However, as the author of this chapter, the responsibility for what is written here is mine alone.

[2] This is the meaning of the 'double presence' concept as the authors' intended (Balbo, 1978; Balbo and Siebert Zahar, 1979). Indeed, 'double presence' should not be confused with the concept of 'double burden', which seeks to stress the additional work burden of employed women who must also attend to household activities. The former concept emphasises the new spaces that have opened up, both in terms of life structure and self-definition, by work experience becoming a 'normal' element in one's biography.

[3] Over time the factory employed about 800 workers and became one of the major exporting firms of 'made in Italy' leather ware.

[4] At the time of the interview, Rita is 'in mobilità'. There is a difference between being temporarily laid off (in Italy, Cassa Integrazione Guadagni [CIG]) and being 'redundant and available for work' ('in mobilità'). In the case of CIG, the contract between the firm and the worker is not broken, whereas with 'mobilità' the worker's contract with the firm is broken and s/he is dependent on the state. In the latter case, the worker is liable to be placed in another firm or in a 'socially useful employment' programme. At the end of the period of 'mobilità, the worker no longer receives any form of benefit. Anyone who does not find a new job gets a pension if s/he has qualified for 35 years of contributions (the years of 'mobilità' count towards the pension), otherwise s/he becomes unemployed.

[5] After the reform of the Italian 'middle school' and the introduction of compulsory education up to the age of 14 (1962), the number of female students increased dramatically. In the 1961-71 period, more than one million new girls entered Italian schools. Nearly half of them continued their studies after compulsory school, but only 14% attended university (33% left school after completing secondary school) (Piazza, 1999, p 11).

[6] Nearly 400,000 marriages per year were contracted in 1971-74 (Marisa got married in 1972). About half of the women born between 1945 and 1953 were already married at 22, and about one third of them had one child. However, with respect to the preceding generation, the number of children decreases: only one quarter of the women of Marisa's age give birth to three babies (Marisa had two babies), vis-à-vis one half in the preceding generation (Piazza, 1999).

[7] See note 4.

[8] From her present perspective, Sonia has no clear ideas about her mother. Speaking of her father's betrayal she says that he had an affair because her mother "entirely devoted herself to us children and obliged my father to live an alienated life". Later, however, Sonia argues that her parents' problems derived from the fact that her mother was "different, because she had travelled around the world and was broad-minded". She was not, therefore, the classical housewife and mother that her father wanted.

[9] Sharing the same historical and social events at the same age is crucial for defining the course and direction of one's life. In our three case studies, for instance, the influence of high unemployment and the weakening of family ties on women is different, according to whether or not they have already gone some way in their biography or, like Sonia, are still planning their future.

[10] Rita can rely on a model where family and work can be reconciled because she belongs to a context with significant premodern features, while Marisa and Sonia, who live in a totally 'individualised' context, do not have the same opportunity.

[11] The comments on the important issue of transmission of change from mothers to daughters seem to point to the overcoming of a linear conception of social change. Sonia and Marisa, for instance, built their identity as workers by opposing a maternal model of the weak woman enslaved by housework. This would imply a trend in gender models orientated towards autonomy and emancipation. However, it is clear that particular social and economic conditions can influence the transmission process. In the case of Sonia, for example, the impact of a strongly male work context, as well as unemployment, seems to push her back to the 'security' of traditional roles. In the case of Marisa, we can speculate whether a daughter, whom she is happy not to have had, would have opted for a model within the domestic sphere as a consequence of her mother's failure in work, or out of her sense of abandonment by a mother who devoted herself to work.

[12] This is what Giddens (1994) described as the post-scarcity order, to which women can offer a greater contribution than men.

References

Balbo, L. (1978) 'La doppia presenza', *Inchiesta*, no 32, pp 3-6.

Balbo, L. and Siebert Zahar, R. (1979) *Interferenze*, Milan: Feltrinelli.

Beck, U. (1992) *Risk society. Towards a new modernity*, London: Sage Publications.

Giddens, A. (1992) *The transformation of intimacy. Sexuality, love and eroticism in modern societies*, Cambridge: Polity Press.

Giddens, A. (1994) *Beyond Left and Right. The future of radical politics*, Cambridge: Polity Press.

Melucci, A. (1991) *Il gioco dell'Io. Il cambiamento di sé in una società globale*, Milan: Feltrinelli.

Merton, R.K. (1949) *Social theory and social structure*, Glencoe, IL: Free Press.

Parsons, T. (1951) *The social system*, Glencoe, IL: Free Press.

Piazza, M. (1999) *Le ragazze di cinquant'anni. Amori, lavori, famiglie e nuove libertà*, Milan: Mondadori.

Saraceno, C. (1986) *Pluralità e mutamento*, Milan: Franco Angeli.

TEN

Gender and family in the development of Greek state and society

Elizabeth Mestheneos and Elisabeth Ioannidi-Kapolou

Introduction

Current European debates concerning the decline of the nuclear family, the forms and implications of new family type structures, and the role of the welfare state in changes in family and gender relationships are hardly on the political agenda in Greece. There are clear indications that aspects of family life are altering. These include the later age of marriage[1], increasing rates of divorce[2], the increase in female participation in the paid labour force[3], and the very slow increase in single parenthood[4]. Other new phenomena indirectly relating to family life, such as increased drug and alcohol use, and homelessness among young people[5], are also indicators of change. Yet the institution of the family remains a core value and practice, even if the foundations are less secure as individualism becomes a stronger force in Greek society.

The effects of family life mark all individual life histories in our Sostris data. Relationships between a child and its parents, parental abilities, characters, weaknesses and absences, the presence of significant kin, and the class, occupational, generational and community affiliations of the family, all have relevance to the individual's life course. In Greece, the institution of family has a strong, extensive and direct influence on the life decisions of its members, including career selection, labour market access, strategies in relation to social inclusion and exclusion, sexuality and marriage. It provides extensive financial, welfare and emotional support, and has always been forced to compensate for the limited welfare state support available in critical areas such as unemployment, dependency in old age, and sickness. In fact, the influence of the family emerged as far more substantial in the southern European countries participating in Sostris than in the northern European countries. Other Greek social theorists confirm this research observation about the critical and extensive role of the Greek family institution in work. Vergopoulos (1989) states that the social control, political authority, economic organisation, ideological and cultural systems are in accordance at all levels with the functioning mechanism of this unique and indissoluble institution. Commenting on the changes in traditional Greek society, caused by modernisation and development, he states that the only predominant central structure that occurs everywhere remains the Mediterranean patriarchal family, at the heart of which is the obedient and passive Mediterranean woman.

This issue of gender and the degree to which patriarchalism is an essential feature of the Greek family institution structure is open to debate, and is discussed later in this chapter. There is widespread agreement that the 'traditional' type of patriarchal family has been changing in line with economic and modernising forces, but it is not clear if the family per se is loosing its sway in Greek society (Meletopoulos, 1997). Gender relations are at the eye of the storm in these changes. Two decades ago, Katakis (1984) discussed the historical coexistence of different types of familial and gender formations and expectations. These she termed the traditional, the modern and postmodern patterns within Greek families. These are evident in the narratives of the individuals interviewed, where all three types of family identity were presented by respondents belonging to different age groups, with consequences for their own life courses. Interviews were selected with individuals at risk of social exclusion, but their narratives illustrate the transformation in family and gender in the development of Greek society. While this is not a representative Greek sample, since some cases appear quite extreme, they do illustrate historical and class structures in Greek society and the coexistence of very different family and gender ideologies and formations.

In the cases of the early-retired and ex-industrial workers, mainly middle-aged, the effects of the tremendous socioeconomic changes in Greece and the historical impact of major political events, have had a direct structuring impact on the life courses of many individuals. These appear in narratives of family and individual histories in the form of poverty, political repression, experiences of being refugees, and of migration (both international and from country to town) that continue to cast a long shadow over many of the interviewees' lives and attitudes. Among those who were younger (unemployed graduates, unemployed unqualified young people and single mothers), the debate in their narratives had moved from older historical and socioeconomic constraints and structures, to newer ones such as unemployment. However, their stories are far more concerned and absorbed in the issue of how to gain adult status and independence, and control over their life choices, and this involves them adopting or confronting patriarchalism. The young people interviewed illustrate not only individual cases with problems in achieving adult independent status but also the nature of the Greek family institution, both its ability to offer meaning, support and care for its members, but also its capacity to entrap.

Structural factors in family and individual histories

Historical events

Historical events scarred the lives of many, from the Asia Minor disaster (1922)[6] to the Second World War and German occupation (1940-45), the Civil War (1947-49) and the dictatorship (1967-74). Niki, a woman born in 1958 in a small, remote village, was the eldest of three children in a poor family whose father had fought with the Resistance[7] and then the communist army during the Civil War[8]. The subsequent repression against the communists meant that the father found great difficulty in getting work and supporting his family. Niki loved school as a child, and wanted to continue her education. However, after primary school her father explained that he could not afford to send her to high school. By the age of eight, she starts distributing milk in the village to help the family finances.

> We went through difficult years. I was constantly sad and worried. We had a very poor house with one room and no bathroom. I remember that I loved school, I liked it very much. I wanted to be educated, to be someone. I had a dream ... but the circumstances just didn't allow it.

Niki, a strong, optimistic woman, still dreams, although the closure of local industry and the loss of her job, the economic depression in her area, and her wish to stay in her local community are presenting her once again with the issue of poverty.

Fotis, born in 1939 in a remote village in central Greece to farming parents with six children, was forced into a different career than the one he wanted. Ideological schisms and family poverty led him to migrate to Athens during the 1950s.

> I finished high school in Lamia in 1957 and, because of the earlier German occupation and the Civil War, the conditions were very difficult. I finished high school with difficulty – for economic reasons, not academic ones. When I finished high school I had no money to go to university, though I was top of the class in the theoretical and natural sciences ... mathematics, physics, chemistry. I tried to persuade my parents to let me go to aviation school for the air force but they didn't agree and the following year in 1958 through examinations I entered the school for sergeants in the rural police force.... I was very young and I respected my parents and I went to the rural police force without being particularly partial to the idea.... I went there because I didn't want to stay in the village. I went because the moment you enter this school you got money as a student and the 10 months I stayed there I got money so I could help my family.

Refugee origins

Refugee origins also had long-term effects. As a middle-aged woman at the time of the interview, Teresa was still living in the poor refugee[9] neighbourhood with low-rise small houses, originally settled by her grandparents fleeing from Asia Minor in the 1920s. She is the third generation of women in her family to lose her husband early, and runs the small kiosk inherited from her grandmother, with no alternative but unskilled self-employment. Many refugees managed to rise up the social and economic ladder, but, in the absence of a male breadwinner over three generations, Teresa's family is condemned to limited strategies for its survival. Historical gender inequalities have always impacted on women's life courses: men, single or married, had the possibility of emigrating, something not available to women alone, especially those with children. This was underlined at the time of the interview when Teresa was entertaining her maternal uncle and his wife, who had emigrated much earlier to Australia and made better lives.

Poverty

Linked to the size of the family and the insecurity of the father's employment, in addition to the relative remoteness of many areas in Greece during the 1950s and 1960s, were factors that had a lifetime impact. Where Greek society differs from many other European societies is in the strong emphasis placed on education. Men and women both commented in their narratives on how early poverty had limited their choices by not enabling them to complete their education or, for some women, compelled them into marriage. Therefore individuals with intellectual ability, and families upholding the dominant Greek value of education, could not get the education they desired, which they regretted decades later, since it had well-understood consequences for their subsequent employment and life history.

Eleni, an unemployed, middle-aged woman who desperately seeks work but has few labour market skills and limited labour market experience, was born not long after the Second World War on an Aegean island. Describing the characteristic poverty of her childhood, she speaks about her father, who was a fisherman on long-haul trawlers, away from his family for six months at a time. Eleni grew up mainly with her mother and grandmother and the other three children, two of which were from the first marriage of her father, who had been widowed.

> We couldn't even dream about getting an education. It was very difficult to attend school. We didn't have books – everyone was poor then. We didn't have a high school in our village and in order to go to the town you had to rent a house there because there wasn't any regular public transport. Now we have a bus every hour, and there is a school bus for the children. My father used to buy one or two books for us, and the rest we had to borrow from the

neighbours. It was hell even to finish the primary school. Our parents worked just to earn enough for bread. What dreams can you have about an education? After that what kind of dreams can you have?

Kostas, an unemployed ex-industrial worker, born into a very poor family on a small island near Athens and whose father was often unemployed, recounted a similar story marked by the migration of the family to Athens. He worked during the day while attending evening high school for two years:

I went to high school not because I was forced to but because I loved school. I had to help at home and that's why I was forced to stop it.... My father never had a steady job and I started very young to do various jobs. The first time I worked was at the age of seven in a shoe shop.

Historical and socioeconomic circumstances that limited the life choices of individuals affected not only the middle-aged but also some of the next generation. Among the most disadvantaged and socially excluded persons interviewed was Roula, a young, unqualified woman in her twenties, whose story shows how her life course had been greatly affected by poverty, historical events and generational choices in her family.

When she was young, she [Roula's mother] came with her brothers to work in Athens. She had 11 brothers and sisters.... My father, or rather my grandparents, came from Cephallonia at the time of the huge catastrophic earthquake [in the 1950s]. There were seven children but my grandfather found work straight away in the local authority.

Roula comments on the fact that her father would not let her mother work, and as an unskilled man took on all kinds of work under bad conditions. The effects were obvious in his later alcoholism and his early death. Her mother took up the responsibility of caring for her family, and also working in unskilled and uninsured jobs. In her lived life, it was evident that the mother had helped entrap the family further by buying a small, old, flat in a poor, working-class neighbourhood. The neighbours could hardly afford to help her and her family when the threat of unemployment and poverty made – and continues to make – their family's survival and the payment of the housing loan a real problem.

However, historical structuring factors were and are not deterministic. Middle-aged individuals scarred by the same historical events and poverty had followed completely different life trajectories. Aphrodite was born in Athens in 1949 into a family with tremendous economic problems, as her father had been expelled from the army for political reasons. She has another two sisters; Aphrodite is the middle daughter. As she says:

[A]nother two girls ... it was difficult, difficult. We were born in very wild years but, okay, we were lucky and we managed. I can remember other families

in our neighbourhood who landed up in the factories.... Despite the fact
that we went through hunger and my father wasn't working, we grew up on
nothing but we managed. We had a saint – we had God with us.

Aphrodite manages to enter modern Greek life: she gets to university, although
she never completes her studies, has a career, marries, has children, divorces and
starts a new career. Her family and individual story are marked by success in
escaping poverty. Despite her achievements through her own efforts and
strategies, she attributes her success to forces beyond herself – God or luck.

Ethnic minority status

A determining factor in the individual's life course was their ethnic background.
Those belonging to ethnic minorities in Greece followed one of two roads –
retention of traditional family structures and membership of the generally
historically excluded minority groups, or else adaptation. However, all individuals
had to confront the issue of integration. Even when some core Greek social
values were shared, such as the need to escape poverty and obtain an education,
resistance to Greek culture and the retention of cultural identity was a part of
their narrative. The two gypsies interviewed had achieved a considerable degree
of integration into Greek society through both their parents and their own
actions. Christos, a legally registered, self-employed gypsy, tells how his parents
started their very young married life living in a corner of the parents' hut:

> My grandfather gave them two spoons, two forks and one mattress and made
> some space in the same room with another 10 people so they could sleep
> there. No work. My father went pickpocketing and my mother told fortunes.

Against the will of his wider family he attended school from the age of eight
until 12 years of age, at which point he began selling with his father. Their
commercial success enabled them to buy land and build a small apartment
block for the family:

> And since I started to help him we got over our economic problems.... We
> each built a little house ... married and had families.

Christos has also sought partial incorporation through membership of the
Communist Party where both gypsies and non-gypsies meet on equal terms.
  Anna, a young married gypsy woman who has finished secondary education,
praises her parents for supporting her education against the wishes of the wider
gypsy kin group:

> My mother acts as a model for me. She is a mother that nobody has understood
> is illiterate. They even proposed to her that she work in a lawyers' office as a
> secretary.

Ahmet and Ali Mohamet, from the Muslim minority in the north-eastern prefecture of Thrace, bordering European Turkey, live in villages inhabited exclusively by this ethnic minority. Their situation has not radically changed during their lives. Although neither of them had significant property from their family of origin, Ali considers himself a fortunate man within a traditional framework of family and village. He managed to ensure that both of his sons learned trades, he built a house for his eldest son and his dreams for the future are straightforward:

> Now, from now on, I will build a house for the young one. I've already got the license. A house for my young son who is now 18.... It's good, all good.... A man in the village, he's 40, 50 now, has lots of money and hangs around. He never married. What can you do with such a life?

In contrast, Ahmet appeared to have initially attempted partial integration by learning Greek[10] and leaving his village to become a seaman, where origins and nationalities may be less important. However, he stops this work, returns to the village and marries but, without skills or property, cannot go on with his integration life course. In talking about his daughter's future, who left school early, stays at home with her mother and works periodically in the tobacco fields, he says:

> She didn't want to continue her education, she didn't even learn Greek. If someone has brains he would learn it, the way I did. She doesn't know anything. Only good morning and good evening. Nothing else to enable her to go out, to be on her own, she just can't. Since she hasn't learned, it's her look out. Can I do anything about that for her? She went to school and she didn't learn it. Am I right? You can't force her to learn. If someone has the will and wants to learn, he does it.

Unemployment

Economic problems over the past 10 years and increasing unemployment have begun to harden the class dimensions of the significant economic inequalities that have existed for some time. Some families are increasingly trapped in irregular, insecure work, in declining and poor neighbourhoods, and with family and social networks that offer them few opportunities for a different vision of their lives. Where once class mobility (mainly through education) was the norm in Greek society, the past two decades have seen a hardening of class divisions. Research evidence from various studies (for example, Mihelis, 1996) of inequalities in the educational system show that that there are growing inequalities between children drawn from the upper and upper-middle social classes and the urban working class, as well as the agricultural population.

Additionally, the economic benefits deriving from a family investing in their children's education is less clear in more recent years, while dependency has become more prolonged with longer years of education. This has led to the creation of an ever-increasing number of young people with high academic qualifications but who are unemployed. Many continue to be supported for many years by their families while 'waiting for the right job'. Economic and emotional dependence has become protracted long into formal adulthood. A worsening position in the labour market has made many young people feel disappointed in the gap between the expectations they had from their parents and their actual experiences in the labour market. In cases we shall meet later, Andreas could feel it was normal to blame his parents for not having obtained proper career advice and information about his future prospects, while both he and Jason reported leaving the task of finding a job entirely to their parents.

Education

During the 1960s, the desire of parents from all social strata – from rural areas and refugee neighbourhoods – was to ensure that their children escaped poverty, and education was seen as the main mechanism for this, associated where possible with subsequent employment in the public sector. Since an employee is seen in Greek society with considerable ambivalence in relation to personal achievement at work, social status is still conferred unambivalently both on the individual and his/her family by having obtained a degree (Vergopoulos, 1989). Greeks have always perceived education as the way out of poverty and dependence (Tsoukalas, 1987) and a way of rising in the social structure. In the previous generation, it was seen as an important investment for the upward mobility of the family and for economic gain by the parents, with the educational successes of the children reflecting positively on them. According to Katakis (1984), parents look for psychological rewards when they educate their children rather than any form of economic reward; they live through their children and are proud or humiliated according to the success of failure of their child in education. The narratives indicate clearly the significance of educational aspirations in many life journeys. Sophia, an unqualified young woman, tried twice to take the Panhellenic examinations to enter the university because her parents forced her:

> I never liked reading…. I also see those who have graduated from university and they are doing different jobs from what they have studied. And I didn't want to study for four or five years at the university and in the end not to do what I've studied…. My mother was disappointed that neither of her children went to university. My mother has a psychosis about the university. I always remember her telling me that "You must go to the university". She's still hoping that I may go. She says, "If you don't go, I will force my grandchildren to go".

Efterpi, a 25-year-old unemployed graduate whose immediate goal was to marry and have a family and who had never worked, reported that her parents pushed her to study in order to have the certificate.

> I wanted to enter university and I didn't mind in what field. I didn't care what.

The consequences of Greek familism for individual life choices

Individualism was less evident in the Greek interviews as the members of the family continued to have multi-stranded relationships with one another and a strong sense of mutual obligation that included fulfilling family expectations. There were cases in all generations of individualised life courses reflected in marital and sexual choices and finding expression too in interests and hobbies. Generally, however, there has been a less individualised trajectory, with many remaining bound within the context of the collective entity of the family. The past three decades have seen a challenge to traditional family values and priorities supporting collective patterns and has allowed choices in individual life courses. Yet the older values necessarily still influence social interaction within and without the family. Triandis (1972) compares the concept of 'in-group' in the US, defined by the individual in terms of 'those who are like me, have the same interests', with the Greek definition of in-group membership in terms 'of people who care about me, and with whom I can create mutual dependence'. This includes not only the immediate family and kin group, but also all those with whom one has managed to create such ties and who may be called on in moments of need. Need is not defined as a failure to cope with individual problems but as a basis for social exchange, which is the foundation for continuing and long-lasting relations. The ideology and exercise of family membership in the form of protection, trust and solidarity is extended to a much wider range of persons: the expression "He is my man" in popular speech indicates the presence or extension of this familial type relationship (Georgas, 1995), linking and protecting individuals. Gifts of goods and services, as everywhere, indicate the continuities as well as the creation of social relationships and dependencies. Requesting help in finding a job, a house, or good healthcare is to reaffirm the interdependency and reciprocity between individuals and families.

Economic and social restructuring has occurred at a variable pace for different social and class groups, and for urban and rural areas. Consequently, more individualistic choices and lifestyles are available in urban centres. Families providing more economic and educational resources for their children may have also allowed more life choices, although these did not necessarily challenge traditional family and gender models. Yet, despite very large differences in income and education, the world view of the majority, and the common goal of Greek families, has involved shared aspirations for economic security and a good income, an urban life style and home ownership (Kouvelli, 1997, p 203), and educational success and social mobility for children[11]. The very limited development of industrial-based class solidarity has meant that there is no alternative collective identification for individuals – goals and values are still oriented to the family. By contributing to its wellbeing and economic resources, individuals help in its upward social mobility that benefits all the members.

Despite the fact that many interviewees were from Athens, where one might have expected a greater degree of individualism and separation from the family, all the young, unmarried people we interviewed were still supported economically and emotionally by their parents and living in the family house. This existed regardless of the social and income background of the parents. Despina, a graduate who can only find part-time work unrelated to her degree, still lives at her father's house with her brother, and says:

> I'd say I'm in a terrible situation.... Meaning ... there is some dependency that ... when one is a student one doesn't feel that way. He believes it's the father's responsibility to offer him some money and ... I began to feel that because I am dependent I have to account to my father and I am still like this to some extent. Although I am not completely dependent, I have to ask for anything I want ... and I'm at an age when one has a lot of need for things ... to go out ... to dress....

However, other events in life histories can be critical. Despina and Andreas are both scarred by the deaths of their parents – Despina's mother and Andreas' father – with repercussions for their achieving independence and adult status. Andreas, an unemployed university graduate, lives off his widowed mother's pension without any feelings of it being inappropriate for a man of 30 and, indeed, he projects a future based on the 'family' pension.

> I'd like to have my own money to make some of my dreams come true, to be economically okay, so I could travel, buy books.... As time goes by, the pension is fixed and it increases very little ... so with inflation this income keeps reducing and doesn't correspond to the family needs.

Therefore, dependency may occur out of damaging life events. Kyriakos, an unemployed and unqualified young man, reported that he lived with his mother in Athens and that they survived from her widow's pension and economic help from his sisters. Kyriakos, affected by the early death of his father and unable to settle down to regular work, says:

> Previously there used to be jobs. One could work six months and then stop, then you looked somewhere else. I don't like the idea of starting a family, I don't want to get married. My mother is doing the housework, is cooking .... I don't want her to be alone.

The symbiosis between the needs of the mother – for protection, company, and emotional support – and the needs of Kyriakos – for an income, the emotional and physical support of his mother – is common, but has personal, long-term consequences. Narratives highlight acceptance of the value placed on mutual support and interdependencies throughout life into old age. Care of older people, as everywhere, falls disproportionately upon women as daughters and daughters-in-law.

Given the process of ongoing social transformation in Greek society, the younger generations are quite likely to confront different attitudes towards the dependency of parents on children. Toula, an ex-industrial worker from a poor background, sees care giving as an asset in her life. She appreciates that her own children were cared for by both her mother-in-law and her mother, and in turn regards care for her mother-in-law with dementia not as a problem or burden but an unquestioned duty. Toula and her husband supported their children through long years of education (and unemployment) with the expectation of receiving care and support in their old age. However, Toula increasingly recognises that this expectation depends on factors over which she has no control any more – the character of her daughter or daughter-in-law – since she realises the ongoing changes in attitudes are producing growing individualism.

The denial of adult status

Among both the young men and women interviewed were individuals for whom the family was not only a nurturing nest, a protector against a harsh and indifferent world, but also a powerful trap that had limited their choices and constrained their actions. In an emotional sense, the individuals had had their wings clipped by their families and could never really take flight. Therefore, although structural reasons (including high rates of unemployment, poor qualifications, poor labour market skills) explained quite a lot about their inability to find work and achieve greater autonomy as an adult, there were also personal, psychological factors that related to the weight of the family on the individuals. Natasha's father has dominated all her education and career choices; she is left unemployed and depressed and unable to become independent:

> Since I didn't want to go against my father's wish, since I've a soft spot for him, I said, "Okay, I won't follow the profession of a masseuse".... My first hidden wish is gone ... Natasha's wings are gone[12].

In cases where individuals assert their own choices, feelings of guilt are expressed, especially where the outcome is continuing economic dependence. Cleopatra, who chose her own studies and career path, felt she had strayed from the wishes of her father in this, in comparison with her sister who followed in her parents' career footsteps. Throughout her narrative, she attempted to convince the interviewer (and herself) that she was right in selecting her profession.

A parent's death, a problematic parent (such as an alcoholic), unemployed or very dominating father, or passive mother – all can paralyse children's adult lives. Although such factors are important in all societies, these structured 'malfunctioning' elements in family lives are likely to have a greater significance subsequently on individuals in Greece, where the family is the central institution. It is worth noting that in Greek society a person can be described as an 'orphan' when one parent (father or mother) dies, and that the description is applied well into adulthood. Teresa, mentioned earlier as a widowed mother, illustrates how being an orphan had scarred three generations in her family:

> Okay, we were unlucky. My father died. Anywhere we passed by they would say, "Here are the orphans". They used to come to our house and call us the orphans. There was no other word in their mouths. This has stigmatised me since then. It even bothers me today, and it bothers me more that they say the same thing to my children.

Natasha, striving to build her identity as an independent woman and having a passive but educated mother as a female model, becomes paralysed in all aspects of her life, unable to form relationships with men or find a permanent job:

> My mother was always unhappy. I never saw her laugh.... She went through a lot of troubles, difficult situations – she's suffered a lot during her life.... I didn't know of a single thing that would give her pleasure.... She grew up with a mother-in-law, with kin .... I never saw my mother as an active person. She was always a pessimist. Not once, not even once was she optimistic ... not because she didn't want to.... The situations she lived through were such that she didn't have the chance to be optimistic. She never enjoyed her children, caressed them, cuddled them.

The consequences of family structures on the lives of individuals are, as this example illustrates, also gendered ones. Not all individuals become paralysed; indeed, Petros reacts to his father's disablement by taking on the responsibilities of the only son as defined in a traditional, patriarchal society. He develops a new career strategy to deal with his unemployment, forced by economic pressure and family expectations.

Gender relations and sexuality

Although Greek society and state still have patriarchal characteristics, even within apparently traditional families the actual nature of power relations between men and women are very diverse (Papataxiarchis et al, 1992). Equality within the family has always been the outcome of a number of variables, including the ownership of property, social class, relationships to non-domestic work, education and age and the personalities involved (Skoyteri-Didaskalou, 1991). Since individual men and women have always been aware of the possible flexibility and variations in gender relationships, they are often not experienced as patriarchal at the personal level. There are structured repercussions for gender relations from living in a patriarchal society (such as lack of power in political and economic life) but at the family or individual level gender relations may be played out by the individuals in a far more equitable and non-traditionally gendered manner[13]. Gender relations are mediated through socioeconomic changes, as well as class and educational backgrounds. However, the emotional relationship between children and their parents, and children's perception of the gender relations between the parents, emerge in narratives as determining their subsequent ability to develop as autonomous, reflexive and gendered individuals. Parental role models greatly affect the extent to which adult children achieve gender equality. Parental relationships and role models seemed critical in determining the extent to which women could identify with the mother figure and were able to generate more equal relationships with men and the society around them. Rosa, a young unemployed secretary, has a very clear idea of equality that she has learned from her own home. Planning to marry soon, she tells us about the problems of being unemployed:

> I'm all the time hovering over the phone and I'm tired and disappointed because I am young. I want to work. I'm planning to get married in a year but I am discouraged because I have nothing of my own. I cannot say I have worked and now I can get married. Because if a couple aren't working in a house, they can't support a family. Like my own house where they are both in the same situation. It isn't the man or the woman in distinctive roles they are the same. And I want to do the same thing.

In some narratives the attempt to control sexuality indicated the persistence of traditional patriarchal values. In anthropological literature on family life in Greek villages, reference is frequently made to the importance of family honour, involving the sexual behaviour of women, men's success in public and social life, and the successful execution of parental and spouse roles (Dubisch, 1986). Strikingly, two generations later in a metropolitan centre, reference to such values still appear to underlie some attitudes and behaviour. Natasha, an unemployed graduate, comes from a poor family that manages to send one brother abroad to study for a degree, enrols Natasha in a private college and ensures that all the children take private language lessons.

> In a few words, we are children of a family with what we call today "children with some principles". Our father insisted that we always keep these principles, not to go astray because of anyone or anywhere or anything.

It is not only girls who are subject to control; boys were pushed into appropriate male forms of sexual behaviour. Jason was a young unemployed graduate whose male identity was a critical issue and the central focus of his narrative. He obviously deeply admired and imitated his father. Despite what may be termed his delayed adolescence in terms of economic independence, there were no implications for his sexual adulthood.

> I had my father urging me on to start relationships with women. Like all boys, the father guides the boys to get what we call manhood.

Some girls with overprotective, conservative parents who tried to control their sexuality, sought escape through the apparently easy and socially approved route of marriage. This was noticeable among single mothers, some of whom, in order to escape this control, had married inappropriately when still very immature and inexperienced. Their inability to develop a relationship of equality with their husband ended in divorce and separation. Others resisted by seeking sexual freedom and an individualised lifestyle. Dimitra is an illustration of this. Born in 1944 into a poor uneducated and conservative family in Athens, her father was an Asia Minor refugee while her mother was from a village in central Greece.

> I'd say I belonged to the working class. The basic characteristic of my family and me was not so much poverty ... it has some consequences on your life later on ... but conservatism. My parents were very conservative, especially my father. He was the person with the first and last word in the house. This influenced me.

Forbidden by her family to have any sexual relations with boys, her reaction is to seek adult status and liberation through education. She enters the university in Athens and gains her sexual freedom.

> I finished high school without any love relationships. I couldn't even think about this. Then I entered university and started.... While in university I began to want to lose my virginity which had become a burden for me.

Although marriage is a central axis in Greek society there are always individual strategies about how to negotiate this essentially gendered relationship. Rena, a woman in a provincial town, takes early retirement because of her clearly stated value of giving priority to her marriage and her roles as wife and mother. Christina married in haste someone who filled the family stereotype of an ideal husband, in order to fulfil family expectations. However, within her own lived life, she begins to seek to escape from the traditional model by seeing herself as an independent woman. She refuses to submit to what she interprets as the domination of her husband who demands that his name be added to her property before he is willing to give any help in building flats for them (to live in and to rent). She asserts her independence partly through using what she has been given from her family of origin, but mainly by demonstrating that she can manage through her own paid work to create resources. She can contemplate taking her husband back to live with her after only when she feels that the relationship will be an equal one. This equality is asserted by Christina through economic independence. However, among some of the middle-aged metropolitan-born such as Georgos, Vasilis, Aphrodite and Dimitra, individualistic life choices and styles were followed, where marriage played a secondary or absent role.

Conclusions

Two different 'modernising' trends in Greek society need to be distinguished. The first concerns the changes that are occurring in the nature of the family, from one with wide influence, saliency and responsibilities – termed 'traditional' – to one where these functions and capacities have steadily been reduced. This can be termed the modernising process, where structural links increasingly give way to the negotiation of individualised, interpersonal relationships between family members. The second dimension is the trend towards greater gender equality and a decline in patriarchalism. This may also be perceived as part of the individualising process. While the general trend is towards greater individualisation and more gender equality, neither age, class nor background is determining. There are always individuals who are not typical of their generation or socioeconomic background, such as the young people in urban settings who act in the framework of a traditional patriarchal family.

Modernisation can be undertaken either as a process that leads to greater individual, negotiated relationships within the family, or as a process involving more equal gender relations. If this perspective is presented in terms of the two axes of modernisation – gender and family – individuals presented in this chapter fall, in line with the life course they followed, into four different categories:

1. Individuals who remain paralysed within the framework of traditional family/ patriarchal gender relations;
2. Individuals who seek more egalitarian and individualised lifestyles and yet stay within the traditional, collective structures offered by the family;
3. Individuals who have chosen not to confront gender inequalities in their personal lives by remaining single and leading highly individualised lives;
4. Those who are firmly on the modernising path, seeking both gender equality within family relationships and more individualistic life choices.

Perhaps not surprisingly, given the high levels of unemployment among the interviewees selected, the narratives presented here included many stories from people who remained within the first category, the patriarchal and collective framework. It is their inability to be reflexive, to take on more individualised life patterns, that condemns them to increasing marginality and exclusion in modern Greek society, which is undergoing radical restructuring and transformation. Nonetheless, there is a dynamic movement towards greater individualism, reflecting ongoing processes in Greek society and making it difficult to characterise it currently as traditional, modern or postmodern.

Notes

[1] Between 1964 and 1976, the average age of marriage declined, but has since risen. By 1998, the average age for first marriage for women was 26 years of age (National Statistical Service of Greece, 1998).

[2] Divorces more than doubled between 1979 and 1995 (from 4,716 to 10,995; National Statistical Service of Greece, 1998), from 82.0 per 1,000 marriages in 1982 to 124.2 per 1,000 marriages in 1993.

[3] Fifty-two-and-a-half per cent of women aged 15-64 were in the labour market in 1983, a figure that rose to 61.4% in 1997 (OECD 1997, 1998).

[4] The number of single mothers increased, with lone parents comprising 5% of all families (Kogidou, 1995).

[5] An increase of 105% among adolescents using narcotics was reported over the past five years by OKANA (Organisation Against Drug Use, 2000). In 1995, one per 1,000 of the population were reported as homeless and included two significant groups, youths aged 17-18 and older people aged over 70.

[6] In 1922, after the defeat of the Greek army in Asia Minor, almost one-and-a-quarter million Greeks became refugees and settled in Greece, then an agricultural and poor nation of approximately five million people.

[7] The Greek Resistance was formed against the Axis invasion of Greece in 1940. Many communists were very active in the fight against fascism.

[8] The Greek Civil War erupted after the liberation from Nazi Germany in 1945. Communists and right-wing governments were in confrontation for several years after this and, although the Civil War ended in 1948, the effects were felt long after.

[9] See note 6.

[10] The majority of the Muslims in Thrace speak Turkish.

[11] In the 1960s, national studies of education and social stratification (Lampiri-Dimaki, 1971) showed that the differences in educational opportunities for those from the upper and lower social classes were at a ratio of 6:1, the lowest in Europe.

[12] She uses the word 'wings' metaphorically, referring to her inability to fly; that is, to be free. She also switches to speaking about herself in the third person, something she does

at other points during her narration, indicating a distancing from her present self that she does not like.

[13] In the recent National Census (2001), a large proportion of women unexpectedly declared themselves as head of the household in the presence of their husbands, indicating the patriarchal assumptions of the state mechanism. It is also the case that women are often the owners of the family house through the old dowry system or continued efforts by families to ensure that their daughters do not have to pay rent.

References

Campbell, J. and Sherrard, P. (1968) *Modern Greece*, London: Benn.

Chrysakis, M. (1996) 'Social exclusion and educational inequalities', in E. Katsoulis, D. Maratou Aliupranti and L. Fronimou (eds) *Dimensions of social exclusion in Greece*, Report for the European Social Fund, Athens: EKKE (National Centre of Social Research), pp 83-136.

Dragona, Th. and Naziri, D. (1995) *The way to fatherhood*, Athens: EXANTAS, (in Greek).

Dubisch, J. (ed) (1986) *Gender and power in rural Greece*, Princeton, NJ: Princeton University Press.

EKKE (National Centre of Social Research) (1996) *The dimension of social exclusion in Greece: Main aspects and orientations of policies with priority*, Athens: EKKE.

European Observatory on National Family Policies (1996) *A synthesis of national family policies*, York: Social Policy Research Unit, University of York.

Filias, V. (1991) *14 Dokimia koinoniologias*, (14 Sociological Essays), Athens: Boukoumanis, (in Greek).

Georgas, D. (1995) *Social psychology*, vol 1, Athens: Ellinika Grammata.

Karagiorgas, S., Katsoulas, I., Georgakopoulos, Th., Karantinos, D., Loizidid, I., Bouzas, N., Yfantopoulos, I. and Chrysakis, M. (1990) 'Poverty, inequality and deprivation in education', in *Dimensions of poverty in Greece*, Athens: EKKE, (in Greek).

Karantinos, D., Koniordos, N. and Tinos, P. (1990) *Observatory on national policies to combat social exclusion: First national report of Greece*, Athens: EKKE.

Karantinos, D., Cavounidi, J. and Ioannou, C. (1992) *EC Observatory on national policies to combat social exclusion: Second national report of Greece*, Athens: EKKE.

Katakis, H. (1984) *The three identities of the Greek family*, Athens: Kedros, (in Greek).

Kogidou, A. (1995) *Monoparental families*, Athens: Nea Synora, (in Greek).

Kouvelli, A. (1997) 'The absence of housing policy for social groups with particular housing problems', in I. Lambiri-Dimaki (ed) *Sociology in Greece today 1988-1996*, Athens: Papazisi, (in Greek), pp 193-206.

Lampiri-Dimaki, I. (1971) *Towards a Greek sociology of education*, Athens: EKKE, (in Greek).

Leontidou, L. (1998) 'On linkages between urbanism and urban restructuring in Mediterranean Europe', in C. Keyder (ed) *Tradition in modernity: Southern Europe in question*, Proceedings of the ISA Regional Conference for Southern Europe, Istanbul, June 20-21 1997, pp 201-5.

Maloutas, Th. (1996) 'Family housing practices and segregation in Athens and Volos', in *Dimensions of social exclusion in Greece*, Report for the European Social Fund, Athens: EKKE (National Centre of Social Research), pp 197-228.

Meletopoulos, M. (1997) 'The end of patriarchalism', in I. Lambiri-Dimaki (ed) *Sociology in Greece today 1988-1996*, Athens: Papazisis, (in Greek).

Mihelis, Th. (1996) 'Educational inequalities in the province of Fthiotida', in *The Greek Review of Social Research*, vol 91, pp 79-104.

Moussourou, L. (1996) 'Greece: issues concerning the family in 1995', in *European observatory on national family policies: Developments in national family policies in 1995*, York: Social Policy Research Unit, University of York, pp 37-45.

Mouzelis, N. (1978) *Modern Greece: Facets of underdevelopment*, London: Macmillan.

National Statistical Service of Greece (1998) *Annual Report*.

Papataxiarchis, E. and Paradellis, Th. (eds) (1992) *Identity and gender in modern Greece: Anthropological approaches*, Athens: Kapenioti, (in Greek).

Safilios-Rothschild, C. (1967) 'A comparison of power structure and marital satisfaction in urban Greece and French families', *Journal of Marriage and the Family*, vol 29, no 2, pp 345-52.

Svoronos, N. (1987) *Untold neo-Hellenic history and historiography*, Athens: Themelio, (in Greek).

Triandis, T., Vassiliou, V., Vassilioy, G., Tanaka, V. and Shammingam, L. (1972) *The analysis of subjective culture*, New York, NY: John Wiley & Sons.

Tsoukalas, K. (1986) *The state, society and employment in post-war Greece*, Athens: Themelio, (in Greek).

Tsoukalas, K. (1987) *State, society, labour*, Athens: Themelio, (in Greek).

Tsoukalas, K. (1990), 'Characteristics of Greek society', in *Prosegisis, social structure and the Left*, Athens: Sichroni Epochi (in Greek).

Skoyteri-Didaskalou, N. (1991) *Anthropological dimensions for women's issues*, Athens: Politis, (in Greek).

Vergopoulos, K (1978) *National and economic development*, Athens: Exantas, (in Greek).

ELEVEN

Corporatist structures and cultural diversity in Sweden

Martin Peterson

This chapter reviews a period of tumultuous structural change and new sociocultural conditions in Sweden. It begins with the paradigmatic shift of the 1980s away from the Keynesian–corporatist–Fordist epoch and looks at the reinvention of the notion of the not-for-profit 'social economy' sector in a Swedish context. Through several cases of different immigrant groups and the 'host' population, the chapter explores the relevance and applicability of these changes for individuals at risk.

The cases portray some dramatic shifts in Swedish history. The lives of some began between the 1950s and 1970s, when both society and the workplace appeared monocultural, and political and organisational messages were rather confident. These cases show that the 1990s brought a fragmentation of messages, and even a lack of belief in coherent ideologies. The development of opportunities for individuals from a range of age groups and ethnic backgrounds in the social economy (the non-profit enterprise sector) are also considered, together with their backgrounds in a number of key Swedish firms.

A common argument in current social policy in Sweden is that, in certain more advanced branches of the economy, linguistic barriers represent powerful and genuine barriers to cross-cultural participation. At the same time, 'cultural excuses' are often deployed as a reason for excluding immigrants, so that they meet 'glass ceilings and doors' that are not necessary. This chapter explores varying strategies of members of immigrant groups in overcoming such obstacles.

Post-Fordism and the welfare state model

Corporatism can be briefly defined as a regime under which corporations on the one hand and trade unions on the other moved from one collective settlement to another with the support of the state as the 'third party'. The apogee of corporatism in modern democratic society (with Sweden as the most developed model) coincided with the age of Keynesianism and Fordism – the standardisation of mass production for mass consumption.

The post-1980 period represented something both new and old. Previous collective settlements were replaced by individualised contracts between employer and employee. Fordism became post-Fordism when flexibility and flexible specialisation were substituted for standardised mass production in the 'imperial centre' of 'the West', and when – under the impact of intensifying International Monetary Fund/World Trade Organisation structural adjustments for outside the imperial centre – the national markets and resources of non-Western societies were increasingly forced open as locations for more profitable material extraction and/or industrial production.

With this paradigmatic shift, the political map became blurred and industrial relations obscured. The new corporation of the age of flexibility tried to give the impression of being based on total teamwork, with management trying to treat employees as partners and not as potential adversaries. It was pretty clear, however, that the successful employer, who often enough would be the chief executive of a transnational corporation, would be calling the shots under all circumstances.

The new corporate structures of the 1980s aimed at solutions other than anything smacking of collective agreements. Labour relations entered a new cultural territory, with individualised contracts and, within the confines of the firm, without any union meddling, work committee colloquia on improved safety and stimulation.

Although none of these principles was fully realised, the old organisational constellation had lost influence. The paradigmatic shift that occurred in the 1980s provided new possibilities for expressions of cultural and social diversity, in labour relations and possibly also in the labour market. The decisive new element was tempo and speed due to automation and above all the introduction of electronics and information technology (IT) into every sector of productive as well as social life. This was the picture in Western Europe and indeed in the West in general.

How would this affect the welfare state model in Sweden, which was in its very foundation based on Keynesianism and neo-corporatism, but also on a relatively exclusive cultural homogeneity of the nationally defined 'citizenry'?

It was difficult to predict accurately. There were, of course, those who expected that a welfare state with a mixed and largely planned economy would continue to provide decent housing and elementary needs for weak social groups, among which immigrants and ethnic minorities were counted. An inherent danger of this scenario was that groups dependent on the welfare system would be deterred from taking emancipatory chances. At the opposite end, there was the perspective of the open-market society. This might well ghettoise most of the ethnic minorities, but simultaneously offer a few chances to move upwards and acquire wealth. There are visible variations among European nations, but most welfare systems are strung between these two – equally unsatisfactory – ideal types.

Trade unions and organised labour, which used to provide not only a shield of protection but also a profound sense of principled strength through solidarity, responded uncertainly to the new phenomenon of cultural diversity in the labour market. Traditional unionism could be patently xenophobic. Postwar unions never achieved the will and the cultural and political resources to step in and give immigrant workers a big solidaristic hand, and to facilitate their entry into more advanced job markets. This 'relative failure' on the part of the now weakened unions made conditions much more difficult for immigrant labour in the new post-Fordist conditions.

Changes in the character of work in the 1990s

The most recent research into the effects of structural rationalisations on working life during the 1990s demonstrates that overall quality change was notable but less than expected. Levels of *negative stress*, which curved upwards during the 1990s, were most harmful among civil servants in higher positions and among women who had opted for higher education as a way to improve their job opportunities. There were on the other hand no notable differences between native Swedes and immigrants in these employment conditions (Nermo and Stern, 2001).

There were three more important changes in the character of work during the 1990s, arising from the IT revolution and more holistic organisational principles. First, the *average level of qualification* was raised due to structural transformation, and professions and branches with higher demands on qualifications expanded. Second, there was notably raised *intensity, pace and demands* on performance at work. Third, *mobility between employers* increased through greater flexibility in employment conditions. One major feature of this transformation was that intensity and quality demands were raised significantly within the public sector services, whereas they remained fairly stable in the private sector (Le Grand et al, 2001, pp 79-119).

The new social economy

A further major change in the 1990s concerns the 'third sector' or 'social economy'. Appealing to social ideals, this is becoming something of a social movement. In-between the public and the private sectors, the social economy has been heralded as a new employment platform for categories at risk of becoming redundant, marginalised and eventually excluded (Amnå et al, 1996; Hermansson et al, 2000).

Conventionally, economic sociology (in contrast to microeconomic theory) conceptualises the economy as a whole as 'social'. This perspective treats economy as part of society and subordinate to the social system (Swedberg et al, 1990, pp 64, 69). Karl Polanyi once distinguished between those who see the economy as a separate system and those who see it as part of the *social* system (Polanyi 1968, p 13). Moral values play an important part in any economy and Polanyi discovered that the human economy as a rule is submerged in social relationships. Individuals act so as to safeguard their social standing, social claims, social assets and social dignity. Neither the process of production nor that of distribution is linked to specific economic interests attached to the possession of goods; but every single step in that process is geared to a number of *social interests* that eventually ensure that the required step be taken (Polanyi, 1957, p 46).

In the context of the more ruthlessly competitive conditions of post-Fordism, the social economy has everything to do with social dignity. In social policy terms, the social economy is frequently seen as a first step towards fully-fledged self-employment and entrepreneurship. Policies across Europe range from support for entrepreneurial initiatives and small businesses to payments and allowances for socially useful informal and voluntary activities[1]. In Sweden the social economy is still in a fledgling state. Whether it develops into a major plank in the sphere of production and/or welfare remains to be seen, but it may grow in importance as a device to procure stability.

Since salaries in the social economy are not market rate, they cannot be accused of generating inflation. The social economy, on the other hand, could have a deflationary effect on wage bargaining. However, in the Swedish context, the social economy is presented as part of regulating the labour market in globalised economic conditions. It is non-discriminatory in so far as it provides a basis for pension entitlements. The social economy transcends the Swedish model, which was safely moored in the pre-1980s world. That model entailed strengthening the flagship export industries while getting rid of unprofitable sectors so as at the same time to modernise the economy and promote equality through a solidaristic wage system. The model did not survive the system shift in 1980 and the onslaught of globalisation.

Individual cases

A homogenous culture was a precondition for the unequivocal reception and implementation of the initial welfare message in Sweden in the 1950s. Hence cultural diversity has presented the Swedish model with a particular test. This is of special interest, given the pre-eminent place of Swedish welfare in the league tables of Europe, and the challenge of multiculturalism to the 'national' foundations of welfare systems in Europe[2]. To explore these tensions in the Swedish system, and set the scene in relation to both structural and cultural change, the first case studies are of prototypical older men who were shaped by the Fordist model of industrial relations.

Two cases of early retirement

'Native Swedes'

Robin is a construction worker, and Christopher a shipyard worker. Both suffered notably from the transformation of business and trade union structures. Despite a wide contrast between them, there is a strong affinity in their historical positioning. Both were socially formed well before the 1980s and find it very difficult to function in the 1990s: they react with physical ailments. Their lifestyles and their respective approaches to the political culture of work are opposite, but when it comes to fundamental values they have virtually everything in common. This common bedrock of values has disappeared for later generations in the 1990s.

Robin

Robin had been a union militant in the 1950s and 1960s. With large-scale rationalisations in the construction industry during the 1960s, aiming to facilitate the so-called 'one million housing programme' over a 10-year period, the building trade went through a centralising transformation. Paradoxically, this coincided with a reverberating call in society for liberation from alienating conformism.

Were life to contain any meaning in the contradictory social situation that unfolded towards the end of the 1960s, then Robin had to confront it in the very mode that the combined effects of his personality and life experience had to offer. Assailed by liberatory social tendencies, the very same society was at the same time constructing increasingly centralised and rigid structural frames within which the space for creative manoeuvre diminished by the day. In Robin's view, only those who were able to adjust well enough could cope with such schizophrenia. The vast majority of the population preferred to put up a face of muted adjustment, regardless of how they actually felt.

Centralisation and concentration of the unions increased with the rationalisation of the construction process. Several of the new buildings, which were intended to do away with blighted inner-city areas, had built-in fungal damage. When Robin made objections to the union leadership, which was by then in collusion with the construction company, he was met with covert hostility. And so, exit Robin from his corporatist 'home', in favour of making his living in a free-wheeling entrepreneurial fashion, in sometimes quite legitimate, sometimes more shady, endeavours.

His efforts to preserve his political and professional integrity aligned with his quest for non-conformism. His rebellions included smoking pot and on occasion consuming more risky stuff, as well as transgressing the law in both small-scale business deals and personal affairs. He became accustomed to a life beyond the frame of the system (the informal economy being severely stigmatised in Sweden), both as a craftsman and as a family man. For many years, he provided an illegal shelter in Sweden for a young girl from India who never managed to obtain a residence permit.

The defiant side of Robin was activated in his creation of a private network of clients, such as magistrates, high-level academics and tax bureaucrats, for whom he illicitly built private houses at the going illegal economy rate. He also enjoyed craft discussions with building partners such as architects and teachers at a technical university.

Like many of his generation, Robin had been prone to taking considerable risks at work during the 1950s. That hard work, together with a lifestyle on the edge, took their toll, leading to a heart by-pass operation when he was in his late fifties. He was then eligible for early retirement. However, his many years outside the official system left him with a minuscule pension, far below any existence level. Therefore, with his ailments and a new life with a former girlfriend he had saved from a wife abuser and who is afflicted with a fatal disease, he had to continue his illicit craftsmanship wherever he was offered a chance.

Robin was a union activist when ideological discussions still counted, and when political progress seemed within easy reach. New structural conditions ditched his long-term trajectory as an intelligent and independent-minded construction worker; the new top-heavy unionism quenched his creative ambitions. Both his political and professional language became peripheral to his workplace existence. By the time the social economy movement entered the fray for market space in the 1990s, he was already early retired. He remained in an entirely different state of mind, symptomatic of his generation. The elements of idealistic voluntarism underlying the new social economy required a completely different mental approach.

Christopher

A similar fate befell Christopher, a former shipyard worker, who had belonged in the 1950s to the electrical workers' union. Christopher was a good facilitator and networker within union and shopfloor contexts. When shipyard times were good, his particular and flexible abilities found favour. In the name of the metalworkers' and the electricians' unions, he called for more independent self-management on the shopfloor.

However, this flexibility was adjusted to a particular working situation – the flexibility of social competence within a Fordist framework. His union ethos was antithetical to post-Fordist flexible specialisation demands on workforce and union behaviour. His mental frame, both as a citizen and as a shipyard worker, were steeped in a climate of conflict, which contrasted sharply with the spirit of corporate cultural communication that permeated industrialism in the 1990s. Christopher was also early retired before the appearance of the social economy.

As a person, Christopher was happily rooted in his social environment, both in the shipyard and in the community where he grew up and lived his life. He made a typical life journey from one of the most solidly working-class districts where he grew up as a child to a modern lower-middle class/middle-class district where he settled with his wife. After some years, the couple had one son, who became especially cherished since his wife could not have any more children. However, his son distanced himself (without hostility) from Christopher and his wife. He did not fulfil any of his parents' ambitions. Instead, he moved to the north of Sweden, where he settled with a young woman who became his wife. There he founded a cooperative movement, which was much more in step with the new social economy of the 1990s, and light years away from the constituting realities of Christopher's experience.

As the shipyard industry died during the latter half of the 1970s, Christopher and his mates were left to take up occupations that had only remote connections to the old-time shipbuilding. The younger generation went off to Norway's oil platforms, while the old-timers had to settle with degrading mopping-up jobs. One reputedly mentally strong and stable person drank himself to death after only one-and-a-half years. Simultaneously, Christopher's brother died from exposure to dangerous chemicals in the shipyard. These tragedies made a powerful impression on Christopher, who began to have headaches and duly received, in the mid-1990s, an early but favourable retirement deal at the age of 60.

Christopher sympathised with radical social democratic politics but never took part in militant activities. On the contrary, with his happy memories of a childhood with his extended family in the Gothenburg archipelago during the Second World War (which he and his mates hardly noticed in spite of their proximity to the war-ridden sea), he turned in his retirement to the pleasures of creating of a new summer house with a rich garden, rather than to continuing any unionised *esprit de corps* with his shipyard mates.

Like Robin and Christopher, none of the newly redundant factory workers among our interviewees found any comfort or fresh opportunities in the social economy. Some of them resigned as early retired in order to develop some other talent, such as painting, a musical instrument or carpentry, for which they could pick up some extra earnings in the informal economy. Others tried frantically to find temporary jobs, which seemed the only ones on offer. They were all anxious to maintain the dignity of their previous identities, and were loath to jeopardise their self-images for short-term material security.

Robin and Christopher are products of a time when the Swedish model counted and they themselves belonged to lifelong, proud and identifiable trades. In the 1980s, when supply-side economics, an employers' market and flexible production systems began to prevail, labour markets became inherently unstable. Employment in temporary projects became increasingly frequent, but new generations easily adjusted to these conditions even if they did not necessarily approve of them. The social economy was a long step beyond the Swedish model and it was anathema to people like Robin and Christopher.

Two cases of unskilled youth

Transnational connections were notable among several of our unskilled interviewees, aged 20-25, both among second-generation immigrants and among talented non-immigrant youth. The former are in general a highly exposed group, whereas the latter have became marginalised for more contingent reasons, such as a difficult divorce between their parents, early drug abuse, early pregnancy or failings at school. Building identities across borders is one way of restoring a sense of identity and gaining confidence in oneself.

Alice

Alice is a bright young woman, who was 24 at the time of our interview. She comes from a disrupted marriage where very bad feelings prevailed between her parents. Since her older sister, as marginalised as Alice, had taken the blame on herself and acted as the family go-between, Alice felt freer to follow her own inclinations. This made her very vulnerable. During her late teens, she suffered from psychotic spells, which have now stopped – thanks, perhaps, to her mother's new partner, who presented her with realistic, constructive and challenging alternatives.

Her stepfather was a remarkable man, a redeemer to her, but also to deprived people in Montevideo, Uganda and Palestine[3]. Once the youngest municipal councillor in Danish history, he represented the Danish leftist party, Socialistisk Folkeparti. He came to Sweden as a shipyard worker for family reasons, from which platform he worked up a tremendous knowledge and documentation on the trade union movement in Sweden, the EU and the Third World. These achievements met with covert hostility from the official representatives of the labour movement.

He presented a young Uruguyan man to Alice. Feeling an urge to realise herself as a woman as one way to meet her challenging world, she married the young man from Montevideo and had a daughter with him. They both went to Norway, where they travelled around looking for jobs. Norway was richer, with more of an unconventional societal culture than Sweden, so she felt their chances were better there.

This marriage failed. Not long after her divorce she married again and had a new child only to get divorced again two years later. The second marriage collapsed because, with this husband, a craftworking Swede, she could not live up to her expectations of herself. Since then, she has studied and worked on a part-time and irregular basis. Her political networks and environmental awareness have brought her into contact with ecological non-profit firms. She studies part time and thinks of a future in the legal profession. It might provide a socially and economically viable avenue through which to discover her true aptitudes.

Sam

Sam is a talented young man in his early twenties. He grew up in a province in the centre of Sweden, where niche production centred on a zinc mine, small-scale forestry and shoe manufacturing. The province had a history of liberally inflected revivalist movements, followed by a solid social democratic majority. The zinc mine provided employment for both his parents. His father was a gifted dance-band musician, who had wanted to become a recognised artist. No break came his way, and he languished in the mine. His unsatisfied creativity led to an unpredictable alcoholism that dominated much of Sam's early life.

At a very early age, Sam, like his father, had one ambition: to develop his musical talent. When Sam reached the age of 16, his father stopped drinking and went on tour and began to help Sam by inviting him into his resurrected dance band. Sam feared that this would kill his creativity. Nevertheless, since none of the rest of the family had a musical ear, he had to rely on his father for advice and encouragement. However, his father represented conflicting aspects of his own self. Both felt bound to express their creativity without holding back, which implied a tendency to take self-destructive risks.

Sam saw how his father's creative mind had been destroyed by the monotony of work in the mine. He himself dreaded what would happen to his musical talent when, after school, his only opportunity to support himself came in the form of monotonous, hi-tech manufacturing of computer components. This fear led him to leave this job after a year-and-a-half.

Sam thus put all his eggs in one basket. He felt he had no alternative in a small urban community where only unqualified jobs were on offer. Recently, he won a nationwide competition. Fame, however, taught him that staying and climbing in the music business required qualities opposite to his talent – for example, a tolerance of compromise and routine that he did not have. So he has been left high and dry with his rare talent, and the 'business-like' social economy cannot come to his rescue by providing him with the opportunity to develop[4].

Alice and Sam occupy polar positions in relation to the social economy and multiculturalism. For Alice, with family resources and years of varied experience behind her, the social economy offers a route to personal and occupational development. She will thrive in the openness of its opportunities. For her, multiculturalism has been a positive spur. Sam, by contrast, lacks the equivalent home resources and breadth of experience, despite his outstanding talent and desire for an independent life. He would need substantial social support to enable him to flourish in the social economy.

Let us now consider the context of immigration in Sweden, as a backdrop to the life journeys of three immigrant cases.

Cultural diversity and business corporations in the 1990s

The new ethnic minorities that have transformed Swedish society from an appearance of homogeneity to one of multicultural disparity cannot be encapsulated into one pattern. Rather, they present an endless variety of cultural expressions.

The concept 'cultural diversity' implies divisiveness – a conflicting approach to the cultural and political institutions of the host country, and between cultural groups. Such double-layered conflicts are manifested in gang wars over urban territories between second-generation immigrants from varying backgrounds, who have the same alienated relation to Swedish society.

Before presenting our next set of cases, we need first to outline the pattern of immigration into Sweden, and describe the employment policies of some key corporations regarding immigrants.

The Swedish story of postwar immigration

Since medieval times, Swedish territory has attracted waves of immigrants, who were eager to help exploit its rich assets of natural resources. These immigrants were both technicians (mining engineers, town builders, road and canal constructors) and technocrats (high civil servants teaching the locals how to operate an administration). Many of these immigrants contributed significantly to the formation of the nation.

Some Nordic, mostly Finnish, labour immigration took place during the 20th century. Just before the Second World War, a few thousand Sudeten Germans arrived in Sweden for specific industrial tasks, as a result of the brotherly relations between the Social Democratic Parties in Sweden and the Sudetenland (a German-speaking area in northern Czechoslovakia, now the Czech Republic). This encouraged expanding export industries such as LM Ericsson (telecommunications), SKF (a multinational ball-bearing company) and ASEA (today ABB, energy systems), to engage in regulated imports of hand-picked workers from Italy and Yugoslavia after the war.

Political refugees from the Baltic countries during and after the war, and from Hungary following the 1956 uprising, were all put in menial jobs in spite of their high professional qualifications. The younger ones who entered Swedish universities were told to forget about their past and begin to 'think Swedish'.

In 1968 and 1969, Czechs and Polish Jews fled Soviet repression and Polish nationalist anti-semitism. At that time, however, due to enlightened immigration policy (from the State Immigrant Agency formed in 1969)[5], these refugees were not explicitly told to think Swedish and many were able to pursue their professional careers more or less as they wished, even though a good number ended up in menial jobs.

Until the 1970s, the pro-immigration faction within the polity was enlightened but small, and the 1969 legislation setting up the State Immigration Agency had little backup within the state apparatus. Often even the Social Democratic Party did nothing to stop xenophobic measures by its local hacks.

However, in general, refugees from Eastern Europe and Latin America (25,000 Chileans and 10,000 Argentineans, plus smaller numbers from Bolivia, Peru and Colombia) testified to the palpable generosity and empathy they received. By the 1970s, there were ample language courses and many other provisions to assist assimilation, such as funds and arrangements for accommodation and education. At the same time, however, the wider population had not been prepared for multiculturalism. Many immigrants from the other areas – in particular Asia and the Third World – found that everyday racism was becoming unbearable.

The 1980s saw a new wave of refugees from the Middle East, East Asia and East Africa[6]. Once again, many had higher education and good professions, but most found themselves in menial jobs until they could identify something better. The refugees from Bosnia and Croatia in the 1990s (totalling 93,000) and the many thousand Kosovo-Albanians, who had come towards the end of the 1980s and then again in much larger contingents 10 years later, met with an even harsher reception. The aim was to encourage their return as soon as a semblance of peace was restored in their lands. In the specific discourse used, there was a move from 'exilic bias', a reactive approach on the part of the reluctant liberal states, to a 'source control bias' or proactive policy. The latter implied making it safe for refugees to return to their home nations (Slavnic, 2000).

In segregated suburbia, such as the dense immigrant suburbs of Stockholm, Gothenburg and Malmö, more than 40 different languages are typically spoken. Such facts were not heeded in the 1980s, when the immigrant population of still full-employment Sweden had higher rates of employment than the 'host' Swedish population. However, the economic crisis of the mid-1990s became a disastrous experience for large sections of the population. No professional line was safe, however qualified, and immigrants were hit the hardest. During this crisis, the worst of the postwar era, 100,000 desperate, war-traumatised refugees arrived from former Yugoslavia, with others from the Middle East.

At first, the authorities made half-hearted attempts to provide refugee immigrants with courses. "Courses for what?", it was generally asked. The policy of preparing immigrants for return became more explicit, and these courses assumed that purpose. However, immigrants who have begun to settle and root themselves, in particular those with children of school age who speak fluent Swedish, are determined to stay. A fear of an underground economy is currently taking over suburbia.

Since rationalisation has reduced opportunities in the traditionally immigrant-friendly transnational industries, new openings are often sought in small service sector enterprises or in the social economy. There has been a reaction by migrants against dismissive expectations on the part of authorities, with many attempting to become entrepreneurs, according to a well-established immigrant pattern. Hence, it seems at least possible that the social economy may offer a bridge between the incommensurate worlds of, on the one hand, modernised Swedish industrial culture representing chauvinism adjusted to globalism, and, on the other, the less regulated tertiary sector reserved for immigrant, entrepreneurial cultures.

Industrial stories: immigrant labour and cultural diversity

Let us look at the decreasingly favourable behaviour of different industrial branches with regard to immigrant labour.

Building and construction – the anti-immigrant story

The building trade and the construction branch represent old-time Swedish companies with almost no recent immigrant employees. Training takes place 'on the job' from apprentice age. The technical knowledge is relatively easy and quick to learn. Yet there are signals or signifiers that are taught at a very early stage, which take a long time for somebody uninitiated to learn (especially anyone who is being cold-shouldered). The high tempo requires an immediate and full understanding of what issue is at stake – for safety reasons, the slightest nuance of communication cannot ever be missed. High salaries have created a closed-shop mentality. The turnover of labour is low, and recruitment is usually from family and friends and cronies from the football team. Therefore, from producers to customers, the construction industry cultivates a macho anti-immigrant climate. Prejudiced and troublesome scenarios are painted in which ghettos, segregation, illegal activities and molecular street wars may easily escalate into full-scale civil wars between Swedes and immigrants (Broomé and Bäcklund, 1998).

We shall now consider a number of firms in which immigrants have played a greater role, and briefly sketch the evolution of their employment policies.

The Plåtmanufaktur story

Plåtmanufaktur (PLM) is a multinational canning concern, which already employed quite a few immigrant workers during the 1970s. The immigrant staff make up less than 10% of the white-collar employees, but between 25% and 30% of the blue-collar workers.

When an important new plant was established in the early 1980s, about half the staff were immigrants, a proportion that decreased in the 1990s to 25%. Less-qualified jobs with a higher proportion of immigrant workers were rationalised away – perhaps hidden discrimination was applied in new recruitment.

The job has become increasingly noisy and stressful, and its higher tempo has become standard over all industry since 1980. Accordingly, the organisation has been slimmed down and trimmed. Middle management has disappeared, including positions as shopfloor work leaders, and with them quite a number of immigrant work leaders.

In general, new employees are recruited from the ranks of ethnic groups already well-established within the plant. New ethnic groups from waves of refugees escaping new wars do not stand a chance of being taken on by PLM, since they lack personal contacts inside the plant.

The company has deliberately tried to break up 'tribal' patterns in order to create loyalty to the efficiency and success of the company. These measures have a double meaning. On the one hand, they strengthen management control over faster communication lines. On the other hand, they facilitate rationalisation, since a staff lacking in ethnic cohesion is less able to resist.

PLM has accumulated a rich experience and knowledge of adjusting immigrants to work patterns and negotiating between different normative systems. Its original philosophy held that from the point of view of both the company and society it was indispensable that people with different ethnic origins took part in the social community that the work situation implies.

However, demands for more communication in the (much faster) production process has brought a new recruitment policy, in which PLM increasingly desists from hiring immigrants.

The Volvo story

Ericsson is a hi-tech industry that normally recruits a large proportion of women. Its Volvo Gothenburg plant, which launched its modern assembly line in 1964, was by contrast a predominantly male industry. A kind of 'Ellis Island' of the Swedish labour market, it symbolised the typically unskilled factory work in which an immigrant first encountered Swedish working life. It offered an unskilled worker a secure and substantial wage, at least by south-eastern European standards.

While business cycles were favourable, any immigrant wanting to work would be hired through recommendations from family, friends or friends of friends. Often entire families were employed, usually from typical immigrant-labour nations of southern and eastern Europe. During the 1980s, many Asians and Africans also gained access to the Volvo assembly line. The company later asserted and regretted that too many had been hired during those years, citing a failure to meet proper criteria, in the first place for knowledge of the Swedish language, and secondly for craft skills.

Volvo personnel managers alleged that these mistakes incurred excessive costs. It may well be, however, that these stories allowed the company to blame its difficulties on its earlier immigrant labour. The ones who stood to lose most from such games of subterfuge were 1990s would-be immigrant recruits. By then, public Swedish policy had already begun to swing against immigrant labour in favour of those 'Swedish' youngsters whose labour market future looked bleak. Beyond that, the gospel of repatriation loomed large.

There is a widely argued view that 1990s society simply became far too advanced for large groups of immigrant populations, especially non-European populations, to be absorbed. This sounded perfectly reasonable in the public rhetoric and was hardly questioned by anybody – least of all the media. Meanwhile, the EC has become concerned about the falling rate of population replacement, and the need to maintain both labour supplies and pension funds (the latter depending on current contributions).

Four refugee cases

Four cases of refugees – representing political upheavals in Chile[7] and Somalia – reveal how people with diverse cultural backgrounds confronted unexpected structural privations, particularly in the 1990s.

Victor

Victor is a young person, in his early twenties, whose existential doubts and difficulties affect both his social and professional outlooks. His family arrived in Sweden during the 1980s as political refugees from Chile. Victor was not yet 10 years old. He received bad marks at school and found few prospects on the labour market.

Many of his siblings and friends from Chile have had similar adjustment problems, in spite of the fact that they all have a command of the Swedish language. Their problems derive from inadequate social and cultural acceptance. Such frustrations are all the more salient for Victor, since his family came to Sweden because of its well-publicised welfare state and opportunities. When you cannot fulfil your expectations, you blame either yourself or the new society.

In Victor's case, as in numerous other cases, it tended to be a mixture of both which provided for self-doubt and existential agonies. Victor saw his elder brother and cousin return to Chile in the mid-1990s, but hopes of finding a life for themselves there were disappointed, so they returned to Sweden where they were treated as newcomers by the authorities and were duly put last in the line for jobs. Devastatingly, Victor's father died in 1994.

The closest he could get to any welfare state solution (meaning public support) emerged in the social economy, where Victor, some years after our interview with him, eventually found, at least temporarily, safe ground under his feet.

Vallejo

Vallejo, who was 21 when he arrived, entered an established Chilean community in Gothenburg. For much of his life, his idealistic family had lived as political fugitives in Chile, and now Vallejo was avoiding his military service. Mechanical engineering, in which he had trained, was in demand so he had no problem finding jobs during the course of the 1980s. This facilitated his fairly early marriage to a Chilean girl who had emigrated with her entire family after the military coup against the Allende regime in 1973[8].

By the 1990s, Vallejo had three children to provide for at the same time that job availability ended. Redundancy made him turn to politics, and he founded a political debating club that doubled as a job-search club. The members also prioritised the wellbeing of their children. Much of the discussion turned on whether Swedish societal opinion would be ready for them to open up their own shop, or whether they should adapt to the grey zone of newly launched ventures in the social economy.

Vallejo sometimes did odd short-term jobs in the public sector (such as unskilled hospital care), or for some private or social economy firm. Events had not convinced him entirely of the advantages of the social economy, even though he recognised its potential for the members of his debating club. He blamed both Swedish political opportunism and the EU's march towards a European Monetary Union, as did his friends.

This disillusionment about 'Europe' reinforced the radical ideals he had preserved from his continent of origin, but gave him no hope of ever realising them. His private utopianism might have facilitated ways of coping with strife, but in fact it alienated him further from Swedish realities. His concern for the wellbeing of his children made him pragmatic enough in everyday life. At the same time as he shared his grievances with his family, he nurtured a hope that his children would not experience such agonies. However, when his eldest son, who had just reached his teens, took part in activist demonstrations against the EU summit meeting and globalism in June 2001 (in Gothenburg), he was much more scared than proud.

In sum, social economy ventures have partly contributed to solving Vallejo's everyday concerns for his family. At the same time, he has become increasingly alienated from the social and political culture (or lack of such culture) of his adopted country without any hopes of doing anything about it. Vallejo found the frames of social activities instituted by Swedish society too narrow for his ideals. His children have become his goals and ambitions. Yet they, as second-generation Chilean immigrants and whether they are politically radical or not, tend to adopt the cultural alienation of their parents, whether out of innate sympathy or because of their own experiences of prejudice (overt and covert) against non-European immigrants.

Ishmail and Farah

Refugees from Somalia tend to be more sophisticated and well-educated than most of their non-European counterparts. Many have been grounded in a socialist party culture at the same time as they come from an upper-class elite. They share a streak of *noblesse oblige*, and their sense of political and social responsibility spills over into other immigrant communities.

Ishmail and Farah were married in Sweden in 1992 as refugees. Both come from upper middle-class families with a deep sense of commitment to improve living standards in Somalia. Ishmail was educated in a gymnasium steeped in an Italian educational culture, where Aristotle and Kant were basic to all learning and Moravia, Gramsci and Silone to an understanding of contemporary society. After completing his schooling, he was obliged to do social service in a remote village community, where he and his peers became politically aware in a more practical and concrete sense.

Ishmail had acquired a radical political philosophy. Feeling that the higher educational climate in Mogadishu was too narrow, he went on scholarships for five years to Kiev in the Ukraine, where he took a degree (BSc) in television and radio communication, an exam in transport economics in Bucharest, Romania, and a financial and planning certificate in Padova, Italy. He is fluent in Russian, Romanian, Italian, French, English, and now also Swedish. With his university qualifications from both Eastern and Western Europe, his experience could obviously be put to broader use. So far, however, it has not.

Farah was a leading figure in the formation and development of the Somalian women's movement. With her organisational talent and powerful influence over the women around her, she was recruited on the municipal level in Gothenburg to head an immigrant women's organisation for health and safety. Ishmail does not have such a possibility, and so he remains unemployed. In order to have a meaningful occupation and a channel for a return at any time, he organises the export and safe shipment to Somalia of essential quality goods, such as medical supplies or communications equipment.

Refugees and the social economy sector

The new social economy coincided with, or rather arrived as a response to, the mass unemployment that hit immigrant communities even harder than other categories. This asymmetry of effect between refugee communities and other redundancy categories of the 1990s is rather shocking in a society that has been so committed to justice and equality. It is compounded by popular and institutional narratives (such as those concerning employment and the linguistic capacities of immigrants), but also perhaps by the paternalism of the Swedish welfare system, a frame of thought that has always assumed that all immigrants are inherently weak and hapless when confronting the Swedish labour market.

What the cases here presented and discussed show is a differentiation between various forms of the social economy and a discrepancy between how immigrant and 'native' realities unfold in relation to them. In short, the social economy may be perceived – and is developing – in several ways. Through the case studies, we see individuals and groups acting in and around this new field and developing their own interests and strategies in relation to it. This suggests how different conceptions and uses of the social economy may influence the development of this alternative approach to, or sector of, the market economy.

Conclusions

Three issues dominate Swedish social policy debate at the beginning of the 21st century. One is steeply rising absenteeism, which results in sky-high costs and insecurities at work. Another is long-term sick leave, with little prospect that the sick person will actually return to the previous job. Both are considered to be due to hyperstress and 'burn out'. When the same phenomena plagued the 1980s, they were blamed on individual exploitation of the generosity of the welfare state. Now that the welfare state is not there in the same shape, the syndrome has to be regarded in a new light. No immediate remedies are in sight and, in the final analysis, not only the production apparatus but basic democratic values are at stake. The third issue concerns multiculturalism and the implied segregation, as well as flawed integration policies in major urban areas. In the Swedish debate, the polity is eager to stress a separate attitude from those xenophobic tendencies which prevail in many EU nations, notably Denmark. Instead, normative multiculturalism and interculturalism (see Peterson, 1996b) are presented as attainable solutions (Barry, 2001, pp 22-3). However, the deep social problems developing in non-integrated neighbourhoods will not go away (Westin, 1998, p 56). The structural inadequacies revealed in the implementation of Swedish immigration and integration policies are not compensated by merely addressing the ideological questions involved, however boldly this might be done. In all three cases – absenteeism, extended sick leave, multiculturalism – social policies remain vague, not because of a lack of will to focus them, but due to the sheer complexities of the issues, which call for much more progressive and imaginative policy outlines than the present political class is capable of.

Notes

[1] Agency studies conducted by the Italian and Spanish Sostris teams focused respectively on an 'honour loan' scheme in Southern Italy to support entrepreneurial initiatives by young people, and neighbourhood exchange and care payment schemes in Barcelona. See Chapter Fourteen of this volume and *Working Paper 8* (Sostris, 1999).

[2] For a fuller account of the Swedish welfare system, see Esping-Andersen (1990).

[3] Tragically, he has died since our interview with Alice.

[4] Rock musicians in Britain have attempted to destigmatise social benefits by pointing out that the dole has often functioned as their main source of support.

[5] For a more elaborate discussion of immigration into Sweden, see Peterson (1999a, p 104).

[6] Most came from Iran after Khomeini (40,000) and Iraq (the vast majority being Kurds and Shiites), Assyrians (20,000) and Palestinians (13,000), Eritreans (11,000), Somalians (9,000) and Vietnamese Chinese (9,000).

[7] For a comparable Chilean case, see Peterson, 1999a.

[8] Allende was a socialist president, who was ousted by a US-backed coup.

Bibliography

Amnå, E. et al (1996) *Medmänsklighet till salu?*, Stockholm: Ministry of the Interior.

Barry, B. (2001) *Culture and equality*, Cambridge: Polity Press.

Broomé, P. and Bäcklund, A.K. (1998) *S-märkt. Företagets etniska vägval*, Stockholm: SNS Förlag.

Dacyl, J.W. and Westin, C. (eds) (2000) *Governance of cultural diversity*, Edsbruk: UNESCO, CEIFO and Akademitryck, Stockholm University.

De Wenden, C. (2000) 'Withold, European citizenship and migration', in J.W. Dacyl and C. Westin (eds) *Governance of cultural diversity*, Stockholm: UNESCO and CEIFO, pp 45-46.

Esping-Andersen, G. (1990) *The three worlds of welfare capitalism*, Cambridge: Polity Press.

Esping-Andersen, G. and Regini, M. (eds) (2000) *Why deregulate labour markets?*, Oxford: Oxford University Press.

Fritzell, J., Gähler, M. and Lundberg, O. (eds) (2001) *Välfärd och arbete i arbetslöshetens årtionde*, Kommittén Välfärdsbokslut, SOU 53, Stockholm: Statens Offentliga Utrednigar.

Geddes, A. (2000) *Immigration and European integration. Towards fortress Europe?*, Manchester: Manchester University Press.

Gundara, J. and Jacobs, S. (eds) (2000) *Intercultural Europe*, Aldershot: Ashgate.

Hermansson, H.E. et al (2000) *Den sociala ekonomin,* Stockholm: Carlssons Förlag.

Le Grand, C., Szulkin, R. and Tåhlin, M. (2001) 'Har jobben blivit bättre?', in J. Fritzell, M. Gähler and O. Lundberg (eds) *Välfärd och arbete i arbetslöshetens årtionde*, Kommittén Välfärdsbokslut, SOU 53, Stockholm: Statens Offentliga Utrednigar.

Nermo, M. and Stern, L. (2001) 'Kappsäck och välfärd – samband mellan tillgång till resurser och välfärdsproblem 1991-2000', in J. Fritzell, M. Gähler and O. Lundberg (eds) *Välfärd och arbete i arbetslöshetens årtionde*, Kommittén Välfärdsbokslut, SOU 53, Stockholm: Statens Offentliga Utrednigar.

Peterson, M. (1999a) 'Migration experiences in an ambivalent society', in *Sostris Working Paper 4: Case study materials – ethnic minorities and migrants*, London: Centre for Biography and Social Policy, University of East London, pp 104-19.

Peterson, M. (1996b) 'From multiculturalism to interculturalism: political contexts of migration in Europe', in *Sostris Working Paper 4: Case study materials – ethnic minorities and migrants*, London: Centre for Biography and Social Policy, University of East London, pp 1-10.

Polanyi, K. (1957) *The great transformation*, Boston, MA: Beacon Press.

Polanyi, K. (1968) 'Appendix' in G. Dalton (ed) *Primitive, archaic, and modern economies: Essays of Karl Polanyi*, New York, NY: Anchor Books.

Salamon, L. and Anheier, H. (1994) *The emerging sector*, Baltimore, MD: Johns Hopkins University.

Slavnic, Z. (2000) *Temporalitet och Existens*, Umeå: UP Umeå.

Starrin, B. and Svensson, R. (eds) (1998) *Sverige efter välfärdskrisen. Mellan hot och hopp*, Umeå: Boréa bokförlag.

Swedberg, U., Himmelstrand, G. and Brulin, G. (1990) 'The paradigm of economic sociology', in S. Zukin and P. Di Maggio (eds) *Structures of capital*, Cambridge: Cambridge University Press.

Westin, C. (1998) 'Temporal and spatial aspects of multiculturality', in R. Bauböck and J. Rundell (eds) *Blurred boundaries: Migration, ethnicity, citizenship*, Aldershot: Ashgate.

Young, I.M. (2000) *Inclusion and democracy*, Oxford: Oxford University Press.

TWELVE

'Migrants': a target-category for social policy? Experiences of first-generation migration

Roswitha Breckner

More and more people share the experience of migration, in the sense of crossing nation-state borders to start a new life in a different society. Theories of globalisation and postmodernism present this experience as a typical occurrence, almost taken for granted, in the lives of growing numbers of people. Even though migration constitutes the 'normality' of many societies to a greater or lesser degree, the public and, not least, the sociopolitical discourses of migration, are still predominantly shaped by the view that the large-scale movement of people somehow constitutes a problem. In the first place, the 'problem' of migration within this perspective is mostly considered from the point of view of the receiving society, which feels 'confronted' by the 'challenge to integrate large numbers' of 'different' people coming from 'elsewhere', 'another place'. This, in general, constitutes a core theme of social policy discourse in most Western societies, which see themselves as the main destination of economic migrants escaping poverty, but also of refugees and exiles[1].

This discourse focuses on the societal integration of those who stay and do not return to 'their place', as is expected of them. Problems with the migrants' legal statuses, and with their access to various social spheres such as the labour market, the educational system and the health service, are most commonly dealt with. At the same time, assumptions are made about the specific kind of 'problems' emerging in the individual life of migrants. From this perspective, the discourse operates with a variety of ascriptions, centred for the most part around the question of identity. Migrants are assumed to have difficulties in constructing stable, coherent identities. They are seen as either stuck in their 'traditional culture', which is regarded as inadequate to adapting to and making a success of life in the 'modern society' where they have settled, or they are perceived as 'torn between two cultures', with 'unstable identities', or as completely 'uprooted' and 'lacking embeddedness'. The latter implies that they are not attached to any culture, producing the pathology of 'identity breakdown'.

Theoretical discussions on migration have already pointed out that these views of identity formation are based on concepts of coherence and consistency that can no longer account for, or explain, the emergence of new configurations of identity shaped by hybridity, fluidity, multiculturality or even transculturality. New concepts have to be developed in their place, concepts that do not regard living in different cultural settings as a problem that has to be 'cured', but as a challenge to which new social responses and solutions to the complex questions of social identity have to be creatively worked out (see the exemplary work of Hall, 1996; Davis and Lutz, 2000; Fischer-Rosenthal, 2000). This conforms to the self-representations of migrants who claim to have created relatively unproblematic and resourceful ways of living in different social and cultural worlds, having achieved flexible and fluid identities in which belonging has lost its relevance. However, we can also find expressions of migrants that confirm their feeling of being torn between two worlds, of confronting disruption to their lives or even 'uprootedness' due to their migration. This raises the question of how these feelings fit in with the image of new fluid, translocal identities.

These considerations indicate that our general picture of how migrants experience their situation is in flux, and subject to social and political debate. This offers an opportunity not to fall back on shared preconceptions of migrants' social situation and personal experience. However, the question remains whether, in principle, it is possible to find patterns that capture the diversity and complexity of migratory situations and trajectories, constituted by different types of migration (the result of marriage, education, refuge from violence and/or political exile), but also by the dynamics of the respective biography in which every individual migration is embedded.

Firstly in this chapter, I discuss, on the basis of classical sociological theory, the position and experience of strangers who might share certain features of their social position with migrants in a receiving society. In the second part of this chapter, I argue that it is mainly the biographical context in which the dynamics of the migratory experience develops. In presenting two case studies, I demonstrate how the biographical meaning of migration can vary, constituting, for example, a turning point in the lives of the respective migrants, or forming part of a biographical continuity unshaken by the changes due to the move to a different society. Finally, I discuss possible conclusions from a social policy perspective.

The social position of immigrants in 'modern societies'

It is no coincidence that theorising about the social position of 'the modern wanderer' – so memorably defined by Simmel "as the person who comes today and stays tomorrow" (1950, p 402) – has reached its peak in the historic periods of mass migration to Europe and the US. It was specifically at the turn of the 20th century as well as in the 1980s and 1990s that theoretical consideration of the social status and situation of 'strangers' was most lively. Whereas the 'classical' debate's core concern was the specificity of the social position of strangers and their role in the development of social relationships typical of modern societies (Simmel), the attempt from the 1980s onwards to explain rising violence against 'foreigners' and their exclusion formed the backdrop to revising the classical concepts (especially Bauman, 1991; Hall, 1996; for a German context see Hahn, 1994; Nassehi, 1995).

The starting point for theorising the social position of the stranger is to conceptualise it *in relation* to that of the 'established'. This means that the specificity of the stranger is not sought in specific attributes of difference such as language or culture. On the contrary, in Simmel's definition (1950) it is the spatial nearness combined with social distance that characterises the relation between strangers and established residents. Strangers are close because they live 'nearby', but – in contrast to the association of spatial closeness with familiarity – they represent another place, and are therefore socially distant and 'far'. Furthermore, they represent a transitory potential, which means one never knows how long they will stay and what kind of relationship the period of their stay will allow. Consequently, the presence of strangers creates a sphere of social distance in close vicinity.

However, Simmel did not conceptualise the stranger merely as an outsider. Rather, he saw the stranger as a constitutive part of the modern community in so far as social relationships in general were less and less based on familiar bonds with clear-cut boundaries to the outside, but increasingly on more socially distant and reflexive interaction. In this respect, the stranger is seen as a kind of prototype of modernity, representing the position of being simultaneously 'inside' and 'outside', which for Simmel had more positive than negative connotations. This meant, for example, that strangers were predisposed to be more 'objective' – that is, as judges in the community life – in which they could participate because they knew the rules, while remaining sufficiently distant from its conflicts in which they were not closely involved.

Zygmunt Bauman (1991) has highlighted in a more recent theoretical approach partly indebted to Simmel's ideas, the rather precarious social position of the stranger in modernity. Strangers, in Bauman's terms, represent ambivalence in societies that, in the form of nation states, are generally based on a social order constituted by a fundamental distinction between the sphere of 'friends' – the familiar and known – and the sphere of 'enemies', who must be kept out. Therefore, in modernity, it has constantly to be defined who belongs to the sphere of friends and who to that of enemies, trying to create clear-cut categories on which the sphere of familiarity and trust can be based. In so doing, strangers appear as a disruptive factor, neither in the sphere of friends nor that of enemies, but occupying a new, ambivalent position of insider and outsider, potentially friends and enemies, at the same time. This challenges the clear distinction between the two spheres, and the response of modern societies is either to assimilate strangers or to combat them, trying to make them either friends or enemies. Therefore strangers in modern societies are exposed to discourses and practices of cultural dominance, aggression, violence and even extermination.

In contrast, the position of the stranger in postmodern societies – which Bauman sees as structurally different to modern ones – is changing, in so far as it is becoming common. In a postmodern structure, the 'natives' potentially develop into strangers. Community bonds have nearly disappeared, and in the light of globalisation, the distinction between the sphere of friends and that of enemies is harder to draw in clear-cut terms either of nation state or internal social boundaries as societies are being profoundly reorganised. This, for Bauman, creates the opportunity to establish a social order no longer based on the juxtaposition of friends and enemies in which the stranger is a profoundly disturbing factor, but on solidarity between strangers since everybody potentially finds him or herself in this position in relation to others.

It is open to question whether this potential of postmodern societies will develop as an empirically dominant pattern. The present debate still focuses on the critique of the nation state and the respective definition of strangers, who in this context have come to be defined as 'foreigners' who are also characterised by being partially included, partially excluded from society. For them, the borders of the nation state have remained a pertinent factor in defining their social position, and determining obstacles and opportunities in many social fields (see, for example, Hahn, 1994; Nassehi, 1995; Davis and Lutz, 2000)[2].

So far I have considered some of the general characteristics defining the position of strangers in modern societies as they are currently theorised. But what about the experience of migrants themselves and their understanding of their situation? Is it possible to assume that there are general or typical experiences of migration according to the social relations that strangers or foreigners are assigned in a society? Last, but not least, what meaning does this experience acquire in a biographical context?

The biographical meaning of experiences of migration

One of the most elaborate approaches to theorising the experience of transition from one social context to another, exemplified by a migratory situation, has been developed by Alfred Schütz (1964). He focuses on the situation of immigration, that is, of *approaching* a new social order with the aim of becoming part of it. In his opinion, a discontinuation and transformation of the respective person's system of (social) knowledge shapes their experience. This system is based on common sense, which guides activity in everyday life, allowing us to take many things for granted. The typical experience in the immigrant situation is therefore that the achieved common sense does not work as it used to. Instead, new ways in which everyday life is organised have to be learnt and explored.

Furthermore, to avoid losing the stock of knowledge and experience built up prior to the move, old and new points of reference for orientation, experience and action have to be integrated. In the process of 'translating' past experiences and knowledge into a new social context with new experiences (a necessarily 'incomplete' and partial process), the typical experience of strangers is that of a profound restructuring of the whole system of knowledge, now based on divergent common senses from different societies. How does this experience become biographically relevant, and in what context does it develop long-term significance?

One of the most discussed features of migration is its association with biographical discontinuities and transformations, constituting turning points or even ruptures. However, looking at the life histories and stories of different migrants, it becomes apparent that, in many cases, migration is experienced not primarily as a biographical discontinuity, disrupting life projects and networks (for example, professional career, family life, peer-group links) but rather as a continuity of specific biographical projects and sometimes, in case of persecution and refuge, even of life itself. Therefore, how the experience of migration is shaped within the biographical context remains an empirically open question.

To explore this dimension, additional assumptions based on concepts from biographical research are needed (Rosenthal, 1997; Fischer-Rosenthal, 2000). In this perspective, the migratory experience is shaped by an ongoing process: the periods of time before, during, and after the actual move are included up to the point at which the experience acquires retrospective meaning (for example, after 10, 20 years or more) for successive generations. Since the process of shaping its meaning is never completed, the biographical meaning of migration has to be conceptualised as a changing, infinite and open process that entails a whole variety of other experiences making up a person's biography (Breckner, 1994, 2001). Within this complexity of life we can, however, reconstruct specific contexts and dynamics in which migratory experiences acquire and change their significance.

In the following cases, migration acquired contrasting biographical significance – as a turning point in one, and as a means of creating biographical continuity in the other. A comparison of the two cases highlights the different impact the changes in social context had on the dynamics of these migratory processes and biographies.

Ana

Flight experienced as a biographical turning point

Ana, 32 years old at the time of our interview in 1998[3], grew up in a small town in Yugoslavia that later became part of Bosnia-Herzegovina. She had a humanistic education and the fact that her parents were relatively well off made it possible to spend her holidays in Sweden in 1982, visiting relatives there. After leaving high school, Ana attended the School of Economics in Sarajevo, where she graduated. In 1987, she started to work as an economist in an import/export company, where she met her husband, a Serb. They married and their first daughter was born in 1990 after the family had bought a flat and a car, and planned to buy a summerhouse. The outbreak of the war in 1991 hit the family while it was in the process of creating a comfortable life. In the case of Ana, who lived in a 'mixed' marriage, the outburst of the war and of hatred shaped as ethnic conflict meant the sudden and irreversible destruction of the foundation on which they were building the present and future of their family. In 1992, and with the help of the Red Cross, Ana escaped with her child to Sweden. Her husband, mother-in-law and brother followed, but her parents remained. Ana and her family remained for three years as refugees in Värmland, where Ana learned Swedish, tried – without success – to get work, and volunteered in projects helping Bosnia. A second daughter was born in 1994, and the family moved to Gothenburg in 1995. However, neither Ana nor her husband, a well-trained technician, could find stable employment there. At the time of the interview, Ana was doing cleaning work and attending a course for foreign economists. Her husband was trying to find work with his taxi and his lorry driver's licence acquired in Sweden. The family was trying to attain Swedish citizenship that would allow them to visit Ana's parents in Bosnia or to acquire visas for them to come to Sweden.

In Ana's case, it is obvious that the outbreak of the war in Yugoslavia and the flight to Sweden were the dominant experiences in her life at the time of the interview. They had rather brusquely interrupted her dynamic career path. Finding herself in the position of a refugee, she had to cope with dramatic changes that simultaneously affected her past, present and future. She had to come to terms with the destruction of the social world she had lived in and trusted. She now found herself in an uncertain present in Sweden, where she could hardly continue life 'as usual'. This was impossible not least because she was professionally and socially downgraded to the lowest level of the labour market. In addition, her own and her family's future were anything but clear, their attempts to acquire citizenship being stuck in a transitional stage, and her parents still stuck in a threatening war situation.

Intergenerational family bonds remain strong in Bosnian society. For Ana to leave her parents behind was a split that was particularly hard to come to terms with. Therefore, building new points of reference for her life in the new society without her parents, and thereby profoundly changing orientations and priorities from those of her previous life, seems to have been anything but easy. Furthermore, it probably invoked considerable feelings of guilt to have escaped from physical violence while her parents were still exposed to it.

In contrast, the fact of having escaped could also be connoted with a sense of having secured continuity, even if at a very basic level. The fact that Ana and her family were able to go to Sweden, a country that she had visited before in a rather relaxed holiday setting probably linked to pleasant memories, could have enhanced the possibility of experiencing the flight in this way. Yet, as we learn from the interview, the separation from the parents together with the circumstances in the new society militated against this. A number of factors – being refugees, the continuation of the ethnic conflict between Serbs and Bosnians within the immigrant community (an uncle of hers refused contact because she was married to a Serb), the long wait for citizenship (and the possibility of a further move if the application were rejected), the impossibility to 'return' even for a visit to see the parents – all deprived Ana of a social basis on which she could develop a greater sense of continuity and confidence that the situation would be resolved.

Instead, Ana's life story reveals that she experienced her flight as a radical turning point, created by external forces. She presents her life story in contrasts and contradictions between the time before and after the war, even as a Greek tragedy, indicating that she sees no way out of the situation either for her or for others, without severe consequences for all. Therefore, it is quite likely that at present Ana suffers from the war and her flight, seeing them as an irreversible disruption to her biographical path. From this point of view, not only does it seem impossible for her to continue her life in the way she had imagined and arranged it before the war, but also for her to trust that solutions will be found to the difficult situations she faces.

However, her action strategy shows that she has tried hard to re-establish a socially secure life, probably now primarily oriented to her children's future. Refusing social welfare in order to maintain autonomy and dignity even at the price of a rather steep professional downgrading is part of this strategy, combined with professional training and changing citizenship, which, in the longer term, may allow her to escape both from her present position in the labour market and her highly insecure future. Should Ana succeed in bringing her parents to Sweden, we can imagine that those aspects of her flight that secured continuity might shape her narrative to a greater extent in the long run. At present, this remains an open question.

Sasa Koaté

Migration in an ambivalent upwardly mobile life trajectory as a means of biographical continuity

Sasa Koaté migrated from Senegal to East Germany (GDR) in the mid-1980s at the age of 24[4]. His case forms a maximal contrast (Glaser and Strauss, 1967) to Ana's case as far as the biographical meaning of migration is concerned. At the time, his migration did not represent a turning point; rather, it was part of his relatively continuous life journey, based mainly on an upwardly mobile professional career path. However, in his case, biographical continuity was challenged by a major historical event as well: the fall of the Berlin Wall created a situation within which his migratory project became *retrospectively* intricate.

Sasa was born in 1961 in a large village of 5,000 inhabitants in the south of Senegal and grew up in his eldest sister's polygamous household. His mother died three months after his birth. His father, the respected 'medicine man' of the village, was living with another women and died when Sasa was seven years old. Despite these events, Sasa's educational career was straightforward. After finishing elementary school in his native village, it was marked by several moves, each time to the nearest bigger town, living in families forming part of his more distant kin, whom he had never met before. After he graduated at a lyceum in the north of the country at the age of 20, Sasa moved to Dakar, the capital city, to begin university studies. Therefore, 'move' – from rural to urban, from close to more distant kin – was part of Sasa's life since his late childhood. Even though the changes brought about by this educational career might not have been easy to digest for Sasa at the time they occurred, now they are presented as unproblematic life events connected to an unquestioned upwardly mobile path, with considerable support from a wider family network. Sasa seems to have balanced his potentially difficult experiences (for example, of being a newcomer in a family several times over) with a successful school career and the support he received in the end in the different family contexts. Through this career, he might also have acquired a highly developed ability to deal with new and changing situations, feeling closely linked to different social and familial contexts, but not bound by them.

In 1985, Sasa luckily obtained a grant from the GDR to study chemistry there. In his university years, he was actively involved in diverse student activities, for example, as the spokesperson for the university's foreign students. This strategy to integrate socially in a new context by engaging in cultural and political activities might have developed already in Senegal. There, Sasa had met and lived with pupils and students from different parts of the country who spoke different native languages, engaging in politics with them and organising strikes.

In 1991, in the first summer after finishing his studies in the GDR, Sasa returned to Senegal in order to look for work there. He came back without any job offers, disappointed not to find 'open doors' as a highly skilled returnee equipped with a skill needed in his country, and decided to continue his studies in the GDR, this time aiming for a doctoral degree.

From these data, it becomes apparent that during the period of studying in the GDR, Sasa was oriented to returning to Senegal to complete his migratory project and to continue a biographical path that had remained strongly connected to his home country. There were two coinciding experiences that forced him to revise his previous plans, and that constituted a biographical turning point initiated by the question of 'returning' or 'staying'. This common dilemma and conflict stage of migration trajectories (Breckner, 2000) is, at present, shaping Sasa's biographical situation. What shook Sasa's formerly straightforward and clear trajectory?

In 1990, the first summer after the breakdown of the GDR, Sasa had started to date an East German girl, an agriculture student. The turning point, however, was initiated only when his girlfriend gave birth to a child at the end of 1994. From then on, Sasa felt bound by the responsibility to provide his child with a stable family context.

> Then I said, the child is here, the PhD is nearing completion, you always wanted to go home. So, this is what the situation looks like. The child will arrive at the time when you perhaps [are in Senegal] some months on, you are completing your PhD, how can you do that, is that human, is that human, would you accept it if somebody would do that to you?... I also said – by the

way, I have been brought up with Islam[5], I'm no practitioner, but I think I believe in some basic values, okay? – every child has the right to have a father with it and a mother and so on, then you should accept your responsibilities. Because the child has not been produced by itself, yeah? And … she has to enjoy all the opportunities other children have, if it is possible.

Based on an ethical commitment to the parental role, Sasa's professional aspirations, as well as his plan to return to Senegal, were now subordinated to the task of maintaining a family.

This connects with his experience that his first attempts to find a job in Senegal, which would allow the family to move there, had failed up till then. Against the background of this experience – which was marked by strong disappointment – a previously stable point of reference in Sasa's life was shaken. This is the second context that makes his plan to return questionable.

However, there is a third context in which Sasa's social position changed: his move from being a 'guest student' to a 'foreigner' as a result of German unification. In the beginning, his migratory situation in Germany was clearly and positively defined in social terms – though only by the state – as one of generosity and welcome of a temporary guest that formed part of international solidarity, one of the relevant, albeit ambiguous, projects of GDR society. The dissolution of this society and the unification with West Germany firstly affected Sasa's private life through new legal restrictions.

> The child belongs to the German mother, that is the law, very definite in this respect. Permission to stay in Germany is bound up with your studies and when they are finished, you have to leave the country immediately, it doesn't matter whether you have family relations, except if you are married…. Then I thought again more realistically: "You always want to respect principles, do you accept the game and say, 'Your studies have finished, goodbye Germany?', or are you taking the responsibility for your child?" Then, I can't say to my daughter one day when she asks: "I left because I no longer had permission to stay". She would say "Why didn't you marry my mom then? Did my mom force you to make a child? And you made a child". Nobody is interested in how it happened, nobody – ok, it doesn't matter. So I said to myself: you have to be realistic, and then we got married in September 1995.

Feeling rather forced into the marriage and family situation that Sasa had neither planned nor chosen, it is not surprising that for him:

> … the family issue is the most intricate and delicate one. You are confronted with the law for foreigners so that you can't make your own decision, just as a person, you can't make a free decision.

Apart from the legal restrictions, it was the restructuring of the chemical industry in the GDR during the transformation process that had severe consequences on his professional life. The big plants near Leipzig, which could have provided Sasa with a job in his profession, were closed down. In February 1996, Sasa obtained his doctoral degree and became unemployed. Even though he applied for a job as a chemist, he was only offered sporadic work as a certified interpreter in French and two African languages for the public administration in Leipzig. After six months, he accepted this career change and began to work at a cultural association, counselling and also organising multicultural events, including an anti-racist school project that he had initiated. In Sasa's presentation of this change, it becomes clear that, for him, becoming a chemist had been his priority.

In addition, Sasa had to confront the xenophobic perspective laid on him by German society, which attributed him with a strategic plan for staying that complicated the already delicate integration of conflicting commitments and orientations.

> All these, um, bad sayings from people: "They all want to stay here" and so on and so forth. That is the image of about – I exaggerate – ninety per cent of the people, that no one wants to go home [sniffs]. They think you can't live somewhere else [laughs tonelessly]. ... Unfortunately, it is confirmed, naturally, "the man has studied, made his PhD, and immediately after finishing he takes the wife, and suddenly he is here". That is what people are thinking, following the motto: "They all want to marry here in order to stay".

With the perspective of a longer-lasting stay, Sasa had to transform his previous social position as a temporary guest into one as a member of the society. Therefore, he had to confront at close quarters German attitudes and behaviour towards foreigners. He had to struggle not only with his own doubts about his decision to stay or to leave, but also with imputations and hostile attitudes that added to the fragility of his situation. This made it necessary to reassert himself.

> But one shouldn't care too much about what other people think, for me it doesn't matter, I know one hundred per cent, my conviction is that I am here because of family reasons ... that I have responsibilities and duties concerning my family and I definitely want to fulfil them, and everything what other people say doesn't interest me.

Sasa accepted that his path might change and he already started to prepare himself for a longer stay and even a change in professional career. He established relations so he could continue his involvement with various forms of voluntary and political activity. Among other things, he leads the local branch of the Green Party that had paid for his doctoral studies, thereby consolidating contacts that might help him to continue his work in the sphere of multicultural and anti-racist activity. Furthermore, he describes his political and voluntary activities as a means of integrating into German society, of taking part in its problems and in its development. Sasa's personal and social capacity to adapt to the new situation and to make his way even under altered conditions is highly developed.

This, however, is still based on the hope that his situation will be transitory, even though his future objectives have become completely uncertain.

> I am still convinced that I would like to go to Senegal to work there, but without the family it's not possible, because my wife has to join in, and at the moment it doesn't look like she is enthusiastic about this idea. Before the marriage it was a bit different, then the child came, and then you have this *anxiety about life* – you think too much about the future of the child, you don't know it. She has never been there, I myself have only been there twice in 12 years – only twice in 12 years – so this is a critical situation.

In spite of feeling in a 'critical situation', Sasa's biographical strategy of focusing on the positive sides of life, looking for possibilities of coping with difficult situations, is still very much in place and enables him to deal with difficulties in a productive way. He is far from being stuck. Nevertheless, he has to deal with a high potential risk which, if his family commitments, his professional life and his desire to return are not kept in a reasonable balance, might become critical in the long term. So, in his case, it is the potentiality of risk that forms the future horizon of his present life situation.

Conclusions

It seems obvious that, as far as the biographical meaning of the migratory experience is concerned, the difference between the two cases could hardly be greater. In Ana's case, the flight from Bosnia-Herzegovina to Sweden represents a profound disrupture of her biography and the start of a difficult period in exile. On the other hand, in Sasa's case, it was to be just another step in his upwardly mobile educational path. In Ana's case, the flight has severely impacted on her life, separating it into a time 'before' and one 'after' that might not be easy to reintegrate. When asking if it was the experience of migration itself that broke her life in two, it becomes obvious that, in her case, it is the experience of the war that has shaken the basis of her existential security. Even though the flight and the concomitant experiences of being a refugee form part of the whole complex of the war experience, in her case, it is not its primary constituent[6].

From this perspective, the difference between the cases is less absolute, and more comparable. In Sasa's case as well, it is not primarily the experience of migration itself that is the most relevant in his upwardly mobile life journey. Rather, this is formed by the experience of getting access to the support and resources he needed in order to proceed on his path. Therefore, for Sasa, the day he was informed that he had received the grant to study in the GDR was much more important than that of his arrival in the country. This was the case even though the move required him to adapt to a rather different cultural life and environment, including another language, and people of different appearance, with different habits and expectations in many aspects of everyday life. Since his biography remained focused on returning to his home country, the GDR – as a place he had moved to – remained a transitory one for nearly 10 years. However, the biographical turning point initiated by the pregnancy of his girlfriend challenged this pattern considerably, which retrospectively and in the long term might change the prior meaning attached to his migration. Then, also in his case, the move might come to represent a turning point, leading his life in a different direction.

As soon as we compare the impact of events and circumstances in their social contexts on both of their lives, the difference again becomes obvious. In Ana's case, it was a radical change in the social sphere that formed part of her life that initiated her move and the disruption of her biography. The fact that she lived in a 'mixed' marriage left few alternatives but to leave in a situation of an outburst of violence and hatred in a war defined as an ethnic conflict (see Morokvasic-Müller, 2000). The personal room for manoeuvre in her case was severely constrained by social – and even global – forces (which developed after the dissolution of the division of East and West Europe) that Ana could not influence.

In contrast, Sasa's decision to move was embedded in a relatively more stable social situation, in which he could decide to apply for a grant and was not forced by anybody or anything[7]. In his case, a major change in the social sphere was linked to his 'return'. If GDR society had continued to exist, Sasa would have been forced to stick to his contract and to leave the country, regardless of whether he had a child or not. In this case, it would have been the decision and responsibility of his girlfriend to join him or to separate with the respective consequences for their child. Under the circumstances of GDR society dissolving in a context in which only a few of the contractual obligations established under its regime were continued in the unified Germany, Sasa was free to make a decision that at the same time forced him into a marriage he did not want. Therefore the societal intervention in his case was substantial, affecting the biographical embeddedness of his migratory project as well. However, it caused more ambivalence than in Ana's case. In both cases, changes at the macro level therefore had considerable influence on the migration process as well as on the biographical dynamics, albeit in different phases and in a different way.

Last but not least, when comparing the two cases, it becomes apparent that they both confronted the experience of being devalued and excluded from different spheres of society (most obviously from the labour market) during their migration process, but at different stages and again in different ways. Whereas Ana experienced a sudden fall, even collapse, as far as social recognition of her professional competence was concerned, Sasa was exposed to a slower process of creeping exclusion from the professional career for which he was highly trained. Moreover, Sasa shared this experience with the 'natives' of GDR society, whereas for Ana it formed part of her situation as a refugee with a specific legal status in Sweden, as well as in most other, Western societies. Therefore it is not surprising that Ana aimed to retrain in order to re-establish herself within her familiar professional field, whereas Sasa followed the opportunities in a transforming society, based on the variety of his competencies that allowed him to try out another professional field.

More generally, we can observe a similar strategy in both cases in dealing with the obstacles they faced. This is based on attempts to escape a situation of state dependency with the aim of regaining a basis for a relatively autonomous life. So the question arises, in what way, if at all, can these two cases be regarded as relevant to developing social policy concepts that address issues of migration? What kind of general conclusions can we draw from them in this respect?

'Migrants': a target-category for social policy?

Even though Ana and Sasa are highly skilled and successful in dealing with the obstacles they were confronted with during the migration process in its different phases, they show us what kind of obstacles they had to face. These might give a picture of typical challenges inherent in migration processes.

First of all, in both cases it was their legal status in the target society that not only restricted their space to make personal decisions, but questioned their future prospects. In both cases, this created a horizon of insecurity and risk that also challenged the relatively stable trajectories developed in the past.

If we compare Ana and Sasa with regard to their biographical situation, it becomes apparent that in Sasa's case the potential risks might become apparent in the family sphere over the long term. Therefore, the potential need for support would be in the family sphere. In contrast, in Ana's case, apart from the legal situation, it is her professional downgrading that at present forms the main obstacle to rebuilding biographical continuity in the sphere of life based on training and skills, and not destroyed by the war. Although Ana's nuclear family seems to be a rather stabilising factor, the split from her parents and the anxiety about their fate is also a considerable source of sorrow. Therefore, providing support to adapt her skills to the new society, as well as potential support to deal with the losses in her life due to the war, would probably be the most appropriate.

From these two cases, we can see already that they both came up against legal, professional and personal obstacles in the course of their migration process. These obstacles led to further difficulties and insecurities, as well as potential risks in different ways, in a unique concatenation of consequences in different life spheres for each of them. Therefore we can conclude that, despite the structural similarity of social positions and biographical challenges occurring during the migration process (be it work or professional migration, war or poverty migration), they are experienced and dealt with differently. Rebuilding biographical continuity by dealing with radical changes in life prospects is therefore also determined by the respective biographical significance the migration process acquires in different phases and spheres of life (such as family, work and friends). Therefore, a huge variety of challenges and strategies to deal with them develops within the social field of migration. Social policy concepts that address migration issues too generally – deducing 'difficulties' purely from people having the status of strangers or foreigners without asking how they are experienced and handled by the respective individual – therefore risk:

(a) failing to capture the specific situation, needs, experiences and competence of individual migrants;
(b) labelling migrants in general as a 'social problem'.

As we have seen in the cases of Ana and Sasa, this does not do justice to the competence they have developed to cope with challenging changes and even disruptions to their lives.

How could social policy concepts take on board the diversity of experiences and strategies without being overwhelmed by the variety of the field? There is not the space to develop this in detail here. Suffice to say, however, that the societal as well as the personal situations of migrants in need of support first have to be explored before specific intervention is offered or proposed. The following questions might be helpful in guiding such a process of examination based on an account in which the respective person has the opportunity to tell his or her story without being pushed into a 'category' that is expected to have specific and already known 'problems'.

- What kind of legal, professional, familial or other conditions have become a problem during the migration process, during all its stages and time perspectives and how do they interact with each other?
- In what way are the difficulties biographically embedded?

Are they due to:

- the migration experience itself (such as trauma closely linked to the move)?
- downgrading experiences in the receiving society?
- problems with the social position migrants being fixed (for example, not allowing them to develop future prospects)?
- difficulties in transforming 'common sense' knowledge?
- conditions of 'return' and their impact on the structuring of the whole migration process?
- other life experiences and problems that are reinforced but not initiated by the migration process?
- experiences and problems that are not connected at all to the migration?

A careful exploration of the peculiarity and typicality of migration experiences with regard to their biographical significance emerging in the stories told so far is probably the most effective way of dealing with problems occurring in the lives of those who have experienced migration.

Notes

[1] For information on global processes of migration, see Sassen (1996), Zolberg et al (1989).

[2] Social science at present attempts to define 'society' not necessarily as an entity finding its constituting borders in the nation state, but in global structures and in the process of developing the EU (see, for example, Sylvia Walby 'Theorizing polities beyond the nation state: rethinking the concept of society in a global era', plenary speech given at the Fifth European Sociological Association Congress in Helsinki, August 2001). However, the issue of whether or not this is an utopian idea, or if it already finds its empirical correspondence in structures that will become dominant in the future, remains open.

[3] This interview was conducted and analysed by Birgitta Thorsell from Gothenburg, Sweden, who has contributed Chapter Eight to this volume. The presentation is based on her case analysis prepared for the Swedish national report on migration and ethnic minorities in *Sostris Working Paper 4* (Sostris, 1999).

[4] The interview with Sasa Koaté was conducted by William Hungerbühler, my colleague in the German Sostris project, who also contributed to the analysis.

[5] Islam is the religion of 92% of Senegal's population.

[6] This cannot be generalised in the sense that, in the case of refugees, it is never the experience connected to the move that is the most relevant. There are many cases of refugees who experience severe threats and physical violence during their move or traumatic events even in the receiving society that then constitute the most relevant and disturbing experience, whereas those experiences connected to the home context, even in a situation of war, can remain in the background as relatively unspectacular.

[7] At the same time, he also faced constraints in making his decision. It was not really possible to choose the target country for his study, which depended on the geopolitical relations his country had with others either in the 'eastern' or the 'western' hemisphere in a politically polarised world.

References

Bauman, Z. (1991) *Modernity and ambivalence*, Cambridge: Polity Press.

Breckner, R. (1994) 'Im Grunde genommen war ich immer ein Entwurzelter. Aspekte biographischer Migrationsforschung in Ost-West-Perspektive', in B. Balla and W. Geier (eds) *Zu einer Soziologie des Postkommunismus. Kritik, Theorie, Methodologie*, Hamburg: Lit, pp 37-50.

Breckner, R. (2000) 'Processes of reconstructing migration biographies: the experience of "Return" from the West to the East of Europe after 1989', in B. Agozino (ed) *Theoretical and methodological issues in migration research: Interdisciplinary, intergenerational and international perspectives*, Aldershot: Ashgate, pp 91-106.

Breckner, R. (2001) *Leben in polarisierten Welten. Zum Verhältnis von Migration und Biographie im Ost-West Europäischen Migrationsfeld*, Berlin: Technical University.

Davis, K. and Lutz, H. (2000) 'Life in theory: three feminist thinkers on transition(s)', in *The European Journal of Women's Studies*, vol 7, no 3.

Fischer-Rosenthal, W. (2000) 'Address lost: how to fix lives. Biographical structuring in the European modern age', in R. Breckner, D. Kalekin-Fishman and I. Miethe (eds) *Biographies and the division of Europe*, Opladen: Leske & Budrich, pp 55-75.

Glaser, B.G. and Stauss, A.L. (1967) *The discovery of grounded theory*, Chicago, IL: Aldine.

Hahn, A. (1994) 'Die soziale Konstruktion des Fremden', in W.M. Sprondel (ed) *Die Objektivität der Ordnungen und ihre kommunikative Konstruktion*, Frankfurt-am-Main: Suhrkamp, pp 140-66.

Hall, S. (ed) (1996) *Questions of cultural identity*, London: Sage Publications.

Morokvasic-Müller, M. (2000) 'Inter-ethnic marriages in the post-Yugoslavian region', in R. Breckner, D. Kalekin-Fishman and I. Miethe (eds) *Biographies and the division of Europe*, Opladen: Leske & Budrich, pp 195-216.

Nassehi, A. (1995) 'Der Fremde als Vertrauter. Soziologische Beobachtungen zur Konstruktion von Identitäten und Differenzen', in *Kölner Zeitschrift für Soziologie und Sozialpsychologie*, vol 47, pp 443-63.

Rosenthal, G. (1997) 'National identity or multicultural autobiography', *The Narrative Study of Lives*, vol 5, pp 21-9.

Sassen, S. (1996) *Migranten, Siedler, Flüchtlinge. Von der Massenauswanderung zur Festung Europa*, Frankfurt-am-Main: Fischer.

Schütz, A. (1964) 'The stranger', in A. Brodersen (ed) *Collected papers*, vol 2, The Hague: Nijhoff, pp 91-105.

Simmel, G. (1950) 'The stranger', in *The sociology of Georg Simmel*, New York: Free Press, pp 402-08.

Sostris (1999) *Sostris Working Paper 4: Case study materials – ethnic minorities and migrants*, London: Centre for Biography in Social Policy, University of East London.

Zolberg, A., Suhrke, A. and Aguayo, S. (1989) *Escape from violence. Conflict and the refugee crisis in the developing world*, Oxford: Oxford University Press.

———

THIRTEEN

Second-generation transcultural lives

Prue Chamberlayne

This was only when I was about six but it's, it's in my head so much that I can remember it today.... It was a table of white girls ... and the teacher said, there's six cubes here, take away five, and nobody would touch those cubes, because I'd touched them, and there was this theory that, oh no, they're dirty, you mustn't touch them now 'cos she's got brown skin, you know and it was so awful and I felt so horrid.... I have seen that all through my life, it made me so tough.... I didn't care, I was so angry. (Djamillah, speaking of her schooling in the mid-1970s in Britain)

This piece of narrative may well evoke memories – and many questions – for you as a reader. What has been the impact on Djamillah's life and identity of that 'misrecognition' of her brown skin as 'dirty'? How did this event affect the children doing the excluding, and the teacher standing by? How widespread were such experiences in the 1970s, in Britain and in other countries, and for Black, Asian and Arab immigrants? How do schools tackle such incidents? In what ways does racialised social exclusion differ from other kinds of everyday social prejudice?

Djamillah's extract may lead you to pessimistic thoughts about the extent of racism in Europe. However, there have also been many positive developments in the direction of multiculturalism. If you went to Germany in the mid-1990s, you might well have seen a widespread wall slogan which declared, "We are all foreigners!" Cleverly, this inverted the process of misrecognition, hailing passers-by to identify themselves as 'foreigners'. While addressing all, the slogan simultaneously differentiated the German readers, inviting them to take the place of the stranger[1]. This kind of sophistication is now commonplace in European countries experiencing their second and third generations of postcolonial cultural mixing. It is highlighted in the lively debates, often led by the university-educated children and grandchildren of migrants, about which concepts best capture the specific features of second- and third-generation migration experience and identity issues, and about how multiculturalism is shaking the foundations of European thinking and politics.

Literature on multiculturalism – and more recently 'transculturalism' – highlights the way many ethnic minority citizens enjoy simultaneous insider and outsider standpoints and a fluidity of cultural identities. It sparkles with the intensity of personal experience, and the excitement of articulating new viewpoints and challenging old ones. These debates are lively within feminism. The philosopher Rose Braidotti, for example, regards herself as a 'nomad', and uses the term to theorise multiculturalism. For her, the feminist nomad is an agent par excellence, always in transit and constantly transgressing boundaries. Having moved between Italy, Australia, France and the Netherlands, she considers Europe an ideal place to look for possible lives and relationships. She argues that 'nomad' avoids idealising the community of origin and the postmodern dissolution of identity. It recognises both the empowering and disempowering features of transitions (Braidotti, 1994; Davis and Lutz, 2000). Seyla Benhahib, who has lived in Turkey, North America and Germany, prefers the concept of 'exile'. The exile chooses to leave home, but then acquires a viewpoint from "outside the walls of the city" (quoted in Davis and Lutz, 2000, pp 371, 374). Challenging postmodern theory, with its emphasis on fragmented disembeddedness. Benhabib argues that exile is fluid and interactive, and that it strengthens universalism. Another feminist, Avtar Brah, who has lived in India, East Africa, the UK and North America, prioritises the concept of 'diaspora space'. This brings into view the transmigrancy of people, capital, commodities and culture, and "the *intersectionality* of contemporary conditions" (p 242):

> It is the realm where the crossing of borders is experienced, transcultural identities constituted, and belongingness and otherness appropriated and contested. (Brah, 1996, p 242)

Stuart Hall, a leading British sociologist who grew up in the Caribbean, regards the development of multiculturalism with some optimism, not least because it challenges the assumption of universal cultural homogeneity which has underpinned the western state since the enlightenment. Through the process of globalisation, the particularised margins move inwards, decentering the West's universalising mission. This also defies the cultural and intellectual heritage of externalising and (often) racialising the 'Other' (Hall, 2000, p 217). Furthermore, multiculturalism promotes the bridging of the long-standing divide between the politics of equality and that of recognition. As well as challenging the deep political injustices of inequality and social exclusion, multiculturalism highlights the subjective and social complexities of attachment, belonging and identity. So it provides an opportunity for 'transformative' thinking, beyond existing political discourses (Hall, 2000, p 235).

Sometimes Hall uses the term 'transculturalism' to capture the fluidity of contemporary identities. He is at pains to emphasise that appreciating cultural particularities by no means endorses ethnic absolutism or segregated communalism. He finds the way forward in Derrida's notion of *différance*, a process in which meanings are woven in a play between similarities and differences. This interplay of similarity and difference is relationally determined, meaning that it occurs in interpersonal and social relationships, and in the reflections and reworkings of those in people's inner worlds (Hall, 2000, p 236).

Hall celebrates the "right to live one's life from within" as a cosmopolitan value, a "concrete universal" (Hall, 2000, p 233). This implies the need for individuals to find an integrated, even if fluid, identity within multiculturalism. A personal settlement may occur in different ways, as the debates on nomadism, exile and the diaspora suggest, but is achieved in and through relationships, rather than by lone individuals.

While theorists provide us with concepts for comparing experiences of transculturalism and thinking about the challenge posed by multiculturalism to European political thinking, they tend not to trace the processes by which they themselves achieved such identities. It is this process of difficult transition that is brought to light through the accounts of our interviewees, implicitly and explicitly revealing their responses to the everyday challenges and structural constraints of their lives.

A major impetus for multiculturalism comes from the responses of ethnic minority members to these challenges[2], including those in the personal and family realm. Bhikhu Parekh writes that in Asian and Afro-Caribbean communities in the UK:

> Every family has become a terrain of subdued or explosive struggles. In every family, husband and wife, parents and children, brothers and sisters are having to re-negotiate and re-define their patterns of relationship in a manner that takes account both of their traditional values and those characteristic of their adopted country. Different families reach their own inherently tentative conclusions. (Parekh, 1991, quoted in Hall, 2000, pp 220-1)

Intergenerational changes in values and attitudes can be highly conflictual, and while the challenge of forging new identities can be invigorating for some, it can be exhausting for others. As our opening quotation from Djamillah suggests, great pain can underlie a tough approach.

The case studies presented in this chapter suggest that, for ethnic minority citizens, achieving a sense of personal fulfilment and purpose (living one's life from within) involves overcoming cultural divides, as well as the external obstacles and internal hurt caused by racism. They point to social, familial and personal resources that allow hurdles to be overcome, and to ways in which institutional and social contexts may support or hinder the achievement of personal stability and creative drive. Spanning lives of some 30 years, they suggest the importance of multicultural spaces – which have developed since the 1970s within certain kinds of employment and within some city areas – for the achieving of integrated identities.

In general, the profile of ethnic minority interviewees in the Sostris project reflected EU policy emphasis on new economic migrants and asylum seekers. Newcomers to Europe – from Africa, Central and South America, from the former Yugoslavia and eastern Europe, from Turkey, India and the Philippines – most of our immigrant interviewees formed part of the 14 million non-nationals who were resident in Europe in the mid-1990s. As Helma Lutz and her colleagues remark (1995), it is ironic that the 'inclusive' postwar welfare systems, which have been central to defining European identity, should exclude such vast numbers of their populations from citizenship and services, and be so concerned to keep out further newcomers. Second- and third-generation ethnic minority members have moved on so far from the experience of their parents that the term 'second-generation immigrants' feels out of place. Yet the operations of Fortress Europe creates a climate of political discourse and everyday racism that directly affects their lives.

Our subjects in this chapter are European nationals in their late 20s, who cherish, even while they struggle with, a sense of multiple belongings and commitments. The three main biographies are of Djamillah, born in Britain soon after her parents arrived from Pakistan, Zenon, born of Algerian and Spanish parents, who lives in Paris, and Steven, born of Caribbean parents in London. Each has dealt differently with the challenges of multiculturalism. Djamillah, a fighter backed by a relatively accommodating family, has achieved an inventive, if precarious, transcultural identity. Zenon, whose family tradition is of removal and avoidance, is pretty stuck: *le cul entre trois chaises* – falling between three stools – trying to gain a footing as a graduate in media. Steven is struggling in the same professional field. A more reflexive character, his account traces the painful process of brokering new frontiers and friendships beyond the defensive strategies of his powerful parents, as an essential part of moving on.

Djamillah

Djamillah's parents married in Pakistan in 1962. Her father, a major in the Pakistan Army, which had been newly formed after Indian independence in 1947, had been injured in the 1950s. He was 29 when he married, whereas Djamillah's mother, who was illiterate, was 10 years younger. Their first child was born after five years, when the father had already left for England to join his brother in a bakery in Luton. The mother came two years later, and in 1971 Djamillah was born, followed by three boys.

In England, the family was supported by an intensive and elaborate kinship network (known as *biradari*). Djamillah's father joined his brother in the baking trade, and they lived together as an extended family until Djamillah was 12, the year her father also stopped work because of chronic illness. The children attended Koranic school, and there was great emphasis on education. All of them grew up to be doctors, lawyers or scientists. The family itself is transcultural: the father was godfather to a child of white friends, and one of the brothers married a white wife, who converted to Islam.

Djamillah recounts her life as a story of fights and decisive choices. Frequently switching between 'we' and 'I', and between then and now, she recalls conflicts in relation to race, gender and generation, within the arenas of family, education, her marriage and her work. Racism at school "seemed so odd", she says, and came as a shock. She raged at her mum and wished she were born in a white family, but relied on Asian clothes to hide her brown skin:

> I tried to, you know, do the things that all the white people would do, and I
> tried to talk like them, and I tried to act like them.... I never used to wear
> shorts or short skirts, I used to wear, like, tracksuit bottoms and full-length
> thingies so that I showed the least amount of my body as possible.

Her father encouraged her in her fights in school, and "All the time he was on our back to study, study, study". More globally she says, "He has opposed me in a lot of things ... but he has been like a pillar of support for me throughout – whenever it has been the hard times, my Dad is the only one that's been there".

At times she and her brothers rebelled against their parents, and at other times she fought alone, as over a white boyfriend, and over living in a mixed hall of residence. She talks dramatically and at length about this:

> I knew I was gonna go to school, I was gonna get to university, and I thought
> I'm gonna – that's when I'm gonna do what I want, because I – they won't be
> there, to tell me what to do and what not to do.... That was another big
> major fight I had to have with the whole family.

She argued that in the end they had to trust her, and despite her father's prophetic worries – "You don't know what men are like" – her mother supported her. University, which gave her a sense of freedom and control, was "wonderful ... I had such a good laugh". She studied law, and proceeded to become a barrister.

It may well be that, in the fights, her parents were (perhaps unconsciously) testing rather than seriously opposing her. Ambitious first-generation parents depend upon their children taking initiatives and crossing new boundaries, but the adjustments and compromises are delicate on their side too. However, the precariousness of maintaining her loyalty to her family while also fashioning her own independence reached a crisis in her marriage. Her husband was wealthy, but uneducated:

> I deliberately went out with my husband because he was a Muslim and because
> he was from [her family's area of Pakistan] 'cos I thought this would be my
> parents' perfect choice.... They tried to get this proposal fixed up but I was
> having none of it, I said no way, I'll marry who I want, even though it might
> be the wrong decision.... I am entitled to make mistakes, I suppose. We all
> are.

Discovering that her husband is already married with children in Pakistan, Djamillah is devastated and returns to her family. Her mother begs her to save them from the public shame of having allowed a modern, free-choice marriage that failed, so she returns to him, feeling sure of their protection. She has met her husband's family, and in any case enjoys visiting Pakistan. Now two of his children live with Djamillah and her husband in London, as does one of her brothers. Her husband partly lives in Pakistan.

Meanwhile, she has left her prestigious career path as a barrister. She works in a community law centre, in an area where she is still regularly spat at and taunted as 'Paki', and is enjoying a part-time evening degree in humanities:

> Everybody keeps asking me, why did you leave that good job, to come here, and you know nobody understands that this work is more important to me, it proves a point to me that I'm fighting against something which I couldn't do as a child.

Within the main theme of her biography as a feisty big fight there appears a more sorrowful evaluation: "It's been a big haul". Her use of 'big haul' rather than the more usual 'long haul' is intriguing. It conveys a weight, evoking the considerable constraints on her life alongside her achievements.

Djamillah's life strategy involves compromising between her own choices and loyalty to her family. Without her loyalty to her family she might well have known her husband better. She might well have lived with him before marrying, and she could have divorced. But her family loyalty springs from her own needs, as well as from having to spare them humiliation. Her family is important to her sense of security and her sense of self; it gives her the confidence to tread her particular and rather precarious path. Her family has backed her in her fights and enabled her to learn skills of accommodation; it gives her access to Pakistan, and protects her against her husband's potential violence (against her independence). Hall reminds us that:

> We often operate with too simplistic a conception of 'belonging'. Sometimes we are most 'spoken' by our attachments when we struggle to be free of them, quarrel with, criticise or dissent radically from them. Like parental relationships, cultural traditions shape us *both* when they nurture and sustain us *and* when we have to break irrevocably with them in order to survive. (Hall, 2000, p 233).

Djamillah's case shows a culture permeating the very fibre of an individual's life and responses. Fights are so central to Djamillah's biographical strategy and to her identity that she even seems to seek them out. Her legal work allows her to seek justice for the everyday discriminations of her childhood, but perhaps also to externalise and relativise her own dilemmas.

The fears evoked by even drinking with a male friend suggest the constraints on her lifestyle and household arrangement:

> I still think one of my brothers is gonna walk past or, you know, my husband'll walk past or my dad'll walk past.... My husband would go berserk [laughs] –

he'd kill me [laughs].... I don't know what would happen to me – I don't even wanna think about it.

The inequalities of race, gender, generation and class that faced Djamillah as a child continue in her life now and still have to be fought. In one sense, confrontation is her father's script. He believed "you have to beat the system", and he "made us, in a way, go through it all" (meaning the confronting of racism). Struggles, however, have enabled Djamillah to define herself, gain her sense of agency, and negotiate her own choices. Struggles in the private as well as the public sphere have formed her skills. In the detail of her arguments over the mixed hall of residence, we see her powers of persuasion being honed, and a bitter struggle finally being resolved, anxiously at first, but then with good humour, affection and reason.

Brah comments that: "Operations of power are the very basis of agency ... marked by the contradictions of subjectivity" (1996, p 243). While power is often oppressive, it is also "at the heart of cultural creativity, of pleasure and desire, of subversion and resistance" (p 243). Amina Mama likewise defines individual subjectivity as produced "out of reverberations between historical-cultural and psychological conditions" (Mama, 1995, p 133).

The literature of transculturalism has greatly enriched our analysis of Djamillah's situation, which we at first constructed as that of a 'modern', individual woman pulled between tradition and modernity (Rupp, 1999)[3]. As we have seen, Stuart Hall likes the way 'the multicultural question' dislodges such binary understandings. He argues that colonised, traditional cultures remain distinctive but inevitably become "conscripts of modernity" (2000, p 225). New and old diaspora are to be found everywhere, ambiguously and anxiously 'translating' between insider and outsider positions. Hybridity displays or highlights

> ... the dissonances which have to be crossed despite proximate relations; the disjunctions of power or position that have to be contested; the values, ethical and aesthetic, that have to be 'translated', but will not seamlessly transcend the process of transfer. (Bhabha, 1997, quoted in Hall, 2000, p 226)

This is often, as Rushdie put it, "how newness enters the world" (quoted in Hall, 2000, p 226).

Intercultural 'translation' requires sophisticated reflexive capacities, and habits of accommodation that Djamillah was fortunate to gain in her family. As we argue elsewhere in this book (for example in the Introduction and Conclusion), reflexive skills are not individually acquired, but nurtured by families and the collective discourses and consciousness raising of new social movements. There is no guarantee that hybridity will lead to creativity in identity and a strong sense of agency, and second-generation experience is, of course, uneven and varied. For personal and/or social reasons, some people will not have shared in collective processes of translation. They will not have the investment – meaning the eagerness, emotion and desire – that the act of 'identification' assumes, identification being necessary to action (Hall, 1996, p 168). For some, the dissonance and disjunction between cultures may be too awkward to be bridgeable. This is the case with Zenon, who feels isolated and alienated.

Zenon

Zenon tells us that his Arab father came to Paris in the 1950s at the age of 17, his parents (Zenon's grandparents) wanting to save him – their only son – from the Algerian war. He found himself doing building and decorating work. Zenon's "stubborn" mother, who came to Paris from Seville aged 32 to resist marriage and escape her overprotective mother, did domestic work. They met in 1968, and despite their different languages, Zenon thinks they understood each other well. Born in 1969, Zenon was sent for his first two years to Spain, where he would have preferred to stay. Having recounted this much, Zenon feels he has said everything. As a coda he adds that his parents have always maintained the three cultures, with frequents visits to Algeria and Spain. They also tried to spare Zenon and his sister from problems of race, by living in bourgeois districts. He concludes: "So that's how we were brought up, straddled between three stools."

In Zenon's life, the disjunctions of family, class and culture remain unbridged, and political and social confrontations with racial issues are avoided. His father's concierge work allows Zenon to attend good schools and pass his baccalauréat exams in humanities and maths in "the normal way". He refused the offer of a larger flat in a mixed area for fear of *la racaille* ("the scum") and "this fauna of immigrants" – to which Zenon comments, "and he's right". The predominantly Spanish and Portuguese children of the concierges in these affluent districts were "more tightly knit (*soudé*) than their parents.... They made a good and rather solid group". Zenon himself now lives in a multicultural area with more night life, which he much prefers.

At university Zenon studied plastic art and film. "Above all I wanted not to, I wanted to do something which would interest me.... It was super". (What lurks in the shadow of "wanted not to" is perhaps his father's kind of work.) He delighted in living independently of his parents, although he felt lonely in a studio flat. He then fell in love and had a perfect time (we are not told the painful ending). But eventually "little jobs" in the informal (and illegal) sector, which he initially did to survive, took over. He got a job as a sound engineer, but had to give it up since he was not properly qualified, and now he is unemployed.

He says that in his teenage years he didn't know who he was, whereas at 18 he adopted a Spanish-European identity. Regarding Algeria with its different relations between men and women, its lack of freedom of expression, the different films, literature and music, he says, "I can take some things from it but I can't be submerged in it all the time". Rather surprisingly, despite intense levels of hostility to Arabs in France, he at no point mentions racism as a general problem or a direct personal experience. Instead, he declares:

> Now I've totally accepted being neither French, nor Spanish, nor Algerian but being the three at once, there.

Djamillah's case revealed the complex interconnections between emotional bonds, personal needs and more externally negotiated identities. Zenon's preference for a Spanish identity is also multiply determined, by his attachment to his aunt and to his teenage peer group, by anti-Arab racism (even though he does not mention it), and by his ambivalence towards his father. He also lacks family models of interculturalism, since his parents are assimilationists. Instead of celebrating her multiculturalism, his mother represses her Spanish identity, and acts Arab in Algeria and French in France. ("My mother married an Algerian, and if you marry an Arab, there is a sacrifice to be made ... you have to completely leave your culture and your family.") His sister, married to a cousin of their father and living in France, adopts an Arab lifestyle. His father assimilates to the milieu of Spanish-Portuguese concierges.

Zenon's life seems at an impasse. He says little about his childhood, his own situation, or his aspirations. Sadness pervades his separate accounts of family life and holidays, the discord between his parents, his mother's unrealised gift for singing, and his Spanish aunt's repressed life. In the interview, he treats himself as an afterthought, a sympathetic observer of other people's problems, which are surely projections for his own feelings of dislocation and unfulfilled potential.

He regrets the unhappiness he must have caused his mother when, returning from Spain as a small child, he called her "auntie". Her father had died in the Civil War in Spain in the 1930s, so that her life was "austere", and the four children had had to work. She wanted to be a lyrical singer, but she kept that "in the bottom of her throat", and now she even forgets she speaks Spanish unless he, Zenon, initiates it. She is resented in Spain for having married an Algerian, though in Algeria, where she veils herself, she is accepted.

Zenon considers his father unintelligent. He drinks, has had some girlfriends, and can be violent. As a small child, Zenon protected his sister from him, and now he watches over his mother. The father sometimes gets angry with Zenon, and Zenon is clearly angry with him: "He ought to know where he's coming from". However, just as Zenon considers his father "not really racist", so his anger is repressed under sympathy with his confusion:

> He who was born French in French Algeria, who married a Spaniard, who has had children who are of French nationality, a daughter who is married to an Algerian and a son who gets to a certain age and is more European. I know that in his head, as well with the problems happening in Algeria nowadays, I know that in his head everything is mixed, so he, in my opinion,

> he doesn't have any bearings.... So that can be very painful, painful psychically, he can't know where he's from any more. Also he's unemployed.

The family does not fight or clarify disagreements. Zenon does not even mention any adolescent rebellion. A culture of removal and avoidance predominates, and both generations are deeply ambivalent, even fatalistic, towards cultural cleavages. Zenon's father was removed from the dangers from the Algerian war, but he did not thrive on this protection. Being wrenched away from his home territory and connections, removed from the working out of political loyalties in the turmoil of the war of independence, and dropped unarmed in a hostile and racist colonial society must have been difficult enough for a young man of 17. In fact, he had been transposed to another set of conflicts between *colons* (long-standing French residents in Algeria, many quite working class), *harkis* (Algerians who sided with the French) and national liberationists. Zenon makes no mention of this. However, his grandparents' strategy of removing their son from the Algerian war was curiously similar to Zenon's father's avoidance of living in immigrant areas. The teenage concierge children, predominantly Spanish and Portuguese, doubtless confronted racism in the schools they attended. Yet they could stand aside from the racial conflicts surrounding North and West African, Caribbean, and other Dom–Tom communities (French overseas departments and territories). These conflicts intensified in the globalised 1990s context of Fortress Europe, and in the new civil war in Algeria. The family strategy of avoidance means that Zenon misses out on the social learning and identity struggles of immigrant areas, and on the supportive social processes that might help in fashioning an intercultural identity, in positioning and engaging himself in the Paris and France of his time.

Following his studies, Zenon still feels in a no-man's land. Now he can find no connection between the cultivated classes concerned with art and cinema and the most oppressed section of the working class, the foreigners in "little jobs" who are forced to work illegally. He has had an education, but no guidance or mentoring in making the transition into professional life, and no help in turning the family romance of music into a career. Nor has he been able to resolve in himself the gender fracture in the family, his sister joining the father's Algerian side of the family, while he himself is emotionally bound to his mother, her music and his Spanish aunt.

Zenon seems to live in a suspended state, with little sense of his own agency. He feels alone, but does not know why. He makes no mention of friends or of networks, of present work strategies, of his own future. Rather than looking forward, his interview ends with further regrets about his aunt in Spain, whom he still feels, perhaps, is his 'real' mother. Zenon regrets not visiting her for several years. Perhaps the pain was too great. Of the last time, he says:

> I looked at her and I thought she has many regrets ... because I think she knows she has forgotten something essential in her life – light, the joy of living.

Zenon finds the disjunctures of multiculturalism unbridgeable. In opposite ways, both he and Djamillah make manifest the considerable biographical resources that are necessary to work across and through cultural dissonance. Compared with Zenon, and despite the precariousness of her situation, Djamillah enjoys numerous advantages: a vibrant and accommodating family culture, a (possibly male-led) model of educational success and professional fulfilment, family support in fighting school and community racism, a sense of combative social solidarity with colleagues and clients in her community law work, and the social status of running a family household. Zenon has lacked supportive family and peer models in confronting racism and in entering a career. His removal from the social turmoil of multicultural society has caused him to avoid – rather than work through – the issues of identity involved in bridging three cultures. Cross-generational splits characterise his family life. Zenon's interview eloquently presents transculturalism as a problem rather than as a cause for celebration or a source of energy.

Steven, our next case, is still struggling with his development in a way that has eluded Zenon, though he is far from achieving Djamillah's assurance and professional success. His narrative provides a more intimate exploration of working through intercultural experience. He is a particularly reflective person, in some ways less well supported than Djamillah, but still guided by strongly partnered parents. He has to struggle against his parents' first-generation strategy of removal, and, like Zenon, lacks supportive male role models.

Steven

Steven's Afro-Caribbean parents prepared themselves carefully for having children. They were married for several years before Steven was born in 1971 (two daughters followed), and his mother rejected an opportunity for professional training on the grounds that she would be away too much from the family. Like many British migrants from the Caribbean, they worked for London Transport, where they met.

The late 1960s saw a growing tide of resistance in British Afro-Caribbean communities to discrimination in housing, employment, and especially education, and Steven's parents had prior experience of school problems. In 1968, they had taken in an orphaned 10-year-old nephew from the Caribbean, to enhance his educational chances. However, "All the teachers ever wanted him to do was play football because he was really good at football". After three years, he knew less than when he had arrived, and he was despatched back to the Caribbean. This threat of removal hung like a sword of Damocles over Steven, who knew his mother's decisiveness: "From the time that I was born her whole idea was, well, I'm not mucking about with you". In Steven's case the parents resisted the teachers' claim that Steven needed educational guidance for his 'disruptiveness', and moved him to a predominantly black private Baptist school, where he leapt ahead.

Many of Steven's reflections concern the extrication of his development from his parents' actions and strategies. His hesitancy suggests that he is still working out his own orientation, but that he appreciates his interdependency with his parents. His mother clearly tends to dominate, yet:

> She's not like, well, "If you don't do this, this is going to happen to you if you don't do". She's never been like that with me at all.... 'Cos like most things she says it takes me a while to kind of, erm, get 'em. But no, there's never any pressure from Mum and Dad and they're just like – like I said my Dad's just like – he's just like, yeah, really cool. It just all passes over him.... He's not particularly, um, concerned about it. Actually, that's a lie. He is. But he's like – he's just not as vocal, that's all. He worries. He does all the same things as my Mum does. It's like my Mum will just do it.

His accounts of his school and university experiences are similarly pensive. Somewhat mischievous at school, at Sunday school Steven was outright rebellious, letting off a stink-bomb during a service, burning a Christmas tree, daubing the church with paint. Steven himself does not theorise this particular incident, but as researchers we saw it as a response to the everyday violence that Steven and his friends sensed and were not able to tackle. The private institution that purportedly protected them from social discrimination was itself framed by a discriminatory and violent reality, and their 'separation' from outside society was pressurising. Finding a way back into the mainstream, forging a more multicultural set of connections, becomes quite a challenge at a later stage.

If removal is one aspect of his parents' anti-discrimination strategy, another is individual self-reliance. When 13-year-old Steven becomes involved in producing a sci-fi magazine with friends at school, and "It dawned on me one day that I was the only person working on the magazine", his mother's response is "You've got certain talents, you don't need anyone". Yet working cooperatively in a team is a prerequisite of the media industry, so that this training in individualism becomes a handicap. It has always been hard to confront his mother directly, but Steven does hold his own against a teacher at the age of 14. Fascinated with religious and philosophical questions, which were argued out in a special discussion group, Steven was furious when the teacher burst out, "Oh stop questioning, just believe". Parents and other teachers complained about this, and the teacher suggested that Steven write an article for the school magazine. Having his opinion published was "one of the biggest experiences".

Making his way out of his parents' ethnic cocoon was a key experience at sixth-form college.

> There was a lot of white kids, there was Asian kids, there was Chinese kids. And they all had, you know, different ways of, you know, doing things.... A long, long common room, the black kids would be there like and then in the middle just about there you'd get like all the Asian kids ... Chinese kids, all

the little mix-ups, you'd just keep going round like that. And then, right at
the front table was always – would be all the white kids.

His account of making friends with a white student is equally graphic and
moving. Implicitly, this involves overcoming his parents' assumption of the
inevitability of white prejudice:

> He was really abrupt, such an abrupt nature, but I was fascinated·by him, I
> don't know why…. I was just like, "Oh, you collect science fiction". He was
> like "'Oh, yeah, yeah!", and then I started telling him what I liked and he goes
> "Oh, that's crap, that's rubbish". But instead of doing like my usual I'd be –
> I'd have just walked off or something but I just sat there and we just ended up
> talking, and even though we had totally opposing views on a lot of things it
> was just really fun being able to talk to him.

He is thrilled by multicultural relationships:

> You just start making friends and you start getting on with people instead of
> like having preconceived notions and going along with whatever everybody
> else has been telling you. You just kind of like get on with them. And now
> I've got such a mixed bag of friends. It is unbelievable.

At university and in his search for employment, Steven has been plagued by
two conflicts: between his own creative interests and market pressures, on the
one hand, and between being both self-directed and a flexible team worker on
the other. The media industry seemed alluring in the late 1980s: "It seemed
like anybody who was in the media business was just earning tons and tons of
money". A new tutor in the third year adopted a market orientation, "making
public relations for Marks and Spencers kind of thing", but Steven was thinking,
"No. I'm at college". He wanted to be creative and was busily reading about
science fiction. Receiving a worse mark than those who had chosen a
commercial theme gave him "the worst day I've ever had".

Despite having gained the highest marks in the class in the tightly directed
first year, the switch into the second was like "swimming in jelly". "All of a
sudden you were like well, am I here, am I there? What's going on?" He
developed a phobia of going on the underground, which was also his parents'
workplace. As researchers attempting to interpret this phobia, we reflected on
the underground as a system of moving on, requiring trust that there is a fully
planned and functioning system, that there will be guidance at decisive points,
that there will be ways of dealing with unforeseen problems. Steven felt lost in
the more openly structured second year, though eventually he overcame these
difficulties and completed the degree.

> The graduation was like three weeks later, and I really enjoyed it…. I don't
> think I was over it but I just kind of like thought, "Well, I've got it, I've got a
> degree". That's what I came here for.

After his graduation Steven was shocked by the difficulty of getting a job: "It
was like, 'Well, okay, you've got some interesting work but, erm, what experience
have you got?'" A relationship with a girlfriend broke up: "I was completely
numb … just yombified for about a few months". He worked for a science
fiction bookseller, but was given mundane jobs, often cleaning and often in an
unheated warehouse. His mother rang up to protest when he was sacked after
he had been off work with 'flu. This was another step in developing more
independence from his mother:

> I really wanted to feel bad about the fact that I'd lost this job but I just did –
> I tried so hard to make myself feel really bad and I didn't. It was really amazing.
> I was, I was more scared of the fact that I didn't feel bad about it.

This seemed to be a turning point, since, based on a friend's recommendation
of his personal communication skills, he then got an interviewing job at a
research agency, which he combined with pursuing science fiction. He seemed
now to have a much stronger sense of self. He was getting on well with his
colleagues and supervisors, their ethnic background did not seem to be an
issue, and he was able to try different strategies and to find solutions.

Steven gives a nuanced account of his struggle to find an independent and
transcultural alternative to his parents' strategy of defiant protectionism. It is a
moving chronicle or *Bildungsroman* of the personal travails of a second-generation
black British young man moving through childhood, teenage, student and
young adult years in the context of Britain in the 1970s, 1980s and 1990s.
Because he is so reflective, but also still so involved in finding his own way in
life, he vividly depicts the milestone experiences, and his choices and decisions.
As we felt with Djamillah, the strands of personal emotional development, an
emerging transcultural space and social discrimination are intimately intertwined.
Steven's growing sense of personal agency is achieved interactively with his
familial and sociopolitical context.

Both Steven and Zenon might be helped by stronger male role models,
within their families and as professional mentors. The 'crisis of working-class
masculinity', which is discussed in several other chapters in this book (see
Chapters Five, Six and Seven) is often couched in terms of the shift to
deindustrialisation, the service economy and network society. That there is a
particularly complex story to be uncovered among Afro-Caribbeans is clear
from persistent patterns of educational failure, unemployment, crime, and mental
illness. Mary Chamberlain's oral history research (1998) suggests that the
humiliation of first-generation black men in British society may have been
especially pernicious. She quotes a 30-year-old woman who had visited
Barbados in 1976 after 20 years in Britain:

I'll never forget this feeling.... Do you know what really got me? The men ... I'm seeing these men. They're tall. Black men in England aren't tall, they're not erect, they're always working as if they've got a burden.... These men look(ed) so proud.... I think the black man in Britain has lost out as a result of living in a culture that is ... alien and hostile.... If you're proud in England, and you're black, you're seen as uppity, or having a chip on your shoulder. (Chamberlain, 1998, p 54)

Neither Zenon nor Steven construct their biographies in terms of a fight against discrimination, even though their main difficulties in education and employment, and in the dynamics of their family situations, manifestly result from living in a racist society. Zenon and Steven are not unaware of racism, but they want to take responsibility for their own situations. It is also a moot point whether casting their position in terms of 'discrimination' would be helpful for either of them. Steven's biographical work has been of a much deeper nature than would normally be associated with anti-discrimination work. It illustrates well the point made by Gunaratnam and Lewis (2001) that anti-discrimination policies are limited unless they tackle underlying emotions, such as fears, anger, envy and shame. Although such feelings often paralyse interracial interventions, they are as yet far from policy agendas.

Conclusion

This chapter began by celebrating the new social spaces and political openings that transculturalism brings to Europe. Djamillah and Steven show awareness of its exciting potential, and huge determination and energy to achieve intercultural lives. However, both their and Zenon's narratives also convey the difficulties that may be involved in second-generation experience. Zenon is impeded by internal uncertainties, and Steven demonstrates the laborious process that may be involved in reconciling inner and outward worlds sufficiently to 'live one's life from within'. Even Djamillah, whose life is inventively transcultural, is in a precarious and constrained situation.

Bhavnani characterises identity as a "complex kind of sedimentation", that we rehistoricise though story-telling practices.

Those story-telling practices themselves are ways of trying to interrogate, get at, the kinds of encounters, historical moments, the kinds of key moments of transition for us – both individually and collectively. (Bhavnani and Haraway, 1994, p 21)

Hesse (2000) uses the term 'transruptions' to capture cross-time processes of cultural unsettlement. These concepts characterise well the biographical work that our subjects have been undertaking in their lives, work that they continue in their interviews.

Intergenerational family strategies, themselves intertwined with political and social histories, were a key factor in processing racial conflict and cultural fracturing in the second-generation setting. Djamillah was supported by a family tradition of working conflicts through, and by, her father's sacrificing of his own status for the sake of his children's. She was both supported and constrained by her closeness to her father. Family dynamics were more negatively rooted in removal and avoidance in Zenon's case, and Steven had to struggle to extricate himself from his parents', and particularly his mother's, strategy of protective closure and self-reliance.

The achieving of transculturalism is not just an individual or family affair, and while second-generation sharing of experience was not explicitly discussed by the interviewees, we sensed its direct presence in the cases of Djamillah and Steven, and its availability in Zenon's case, were he to be open to and identified with it. How social policy might give more support to the difficult process of achieving transculturalism requires some imaginative thinking. One approach might be to find ways of recreating the intense sharing of the forging of new self- and collective understandings and identities, which have been so fruitful among ethnic minority feminists and intellectuals, and in new social movements more generally. These are issues to which we return in Chapter Fifteen of this volume.

Notes

[1] In her fascinating book, *Strange encounters* (2000, pp 22-4), Sarah Ahmed discusses (mis-)recognising the other/stranger as central to the forming of subjectivity.

[2] However, treating ethnic minority members as the key protagonists of multiculturalism omits the much bigger process of challenging 'white' identity in the population at large.

[3] Warm thanks to Yasmin Gunaratnam for comments on this and several other key points in this chapter.

References

Ahmed, S. (2000) *Strange encounters: Embodied others in post-coloniality*, London: Routledge.

Bhavnani, K.-K. and Phoenix, A. (1994) *Shifting identities, shifting racisms: A feminism and psychology reader*, London: Sage Publications.

Bhavnani, K.-K. and Haraway, D. (1994) 'Shifting the subject: a conversation between Kum-Kum Bhavnani and Donna Haraway on 12 April 1993, Santa Cruz, California', in K-K. Bhavnani and A. Phoenix (eds) *Shifting identities, shifting racisms: A feminism and psychology reader*, London: Sage Publications, pp 19-39.

Brah, A. (1996) *Cartographies of diaspora: Contesting identities*, London: Routledge.

Braidotti, R. (1994) *Nomadic subjects: Embodiment and sexual difference in contemporary feminist theory*, New York, NY: Columbia University Press.

Chamberlain, M. (1998) 'I belong to whoever wants me', *New Formations*, no 33, pp 47-58.

Davis, K. and Lutz, H. (2000) 'Life in theory: three feminist thinkers on transition(s)', *The European Journal of Women's Studies*, vol 7, pp 367-78.

Gunaratnam, Y. and Lewis, G. (2001) 'Racialised emotional labour and emotionalising racialised labour: anger, fear and shame in social welfare', *Journal of Social Work Practice*, vol 15, no 2, pp 131-48.

Hall, S. (1996) 'Introduction: who needs identity?', in S. Hall and P. du Gay (eds) *Cultural identity*, London: Sage Publications.

Hall, S. (2000) 'Conclusion: the multi-cultural question', in B. Hesse (ed) *Un/settled multiculturalisms: Diasporas, entanglements, transruptions*, London: Zed Books, pp 209-41.

Hesse, B. (ed) (2000) *Un/settled multiculturalisms: Diasporas, entanglements, transruptions*, London: Zed Books.

Lutz, H., Phoenix, A. and Yuval-Davis, N. (1995) *Crossfires: Nationalism, racism and gender in Europe*, London: Pluto.

Mama, A. (1995) *Beyond the masks: Race, gender and subjectivity*, London: Routledge.

Rupp, S. (1999) 'Living between two cultures', *Sostris Working Paper 4: Case study materials – ethnic minorities and migrants*, London: Centre for Biography in Social Policy, University of East London, pp 40-55.

FOURTEEN

Biographical work and agency innovation: relationships, reflexivity and theory-in-use

Tom Wengraf

Introduction

Why do people do what they do? What policies could improve our understanding of what people need at key points of their life?

> A colleague once recalled his satisfaction when, after weeks of painstaking advocacy for a recently bereaved woman, he had helped her to resolve her housing problems. But then, on the eve of gaining her new tenancy, she killed herself. (Froggett, 2002, pp 9-10)

Only her personal history would tell us why the sort of help that was being offered was not the sort of help that at that moment was most important for her to receive. We can, however, speculate that, for her, the crucial transition was not that of 'a transition into better housing' but some 'transition into widowhood' that the available support was not addressing. In retrospect, her priority needs were 'misrecognised' (see Chapter Thirteen of this volume).

The chapters so far have focused on the question of 'difficult transitions' (predictable and unpredictable). Difficult transitions occur at different points in an individual's and a family's life course (for example, school–work, country–country, couple–parent, worker–non-worker). Although they are experienced by the individual or family in singular ways, they are only fully understandable if they (and we) take into account both long-term trends and dynamics and also sudden collective events of the macro-history and context of the society in which they are living: sudden wars, deindustrialisation, removal of protections for labour, transformation and loss of state welfare regimes for personal protection and support, changes of state rules and practices, sickness, changes in the balance of gender relations at home and at work, and so on.

However, knowing all this does not excuse us from understanding how the same collective trends and events can enter differently into each person's individual history. How did all these trends, dynamics and sudden collective events enter into this woman's decision to kill herself?

At any given moment, each person has been formed by their previous life history and choices and now can, has to, re-form them again. Constructed by their previous biography, they have to reconstruct. To come to terms with these life transitions, individuals are constantly under pressure *to do* biographical work.

What do we mean by 'doing biographical work'? As well as struggling to ensure sufficient continuity, it can involve changing oneself, one's practice, one's self-understanding and relationships, one's understanding of our life world and our life so far – in ways that are by no means obvious nor achieved by a simple effort of individual will (but in ways that we hope this volume has illuminated).

Having completed our Sostris case interviews, we looked for organisations doing work 'in the spirit of' our approach to social exclusion and its prevention. We were looking for agencies that conceived these risks in the way that we did, in person-centred and individualised terms, and that – although they might include the provision of material help or supportive care – were committed primarily to developing the 'strategies' and the personal resources and resourcefulness of their clients, to help them do what we call biographical work.

Despite being rather sceptical initially as to whether we would find such organisations in sufficient number and variety, we were very excited to find many working in the same direction.

Although social agencies are not individuals, our methodology for studying these agencies continued to be biographical–narrative in character. We wanted to see whether, with an organisation, too, story-telling would be productive. We wanted to experiment with the 'lived life'/'told story' methodology, adapting it to the understanding of an institution[1].

National teams conducted biographic–narrative interviews with the individual founders and/or leading members of the (often small) teams involved, and/or typical members of front-line staff and/or clients. They were asked to tell the history of how they came to be involved in the organisation (or set up the organisation) and what happened after that. Where they could, the national teams also collected self-presentational documents produced by the institution and engaged in some (very limited) observation.

Within a common commitment to 'capacity-building' and to facilitating personal transitions, we found a great variety of organisational forms and practices, some manifestly very effective, and some less so or even counter-productive. We found that the successful organisations were primarily those concerned with 'innovating':

- both in their *internal relations* (staff/staff, staff/client, client/client, the role of volunteers) and in their *external relations* (organisation/partners/ neighbourhood);

and also

- with working constantly on *the relation between the two*, in what we might call a biography-narrating and biographically reflexive way.

> **Our findings may be summarised as follows:**
>
> - Biographical narrating was our method of research; it also turned out to be a feature of successful helping organisations.

Of the original 13 institutional studies, I present one exemplary case: a community centre in Bromley-by-Bow, London, which embodies a variety of positive features[2]. I consider more general issues in the second part of this chapter, theorising this case in part by comparing its features with those of some other cases.

I. The Bromley-by-Bow Centre[3]

Keeping the 'social' in social entrepreneurship

New initiatives require initiators. To fit into the dominant neoliberal discourse, and perhaps foster government and business support, the term used in England is 'social entrepreneurs'. However, though the term always lends itself to – and is very much pushed towards – such a limited understanding, the notion of social entrepreneurship is not just shorthand for 'being a business entrepreneur in a not-for-profit context'. Social entrepreneurship involves a mobilisation of social resources that often cannot be mobilised by – and are even demobilised by, and sometimes can only be mobilised *against* – the search for private corporate profit by business entrepreneurs and corporations or a regime of top-down state bureaucracy. For a collective to function as a social entrepreneur, the entrepreneurial process has to focus on mobilising the 'social', enabling it to mobilise and develop itself.

Bromley-by-Bow is a 'whole community' in a deprived and demoralised part of London. In this context, social entrepreneurship denotes a newly creative relationship between the business and social sectors organised to promote innovative action at the community level. In a highly diverse and divided area, the centre welcomes all local people who wish to participate. As the primary source of energy and outreach, it has a *volunteering base*: individuals help those worse off and develop themselves in the process, occasionally becoming part- or full-time workers if they so wish, and thereby fulfilling the general strategy of:

(a) overcoming internal boundaries and community divisions; and
(b) promoting individual initiative and eventual group reflexivity.

The intertwining of the two facets, local activities and business sponsorship, arose pragmatically. Starting from a near-derelict Church and church building in 1984, Andrew Mawson – the newly appointed United Reform Church minister – had by 1990 developed a thriving set of community activities.

Mawson had long considered public services 'a Sargasso sea' of bureaucracy and self-serving professionalism that actively created poverty. "The word was made flesh, not minutes!" he declares. Emblematic of this frustration was, for a parent in the community dying of cancer, the fact that there was no provision by the state statutory services of any adequate support for her or her family. Given this failure or abdication by the state, members and volunteers from the centre organised ongoing care, and became involved in the conflictual negotiations concerning which aunt should become the children's guardian. In the course of this, an offer of caring help from a deeply disturbed and childless woman (who was convinced *she* was called to be the children's guardian) was originally rejected by the volunteers. Negotiating that conflict, leading the volunteers to understand the woman's distress, finding ways of accepting and using her desire for social engagement to break the pattern of ostracism and exclusion (which was achieved through a gardening project and much group discussion), is also emblematic of the centre's work. Nobody who wants to join is to be excluded. As the second director, Alison Trimble, puts it:

> Whatever baggage there is has to be included and managed.

From the collective caring for the woman dying of cancer sprang the idea of a locally owned health centre. Starting off in prefabricated huts, this clinic moved into a beautifully designed new building in 1998. By that time, it had attracted government attention as a model of an arts-based 'healthy living centre' and was extolled in a government Green Paper on public health.

Narrations and stories (such as that of the woman dying of cancer) are central to the identity and functioning of the project. They are the main means by which its development and approach are explained to others, both outsiders and insiders.

One of the day centre workers, who started off as a bored housewife whose playgroup had collapsed, moved through a women's DIY group, to a mosaics and pottery class, to National Vocational Qualification training in welfare rights and business – "I've done a lot with me life in 10 years", she says. Her daughters, meanwhile, joined art, woodwork, drama, music and gardening activities, and both performed live on stage "with all the stars", and her husband became a community transport driver.

> Once you're in, it's like a family. Once you're in, you're in. You'd come back every day and every day there's something new.... I call this place the web, you get in and you don't wanna get out.

A primary technique is that of drawing vulnerable people into activities by inviting them to give help to those who are even more vulnerable to exclusion. This community work method, which builds on local people's personal understandings of what it is to be 'down' and dependent on their skills for survival, has so far turned out to be work done mainly (but not exclusively) by and with women[4].

Crossing boundaries

As has been said, the project began in and around the church building. With 45 languages spoken in the area, a multitude of religions are represented among the participants. Religion represents openness, a person-centred approach, and a way of accessing different levels of personal experience and reality. Andrew Mawson sees this in the children's games and dressing up in the church nursery, constantly changing their identities and on the edge of danger, shifting between benign and frightening situations, surprising and being surprised.

One of the project workers relates her response when realising she was being helped by, rather than helping, a disabled person:

> I thought, "How do you do pottery?" … I was dreading it…. And this guy in a wheelchair amazed me … he just said to me "Sit there. I'll demonstrate", and he just talked me through it as if he was my teacher … and I was amazed. I thought, "I've come here to help somebody with his disability who is sitting there teaching me what to do", and that's when I thought I really like this place.

Crossing boundaries is also the way the day centre manager describes the way the artists work with service users. The very emphasis on garden and architectural design, fountains, sculpture and paintings that one encounters at every turn in the centre already breaks the boundaries of an ordinary community centre in a deprived area. Such reorganisation of the material elements of 'routine living' in a deprived area, the organisation of 'unusual inside events and outside trips', are part of providing and permitting innovations in lived lives, changing the stories that can be told.

The centre's openness and willingness to cross boundaries can also be very difficult for the project workers themselves:

> One of the people who was probably one of the most racist women I've met here would lead her children out of school when Bengalis songs were being sung. She used to come with me on the bus to pick people up from the community, welcome the person, bring them out of the house, and bring them onto the bus. She wouldn't do it with this one Bengali man and the question for me was, well, what do I do?… And I remember one day we were in the hall and this man had just had a stroke and he could only communicate by stamping his hands and his feet, and he wasn't feeling very well, and I just

said to this woman, the first person that I saw, just sit for a minute while I find someone to take him home, just sit with him till I sort something out. And I rushed off, hadn't realised – well I realised when I said it that it was this women who wouldn't even go to his house…. And I came back half an hour later and saw her sitting there stroking one of his hands and talking to him quietly … and after that she would get out of the bus and go and pick him up every morning, and so that pattern was broken. Now if we'd said "You're being racist, either do it or don't take part", we would have lost the opportunity. It's a bit like allowing space for somebody to grow, really.

The day centre manager contrasted the emphasis at the centre on communication, much of it generated through arts work that "gets the creative juices going", with the personal isolation characteristic of a residential home. He remarks on the excitement of seeing people in the day care sessions "visibly change. That's quality, that's touching people at the core of their being really, and people are feeling good … and they've had a good time". He came to the project from a local authority social services department, where "my work environment was pretty miserable. And I was struck by how happy people were here…. They seemed to enjoy their work", including those who had worked at the project for many years.

In the opinion of those involved, what helps this to happen?

Giving time and space

'Giving space' is a key theme in the centre's approach to personal and leadership development. Allison Trimble describes how she arrived to take up her post armed with a sheaf of ideas. Her designated role was to "help mothers in the nursery to connect with other parts of the project [and to] enable the women to become involved".

On my first day Andrew, he's the chief executive, said to me, "Well your job is a blank sheet of paper, and you call it how you want, we've got funding for it, for you to set up some projects, and there's lots of needs". When I came for my interview I had a book about that thick, full of ideas and things, and I got the job, and he says, "Put that book on a shelf for a moment, in a drawer, and after three months of hanging around, have another look at it, and then decide what you want to do"…. I never looked at it again.

Personal space allows staff to think about 'principles' and not obsessively implement 'policies'. The six key principles are:

- flexibility;
- creativity;
- quality;
- pragmatism;

- backing people;
- rhythms.

Principles are agreed through discussion, but allow a certain fluidity in their translation, a 'dancing either side of the line', the crucial process through which the local survival-oriented 'rip-off' culture becomes broken by experience of the rewards of giving and trusting. These are messy and very personal transitions, which have to be worked through and managed by people themselves. Understanding such work, and providing the time and space needed for it, is an essential part of leadership.

In the face of obstacles, the project's response is to have brainstorming sessions. Such sessions – 'cluster meetings' – are typical of the project's organisational structures that develop around particular projects and, while designating responsibilities, avoid primary reliance on formal hierarchies. This approach involves understanding the circles of oppression within which those with power often block the pathways for others to change. Allowing space involves taking risks, but by no means involves a relinquishing of responsibility. As embodied in the story of Trimble's initiation by Mawson related earlier, the leader has to model the mode of relating, the style of being and task handling, to be promoted within the organisation.

An explicit mechanism for the right sort of different 'internal relations'[5] is the provision of space for experiment and reflexivity:

(a) for the community as a whole;
(b) for the volunteers (a place to combine freely self-developing and other-focused activities);
(c) for full-time staff (principles rather than policies, support for staff, collective brainstorming and experimentation);
(d) to allow an enormous amount of informal working with individuals in trouble, even if this means that some other priorities have to be set aside.

2. What questions and issues arise?

We have considered the case of one innovative organisation. Sostris's full report (Sostris, 1999) on innovatory organisations covers some 13 organisations in seven countries. What more general questions and issues arise?

The impulse to innovate: origins

All innovative initiatives require strongly committed individual or collective entrepreneurs to perceive a need for something new and to work towards it. Where do they come from? How does one imagine the possibility that there *could* be an alternative, that the story does not *have* to be like this?

A small, ideologically motivated group seems to be a precondition. The ideological motivation appears often to be that of religious or political 'activism', or simply 'humanitarian frustration'. The outburst of one Spanish professional is quite representative:

> I'm desperate about being in a structure with no way out. We are becoming bureaucrats dealing only with files, not allowed to take decisions even if we see things which should be changed or improved. (Tejero et al, 1999, p 107).

In general, the direct experience both of glaring need and of the uselessness of existing provision is what helps to produce the 'innovatory impulse'.

However, this is not sufficient, otherwise all frustrated personal service and community workers would have transformed their organisations or created new ones. If secular or religious ideology is part of the imagining, it is only the start. Once an alternative *has* been imagined, what else has to be envisaged and accomplished?

Mobilising human and funding resources: networking

Successful network mobilisation

For innovative initiatives to take off, the originators must be able to find sufficient and mobile human and funding resources for what they are trying to do. This means building alliances, enlisting energies, attracting funds, compelling the interest of possible local partner institutions. The capacity to do this varies immensely. Being located close to the heart of the City of London has probably been crucial for attracting sponsorship for the Bromley-by-Bow project. The promoter of the Bauhof youth training programmes in Halle, East Germany, was already part of the Protestant Church and when the 'challenge' of the West German devastation of the East German economy left the authorities struggling in the early 1990s to find viable interlocutors and entrepreneurs to fight against the rising tide of structural adjustment unemployment, such respectable non-political affiliation was important[6]. Both in the Spanish neighbourhood networks[7] and in the London Camden Refugee Education Project[8], the support or initiative of existing or former social workers with a network of contacts in local government and local organisations and communities was crucial for alliance building. In Sweden, the head of the Gothenburg Women's Resource Centre was a veteran of the municipal administration and a woman with considerable networks and personal influence with central departments of the municipal government[9].

The Camden Refugee Education Project (REP) emerged from one-person lobbying action (which then became a four-person pressure group) that concentrated on the Camden Education Services. The project felt it was important to enable refugee community parents to help 'educate' the local schoolteachers whose personal experience and whose training had given them no preparation for handling the needs of children in families fleeing war, persecution, torture and generally appalling and traumatic conditions. The Camden REP mediated between teachers, the parents in the refugee communities, and other social services, thereby enabling individual case handling and collective understanding to be considerably improved. A Camden education officer remarked:

> Whatever the shortcomings of the work they do, it's in many cases unique to have such a dedicated and coherent approach towards the settlement of refugee children ... and the active attempt to involve refugee communities in educating our existing staff and other Camden employees. (Kowarzik, 1999)

Another feature of successful organisations is their concern to have more than a local resonance, to spread news of their mission and their methodology to a national level. For example, the Camden REP struggled to 'spread the word', to find an pan-London and even national resonance for its research and development work. Despite its minimal resources, it nonetheless has done much to raise consciousness beyond its London borough about refugee children, and in 1997 the project received the prestigious 'Race Award' from the UK Commission for Racial Equality.

Perhaps the most successful agency in our study was the Italian Development of the South agency (Caniglia and Spanò, 1999). If social entrepreneurship means transforming the personal culture of significant numbers of people in the target population, this can only be seriously addressed by creating network structures (structures of collectivity) in which normal depressing relationships are replaced by energy-promoting ones. This project, aimed at developing youth entrepreneurship in the Italian South, started with individualised working (advertising for and finding individual youth entrepreneurs). In a second phase, it promoted the regional networks of actors and institutions within which any individual would-be youth entrepreneurs would find support. It discovered that the key to the liberating of individual energies was transforming the networks of relationships in which such individual entrepreneurs would find themselves. The project led to new national legislation that further transformed the possibilities of local action.

Unsuccessful attempts

Not all innovations 'take'. Why not?

The social worker who attempted to get the gypsy children begging at traffic lights in central Athens into education found herself faced by (a) the extreme disinterest of the police and the school authorities, all of whom prefer 'not to know' that these children are not undertaking the schooling that is theoretically compulsory; (b) the tacit hostility of many of the parents of the children for whom the children's takings represent all or often the lion's share of 'the family wage'; (c) the disinterest of Greek institutions in funding or supporting such 'non-Greek minorities'. These local networks mobilised against her. She had no allies (Mestheneos and Ioannidi, 1999).

Another attempt to innovate, the Watch for Women's Rights set up in Athens by women from different political parties, depended on the political fortunes of its female politician leader and on a three-year EU grant. There seemed to be no connection between its research function and its drop-in or phone-in Social Services Bureau. Volunteers were neither selected nor trained, nor perhaps particularly supervised, mentored or supported. The end of EU funding probably meant its disappearance. The organisation, though small, had no internal mutually supportive relationships (Mestheneos and Ioannidi, 1999).

The French municipal politicians who insisted on the creation of a Municipal Advice Centre in a disadvantaged area of a town near Paris did not even attempt to gain the participation of such local interest groups and organisations as there were (only 'big' politicians were invited to the opening). They did not even gain the support of the different municipal services that were supposed to staff the advice centre. They designed the building in such a way that there were no rooms large enough for local groups to meet or small enough for one-to-one interviews to take place. Neither internal nor external relations were attended to (Murard, 1999).

Less successful organisations often failed to mobilise a sufficient 'external network' of personal and organisational support, either from the community of actual and potential clients, or from government (local or central), business or the social sector. If being part of a network is a vital way in which *individuals* avoid social exclusion, it also seems that being part of a network – or building a network – of material and emotional-intellectual support is vital also for *organisations*. In some cases, would-be organisations were struggling to avoid the fate of being as 'excluded' as the clients they wished to serve. They were – often through no fault of their own – limited in their external networking capability.

Some of the less successful organisations had inappropriate external *and* internal relationships. They had either virtually no inter-organisational network to provide partner support (such as the Greek gypsy children agency) or, being locked too tightly in a subordinated position, had insufficient autonomy. In addition, they operated without any realisation that, to change the 'capacities' of the people they intended to help, they needed different internal social relations from those 'normally prevailing'.

Between funding regimes and internal regimes: are there transmission belts or buffers?

In general, the funding regime is liable to dictate the limits of the management's capacity to relate well to the front-line workers. This relation, in turn, is liable to dictate the limits of how the front-line workers (individually and collectively) are able to relate well to their clients (individual and collective).

Perpetual emergencies block long-term thinking. The funding regime of the Bauhof in Halle means that only a one-man 'mastership' holds the centrifugal forces of yearly funded projects together, and the lack of transparency means a further drain of coherence. A harsh, output-oriented funding regime tends to prevent creative thinking – or even any serious thinking at all. Panic and chaotic emergencies prevail.

Where the state imposes short-term behavioural targets on those who tender for funding (the typical pattern of Anglo-Saxon contractualism), then such short-term behavioural compliance *can* become what management dictates to its workers and what the workers furiously dictate to their furious and frustrated clients[10]. Neither disempowered nor falsely empowered staff can support the genuine self-empowerment of clients.

The context of social relations between management and front-line staff does not *dictate* the way relations between actual agents and actual clients work. They just render some *more probable* than others. Institutional leadership is a crucial variable: will outside pressures be simply transmitted or complexly contained (for the latter concept, see Stokes, 1994)? Much depends – particularly within a targets-and-audit-maddened general culture (such as that of the UK) – on the management regime's ability and readiness to provide a buffer, to protect their front-line agents' capacity for getting to know their clients as persons, to give them time and space and knowledge to work biographically.

What individual and group work helps clients in organisations?

Some organisations that do work biographically (at least in part) focus largely on an individual professional 'relating to' an individual client. This is the case of the Bauhof in Halle, where a fortunately generous provision of social workers (1:10) supports the biographical work of the troubled youths as they continue with their employment training. There are bimonthly case conferences in which all the staff involved review the progress of the case with the individual concerned (Breckner et al, 1999). The same concept of professional–client relationship marks the rather less successful Athens Social Services Bureau of the Watch for Women's Rights. Here, unfortunately, there is an inadequate supply of appropriate professionals – no psychologist or social worker, only a lawyer, and no case meetings (Mestheneos and Ioannidi, 1999).

Given the high cost of paid professional to individual work, this pattern of professional–individual casework (as in the UK before the 1980s, and in some German *sozialpädagogik*) is not likely to be the main way in which, most of the time, innovative organisations can allow themselves to work.

A more economical use of scarce resources is that of *facilitated group work*. In the form of a formally distinguished special activity, this was rare. We found it far more frequently – as in the Bromley-by-Bow practice, and the practice of most peer-support organisations (such as the Spanish neighbourhood networks) – as a practice as far as possible *normalised* into the ordinary working of task-oriented groups. Volunteers learn to function as informal mentors to new volunteers (the case of the Bengali woman discussed later in this chapter) and informal counselling is done by a variety of people.

Whether virtually unfunded (such as the LETS scheme in Barcelona), or very conditionally funded (like the German Bauhof), or relatively core-funded (like the Bromley-by-Bow Centre), the most promising organisations were those that provided a matrix of social relations for innovative action by the targeted population. They worked to replace depressing individualised social relations by mutually self-helping and other-helping reflexive social relations. For the professionals in them, a crucial task, perhaps the primary process task, was to model and support expressive, reflexive and relationship-focused sensitivity among the volunteering pioneers from the 'client' community.

Mentoring/modelling styles of relating: peers and leadership

It is implicit in what has been said so far that a major function of the strong 'part-time volunteer structure' of the more successful projects was the development of de facto individual or small-group mentoring, not usually known by that name. Sometimes hidden behind a concept of 'peer support', or institutionalised as 'mentoring', the modelling of good practice and the provision of space and resources for a caring relationship between mentor and mentored (individual or small-group collective) was often critical in fostering the belief that: "If she could do it, I could do it, too".

An example of how volunteers are recruited – often by one another – is a Bromley-by-Bow Bengali outreach worker's account of how she developed a sewing class.

> We got no money to open the sewing class.... So then I've been to the local – to find out from people mouth-to-mouth – the factory there. Then I asked for the cotton, I asked for the material, and then one day I found out about a machine, from an old class. So with one machine or two machines I started my first class. I am not a qualified teacher you know, I only know basic sewing, so I myself was both a sewing teacher with two or three ladies and an outreach worker. So then after a few months, one lady said that she would like to come to my women's group, and her sewing is better than me, so I said do you mind if you help me as a voluntary worker in the same class, so she is a voluntary worker without money for two or three weeks. And then I find out from the project about £5 for voluntary work so I give her £5 and then she helping.

Negative cases involve the refusal of relationship. The Foyer is a project for unqualified homeless youth in East London[11]. Originally, it felt no need for staff with any relational skills in order to cope with people it saw just as tenants; consequently, its untrained, unskilled and poorly paid staff were unable to deal with the human difficulties of the Foyer's troubled young people. An accommodation officer at the Foyer insisted, counter-productively, that they were here to manage space not the person:

> I don't want it to be like I'm their father or their uncle, but just as somebody who has a responsibility to manage this space.... When you've got people [who are] absent from their families and missing God-knows-what and life is very, very confusing ... the last thing I want is confusion of roles as to what somebody like me is here for. (Petrie, 1999, p 17)

Such a desperate demand for a non-fuzzy role is at the other end of the spectrum from awareness that all relations are fuzzy. The question is whether this *inevitable* fuzziness of interpersonal relationships is accepted and worked with, or (as in this case) denied. At the Foyer, the accommodation officer's denial of the fuzzy realities meant that he could not do his work. What model of 'persons' do organisations have?

3. Our conception of the person controls our understanding of the task

Less successful organisations conceived of their work with those 'at risk' in a partial and non-holistic way. Sometimes this involved seeing their clients merely as 'tenants' or as 'claimants', or in some part-object way. Sometimes they did attempt to work with 'the whole person' but saw the person in shallow 'behaviouristic terms' (teaching tenant reliability or work discipline), abstracting from the biography of the whole person and their milieu. These tended to be unsatisfying both for front-line staff and for clients. They had a behaviouristic – and not a biographical – approach to the person, or 'subject'.

Froggett (2002) identifies four levels at which the 'subject of social policy' is imagined and operates:

> *First*, at the macro level, most public debate about the welfare state is in terms of *social and economic relations*, and the political intentions and conflicts behind policy and opinion formation.

> *Second* [imagined subjects of social policy] are reproduced in the *institutional culture* directly implicated in welfare provision, the values that inform them, and in formal and informal representations of help and helping.

> *Third*, they are reflected in *interpersonal relationships* between people. A growing body of service evaluation attests to the fact that the quality of the helping relationship is at least as important as practical and financial assistance.

> *Fourth*, they become bound to *intra-psychic* material. Helping relationships imply particular states of mind which mobilise different socially structured defences. The relative neglect of this dimension has entailed a silence about

> the ways in which welfare arrangements affect how, or whether, we become responsible caring subjects. It also means we are deprived of a language in which to speak of the irrational, chaotic, fearful experiences that accompany the sociologically defined categories of exclusion, poverty or disadvantage. (Froggett, 2002, p 17, emphasis original)

Developing an institution devoted to helping the socially excluded or those in danger of such exclusion involves understanding the implications for the 'irrational, chaotic, fearful' experiencing of the troubled individuals, categories and communities involved of the historical transitions of (and in) life worlds[12]. If public social policy has an image of 'the subject of welfare' that excludes this experiencing from consideration or treats it as epiphenomenal, then public social policy will produce perverse results (for example, the woman who killed herself after obtaining a new flat, young people who cannot 'use' educational opportunities, or can only use them in an extremely limited and self-limiting way, and so on).

What our material and argument suggest is that overcoming the primary isolation of individuals 'at risk' in EU societies means that individuals, their families, their networks and communities need to develop a sense of belonging and a sense of contributing. This requires *sufficient time* in an appropriate social space and setting, as well as *appropriate leadership* and *relationship styling*. For this to happen to clients, it must have happened and be happening to front-line staff. Time and space and relationships appropriate for mutual 'getting to know one another' and therefore for mutual 'getting to be able to become different' were found.

The time is above all time for people to *become known*, and be able to *learn from their life*. Without the flow of biographical story-telling, the change managers do not know in the necessary detail – and in its unique configuration – what they need to know in order to manage. This is especially true when the change manager is the 'troubled person' him or herself.

Should authentic intimacy require encouraging and proliferating *any* biographic narration, a further question arises with regard to the *type* and *depth* of understanding given to it. Our theory-in-use questioning must go still further. *How* do we learn from the told lives – our own, those of other people, those of institutions?

Biographic work tends to promote some level of reflexivity. But what are the most (and least) productive mental and emotional frameworks for 'understanding' the biographical narration? As participants in our institutions, with what *mental and emotional framework* should we encourage ourselves to listen, and so understand, the biographical narration we hear?

This final and crucial question rejoins the original Sostris issue: with what *methodology* should we analyse and interpret the material of the biographic narration our interview method generates?

Early oral historians perceived their task as collecting oral histories and then presenting them directly to the world with minimal editing, in order that such 'voices hidden from history' could express themselves without mediation. More recently, there has been a shift from simply 'recycling' the self-expression and self-understanding of the narrator to presenting, in addition, that self-expression and self-understanding for readers to understand in ways that the narrator would not necessarily accept, ways that go beyond the subject's spontaneous self-understanding (Chamberlayne et al, 2000).

It is not enough for an institution to foster biographical narration to facilitate reflexive self-understanding – though, if they did so, it would already be an incomparable leap forward. Just as Sostris researchers were required to undergo training in order to explore and relate the lived life and the told story (see Appendices A and B; Wengraf, 2001, pp 231-300), so too do peers and professionals in institutions that help socially excluded people. For their part, they require modelling and support to deal with biographical narration in a way that distinguishes *real events* from *the states of mind* embodied and embedded in the telling of the story of those events, as well as models of appropriate intervention. The life journey stories that have been told and discussed in previous chapters indicate, in the main, the insights that can be gained by using a method of biographical inquiry and a method of narrative analysis that understands the psychosocial dynamics of the 'defended self' (Hollway and Jefferson, 2000; Wengraf, 2001, pp 158-9).

By distinguishing and relating the lived life and the states of mind of a story, participants in working welfare institutions can support the development of the biographical narrator's psychosocial capacity; in other words, develop a less defended understanding of themselves[13].

In an institution, the theory of 'persons' in use is critical in this regard. This institutional theory is embodied in the stories that we tell and hear – and fear to tell and fear to hear – about ourselves, about each other, about the institution, and about other institutions and our overall historical context[14].

Conclusion

We have considered some of the results of the Sostris study of agencies (see also *Sostris Working Paper 8*, 1999). We have indicated the varying ways in which the organisations see themselves as handling 'the whole person' or as being restricted to dealing with particular issues or aspects of activity (counselling for the soul, meals-on-wheels and home helps for the body, or biographical reflexivity for the client's self). We have suggested that organisations with strong external relations *and* empowering internal relations, *and* oriented to (pre)figurative work concerning relations and reflexivity for the 'whole person in their whole situation' are likely to have high leverage effects on improving the resources, strategies and 'states of mind' of the individual.

However, we have also stressed that the adequacy of those organisations that do wish to deal with the whole person depends very much on the *particular theory-in-use*[15] of whole persons that their practice (whether they realise it or not) enacts. It varies greatly from the adequacy of that theory-in-use.

> It seems that different perspectives on unconscious aspects of mental life give rise to characteristically different political and social outlooks. Outright denial of the existence of the unconscious domain, within the behaviourist psychological tradition, characteristically generates interest-based and coercive models of organisation.... The view of mental life upheld by [a tendency within] the British psychoanalytic school ... holds that engagement with the inner world, the toleration of uncertainty, and intense states of feeling and intimacy, can only be sustained at a micro-level, in face-to-face relationships, or through the practice of art or other kinds of creative thought.... (Rustin, 2001, 158-9, rearranged)

"Institutions where inner states of mind (notably anxiety) are taken seriously and as matters for reflection rather than for onward projection or punitive reprisal" (Rustin, 2001, p 158) will want to be judged by the *quality* of the face-to-face micro-intimacies and engagement with the expression of people's inner world that they promote at all levels of the organisation.

In a competitive world (generative of schizoid/paranoid relationships), such interactions will not occur by default but only by deliberate purpose, principle, modelling and design, with management functioning as a necessary buffer and, in their individual and collective behaviour, providing a purposeful internal modelling.

Our evidence suggests that only where there are the material and human resources for appropriate space and appropriate time for reflexive and relational group work that fosters 'getting to be known as a (hi)storied person' can significant changes be made of a *supportive* and *remedial* sort.

In addition, we argue (but without the space to explore the argument) that *preventative* social policy requires at least the promotion of biographically sensitive reflexive and relational group work in schools and youth training and in further and higher education[16].

One line of argument runs as follows: "Respect for autonomy ... moves professionals towards a more biographical approach" (Stroobants et al, 2001). A more biographical approach to clients by bureau professionals in a learning organisation (see note 5) means a more biographical approach by the learning organisation to its own biography. This can emerge only from encouraging the personal biographical 'narration' of its managers and bureau professionals, as well as its clients. The amnesia of this (behaviourist) age must be tackled because only our history can tell who we are[17].

The struggle to keep an organisation learning and innovating, and to maintain a balance between order and disorder in this process, is always a dance on the edge of chaos, running the dangers of becoming either a destructive or irrelevant routine (Weick and Westley, 1999). Biographic interviews with individuals in respect of their whole lives and in respect of relevant organisations can combine with ethnographic and other research to produce better understandings of the often hidden dynamics[18] of such situations and the complex relations of internal and external processes[19].

Notes

[1] These distinctions between the 'lived life' and the 'told story' have been crucial to Sostris' method. See Chapter One and Appendices A and B.

[2] For further details, see *Sostris Working Paper 8* (1999). This chapter has been considerably improved by the comments of Prue Chamberlayne, Jeff Evans, Lynn Froggett, Richard Freeman and its anonymous reviewer.

[3] For a later analysis, based largely on the same research material (Chamberlayne and Rupp, 1999) but from a more psychodynamic perspective, see Froggett (2002, pp 129-54).

[4] Sports and fitness seem to be the main ways of accessing men, and the centre is making great efforts to find ways of drawing in the young men who are difficult to involve (particularly white men).

[5] Most of the agencies we studied seemed little aware of research and discussion in contemporary business literature of the concept of the 'learning organisation' (Senge, 1990; Dougherty, 1999; Weick and Westley, 1999). For a recent collection, see Easterby-Smith et al (1999).

[6] The Bauhof is an umbrella organisation for the training and employment of unqualified youth in Halle. It has a staff of about 40 and a clientele of 150 mainly young people involved in different training projects. By participating in different sub-projects within the Bauhof, an individual can theoretically go all the way from the first step of 'hanging around on the street' to a full-blown, three-year apprenticeship (for further details, see Breckner et al, 1999).

[7] The Spanish Sostris team (Tejero and Torrabadella, 1999) investigated two projects – La Broca and La Xarxa. La Broca, situated in a working-class suburb of Barcelona affected by industrial decline, operates a network of exchange that combines institutional and community participation. It aims to increase personal esteem and foster new ways of mutual self-help, without and against the use of money. Based on the LETS (local exchange trading system) principle, it has a unit of resource, the *broca*, the equivalent of one hour's labour. At the time of inquiry, some 50 different services were being offered through the project, one-third involving caring or domestic tasks. It is interesting that, unlike some LETS schemes, there were more offers of services than takers. La Xarxa is located in a more residential neighbourhood with a high percentage of early-retired and older people suffering from loneliness and isolation and who want to be 'useful'. The aim of the project is to interchange goods and services but, unlike La Broca, it has a solidarity fund for those unable to make a contribution themselves. Most of its activities take the form of an extension of caring outside the home, and some 200 families are involved. The initiative began in 1990 and is organised by the Neighbourhood Association

that carries out the 'banking'. Supported by both the local authority and the Catalan government, it is also followed by a social worker and a psychologist.

[8] The Camden Refugee Education Project began in 1990 with one temporary teaching post within the Camden Language and Support services. Its aims are to (a) offer support with assessment and induction of newly arrived refugee pupils; (b) develop educational support for unaccompanied children and young people; (c) develop home–school–community links; (d) develop policy, resources and curriculum materials that reflect refugee and human rights issues; (e) provide schools, school governors and other services with in-service training on meeting the educational needs of refugee children. For further details, see Kowarzik (1999).

[9] The Women's Resource Centre in Gothenburg, Sweden, began with a proposal for a network of centrally funded but decentralised women's resource centres, which by 1996 was well in place, with EU funding and international links. The orientation was to foster empowerment and creativity, on the basis of knowledge and proper counselling and advice. The centres were to be accessible, geared to generating employment, providing supporting links to the authorities and to credit unions, and seeking to end male domination in the fields of employment and politics. They also aimed to draw on and to integrate the networking traditions of rural women into the urban process. For further details, see Peterson and Thorsell (1999).

[10] The founders of the Bromley-by-Bow Centre felt that business sponsorship was more interested in organisational innovation than were UK local authorities, while central government agencies were looking for competitive tendering for stand-alone, short-term behavioural projects. Hoggett (2000, pp 199-201) describes very well the spiral of competitive distrust generated in the British public services in the Thatcher-Blair epoch.

[11] The Foyer, a public sector partnership agency that opened in 1996, provides combined accommodation and training for 210 young homeless people, in partnership with a variety of public, private and commercial stakeholders. The fact that the original bid was put forward without a clear conceptual framework for understanding the group (its provision was aimed at the levels of professional support that would be needed to support them) has meant that a very sharp and difficult learning curve has had to be developed, together with reorganising of the funding arrangements (its intended self-sufficiency is based on room rental) and institutional self-definition. It took the Foyer three years to have its own bank account separate from that of the parent organisation! For further details, see Petrie (1999).

[12] This has implications for the 'model of governance' of such institutions (Newman, 2001, p 87).

[13] Such a change in psychosocial capacity might show itself in a change of self-understanding revealed in a new way of telling the person's life story. Narrative therapy – as recommended by Jordan (2000, pp 214-18) – may be useful in this context, but

narrative 're-engineering' and mechanical use should be avoided (see, for example, Freedman and Combs, 1996). It is experienced 'being' that determines narrative, rather than narrative that controls being. And being is modified by new 'doing', or acts, in new social relations. Shared biographical narrating and listening is part of that new doing, but only a part of it. Just learning to parrot 'positive narratives' while changing neither behaviour or one's social relations is not a forward step.

[14] The [second-order] stories that we tell about the [first-order] biographical narratives fostered by biographically oriented institutions are key to the states of mind and types and level of understanding that the local narrative culture fosters or represses. (For 'states of mind and mindlessness', see Bion, 1967, 1988).

[15] Chris Argyris's term. For a summary, see Edmondson and Moingeon (2000, pp 160-2) and discussion in Hoggett (2000, pp 49-51).

[16] This does not mean adding a few Civics classes to an already ludicrously busy curriculum. It means seeing the internal organisation of schools as the set of social relations, which cannot but have a profound effect on the development (or devastation) of people – our human and cultural capital.

[17] Delcroix (2000) argues convincingly that the transmission of life stories from fathers to their children is a crucial and personal resource that promotes their children's integration. She cites a 'genealogical principle': "If an individual is not aware of their genealogical history, then life cannot be fully lived". The same is likely to be true of transmission from organisational seniors to organisational juniors.

[18] Much more intensive study is required of the unconscious dynamics of organisational behaviour, since interpersonal and inter-category relationships cannot be understood without them (Menzies Lyth, 1960; Obholzer and Roberts, 1994; Hinshelwood and Skogstad, 2000).

[19] The funding regime of Sostris did not permit anything more than an exploratory studies of organisations. A fuller, three-year evaluation programme of the Bromley-by-Bow Centre is currently under way.

References

Bion, W. R. (1967) *Second thoughts: Selected papers on psycho-analysis*, New York, NY/London: Aronson.

Bion, W. R. (1988) *Attention and interpretation*, London: Karnac.

Breckner, R., Hungerbühler, W. and Olk, T. (1999) 'An agency in times of transition: the "Bauhof" in Halle', in *Sostris Working Paper 8: Case study materials – innovative social agencies in Europe*, London: Centre for Biography in Social Policy, University of East London, pp 65-74.

Caniglia, P and Spanò, A. (1999) 'The analysis of an opportunist but effective institution: the Italian national report', in *Sostris Working Paper 8: Case study materials – innovative social agencies in Europe*, London: Centre for Biography in Social Policy, University of East London, pp 91-8.

Chamberlayne, P. and Rupp, S. (1999a) '"Only connect": report on the Bromley by Bow project', in *Sostris Working Paper 8: Case study materials – innovative social agencies in Europe*, London: Centre for Biography in Social Policy, University of East London, pp 42-51.

Chamberlayne, P. and Rustin, M. (1999b) *From biography to social policy: Final report of the Sostris project*, London: Centre for Biography in Social Policy, University of East London.

Chamberlayne, P., Bornat, J. and Wengraf, T. (eds) (2000) *The turn to biographical methods in social science*, London: Routledge.

Clegg, S., Hardy, C. and Nord, W. (eds) (1999) *Managing organisations*, London: Sage Publications. (I am indebted to Richard Freeman for this reference.)

Delcroix, C. (2000) 'The transmission of life stories from ethnic minority fathers to their children: a personal resource to promote social integration', in S. Arber and C. Atteas-Donfut (eds) *Generational conflict*, London: Routledge.

Dougherty, D. (1999) 'Organising for innovation', in S. Clegg, C. Hardy and W. Nord (eds) *Managing organisations*, London: Sage Publications, pp 174-89.

Easterby-Smith, M., Burgoyne, J. and Araujo, L. (eds) (1999) *Organizational learning and the learning organization*, London: Sage Publications.

Edmondson, A. and Moingeon, B. (1999) 'Learning, trust and organisational change: contrasting models of intervention research in organisational behaviour', in M. Easterby-Smith, J. Burgoyne and L. Araujo (eds) *Organizational learning and the learning organization*, London: Sage Publications, pp 157-75.

Freedman, J. and Combs, G. (1996) *Narrative therapy: The social construction of preferred realities*, New York, NY: Norton.

Froggett, L. (2002) *Love, hate and welfare: Psychosocial approaches to policy and practice*, Bristol: The Policy Press.

Hinshelwood, R. and Skogstad, W. (eds) (2000) *Observing organisations: Anxiety, defence and culture in health care*, London: Routledge.

Hoggett, P. (2000) *Emotional life and the politics of welfare*, Basingstoke: Macmillan.

Hollway, W. and Jefferson, T. (2000) *Doing qualitative research differently: Free association, narrative, and the interview method*, London: Sage Publications.

Jordan, B. with Jordan, C. (2000) *Social work and the third way: Tough love as social policy*, London: Sage Publications.

Kowarzik, U. (1999) 'Valuing refugees – developing multicultural services', in *Sostris Working Paper 8: Case study materials – innovative social agencies in Europe*, London: Centre for Biography in Social Policy, University of East London, pp 24-41.

Menzies Lyth, I. (1960) 'The functioning of social systems as a defence against anxiety: a report on a study of the nursing service of a general hospital', in *Containing anxiety in institutions: Selected essays volume 1*, London: Free Associations Books, (2nd edition, 1988), pp 43-90.

Mestheneos, E. and Ioannidi, E. (1999) 'Confronting the position of women and minorities: Greek national report', in *Sostris Working Paper 8: Case study materials – innovative social agencies in Europe*, London: Centre for Biography in Social Policy, University of East London, pp 75-90.

Murard, N. (1999) 'From confidence in biographic narratives to confidence in social policy', in *Sostris Working Paper 8: Case study materials – innovative social agencies in Europe*, London: Centre for Biography in Social Policy, University of East London, pp 52-64.

Newman, J. (2001) *Modernising governance*, London: Sage Publications.

Obholzer, A. and Roberts, V. (eds) (1994) *The unconscious at work: Individual and organisational stress in the human services*, London: Routledge.

Peterson, M. and Thorsell, B. (1999) 'New networks, new democracy: Swedish national report', in *Sostris Working Paper 8: Case study materials – innovative social agencies in Europe*, London: Centre for Biography in Social Policy, University of East London, pp 112-18.

Petrie, G. (1999) 'It's just a big step: an East London Foyer for young people', in *Sostris Working Paper 8: Case study materials – innovative social agencies in Europe*, London: Centre for Biography in Social Policy, University of East London, pp 14-23.

Rauner, D.M. (2000) *'They still pick me up when I fall': The role of caring in youth development and community life*, New York, NY: Columbia University Press.

Senge, P. (1990) *The fifth discipline: The art and practice of the learning organisation*, New York, NY: Doubleday.

Rustin, M. (2001) 'Lacan, Klein and Politics', in M. Rustin (ed) *Reason and unreason: Psychoanalysis, science and politics*, Middletown: CT: Wesleyan University Press, pp 135-61.

Sostris (1999) *Sostris Working Paper 8: Case study materials – innovative social agencies in Europe*, London: Centre for Biography in Social Policy, University of East London.

Stokes, J. (1994) 'Institutional chaos and personal stress', in A. Obholzer and V. Roberts (eds) *The unconscious at work: Individual and organisational stress in the human services*, London: Routledge, pp 121-8.

Stroobants, V., Jans, M. and Wildemeersch, D. (2001) 'Making sense of learning for work. Towards a framework of traditional learning', *International Journal of Lifelong Learning*, vol 20, nos 1-2, (Jan-April), pp 114-26.

Tejero, E., Torrabadella, L. and Lemkow, L. (1999) 'Biography, networks and social policy: Spanish national report on flagship agencies', in *Sostris Working Paper 8: Case study materials – innovative social agencies in Europe*, London: Centre for Biography in Social Policy, University of East London, pp 99-111.

Weick, K. and Westley, F. (1999) 'Organisational learning: affirming an oxymoron', in S. Clegg, C. Hardy and W. Nord (eds) *Managing organisations*, London: Sage Publications, pp 190-208.

Wengraf, T. (2001) *Qualitative research interviewing: Biographic narrative and semi-structured method*, London: Sage Publications.

FIFTEEN

Conclusions: social transitions and biographical work

Prue Chamberlayne

This volume's introduction asked how we can come to understand the complex and rapidly changing societies of today, and what such new understanding implies for social policy. Now, from the thick texture of the case studies, we can draw together some more general conclusions concerning emergent gender, class, intercultural and intergenerational relations. We can ask more grounded questions:

- What the biographies imply for the future of the European project.
- What they suggest about the 'nature of the epoch' at the turn of the millennium.
- How biographical methods might contribute to a movement for change within (comparative) social policy.

We invite you to join us in thinking about these questions. The core chapters of this volume have made a number of comparisons between cases, and offered some suggestions on policy issues. However, they have by no means exhausted the process. There is no end to case comparison, since each comparison draws out different issues, as will a reader's own experiences and reflections.

This chapter is made up of two parts. The first reflects initially on some key terms of debate, and on the historical 'moment' in which Sostris was conducted. It is mainly concerned with the extent and patterns of social transformation that are revealed by the interviews, and how these burst out beyond the key categorisations of conventional social policy. The second part, drawing on policy proposals from the earlier chapters, constructs a profile of supportive social interventions, and discusses their implications for training and organisational settings. It considers signs of support for such 'utopian' thinking, and prospects for the social model of welfare given the strength of contrary indications at the economic level.

The extent of social change

Framing the issue

Our initial focus was on 'individualisation' and 'risk', rather than social exclusion, despite this being the title of the EU programme under which our research was funded. Reviewing how social exclusion had entered social science discourse in the seven countries studied, we found that many social scientists had resisted the term. Some argued that it "located at the margins" what belonged at the centre of society, and bore the usual dangers of pathologising poverty. Some preferred the term 'precarity', a broader concept that also indicated the need for preventive measures. In fact, as a mainstream term, social exclusion has gathered about it considerable sophistication (Sostris, 1997; Levitas, 1998; Askonas and Stewart, 2000).

Few of our subjects could be said to be experiencing out-and-out social exclusion, despite their state of uncertainty, even foreboding. Many share a common plight, yet they feel individually situated. Common frames of reference have been lost, even a shared social calendar to make sense of life (Spanò, Chapter Four), and many have been ill. Murard (Chapter Three) identifies 'guilt' (which is internalised) as the prevailing feeling state in contemporary society, as compared with the (collectively derived) 'shame' that characterised the 1970s.

We need to ask to what extent these themes of loss and uncertainty may be accentuated by our research design and by our implicit, even unconscious, assumptions. Our generalised categories of risk and individualisation oriented our sampling to 'range' rather than extremities, although, in evaluating the range we were achieving, we felt we were not accessing as many people at the margins as we would have liked[1]. Nevertheless, in our minds and in our choice of social categories, we were oriented to people making negative transitions. As we have described, we became increasingly drawn, despite our initial misgivings, into the frame of social exclusion, and this has undoubtedly influenced our selection of cases to analyse in depth, and the stages of interpreting, comparing and then theorising cases. Therefore, it has influenced the writing of this book.

On the other hand, we feel that the themes of loss and uncertainty do characterise well the 'epoch' – 1996-2002 – in which we have been working. It was a period in which nothing was resolved. The single European currency has been installed, but 'the European project' remains deeply uncertain, given the strength of the neoliberal dictatorship of the World Trade Organisation within global developments, and the inevitable state of flux arising from such a large scale of European expansion. The Old Left has long been discredited, even in the French elections of 2002. The 'third way' – or New Left of Blair and Schroeder – which claimed to offer a distinctive way forward, has foundered in political corruption and apologies for the deregulation of markets. And the emergent New Right is steeped in a defensive imaginary rather than any viable vision for the future.

The current epoch is a crossroads, but the way ahead is not decipherable, and going back is not an option. From the Second World War until the end of the 1980s and the beginning of the 1990s, redistributive and democratising forms of organisation in the European 'tradition' seemed to maintain their progressive potential. Many people believe there has to be an equitable and sustainable solution to world problems (it is surely no longer possible to maintain the fiction of solutions for Europe separated from the rest of the world). Yet it is quite unclear what viable forms of economic, social and welfare organisation will emerge, or if there are coherent alternatives to the market order. Our claim that biographical methods offer a new approach, even a new paradigm for welfare, has to be relativised. We can point to some salient ingredients, some glimmerings in the dark, but we do not have an overall recipe.

We are clearly in a period of transition, but are we in a period of transformation? Transformation implies fundamental change in a whole society, and suggests that the successor form is known, defined and progressive. It is used by Western politicians to put a positive spin on the restoration of the market and democratic freedoms in Eastern Europe, processes, in fact, which have brought massive waves of social exclusion. It is not used to refer to de-industrialisation and deregulation in Western Europe, however comparable the scale of social destruction and disorientation may be. Rather, the key term in the language of European policy is *social exclusion*. In Murard's view (Chapter Three), social exclusion minimises and offloads the responsibilities of the capitalist classes for social devastation, while simultaneously reflecting their guilt and fear.

Social exclusion refers to a process, inviting the question of who or what is doing the excluding. Yet it lacks historical depth. Understanding social relationships in the past is often helpful in designing social interventions in the present. It is only by understanding how we got to the present, that choosing paths to preferred futures makes sense. Biographies have a real purchase here, since they throw intense light on multiple dimensions of social change over a period of time.

Q. Why have social exclusion and social transition become key terms referring to major social reorganisation in the West, and social transformation become the term referring to major social change in Eastern Europe? Which concept do you prefer, and why?

Q. What is your sense of where the world will be in 10 or 20 years' time? What do you see as the instruments and drivers of progressive developments?

A political impasse?

Through the cases we see a number of things: economic restructuring combining with intergenerational, gender and ethnic shifts, issues of personal character, and the complex intertwining of different aspects of social change. Some of the changes our subjects confront are life transitions that are characteristically difficult in any society or historical period. Combined with major shifts in employment, gender relations and experiences of immigration, however, they become extremely challenging.

While highlighting concepts such as risk, individualisation and fluidity in contemporary experience and in contemporary sociology, our introduction relativised these terms, insisting on the importance of reflexive and enduring social relationships, for both individual and societal wellbeing.

Contrasting the life journeys and prospects of younger cases with those of their older counterparts provides dramatic insights into the way societies have changed, and presents the disorientation of unqualified young people in a new light. Through Harold (Chapter Five), we see an unqualified young man from a broken family in the 1960s and 1970s becoming integrated through the labour market, mentored and teased through rites of passage into adulthood, imbued with a sense of collective responsibility, and trained in negotiating skills through industrial and union concerns. This supportive 'apprenticeship' model has largely disappeared. Instead, the model of Franco (Chapter Four), a leatherworker from Naples who began work aged 11 to become 'early retired' at the age of 18, who remains uneducated and is now unmarriageable because of his poor employment prospects, suddenly assumes a wider significance. Child and student labour, racism against immigrants, family and institutional abuse, school exclusions, drugs, and personal disorientation all contribute to the diminution rather than enhancement of education. In comparison with past apprenticeships, current employability training programmes are superficial in their effects and socially impoverished.

However, the case studies also show the losing of solidarity in very different contexts. In Britain, the liberal project was forced through in the early years (1979–82) of Thatcherism, and then consolidated over a much longer period, while in East Germany and in Bosnia, the substantially more collectivist systems were blown away in a matter of months[2]. In Sweden, the 'shock' of global competition came suddenly, if a little later. Once the corporatist combination of egalitarian inclusion with technological investment proved unviable, latent racism shot to prominence. Countries with less-developed welfare systems might be equally unsettled by a reversal of expectations. In Spain, the promise of social mobility that had been so warmly embraced by the post-Franco generation crumbled in the next. Nicolás (Chapter Two), a 'child delegate' for the aspirations of his parents, shows how difficult it can be to escape from the family mission. The Mediterranean countries in particular show how necessary – and yet how entrapping – family dependencies can be. In Greece, family dependencies continue, in the absence of industrial and social democratic solidarity, as the only basis for protection, education, and the acquisition of negotiating skills. Moves towards individualisation in Greece are occurring within the frame of restrictive family relationships.

As has often been remarked in social science, historical change ushers in new relations between the public and private spheres. While this is an old theme for feminists, our case studies suggest that such shifts now confront all social groups. The importance of employment to men's identities is reflected, as Murard observes (Chapter Three), in the way that work remains the backbone of their narratives, including those of our study. So unused are many men, for example, to appreciating and using the resources and networks of the private and informal spheres, and so unable are they to find self-esteem in domestic activities and roles, that for many of them the loss of waged work means social death. Donald's back problems (Chapter Five) directly express the paralysis he feels at home, as compared with the huge vigour he found in the challenge of underground maintenance work.

Of course, individual responses vary according to both social context and more personally acquired strategies. Harold (Chapter Five), from much the same locality as Donald, has no such problems, having been a family carer since boyhood. Oppositely, Marisa from Southern Italy (Chapter Nine) has so committed herself to an outside identity that redundancy is a catastrophe; by fashioning her life in the image of a man's, she lacks a family or other alternative identity to fall back on. Filippo (Chapter Four) was similarly trapped by his own life strategy as well as by events in society. As long as he was supported institutionally by the Communist Party and the printing industry, he survived. However, once having lost those, and seeking a job in his own right, he floundered.

While biographical case studies sharpen insights into particular social contexts, they do not provide grounds for generalising. This becomes evident as soon as we compare cases in one society. That Rita (Chapter Nine) and her family thrive so well in a postmodern setting (leatherwork–taxis–knitting business) does not allow us to postulate more generally that the informal sphere in Southern Italy eases the transition towards deregulated society (although her case did make us feel that we were discovering and identifying a pattern concerning affinities between premodern and postmodern resources, which further investigation and reflection might show to be a significant and even widespread one). Since Rita has never been concerned with the conflict between a domestic or professional identity, or with the modern feminist question of 'Who am I?', her transition to home-based employment is no problem to her. The opposite is true of Marisa. Nor does the 'Southern' informal economy offer a solution to Franco, following his expulsion from employment at 18.

Lest any reader think otherwise, we are not implying that, by reacting so differently, individuals demonstrate the lack of need for welfare provisions. Individual strategies are as much socially produced as personally derived. They are a fact of life, and it helps little or not at all to tell Donald, Marisa or Filippo to model themselves on Harold or Rita. Each of the former three needs personally tailored and contextually sensitive support.

Our immigrant subjects, such as Ana and Djamillah's father (Chapters Twelve and Thirteen), highlight the extremes of downward mobility that may be involved in contemporary transitions, and the need to change strategies between generations. Racism and social prejudice are still rampant in Europe, even at this moment increasing, also for professionals such as Djamillah. Steven and Zenon (Chapter Thirteen) show how painful and uncertain making a generation break from their parents and achieving professional status can be. Although in some ways Steven's situation is less pressurised than that of Nicolás, who is caught in a regional family divide involving historico-political rifts. Migrant parents want their children to move on from their position – and first-generation parents often recognise that they do not have the answers, that their children have to find their own way. So they may not make their children 'delegates' in the way some upwardly mobile families do.

It may be that that migrants' adaptability makes them the 'best Europeans' (an hypothesis put forward by Jude Bloomfield, Senior Visiting Research Fellow at the University of East London), although they meet many structural obstacles that can only be surmounted by extreme sacrifices. Sasa's adaptability (Chapter Twelve), following his studies in East Germany, cannot protect him from the vagaries of immigration legislation, and the only way he can honour his responsibility as father to his daughter is to make a not very happy marriage. Without that he would have to leave the country and so abandon her. Having gained his doctorate, however, he is able to maintain his educated status in Germany following unification, even if not in his own field. Ana, having come to Sweden at a later life stage, is unable to regain her status as an educated professional. She becomes a cleaner, and family dignity prevents her from claiming any social benefits.

Welfare measures are vital in extending life chances and in improving the emotional quality of life, even though few of our cases talk directly of services. Murard (Chapter Three) argues that, in working-class life, willingness and need for love are all too often undermined by lack of resources, and it is striking among our subjects that those most likely to sacrifice their personal and sexual happiness lack welfare support. Mercia (Chapter Eight), by leaving (then) 'backward' Spain and her family history of abusive relationships, is able to move on in her career and in her personal life, but at the expense of romantic love and at the cost of feeling that she has not loved her children enough. Dionysios (Chapter Seven) sacrifices his independence for the sake of caring for his disabled, widowed mother. Carolina and Janette (in Sostris, 1998) prioritise care for their children and their education over any personal relationship for themselves. Welfare services can protect people from these stark choices, and could do so much more. Through social mobility and self-realisation through her work and politics, GunBritt (Chapter Eight) gains the confidence to develop a real love relationship, and her generous early retirement pension allows her to enjoy this to the full.

———

In the case of Suzanne from East Germany (Chapter Eight), we see someone from a disadvantaged background with a rather poor capacity for love, being supported by collective services to advance professionally and make a new family life. However, welfare measures are no guarantee against abuse in families. The extent and frequency of family violence in life accounts from Spain and Greece are a shocking reminder of the scale of violence and drunkenness that was 'normal' in working-class life in pre-welfare state Britain of the 1930s. However, there was significant mention of it in northern welfare states – examples being GunBritt, Harold and Bernard (Chapters Eight, Five and Seven).

We have mentioned gender as a major dimension in the social changes confronting our subjects. Regarding the shifting relationship between public and private resources, for example, it is not only that returning to a domestic and neighbourhood *habitus* could be traumatic for early-retired or redundant men, but having their husbands intruding in this sphere could be deeply unsettling for their wives. The life of Sonia (Chapter Nine) reveals a more complex process. Sonia faces the gender revolution, both in terms of reconstructing home and work roles (the 'double presence', which leaves the woman asking 'Who am I?' as Antonella Spanò puts it), and of throwing off a family tradition of male abuse, which has left her hating and vilifying men. Having structured her life around taking up arms against her father, she is unable to make relationships with men, nor can she leave home to become an adult. She is trapped by her own strategy. Janette's deep resentment and hurt at her father's absence carries much the same problem (see also Sostris, 1998).

Q. Our chapters have made some comparisons between cases. We invite you to return to a careful reading of the case studies to make some more. Some suggestions are:

Ana and Mercia	Nicolas and Sonia
Ana and Djamillah	Marisa and Donald
Sonia and Nicolás	Franco and Rita
Zenon and Nicolás	Mercia and Zenon's mother
Robin and Gérard	Bernard and Christopher

You could bring in contrasting cases of your own personal experience. You may be interested in contrasting both life journeys and social situations. A starting point might be the different social, legal and welfare contexts into which migrants arrive, another the different conditions in which workers are laid off work, or young people, and not-so-young people, struggle to find work, another the responses of workers to changing trade union cultures. Or you might like to compare all the older (ex) trade unionists, or all the younger men, or women. You might also compare the perspective brought by biographical material to such questions, with a single discipline approach, such as labour market studies or social psychology, or with traditional social policy.

Biographical work

We know from the earlier chapters that life and social transitions have entailed a great deal of biographical work. A particular feature of biographical interpretation lies in identifying shifts in self-understanding over time, and going beyond the self-perception of the narrator. In many instances, we felt that our method of interviewing was helping our interview subjects to organise their thoughts, giving them the space to think emotionally. For those whose lives were manifestly stuck, the interview might nudge them towards seeking out further opportunities for such emotional work, as in counselling or various forms of therapy. Thorsell (Chapter Eight) suggests that this would be helpful in the case of Suzanne. Spanò (Chapter Four) suggests that identity work needs to become a matter of public responsibility, that in the quest for a professional path, self-confidence is just as important as technical skills. And indeed, some countries, such as Holland, do now offer free counselling following any job severance.

Several of the cases, with migrants foremost, detail processes of biographical change. Breckner refers to the typical experience of 'strangers' as 'translation': "a profound restructuring of the whole system of knowledge, now based on divergent 'common senses' from different societies". Murard (1999) describes Mercia as purposely moving to France in order to learn what life is, who others are, who she herself is. Social transformation does not happen *to her*; rather she repositions herself in a new society, and makes herself open to new relationships and experiences. She takes the risk herself, treating new opportunities as welcome challenges rather than difficulties or threats. By contrast, Suzanne, Nicolás and Sonia (Chapters Eight, Two and Nine) do not seem ready or able to open themselves in this way. Mercia's secret (Chapters Eight and Three), an early love relationship, enables her to believe that good things can come from elsewhere. Many of our subjects, lacking a belief in 'other' possibilities, seem stuck. Donald has lost a very particular occupational niche (Chapter Five) and Sonia feels suspended between home and work (Chapter Nine); Nicolás between two political cultures (Chapter Two), Filippo between two generations (Chapter Four) and Zenon between three cultures (Chapter Thirteen).

It is those who are unable to conceive of their future who become stuck. There is a big difference, however, between those who become temporarily stuck (such as Heike) and those who seem more seriously blocked (like Zenon) (Chapters Two and Thirteen). In very many cases, a period of being ill and seeming stuck is actually a 'moratorium' – a period of crisis and reorientation. Such a period is necessary even for someone like Harold, with his wealth of biographical resources (Chapter Five). Certainly an inability to be reflexive can be restrictive, as is clear from the case of Zenon. Among the Greek cases, Mestheneos and Ioannidi-Kapolou (Chapters Seven and Ten) link an inability to be reflexive with paralysis within the traditional family frame. Reflexivity distinguishes those who take on more individualised life patterns from those who do not, or cannot. Steven, who is still doing intensive biographical work, depicts his reflective processes most graphically, giving the impression that he will move on.

Men who are bounced out of the world of work often face a crisis in their gender identity. Beyond this, most men are confronted with women's struggles for emancipation at work, at home, in social life. These are varied, complex and contradictory projects of gender identity, as Chapters Eight and Nine suggest. So gender reconstruction affects almost the whole of society, and yet traditional equality and anti-discrimination measures miss this subjective dimension.

A comparable situation prevails in the realm of cultural identities. Our case studies show the personal pressures involved in dealing with everyday racism, and Chapter Thirteen (transculturalism) asks the reader to consider the formative effect of a racist classroom incident on all the participants. We see the strategies of Sasa, Steven, Zenon, Ana and Djamillah (Chapters Twelve and Thirteen) in dealing with oppressive situations. For them to be comfortably integrated, whole populations, institutions and dominant groups need to do biographical work (individual and collective) on their respective institutional and 'invisible' racism. Europe has hardly started to address the multicultural identity work that is necessary in all regions and localities.

Life transitions involve both maintaining a sense of biographical continuity and flexibly adapting to change. As we commented in the introduction, the very concept of biographical dynamics challenges the postmodern idea of freely adopted identities. In our understanding of human subjectivity, deeper levels of biographical dynamics, orientations and strategies, which build up in different phases of a life, are not easily altered, even by conscious effort. There is also a 'thread' to be found, linking individual agency and experience in different fields and phases of the life[3]. Sasa maintains a sense of continuity in his quest for educational development, despite his rough ride amid East and West German legislation and employment.

> **Q.** The oppressive social relations that surround and permeate the lives of Sasa, Djamillah, Steven or Zenon, result in large measure from the everyday racist behaviour and thinking of those they encounter. What kinds of social interventions could radically change the behaviour of those who generate the oppression? You might pick out particular situations or incidents from the life journeys in the book. More daringly, you might use examples from your own experience, or those of your family members.

> **Q.** Our case studies give numerous examples (and you might think of others) of painful processes of changing gender identities, and how these are affected by patterns of work and family life. You might like to think of a duo or trio of contrasting cases from your own experience, following the structure of Chapter Nine. In what ways could people's (often conflictual) experiences of gender reconstruction be eased and given support?

A new design for social policy

Biographical resources

To what extent can people be helped in conducting such biographical work? This question seems crucial in new designs for social policy. Despite the intensely personal nature of these processes, permeated with intimate feelings of guilt, we can identify a number of ways in which people could be helped:

1. Help people to *identify their own biographical resources*, from recognising their own talents and feelings (such as fortitude and anger), to appreciating resources in their family, neighbourhood and milieu.
2. Help people to recognise the *shared and public nature of their situation*, as a generational or economic process in which they have rights to moral and political as well as material support. Discussion with peers can be a powerful means of individual and group development, as some of the new social movements have demonstrated. It can help unravel feelings of guilt. People need to feel themselves as part of a collective whole, even a political constituency. Often this can start from 'naming' the pioneering nature of people's situations and experiences. Far from being left behind, our subjects are protagonists of the new society. Politicians and policy makers could actively support people in coming to terms with new and challenging situations by recognising and celebrating the pioneering nature of their experience and discussing the problems.
3. People need *models and mediating relationships*. It would be hard for services to provide an equivalent of Mercia's love dream (Chapters Eight and Three), but meaningful relationships, often of a mentoring and bridging kind, can be crucial to processes of personal change. This was a key argument in Chapter Fourteen.
4. Biographical work needs *space*, the time to make adjustments. Even with help it takes time to find a flexible balance between resources, opportunities and aspirations.

> **Q.** Return to the cases you have compared, and think through what they imply for the design of social policy. Suggest what kinds of service provision would be helpful in overcoming difficulties, and also what the 'success' stories or aspects imply for others in comparable situations. The concepts we have just listed may be helpful as prompts to your reflections: biographical resources; shared scripts; models and mediating relationships; time and space.

Social policy principles

If our study of life journeys points to changes that amount to a social transformation of society, then social institutions need to make comparable adjustments. The design of social policy has not traditionally been designed to help people make life transitions, let alone to navigate a major social transformation. As we have seen, in the past young men with few qualifications gained adulthood in the rough and tumble of work place socialisation. In northern European societies, workplaces were the main vehicle for social integration, even to the extent of providing pensioners' activities. Throughout Europe, there was sufficient continuity in the occupational world for parents' advice to be relevant, and for many people to build secure identities on their work. The social policy tradition, rather, was to provide a basic platform of goods and services, such as income maintenance, health and education. Students received grants, but it was not the role of universities and colleges to guide them into professional careers (see also Sostris, 1999). Early retirees received a compensatory lump sum.

In flexible labour market conditions, it may take graduates many years to establish themselves in satisfying employment, and they may have to make major compromises. Young people cannot take their cues from their parents' generation, and there is little job security. They need to find realistic ways of balancing their hopes, resources and opportunities, and settle an identity in the midst of this state of flux and uncertainty. Older people, finding themselves in a community that has lost its moral and cultural moorings following the closure of an industry, have to find new bases for self-respect. Social policy needs to support people through these uncertainties, and promote the generative process of reflexivity. At a minimum, it needs to help people "stay the course of their existence" (Spanò, Chapter Four). As Murard and Spanò put it, the new social policy needs to work with quite different determinants from those that are widely used in applied social science. Lives defy existing administrative categories and linear concepts of social change. Not only is it a question of recognising the shifting multidimensionality of lives, but also the difference between what Taylor (1998, p 345) calls 'categorical' and 'ontological' identity – the former recognising a common belonging, the latter the uniqueness of the individual. Social policy needs to work with both these aspects of identity, and also take into account the force and interplay of past and present-time perspectives, whether these are historical, generational or those of more personal trajectories (see also Vobruba, 2000).

> **Q.** Brainstorm with some friends about situations you know of in which services or administrative categories are badly matched to the needs of particular individuals or families, particularly those who are involved in making transitions in their lives. How might services become more accommodating to differentiated and fluctuating situations and needs? Can you give examples of situations in which it is essential to use categories, and others when it is equally essential to recognise 'who' a person is? Is it possible to think in both terms at once?

Expertise

If the central role of social professionals and educators is to help people to find their own way, they have to understand the social and cultural contexts – and also the inner worlds – of their clients. They need to understand the specific situations individuals are in, their needs, experiences and skills in meeting challenges. Referring to the tradition of social pedagogy that forms the basis of social work training in Germany, Lorenz (2000, p 3) argues that pedagogy is "about the renewal of culture and the harnessing of the creative potential inherent in individuals". Jordan asserts that the practitioner's mode of address should be "one of 'curiosity and respectful puzzlement' at the service user's unique way of making things better" (Jordan with Jordan, 2000, p 215, quoting Parton and O'Byrne, 2000, p 137).

A focus on detailed knowledge and understanding of individual strategies and social contexts redefines expertise, and draws attention to socially and personally embedded structures of acting and feeling. Where are professionals and welfare organisations to gain such knowledge, if not from their clients themselves? Jordan invokes constructive social work, and "creativity and imagination in making sense of experience, self and relationships" (2000, p 214). Encounters between professional and client are shaped by their two biographies, and internal personal reasons may influence the extent to which the professional can hear and appreciate a particular client.

Murard (Chapter Three) suggests that professionals need to find ways of helping young people search for an incentive to become adults, to free them emotionally and normatively from the weight of family expectations. They need to find a spark that will light the way between their class milieu and the outer world, and it can take a lot of courage to take such steps. Many young people do so recklessly and become victims of their own vulnerabilities. Paradoxically, says Murard, casual or illegal work provides a rather good, if dangerous, apprenticeship for modern work conditions. In helping young people to take risks, professionals will need to do so themselves.

Focusing on decisive situations banishes 'underdog discourse', and sets about enhancing people's resources for action (Vorbruba, 2000, pp 604-5). An active approach, which understands the evolving dynamics of lives, promotes social and cultural as well as individual change. It treats clients as a source rather than an object of understanding (Froggett, 2002). Jordan's notion of constructive social work relies on narrative:

> [T]he service user is encouraged to tell the story of the problems in a way that externalises it, giving more control and agency and creating a new perspective on how to manage or overcome it. These narratives construct the future and anticipate change. (Jordan, 2000, p 215)

A biographical approach provides a rich resource for reconnecting social policy with the realities of social change, life worlds with systems. Again and again, we were struck by the evident personal capacities of our interviewees, many of which were unrecognised by society, and by the interview subjects themselves. In orienting to the enhancement of social capital and personal capacity building, social policy programmes need to start from the actual lives and resources of its citizens, rather than from what are often disempowering stereotypes and categories.

We are arguing for a considerable set of skills from the professional worker: biographical sensitivity to the client and to him/herself, awareness of the fluidity of time, understanding of multicultural social contexts, and a dynamic action approach to the individual and the society. This is a far cry from the legalistic, administrative skills required by Britain's Third Way approach to social work.

> **Q.** What do you think of as positive experiences of relating to social workers, teachers, doctors, career advisers, and so on? What about negative ones? If you are a social worker (or in a comparable profession), in what ways do you feel that reading this book has helped you, or hindered you?

Transformative agencies

Individual social professionals cannot invent and sustain biographically sensitive work without organisational and supervisory support. As Chapter Fourteen argued, the internal dynamics of agencies are crucial in mobilising 'the social', and enabling 'the social' to mobilise and develop itself. The innovative agencies we encountered seemed to combine personally sensitive work with quite intricate forms of networking, both inside the agency and in its external relations. There is a danger of the concept of 'social entrepreneurship' highlighting flamboyant rule-breakers and business sponsorships, while downplaying the crucial importance of flexible processes and quality relationships.

The most attentive agencies to the subjectivity and creativity of their clients reflected an open-ended and creative mode of being in their own formation and ongoing organisational lives. Often they had charismatic founders and key members with unusual life journeys, who were themselves 'boundary-crossers'[4]. Agencies that tried to address the whole situation of a person or of a community were more unruly and non-hierarchical than more conventional ones, where workers and clients might be locked into closed definitions, and sometimes separated by glass screens. Experience at Bromley-by-Bow demonstrated that people have to be recognised and acknowledged as they are, before anything can be done for them. Therefore time and space are needed in a 'containing' process, to use a psychoanalytic term; that is, a space in which people feel respected and cared for enough to be able to think and hope, a space in which workers listen, and absorb the meaning of what they are hearing.

The *Cultures of care* project (Chamberlayne and King, 2000) demonstrated the value of building on life worlds and encouraging moral agency, since 'outwardly oriented' carers became flexible, independent and energetic agents, able to make long-term plans and manage crises, and a source of social capital to others[5]. Jordan, advocating a community development approach to social work, also argues:

> ... that individuals, however isolated, oppressed, problem-ridden, preoccupied, deprived or deluded, can quickly learn to work together and to manage jointly owned or collectively shared resources, given a democratic voice. The fact that most present-day mainstream social work does exactly the opposite ... is a waste of the potential of both staff and service users, and a squandering of the social capital that would be generated by more imaginative methods. (Jordan, 2000, p 181)

In an exploration of the social relations that produce welfare, Froggett (2002) emphasises the need to recognise emotion and personalise relationships:

> We are deprived of a language in which to speak of the irrational, chaotic, fearful experiences that accompany the sociologically defined categories of exclusion, poverty or disadvantage. (Froggett, 2002, p 17)

Designing social policy interventions that take account of such fears means that "the quality of the helping relationship is at least as important as practical and financial assistance" (Froggett, 2002, p 17).

> **Q.** What collective solidarities have decayed or emerged during your lifetime, and during the lifetimes of those close to you? How has this affected your personal biography?

Welfare contexts

It is hard to believe that the social tradition in Europe will be easily swept away, given its firm embedding in institutional arrangements and intellectual thinking. In our study we found plenty of confirmation of European social values, arguments for the need to reinvent reciprocal collectivity, to recognise and build up informal resources, to realise human potential by social means. Such thinking was particularly strong within the agencies.

Hermann and Lorenz (1997) endorse this optimistic view of welfare trends, arguing that non-governmental or 'third sector' organisations are resisting market principles, generating new forms of social solidarity, challenging the way welfare is conceptualised and delivered. They argue that policy makers need the third sector's closeness to users and to changing social realities, and that the third sector plays a critical role in challenging and reordering the relationship between society and the state. It forges new parameters for civil, political and social citizenship, and creates a more dynamic connection between policy and politics.

A more sanguine standpoint might argue that, in a period of welfare retrenchment, policy makers inevitably turn their attention to the informal sphere. And 'partnership' may be a crucial vehicle for the incursion of capitalism into the service sector, the recolonising of public services for the market[6].

It is difficult to know to what extent the neoliberal model, so advanced in Britain, will come to dominate institutional structures and thinking in Europe. In our study, partnerships vary considerably in different welfare contexts. They are significantly more representative and socially differentiated in France than in more 'corporatist' Germany. Cooperative, neighbourhood and family solidarities in Spain, marked by the particular history of civil society in Franco's Spain and the period of democratisation following 1975, are backed by legislation (Garcia, 1994; Tejero et al, 1999). Loans of honour, designed to change the culture of welfare dependency in Southern Italy, have also been supported by legislation (*Innovative social agencies*, (*Sostris Working Paper 8*), 1999, p 96). In East Germany, a humanist tradition survives from the churches, and as a legacy of socialist ideals.

There seemed to be a greater affinity and ease of communication between agencies doing biographically sensitive work and mainstream services in other countries than in Britain. In France, the Caisse Nationale d'Allocations Familiales (National Families Allocation Fund; CNAF) adopted the biographical approach in a pilot training scheme, with a view to developing a national programme (Murard, 1996b)[7]. Catherine Delcroix's powerful study (2001) of a Moroccan family in France likewise demonstrates a range of public services acting in concerted and biographically sensitive ways. It describes key crises in the lives of individual family members being dealt with by the family, friends and by health, educational and social work personnel. It shows impressive service networking around the needs of babies and young children, and committed mentoring at later stages. Several of the new agencies in our study had been initiated by public sector officials, suggesting that their methods and aims were supported by public authorities. Third sector funding also seemed more secure in France, Italy, Spain and Sweden, than in Britain[8], Greece and Germany (where resources were particular strained by unification costs).

While neoliberalism is based on the notion of a 'desocialised' individual, the social model of welfare is underpinned by a common notion that the fabric of society must be publicly supported and acted upon. French civic republicanism aims to maintain the identity and continuity of the community by which individuals are sustained, and widen opportunities for responsible self-government (Oldfield, 1990, p 181). German social policy of the 1980s abounded with appeals for a terrain of self-help in which sociopolitical actors could work on the social order on the basis of their own social goals. A 'new grammar of life forms' within services would generate a sense of belonging among excluded groups (Plaschke, 1984; Heinze and Olk, 1984).

Concepts that understand personal experience and meaning as interactive social processes facilitate debate between biographical researchers and policy makers[9]. In Germany, biographical researchers played a key role in criticising a new government strategy of 'activating social policy' in the late 1990s. This new strategy proposed that benefits would be worked out with the client, supposedly giving more control. The metaphor of a trampoline suggested that social policy should enable clients to 'jump out' of their situation. Against this, researchers argued that the problem of many clients was not to be more active, but to become more appropriately oriented, through strategic reflection and biographical work (Chamberlayne and Rustin, 1999, p 116; Leisering and Leibfried, 1999).

This is not to say that the Anglo-Saxon tradition has nothing to contribute. Accommodating difference often seems more difficult for Continental than for rights-based, Anglo-Saxon political cultures. The concept of 'transversal' dialogue or politics illustrates the way postmodern concepts of flux and multiplicity are being combined with relational approaches to citizenship and communication. A group of Italian feminists has termed this 'rooting' and 'shifting' – a process "in which those involved remain rooted in their own (multiple and shifting) identities and values but at the same time are willing to shift views in dialogue with others" (Lister, 1998, p 33).

> **Q.** What are the arguments for institutions such as schools, clinics, social security offices, prisons, and so on, to remain in the public sector? How could their work, often concerned with painful and difficult life transitions, be improved?
>
> **Q.** Which kinds of factors are working in favour of a biographically sensitive, social model of welfare in Europe, and which against? Where do you stand, and what can you do, with whom, to make a difference?

Conclusion

We have stressed the radical nature of a social policy approach that focuses on biographical strategies and resources. Chapter Fourteen proposed a method of thinking about agencies that may promote dialogue within them and with outside stakeholders. Biographical methods offer a means of bringing research, practice and policy into closer connection, in ways that may support the renewing of democratic impulses.

We have outlined a range of conceptual resources and social practices that are experimenting with an exciting mix of biographically sensitive and network-based methods. Such developments, however, need support. And that depends on whether the social model of welfare can thrive in the context of global competition. The European Presidency of Delors – that is, until the early 1990s – brought such concepts as the social sphere, social solidarity, social cohesion, social integration, social partnership, social dialogue and European citizenship to the fore, and gave rise to a commitment to combat social exclusion (Hantrais, 1995; Ditch, 1996). Conditions laid down under the Maastricht criteria, accompanying the Euro (see Teague, 1998, p 119), and through the General Agreement on Trade and Services, are based on quite different principles:

Developments at European level are in the balance between becoming more explicitly a system of economic regulation which expedites the process of deregulation in many traditional areas of national social security on the one hand, and containing the potential for strengthening the progress of civil society on the other. (Hermann and Lorenz, 1997, p 25)

The struggle for a redemocratised vision of social policy, fully adapted to new global as well as European realities, depends in important ways on the survival of the European social model. And within this quest, social policy and practice must prioritise mobilising and supporting biographical resources, and recognising and understanding the dynamics of lives.

Notes

[1] Our schedule allowed about three months' work on each of our six social categories, for access, interviewing and analysis. Extreme cases require specialised routes of access, which take time to establish. We failed to access homeless people, for example, despite numerous attempts.

[2] None of these changes has been 'structurally inevitable'. Without the Falklands War – and had Margaret Thatcher lost the 1982 General Election – there could have been a rather different outcome in Britain.

[3] In analysing 'biographical dynamics', it is the reconstruction of this thread that enables us eventually to understand how one thing led to another (personal communication with Sostris researchers Hungerbühler, Torrabadella and Tejero).

[4] Jordan (with Jordan, 2000) cites Weber (1922), who regarded "charismatic authority as appropriate in situations where order and organisation are at a discount and more informal, less structured relations prevail" (p 220). As Jordan puts it, "Charisma does not mean wild prophetic visions or demagogic ranting, merely the capacity to surprise, to say and do the unexpected" (2000, p 220).

[5] This study, which compared the informal sphere of caring in different welfare regimes (East and West Germany and Britain), was also concerned with the generation of creative relations between the public and private spheres (Chamberlayne and King, 2000).

[6] For this to be successful, services must continue to grow. Such growth can greatly exacerbate inequalities, as the British example shows.

[7] This research explored the impact of professionals' own biographies on their work. It found a contrast between workers who keep a personal distance from clients, fearful of contamination by them, and those who identify with them and want to share their good fortune with them.

[8] Two major studies of poor communities and self-help activities in Britain (Ginsberg et al, 1999; Williams and Windebank, 1999) found they "suffer from underfunding from outside the districts, and lack of recognition and support from official agencies, either in local or in national government" (Jordan with Jordan, 2000, p 169).

[9] French concepts such as proximity, animation, or *habitus* and German concepts such as social pedagogy, *Vergesellschaftung*, or hermeneutics, have no easy Anglo-Saxon equivalent.

References

Askonas, P. and Stewart, A. (eds) (2000) *Social exclusion: Possibilities and tensions*, Basingstoke: Macmillan.

Chamberlayne, P. and King, A. (2000) *Cultures of care: Biographies of carers in Britain and the two Germanies*, Bristol: The Policy Press.

Chamberlayne, P. and Rustin, M. (1999) *Sostris Working Paper 9: Sostris final report – from biography to social policy*, London: Centre for Biography in Social Policy, University of East London.

Delcroix, C. (2001) *Ombres et lumières de la famille nour: Comment certains résistent face à la précarité*, Paris: Payot.

Ditch, J. (1996) 'The prospects for social policy in the European Union', in N. Lunt and D. Coyle (eds) *Welfare policy: Research agendas and issues*, London: Taylor and Francis, pp 159-75.

Froggett, L. (2002) *Love, hate and welfare: Psychosocial approaches to policy and practice*, Bristol: The Policy Press.

Garcia, S. (1994) 'The Spanish experience and its implications for a citizen's Europe' in V. Godard, J. Llobera and C. Shore (eds) *The anthropology of Europe: Identity and boundaries in conflict*, Oxford: Berg, pp 255-74.

Ginsberg, N., Thake, S., Bieler, E., Ford, J., Foreman, J., Joyce, P., Lewis, J. and Ocloo, J. (1999) *Socio-economic assets in poor communities: Case studies of diversity: Interim findings*, London: School of Applied Social Sciences, University of North London.

Hantrais, L. (1995) *Social policy in the European Union*, London: Macmillan.

Heinze, R. and Olk, T. (1984) 'Rückzug des Staates: Aufwertung der Wohlfahrtsverbände?', in R. Bauer and H. Diessenbacher (eds) *Organisierte Nächstenliebe*, Opladen: Westdeutscher Verlag, pp 173-87.

Hermann, P. and Lorenz, W (1997) 'Towards a European welfare state – a European welfare regime by design or default?', in M. Mullard and S. Lee (eds) *The politics of social policy in Europe*, Cheltenham: Edward Elgar, pp 12-28.

Jordan, B. with Jordan, C. (2000) *Social work and the Third Way: Tough love as social policy*, London: Sage Publications.

Leisering, L. and Leibfried, S. (1999) *Time and poverty in western welfare states: United Germany in perspective*, Cambridge: Cambridge University Press, (2nd edition).

Levitas, R. (1998) *The inclusive society? Social exclusion and New Labour*, Basingstoke: Macmillan.

Lister, R. (1998) 'In from the margins: citizenship, inclusion and exclusion', in M. Barry and C. Hallett (eds) *Social exclusion and social work: Issues of theory, policy and practice*, Lyme Regis: Russell House Publishing, pp 26-38.

Lorenz, W. (1994) *Social work in a changing Europe*, London: Routledge.

Lorenz, W. (2000) 'Contentious identities – social work research and the search for professional and personal identities', Paper presented to the ESRC-funded seminar series *Researching social work as a means of inclusion*, University of Edinburgh, (www.nisw.org.uk/tswr/lorenz.html).

Menzies Lyth, I. (1960) 'The functioning of social systems as a defence against anxiety: a report on a study of the nursing service of a general hospital', in *Containing anxiety in institutions: Selected essays volume 1*, London: Free Associations Books, (1st edition, 1988).

Murard, N. (1999a) 'Risks and opportunities in experiences of migration and ethnicity', in *Sostris Working Paper 4: Case study materials – ethnic minorities and migrants*, London: Centre for Biography in Social Policy, University of East London, pp 30-9.

Murard, N. (1999b) 'From confidence in biographic narrative to confidence in social policy', in *Sostris Working Paper 8: Case study materials – innovative social agencies in Europe*, London: Centre for Biography in Social Policy, University of East London, pp 52-64.

Oldfield, A. (1990) 'Citizenship: an unnatural practice?', *Political Quarterly*, vol 61, pp 177-87.

Parton N. and O'Byrne, P. (2000) *Constructive social work*, Basingstoke: Macmillan.

Plaschke, J. (1984) 'Subsidiarität und "Neue Subsidiarität"', in R. Bauer and H. Diessenbacher (eds) *Organisierte Nächstenliebe*, Opladen: Westdeutscher Verlag, pp 134-47.

Sostris (1997) *Sostris Working Paper 1: Case study materials – social exclusion in comparative perspective*, London: Centre for Biography in Social Policy, University of East London.

Sostris (1998) *Sostris Working Paper 3: Case study materials – lone parents*, London: Centre for Biography in Social Policy, University of East London.

Sostris (1999) *Sostris Working Paper 7: Case study materials – unemployed graduates*, London: Centre for Biography in Social Policy, University of East London.

Taylor, D. (1998) 'Social identity and social policy: engagements with postmodern theory', *Journal of Social Policy*, vol 27, no 3, pp 329-50.

Teague, P. (1998) 'Monetary union and social Europe', *Journal of European Social Policy*, vol 8, no 2, pp 117-37.

Tejero, E., Torrabadella, L. and Lemkow, L. (1999) 'Biography, social networks and social policy: Spanish national report on flagship agencies' in *Sostris Working Paper 8: Case study materials – Innovative social agencies in Europe*, London: Centre for Biography in Social Policy, University of East London, pp 99-118.

Vobruba, G. (2000) 'Actors on processes of inclusion and exclusion: towards a dynamic approach', *Social Policy and Administration*, vol 34, no 5, pp 601-13.

Weber, M. (1922) *Economy and society*, New York, NY: Bedminster Press, (2nd edition with G. Roth and C. Wittick, 1968).

Williams, C.C. and Windebank, J. (1999) *Empowering people to help themselves: Tackling social exclusion in deprived neighbourhoods*, Leicester: Department of Geography, Leicester University.

Williams, F. (1998) 'Agency and structure revisited: rethinking poverty and social exclusion', in M. Barry and C. Hallett (eds) *Social exclusion and social work: Issues of theory, policy and practice*, Lyme Regis: Russell House Publishing, pp 13-25.

Discovering biographies in changing social worlds: the biographical–interpretive method

Roswitha Breckner and Susanne Rupp

The use of personal documents in a historical perspective

The use of 'personal documents' in social sciences and related disciplines can be traced back to the time when the insight emerged that understanding social reality requires a profound knowledge of how people experience and interpret 'their' social reality. In sociology, it was the growth of the American cities during the second half of the 19th century, especially the situation of the immigrants who gathered in the cities, that formed the backdrop of the first approaches using written or told biographies. In their research *The Polish peasant in America and Europe*, which was formative for the evolving Chicago School, William Isaak Thomas and Florian Znaniecki developed a biographical approach to social reality for the first time.

Thomas and Znaniecki used mainly written biographical material. This was neither 'accidental', in the sense that they were the only available data, nor were they regarded as a mere illustration of general theoretical considerations. Thomas and Znaniecki gathered them intentionally as basic data to *reconstruct* and *analyse* changes in community life and the way these were manifested in and processed through the lives of their members. By examining the extensive migration process from Poland to America at the turn of the 20th century, they showed that the changes in migrants' lives were not only a result of social changes in Polish society and the Polish community in America. Rather, changing life orientations had become a constitutive part of change in the community and societal sphere. Therefore, the biographical accounts were not solely analysed as an *indicator* or *illustration* of social change. The change of orientations and patterns of activity, based on attitudes and values – as Thomas and Znaniecki theorised their observations – were regarded as pivotal to the change in social institutions such as the family, community and political institutions. The personal life of tangible people was thereby regarded for the first time as a social field in which (radical) social change took place. The concrete or actual individual moved to the centre of sociological interest and investigation[1].

This is illustrated in the research of the Chicago School, where single case studies were carried out as part of community studies. This opened up the perspective of seeing individuals not only as victims of 'objective' social processes but also as actors, albeit struggling ones, who try to cope with difficult situations by seeking and developing solutions that do not appear as such at first glance. Furthermore, these studies implied a sociopolitical dimension, since, by exerting political pressure, they aimed to help manage the consequences of rapid and explosive growth of the city that had resulted in precarious living conditions for many people, segregation and general social tension.

Yet, although the Chicago School was working with personal documents and biographical material, a coherent *biographical method* guiding the data collection, and especially its analysis, was not really developed at that time. This was a point of general criticism of the 'qualitative approach', and the demand grew to develop more scientific methods in sociological work. The positivist paradigm with its criteria of validity and representativity to be ensured by the principles of measurement became dominant also in the Chicago School, and, after the Second World War, in Europe as well. During this period, personal data were barely used in social sciences. Rather, they were regarded either as 'too biased', 'too subjective' or 'not representative' enough. To explain a social world that now was predominantly perceived as being ruled by 'objective laws'[2], they seemed of very minor importance or no use at all. Sociological research became guided to a great extent by the search for objective conditions, that is, social dynamics, constraints and opportunities that were regarded as a result of social laws in a specific social field. In this perspective, the individual seemed either to be a victim or beneficiary of social structures that developed autonomously from the intentions of individuals, and could not really be influenced by them. Only 'collective actors' (such as unions or economic leaders, political parties and other institutions advocating specific interests) were regarded as potential candidates for manipulating or changing social structures.

However, the assumed collective actors seemed to disappear during the development of postwar Western societies, and a general dissolution of 'classes' seemed also to be part of post-war structural changes. Gender and majority/minority statuses, age and other factors became apparent as life-shaping conditions. The differentiation of structural categories brought an elaborate theoretical understanding as to why our lives had become 'fragmented' (Bauman, 1995) and 'individualised' (Giddens, 1991; Beck, 1992), and our society 'detraditionalised' (Heelas et al, 1996). However, the theoretical differentiation of social categories within a general picture of increasing 'fluidity' of social positions did not suffice to explain concretely *how* individuals experienced and perceived, oriented and acted, maintained or changed specific conditions of their lives.

It was in this historical situation and at the beginning of these theoretical discussions in social sciences in the 1970s and 1980s that the use of personal documents was picked up again, broadly, as oral history or as a developing 'biographical approach'. Biographical research consolidated itself in nearly all fields of social research where the character of social beings as actors is prominent[3]. In this strand of research Sostris is also embedded.

Notwithstanding the growing field of biographical research, the question remains: *in what way*, if at all, do personal documents represent social processes? Different answers to this question based on different epistemological assumptions have triggered methodological debates from the early 1980s up to today (see, for example, Newsletters of the International Sociological Association Research Committee 38 'Biography and Society', 1996-2001). On the one hand, we find the idea that life stories are direct reflections of a social reality 'out there', and therefore telling us more or less well 'how it was' in the past, in a milieu or society otherwise inaccessible to historians, sociologists and anthropologists. In this perspective, biographical material is mainly seen as an authentic representation of what we assume was 'going on out there'. This realist approach confronts, however, the difficulty that different people tell different stories about the same reality – that is, events and circumstances they have shared – and that their stories are modified within their own narratives when recalling them in different thematic or time contexts.

On the other hand, one encounters the perception of life stories as constructions, which do not tell us anything about a reality outside of themselves. They can be understood not as a reflection of an external reality but only as a *textual* reality, which is the basic means by which every reality is formed. Reality, in turn, is then only accessible by reconstructing those processes in which textual meaning is produced. In this perspective, life stories are not material or data to be used in order to understand or explain something else, but rather, they are the topic: respectively 'the realities' themselves[4]. However, if life stories are only texts, what distinguishes them from fiction? What is the difference between a completely 'invented' story (like a novel) and an (auto)biography referring to actual events and sequences of events? If there were no difference, we would not need to collect autobiographical accounts but could work – as sociologists – with the whole stock of world literature, without caring about their reference to empirical, historical, reality.

This might suffice to show that the main challenge in using biographical material and developing a biographical approach in social sciences is to answer these questions:

• What status are biographical accounts assumed to have in relation to reality?
• What kind of reality is of concern to the social sciences?

The principles of hermeneutic case reconstruction

In the approach underlying the methods used in Sostris, the key analytic distinction between the 'lived life' – that is, the life history – and the 'life story'[5] (Rosenthal, 1993) conceptualises the relation between a text and the actually lived life. In this understanding, the text in the form of a narrated life story relates to a sequence of situations and events that have taken place in the flow of time, and have left their traces. However, the reality of this sequence of situations and events is also a product of the meaning they gain in every act in which they are communicated, every telling of them in an actual situation. Only through an analytical approach that takes the actual production of meaning into account can we gain some insight into the building up of this reality, its principles of construction and modifications.

In this perspective, the fact that we talk about our experiences from different points of view that have developed in different spheres and periods of life does not indicate that our accounts are unreliable (Fischer-Rosenthal, 1989). It is just a manifestation of the fact that the recollection of an event or of specific circumstances is always embedded in a context of meaning. This develops at the time the event took place, and is reworked in the light of the later consequences during its retrospective recollection and reconstruction (see Schütz, 1962; Ricoeur, 1979; Mead, 1980; Fischer, 1982; Rosenthal, 1995).

In the process of constructing and communicating biographies, past, present and future perspectives are thereby interrelated. The reference to past experiences is necessarily selective, since we cannot tell each and every aspect of the past, not least because to do so would take as long as living it all again. Relevant aspects are separated from irrelevant ones, those that can be communicated from those that cannot. The principle of selecting the relevant from irrelevant follows a general pattern. This pattern forms the perspective of how to understand and communicate the past in a present situation, and in a horizon of expectations for the future (Rosenthal, 1993).

In summary, the perspective from which something is told is the result of a biography, in which social and personal contexts and experiences have created specific patterns of perception and attitudes of action that shape the person's trajectory (Riemann and Schütze, 1990). Furthermore, these general perspectives change in the course of our lives.

Biographical texts can be regarded as part of the strategies people have developed to get along with their lives, their experiences and the sense they make of them in the context of their biographies. However, these strategies are not only, and not even primarily, conscious plans and goals that a person pursues in the different spheres and periods of their lives. Rather, biographical strategies – as we understand them – are those partly conscious, partly unconscious patterns that indicate in what way a person has moulded their perceptions and reactions specifically as a result of difficult situations in their life. The assumption is that a difficult situation can be faced in different ways, and that the way in which a person handles it partly evolves from the situation itself, and partly is embedded in more general patterns of perceiving and acting on this kind of situation. These, on the one hand, are collectively developed and shared, and, on the other, are individually adapted and created.

The advantage this approach offers in terms of social policy is, that people are not labelled by their 'problem', not defined from an external perspective. 'External' definition tends either to victimise them or to de-emphasise a problem they have that outsiders consider to be less important or even trivial. Instead, the Sostris interviewees were encouraged to present their lives and to relate the complexity of their experiences in one specific aspect (lone parenthood, unemployment, and so on) in the way it had become relevant to them. This allows researchers to answer relevant questions:

- Is the assumed problem (lone parenthood, unemployment and so on) really the main problem in their actual situation?
- For example, is it the status and condition of being unemployed that excludes the person from relevant parts of social life, or are there other problems – such as health problems – that restrict his or her participation in social life much more?
- Which role does the assumed problem play in the interviewee's biographical context? For example, lone parenthood could be an event that destroys a person's career, but it could also be the 'solution' to an unsatisfactory family situation.
- Does an assumed problem always have the same meaning for different people? Early retirement, for example, can be experienced as dismissal from employment, but it can also be experienced as an opportunity to regenerate and to restructure a biography centred on work. Moreover, such different and often contradictory meanings can appear in the same person's story, suggesting an ambivalent attitude in his or her perception and handling of the situation.

The variety of meanings of an assumed, difficult life situation cannot be known in advance of the research. If it could, we would not need to do empirical investigation. Nor is it fully accessible to the consciousness of those concerned. Consequently, we need research methods that allow for the discovery and emergence of the complexity of situations and trajectories in which an actual problem is embedded. The narrative biographical interview developed by Fritz Schütze (1983), based on communication and narration theories (see, for example, Labov, 1972; Kallmeyer and Schütze, 1979; Ricoeur, 1988), seems to meet this demand as a tool for collecting biographical data in the form of life stories.

The biographical narrative interview[6]

The main principle of the narrative interview is its *openness*. The interview and the questions are not determined by theoretically deduced hypotheses constructed in advance, but depend, rather, on the themes and the way they are presented by the interviewee. The narrative interview operates with the notion that the relevant patterns and interconnections in the field under investigation will emerge in the course of the research. A precondition for this is that our interviewees (as actors in the field) are given the possibility and space to develop accounts of their experiences that are not guided by the researcher's questions. Therefore, the narrative interview begins with a very general 'initial question' about a topic that is connected to the interviewee's biography. Uninterrupted by further questions, it allows the interviewees to develop their own relevance around the topic and to relate it to their own biographical experiences (Schütze, 1983; Rosenthal, 1995).

In general, too direct and too concrete a question, addressing a specific researcher-defined problem, might focus the narration too much, and consequently foreclose the generation of a more complex account in which the meaning of a topic (such as unemployment) emerges in more *implicit* terms. If we ask the interviewee to address a highly specific topic very directly, then, for the interviewee, it might not be the most relevant one or, alternatively, it might be too sensitive or close to the bone. In the first case, the interviewee would not feel very motivated to talk about something he or she is not really concerned about; in the second case, the direct addressing of a critical experience might raise a strong defence[7]. Less direct and less concrete questions facilitate, in general, the emergence of a more complex and multi-layered picture than a strongly focused and very controlled presentation would allow.

When told by the interviewer that he or she is interested in the experience of unemployment in the context of their whole life history, and would like to listen to their account of their life story from the start until today[8], it is then up to the interviewees to define the thematic context in which they introduce the topic of unemployment and the loss of a traditional economy (for example, in the context of ill health, or poverty, or the loss of a traditional community). It is up to them in which time period they recall themselves experiencing unemployment as a relevant biographical topic, whether related to a state policy of economic deregulation, the strikes in Wales, the closure of other pits or merely the day of dismissal.

Such an open interview method assumes that every story has a *gestalt* (Gurwitsch, 1964; Schütze, 1983; Rosenthal, 1993) that condenses the latent as well as manifest perspectives and meanings in which a situation, an event or life phase has been experienced, recollected and accounted for. From this *gestalt*, we can reconstruct the way in which the past and the present meanings, as well as the future expectations related to an event or topic, are interconnected. This requires a situation in which every interviewee can develop his or her *gestalt* during the main narration without being interrupted by the interviewer.

In the second part of the interview, after the interviewee has signalled that she or he has finished the narration, the 'internal narrative questioning' then explores previously mentioned experiences, events and life phases and spheres in greater detail, evoking further narrations still oriented to the interviewees' relevancies, supporting their processes of recollection.

In addition to careful formulation of narrative questions[9], attentive, empathetic and active listening is needed (Rosenthal 1995), all aiming at evoking further narration of experiences relevant to the interviewees.

In contrast to description and argumentation, narration is regarded as the sort of text through which the meaning of an experience that has been constituted in the past is most likely to emerge. When telling a story the interviewee does not only speak from today's perspective but also recalls the situation as it was for him or her in the past. Furthermore, narration entails detailed information about the context and situation in which an event has taken place, details which would not be remembered so well if the interviewee were asked directly about them. Therefore narration also creates evidence for evaluating the plausibility or implausibility of a story. Last but not least, stories provide evidence about the flow of events because they entail a meaningful development. Narration starts at a certain time at a certain constellation of people and circumstances involved, and, during the events recounted and connected through the narrative stream, a change occurs and is made plausible for the story-teller as well as for the listener. In this way, meaning is created in a very basic sense by integrating different events in a temporal and thematic order (White, 1984; Bruner, 1987; Ricoeur 1988).

Hermeneutic case reconstruction

The awareness of the time-related configuration of experiences and their meanings is already a basic concern during the process of interviewing. Even more attention is paid to this in the process of analysing the narrative interviews. The main aim is to find out in what way the present meaning of a topic (in our case, a problem relevant to social policy) is based in past experiences – that is, in the lived life – and vice versa, in what way the present perception of life, the life story, is also moulding the problem of concern and the past experiences related to it. Finally, we must bear in mind that the individual's expectations of their future also cast a specific light on the whole complex of any given problem. Furthermore, every life history and life story is embedded in a social context that enables or restricts certain patterns of action and paths, as well as certain patterns of communicating them via specific discourses. So the life history and the life story are not regarded as something merely 'individual' but as part of a social context that is, in turn, based on the kind of activities and communication of its participants. The field of interest in biographical analysis in the Sostris project was in reconstructing the interrelation *between specific social contexts* (their opportunities and constraints as well as the specific conditions and relations in the family, at work and in the community at a certain time) and *the responses* of actors. The aim was to reconstruct how people undergo development and changes in contexts with specific problems.

In order to see how this method works in practice, let us look at the case of

Donald[10]. Born in 1944 into a Welsh mining family, Donald had continued with college education after finishing an apprenticeship, probably following the ambitions of his mother to gain a higher education. After one year, however, he gave up the course. Instead, he decided to orient his life around physical work, as a craftsman in the mines. He married the young librarian of his community, with whom he had one child. In this position, Donald was part of the community, but had the training and social status to establish himself elsewhere as well. In 1994, when British Coal closed down the last pit, Donald was made redundant at the age of 50. Since then, he has suffered from physical and mental health problems, from pains in his muscles and joints, sometimes unable to move at all, and from depression. He has taken psychiatric drugs, and began psychotherapy in 1997. Redundancy led to a breakdown; Donald became literally unbalanced and lost his ability to move.

Seen just from the point of view of his 'objective' chances and opportunities when redundancy struck, Donald's situation did not seem hopeless. He was a well-trained and experienced craftsmen who once had started an educational path, which he could, then, have taken up again as an opportunity to get out of his precarious situation. Yet for Donald this did not seem to be an opportunity. Why not? This can only be understood if we turn to his perception of the situation, in the context of how he sees his whole life and future prospects inherent in his (implicit) life concept, which evolved and formed part of the community structure of this (and maybe other) mining communities, based on strong bonds of solidarity.

Donald presented his life story from the perspective of his professional identity as a miner. Other themes of his life – his family and leisure-time activities – were scarcely mentioned, if at all. Surprisingly, Donald told his life story in the form of a love story, from the perspective of somebody who has lost the love of his life, and who struggles to come to terms with his life afterwards.

As we learn in the interview, Donald's love relationship with mining was based on three pillars: his fascination with technology, the danger of the work and, most important, the comradeship he had experienced as a coalface worker.

> I just miss, I miss my mates. I miss being chased because I was, I used to be a bit wicked, you know, in work, and ... I mean, we were always arguing. He used to sit me on his lap, saying we looked like a ventriloquist type.... We used to physically fight, you know, like kicking and punching, he used to sit on me, sit in the coal dust. Oh, that was just one of the things.

For Donald, it is this comradeship that is not replaceable in another industry, which makes it meaningless to aim at retraining or an education taking him out of mining, to which he had been wedded since his late adolescence. Donald could only stick to the mining industry because this was the only place he could conceive of to fulfil his needs. This is why, for Donald, redundancy could not be perceived as a chance to change a life track that had become dissatisfying (for similar cases, see *Sostris Working Paper 2*), but only as a catastrophe that just destroyed the basis on which he had built his life. Therefore, Donald has to restructure his whole life concept to get out of his present painful situation. Here the future dimension also plays a role. Being in his 50s, Donald has used up a great deal of his working life, but there are still 10, even 15, years left. This could be too short to develop a completely new path, but too long just to wait for retirement. This, too, may have contributed to Donald's current paralysis. Furthermore, as the mining community was dissolving, there were no collective strategies at hand.

In short, this analysis is based on different steps of interpretation, focusing on Donald's lived life and told life, trying to elucidate how they are interconnected. The whole process of analysis is organised according to the following steps[11]:

1. *The biographical data of the interviewee, which are extracted from all sources we have from the person, and organised in chronological order, are analysed purely as 'data'.*

We hypothesise about their meaning *without* referring to the text and therefore to the perspectives and meanings attributed by the interviewee. Consequently, it is possible to detect connections and interrelations that were not discussed explicitly in the interview. In general, this step aims to gain a picture of what happened in a life in the sequence of its events, what happened concomitantly and in succession, and where crucial decisions or events might have occurred, creating a turning point and reshaping the interviewee's life. Furthermore, the societal, generational, age-, family- and milieu-related contexts the individual has lived through, are reconstructed. Through this, we acquire insight into the variety of possibilities inherent in the social contexts and we are able to identify those chosen, ignored or rejected by the interviewee.

In Donald's case, we can detect an initial turning point when he decided not to follow the opportunity for a higher education (which *had* been an opportunity in his family and religious milieu) but to remain in the world of physical work in the mining community. This decision had fixed his life and shaped his consequent path. The second turning point obviously came with redundancy, which turned his life into an unstable, precarious one, with severe health consequences.

2. *We turn to the interview text, which is scrutinised following the topics and events in the sequential order that they have been talked about or mentioned in the interview.*

We do this in order to find out how the interviewee perceives his or her life at present. How are topics related to each other and in what way are they elaborated – as an extended narration, a short or extended description, or an argumentation? With which topic does the self-presentation begin, how does it end and what has been left out? What is the general 'dramaturgy' of the story? Following these questions, the analysis aims to reconstruct the structuring principle of the story, its *gestalt*, which is assumed to guide the selection and way of presentation of either topic (Rosenthal, 1993).

In Donald's case, it became apparent that he structured his life story as a love story, more precisely as the story of lost love. The respective topics and stories were predominantly organised along the lines of 'I was in love with my work', implicitly saying what he had lost through redundancy. Through this angle of vision, the more unpleasant and problematic aspects of his working life receded into the background, and, in this perspective, family life also lost its relevance, even though the biographical data indicate it had played quite a vivid role. Furthermore, in this perception of his situation focused on loss, it is difficult to develop future visions of how life could be filled with other things. For Donald, it seems necessary first to deal with his strong feeling of loss before he can develop future perspectives and prospects.

3. *Having found out the present perspective of our interviewee, we must ask how the interviewee might have experienced the past events, crucial periods and turning points, and how his perspective might have developed and changed over time move to the foreground?*

In order to find the answers, all the texts relating to the most relevant stages and turning points are examined to find out from the thematic context in which they are embedded, as well as from the manner of their narration, what they might have meant *in the past* – in contrast to what they might mean at present.

In Donald's case, we turned to the text where he talked about his decision to quit college. He found that he felt threatened by this path because it would have taken him away from the community, something that had happened to friends who had continued their studies. Furthermore, we examined the passages where he talked about his work in relation to his family. We found that, in the past, these life spheres seemed much more balanced than at present. It became apparent that Donald had experienced two work accidents after which he turned more to his family each time, extending his activities there, for example by taking regular holidays abroad with them.

4. *A general comparison must be made between the lived and the told life, which aims to summarise the way in which the life history and the life story are connected.*

We can state briefly that, in Donald's case, he had chosen to live his life as a member of the mining community and had found an equilibrium for his life aspirations and needs, including a balance between his working and family life there. The community had provided the basis on which work and family was integrated. When the pit closed down, he lost his work and with it one of the main elements of his life. Moreover, he also lost the community that was the integrating basis of his life, which started to dissolve after the pit was closed. It is because of this loss that the family life, even though it had also developed as a relevant pillar in Donald's life, could not compensate for the loss of work. The experience of irreversible loss became dominant for Donald and shaped his life story, which focused nearly exclusively on the sphere of work. Thereby he also risked losing the potential of other experiences, for example family relationships that could have compensated for the present loss. Therefore the *gestalt* of the story as one of a lost love forms part of Donald's present situation and problem. It is important to understand that the 'love relation' to work in the way it was presented evolved mainly after Donald had lost it. This makes a difference when thinking about how to support him in his struggle to overcome this loss.

After having understood and explained a case in this way, the following question arises: what does this single case tell us about the social context and strategies that can deal with the specific social problem with which our research started? We are also interested in how this case can be related to other cases. In other words, the question at stake is: what kind of general observation can be derived from a case study, and how can this be shown in the writing up of the case?

The question of generalisation

When we select interviewees and then again choose some of them for in-depth analyses, we presume that these cases will reveal something general or typical. There are, however, different levels on which we can generalise from a case. The 'case structure' that we have analysed already reveals something general – for example, the concept or strategy of an individual around which the line of action and perception is organised. The 'case structure' thus gives us an insight into how an individual develops certain ways of reacting to difficult situations and experiences in the past, present and anticipated future in the framework of his or her life. In Donald's case, we could reconstruct a pattern of a life concept fixed voluntarily in a specific community. This structure – and also this life strategy – is not fully intentional, but nor is it fully unconscious in a psychoanalytic sense. Rather, the assumption is that its genesis takes place in the field of conscious and preconscious social frameworks, habits and preferences emerging in reaction to different kinds of sociostructural conditions and emotional needs, such as the consequences of heavy disappointment, betrayal, love sickness or even of trauma. In addition, the general concept of orientation and action of an individual operates in different situations and spheres of life and is not bound to any specific problem (such as lone parenthood, unemployment or migration). Its general dynamic and structure can be found in every sphere of life and can be shared by individuals belonging to different, or even opposite, social categories.

How far a specific problem and pattern of response to it in one case is shared in other cases, or in what way it represents a relevant aspect of the whole social field under investigation can only be detected, however, by comparison with other cases. In Donald's case, this means that it is quite possible that there were more cases like him, people who adhered voluntarily to a specific community and that they share the experience of having lost a love when a relevant element of their life that was based on community disappeared. Even if the pattern of lost love were the only one in Donald's community, or in others, it would still show one possible reaction within disintegrating communities, based on a specific work culture and industry, which could be relevant to understanding a general feature of the whole social field under investigation.

In contrast to the reconstruction of the case structure, which takes into account every relevant topic in the life of the interviewee, in the attempt to understand and explain its general dynamic, a *systematic comparison* with the patterns of other cases aims at the construction of specific 'types' of responses to a *specific topic*[12], for example long-term unemployment, lone parenthood or migration. With the construction of a type, we can understand how a general action strategy of an individual operates in a specific sphere of life or social field, constituting a specific way of experiencing and coping with a problem, issue or change. Therefore, the construction of a typology refers to a specific field of social action, aiming to show the diversity of possible and – following Glaser and Strauss[13] – similar and contrasting trajectories within such a field. In Donald's case, we can state that he represents a type for whom early retirement led to a biographical crisis with severe health consequences, in contrast to other cases in this field representing a type who experiences early retirement as an opportunity for reorientation and development of new prospects. Finally, a reconstruction of the interactive relation between different types (for example, the relationship between those who suffer from the challenge and those who profit from it), their position in a certain field – for example, in the social welfare system or in public opinion – help us to understand how the different ways of dealing with the challenge are represented in the social field. Which type dominates? Which is 'marginal'? Which is socially supported, and which one experiences restrictions and exclusion?

Before we discuss further conclusions that can be drawn from hermeneutically reconstructed case studies and their comparison, we would first like to show the different levels of comparison that are possible within an international research project and to which discussions can contribute at every level.

In Sostris, it was mainly the interrelation between the social conditions of the lived lives of our interviewees (the peculiar constraints and opportunities, the family and class situation, the peculiarities of local milieus and of national and local traditions, the specific political and historical context) and the responses to these conditions that determined the scope of each biographical analysis. The aim was to reconstruct how people had been affected by social changes that were marked by specific risks, and how they formed an active part in the development of the societal context by responding to personal, as well as sociostructural, challenges in particular ways.

As we investigated six different categories of risk situation in seven different countries, a huge variety of possible comparisons opened up. First, the cases within each category were compared by each national team in order to find contrasting or similar responses to the specific problem under investigation. The choice of a 'main case' that was analysed in depth against the foil of another six 'profiled' cases aimed at reconstructing the most 'typical' or the most 'interesting' pattern. This pattern, which could also be the most 'atypical', throwing light on the 'typical' by contrast, could be observed in either category and in either local or national contexts[14]. Then the question arose, in what way the local and national context formed part of the reconstructed pattern of response, or in what way could it be found in other national and local contexts as well. Therefore, case comparisons of the same categories from different countries were undertaken as the next step[15].

In the further process of analysis, it became apparent that 'typical' responses were not only structured by the specific category (for example, long-term unemployment or single parenthood) in which an interviewee had originally been recruited. Similar patterns of biographical response to risky life situations could be found in the lives of interviewees recruited under different categories, in addition to which an accumulation of several different risks could be observed in many cases. Therefore, a comparison between cases *across* the different categories in *one* national context appeared as a fruitful next step of comparison, even though in Sostris this, and subsequent stages, were not always completed. The question of how far a pattern of response derives from the individual background of a person, pending on previous experiences and ways of handling them, and how far it was grounded in a specific local milieu or national peculiarity (for example by forming part of established ways and a specific 'logic' of sociopolitical intervention), could be approached at this level of comparison.

On the next step of comparison, the similarities and differences between the different fields of problems under investigation (such as lone parenthood and long-term unemployment) could be approached with the aim of constructing hypotheses about the general and specific mechanisms operating in different social fields and the challenges. This step can be extended to an unlimited variety of social phenomena and social fields, aiming at gaining more and more wide-ranging and abstract theoretical concepts that can explain common mechanisms of social action and perception while remaining empirically based at the same time (Glaser and Strauss, 1967). In Sostris, the question of how the analysed responses formed part of general biographical and sociostructural patterns developing as a response to risk situations and social exclusion in Western European societies (in comparison with East Germany as representing an Eastern European society in transition) and how these patterns were bound to national and local conditions could have been approached by a comparison *across* different categories and *across* different countries. This was the most general level that the Sostris research was designed to attain.

This systematically outlined procedure of generalisation may sound as if it is following a path paved with clear methodical rules, which could be accomplished by every researcher in the same way. The practice of analysis shows, however, that each process of interpretation, and therefore of generalisation also, depends on the perspectives, knowledge and experience of the researcher. This interacts with every case and social field. Therefore, self-reflection on the researcher's side, for example clarifying identifications and distinguishing one's own experiences (and projections) from the experiences of the case under analysis, accompanies every process of analysis. In order not to remain too limited to a researcher's own background of experience and knowledge, every analysis should be carried out, or at least checked with colleagues, preferably on a cross-cultural basis. This is the basis on which every generalisation is built upon and is also decisive for its quality, coherence and plausibility. In this approach, therefore, the case is always part of the writing-up of the research results. If we were just to formulate generalisations, derived from the case study, the thesis put forward concerning a specific type or social mechanism observed, the empirical basis of its development would be lost. On the other hand, every presented case study has to accomplish the task of showing what is of general interest in the specific case. In this process, the readers of every case study are involved. They will decide for themselves if they can follow the interpretation of the case, if they would come to different, conclusions, or if they see a different, interesting, general topic in the case that has not been worked out by the author. Hermeneutic research is validated by interaction and discussion, at every step of the interpretation, as well as at the moment when conclusions – on every level of the interpretation, generalisation and theorising process – are drawn.

Case reconstruction in the field of social policy?

In this chapter, we have presented the biographical–interpretive method in order to show how it can contribute to social policy discussions. Biographical research, which includes from the start a policy orientation, brings profound knowledge about a social field and its actors. Hermeneutically reconstructed biographies show how actors depend on and create the social field in which they live. As researchers and policy makers, we gain insight into the principles that make people act. Donald was chosen as an example in order to show how we can draw conclusions for policy and further research just from one case (which was, of course, interpreted against the backdrop of knowledge of sociological theory, of policy discussions and, last but not least, of knowledge from more than 200 other cases from the Sostris project). Donald's case can be related to the question of why further education – as a policy measure that has been offered as a remedy for those affected by the restructuring of the economy – did not help at all, even though he had had access to higher education before he became a miner. Donald represents a type who longs to be part of a community that allows him to balance work and family life. This type is possible in all communities based on close social networks and bonds of solidarity. It is not surprising that the destruction of such communities triggers a crisis for people of Donald's 'type'. If policy had learnt from case studies, it could have developed concepts either of 'replacement', which would have allowed Donald to maintain his belonging to the community, or of how to change the dependence of life concepts on the specific kind of community. For cases like Donald's, this would require intensive support to develop his own self-understanding and a further reconstruction of his own biography. Instead, the mere offer of education did not match Donald's needs. Furthermore, it was actually experienced as a threat because, for him, education meant leaving the community.

With the theoretical and empirical loss of the collective actor, as indicated at the beginning of this chapter, the 'individual' emerged – not the singular actor. Policy has to take this into account. If it addresses actors as 'collective' or places individuals just as members of a 'category', it will not meet the needs of individualised actors in a risk society. On the other hand, a case-oriented concept of social policy has to deal with the risk of apparently advocating and accelerating the general tendency of 'individualisation', by putting the burden of dealing with collectively created social problems mainly on the 'individual', singularising those concerned. Therefore, the effect of case-oriented social policy concepts will depend on the way and the purposes to which biographical knowledge is put[16].

Notes

[1] This was also based on sociological theories developing at that time (such as the work of Georg Simmel), the phenomenological tradition (as outlined by Alfred Schütz), and symbolic interactionism of the pragmatist tradition (mainly represented by George Herbert Mead).

[2] In Marxist terms, *objective laws* of capitalist economy determine the social world. In Durkheimian terms, on the other hand, our social world is ruled by *social facts* that exist or develop independently from individual aspirations, wishes or meanings.

[3] For insights into this development see: Thompson (1978); Niethammer (1980); Schütze (1983); Bertaux (1981); Bertaux and Kohli (1984); Kohli (1986a, 1986b); Passerini (1987); Inowlocki (1993); Fischer-Rosenthal and Alheit (1995); Hoerning and Alheit (1995); Rosenthal (1995 and 1998); Wohlrab-Sahr (1995); Dausien (1996); Rupp (1997); Alheit et al (1999); Apitzsch (1999); Leisering and Leibfried (1999); Miller (1999); Apitzsch and Inowlocki (2000); Chamberlayne et al (2000); Davis and Lutz (2000); Fischer-Rosenthal (2000); Roberts (2001).

[4] This position has been formulated mainly by 'radical constructivism' (for example, in the version of Glasersfeld, 1989). An overview and a discussion of its consequences for biographical research is laid out in Jost (2001).

[5] Elsewhere in this volume these are referred to as the 'told stories'.

[6] For the structure of the interview and the techniques of questioning, see Schütze (1987); Rosenthal (1995); Hollway and Jefferson (1997, 2000); and an English adaptation of Schütze and Rosenthal in Wengraf (2001).

[7] This aspect has been discussed in detail by Jefferson and Hollway (1997, 2000).

[8] This was the form we applied as the initial question in Sostris. It has been developed by Gabriele Rosenthal (see Rosenthal, 1995).

[9] Avoid 'Who?', 'Why?', and 'Where?' questions. Formulate questions such as: "Could you tell me more about ...?", "Can you recall the situation in which ...?" (See Rosenthal, 1997; Hollway and Jefferson, 1997; Wengraf, 2001.)

[10] The interview was conducted by Prue Chamberlayne and Tom Wengraf, and has been analysed by Susanne Rupp (see *Sostris Working Paper 6*). The case is also presented in Chapter Five of this volume, pp 82-7.

[11] For a more detailed exploration of these steps, see Rosenthal (1993, 1995) and – as a concrete example – Breckner (1998).

[12] This very helpful distinction between generalising the 'case structure' and constructing a 'type' has been worked out by Monika Wohlrab-Sahr (1994).

[13] The procedures of comparison by creating minimal and maximal contrasts between different types of social action on different levels of creating grounded theory has been developed by Glaser and Strauss (1967).

[14] In the process of adapting biographical methods in Sostris, every national team dealt first with their main case (in their own language) before they presented the biographical data and the so-called sequentialisation (an overview of the topics of the interview and the way they are presented as narration, argumentation or description, following the sequential order of the interview) in English during the international workshops in which the whole Sostris team participated. Despite the inevitable loss of meaning through translation, we enlarged our knowledge base for the reconstruction of case-relevant social contexts – as well as for further theoretical hypotheses – by a highly differentiated discussion between 17 participants from seven countries. This constellation led to a very rich background for specifying the particularity *and* the generality of the social contexts of the respective cases. At the same time, this complexity made it difficult, within restricted time limits, to complete the hypotheses-building process and to identify general patterns.

[15] See the composite reports in every category in the Sostris working papers, and Chapter Two of this volume.

[16] See the flagship agency studies in *Sostris Working Paper 8*.

References

Alheit, P., Dausien, B., Hanses, A., Fischer-Rosenthal, W. and Keil, A. (eds) (1999) *Biographie und Leib*, Giessen: Psychosozial.

Apitzsch, U. (ed) (1999) *Migration und Traditionsbildung*, Opladen: Westdeutscher Verlag.

Apitzsch, U. and Inowlocki, L. (2000) 'Biographical analysis: a 'German' school?', in P. Chamberlayne, J. Bornat and T. Wengraf (eds) *The turn to biographical methods in social science*, London and New York, NY: Sage Publications, pp 53-70.

Bauman, Z. (1995) *Life in fragments. Essays in postmodern morality*, Oxford: Blackwell.

Beck, U. (1992) *Risk society. Towards a new modernity*, London: Sage Publications.

Bertaux, D. (ed) (1981) *Biography and society. The life history approach in the social sciences*, Beverly Hills: Sage Publications.

Bertaux, D. and Kohli, M. (1984) 'The life story approach: a continental view', *Annual Review of Sociology*, vol 10, pp 215-37.

Breckner, R. (1998) 'The biographical–interpretative method – principles and procedures', in *Sostris Working Paper 2: Case study materials – the early retired*, London: Centre for Biography in Social Policy, University of East London, pp 91-104.

Breckner, R., Kalekin-Fishman, D. and Miethe, I. (2000) *Biographies and the division of Europe. Experience, action and change on the 'Eastern side'*, Opladen: Leske & Budrich.

Bruner, J. (1987) 'Life as narrative', *Social Research*, vol 54, no 1, pp 11-32.

Chamberlayne, P., Bornat, J. and Wengraf, T. (eds) (2000) *The turn to biographical methods in social science*, London and New York, NY: Sage Publications.

Chamberlayne, P. and Rupp, S. (1999) 'British report on category 6', in *Sostris Working Paper 6: Case study materials – ex-traditional workers*, London: Centre for Biography in Social Policy, University of East London.

Dausien, B. (1996) *Biographie und Geschlecht. Zur biographischen Konstruktion sozialer Wirklichkeit in Frauenlebensgeschichten*, Bremen: Donat.

Davis, K. and Lutz, H. (2000) 'Life in theory: three feminist thinkers on transition(s)', *The European Journal of Women's Studies*, vol 7, no 3, pp 367-78.

Fischer, W. (1982) *Time and chronic illness. A study on the social constitution of temporality*, Habilitation thesis, California: University of Berkeley.

Fischer-Rosenthal, W. (1989) 'Life story beyond illusion and events past', *Enquête, Cahiers du Cercom*, no 5, pp 219-25.

Fischer-Rosenthal, W. (2000) 'Address lost: how to fix lives. Biographical structuring in the European modern age, in R. Breckner, D. Kalekin-Fishman and I. Miethe (eds) *Biographies and the division of Europe*, Opladen: Leske & Budrich, pp 55-75.

Fischer-Rosenthal, W. and Alheit, P. (eds) (1995) *Biographien in Deutschland: Soziologische Rekonstruktionen gelebter Gesellschaftsgeschichte*, Opladen: Westdeutscher Verlag.

Giddens, A. (1991) *Modernity and self-identity. Self and society in the late modern age*, Cambridge: Polity Press.

Glaser, B.G. and Strauss, A.L. (1967) *The discovery of grounded theory*, Chicago: Aldine.

Glasersfeld, E.V. (1989) 'Constructivism in education', in T. Husen and T.N. Postlewhaite (eds) *The international encyclopedia of education*, Oxford: Pergamon Press, pp 162-3.

Gurwitsch, A. (1964) *The field of consciousness*, Pittsburgh, PA: Duquesne University Press.

Heelas, P., Lash, S. and Morris, P.M. (1996) *Detraditionalization*, Oxford: Blackwell.

Hoerning, E. and Alheit, P. (1995) 'Biographical socialization', *Current Sociology*, vol 43, nos 2-3, pp 101-14.

Hollway, W. and Jefferson, T. (1997) 'Eliciting narrative through the in-depth interview', *Qualitative Inquiry*, vol 3, no 1, pp 53-70.

Hollway, W. and Jefferson, T. (2000) *Doing qualitative research differently. Free association, narrative and the interview method*, London: Sage Publications.

Inowlocki, L. (1993) 'Grandmothers, mothers and daughters: intergenerational transmission in displaced families in three Jewish communities', in D. Bertaux and P. Thompson (eds) *Between generations. Family models, myths and memories*, Oxford: Oxford University Press, pp 139-53.

Jost, G. (2001) 'Radical constructivist views on biographical research', Paper presented to the conference *Methodological problems of biographical research*, University of Kassel, May.

Kallmeyer, W. and Schütze, F. (1977) 'Zur Konstitution von Kommunikationsschemata der Sachverhaltsdarstellung', in D. Wegner (ed) *Gesprächsanalysen*, Hamburg: Buske, pp 159-274.

Kohli, M. (1986a) 'Biographical research in the German language area', in Z. Dulcewski (ed) *A commemorative book in honor of Florian Znaniecki on the centenary of his birth*, Poznan, pp 91-110.

Kohli, M. (1986b) 'Social organisation and subjective construction of the life course', in A.B. Sorensen, F.E. Weiner and L.R. Sherrod (eds) *Human development and the life course*, Hillsdale, NJ: Lawrence Erlbaum, pp 271-92.

Labov, W. (1972) 'The transformation of experience in narrative syntax', in W. Labov (ed) *Language in the inner city*, Philadelphia, PA: University of Pennsylvania Press.

Leisering, L. and Leibfried, S. (1999) *Time and poverty in western welfare states: United Germany in perspective*, Cambridge: Cambridge University Press.

Mead, G.H. (1980) *The philosophy of the present*, Chicago, IL: University of Chicago Press, (Arthur E. Murphy edition).

Miller, R. (1999) *Researching life stories and family histories*, London: Sage Publications.

Newsletters of the International Sociological Association Research Committee 38 'Biography and Sociology' (1996-2001) *Biography and society*.

Niethammer, L. (ed) (1980) *Lebenserfahrung und kollektives Gedächtnis. Die Praxis der 'Oral History'*, Frankfurt-am-Main: Syndikat.

Oevermann, U., Allert, T., Konau E. and Krambeck, J. (1987) 'Structures of meaning and objective hermeneutics', in V. Meja, D. Misgeld and N. Stehr (eds) *Modern German sociology*, New York, NY: Columbia University Press, pp 436-47.

Passerini, L. (1987) *Fascism in popular memory. The cultural experience of the Turin working class*, Cambridge: Cambridge University Press.

Ricoeur, P. (1979) 'The model of the text. Meaningful action considered as text', in P. Rabinow and W.M. Sullivan (eds) *Interpretative social sciences*, Berkeley, CA: University of California Press, pp 73-101.

Ricoeur, P. (1988) *Time and narrative*, Chicago, IL: University of Chicago Press.

Riemann, G. and Schütze, F. (1990) 'Trajectory as a basic theoretical concept for analyzing suffering and disorderly social processes', in D. Maines (ed) *Social organization and social processes*, Hawthorne: Aldine, pp 333-57.

Roberts, B. (2001) *Biographical research*, Buckingham: Open University Press.

Rosenthal, G. and Bar-On, D. (1992) 'A biographical case study of a victimizer's daughter', *Journal of Narrative and Life History*, vol 2, no 2, pp 105-27.

Rosenthal, G. (1993) 'Reconstruction of life stories. Principles of selection in generating stories for narrative biographical interviews', *The Narrative Study of Lives*, vol 1, no 1, pp 59-91.

Rosenthal, G. (1995) *Erlebte und Erzählte Lebensgeschichte*, New York and Franfurt-am-Main: Campus.

Rosenthal, G. (1998) *The Holocaust in three generations: Families of victims and perpetrators of the Nazi Regime*, London: Cassell.

Rupp, S. (1997) 'Zur Herausbildung von Generationseinheiten und Generationenbeziehungen bei Angehörigen der Weimarer Jugend- und Hitlerjugendgeneration', in J. Mansel, G. Rosenthal and A. Tölke (eds) *Generationen-Beziehungen, Austausch und Tradierung*, Opladen: Westdeutscher Verlag, pp 205-17.

Schütz, A. (1962) *The problem of social reality. Collected papers*, The Hague: Niejhoff.

Schütze, F. (1983) 'Biographieforschung und narratives Interview', *Neue Praxis*, vol 3, pp 283-94.

Schütze, F. (1992) 'Pressure and guilt: the experience of a young German soldier in World War II and its biographical implication', *International Sociology*, vol 7, nos 2-3, pp 187-208, 347-467.

Sostris (1998-99) *Sostris Working Papers 1-9*, London: Centre for Biography in Social Policy, University of East London.

Thomas, W.I. and Znaniecki, F. (1918-20, 1923) *The Polish peasant in Europe and America. Monograph of an immigrant group*, vols 1-5, Boston, MA: Richard G. Badger.

Thompson, P. (1978) *The voice of the past: Oral history*, Oxford: Oxford University Press.

White, H. (1984) 'The value of narrativity in the representation of reality', in W.J.T. Mitchell (ed) *On narrative*, Chicago, IL: University of Chicago Press.

Wengraf, T. (2001) *Qualitative research interviewing: Biographic narrative and semi-structured method*, London: Sage Publications.

Wohlrab-Sahr, M. (1994) 'Vom Fall zum Typus. Die Sehnsucht nach dem 'Ganzen' und dem 'Eigentlichen' – Idealisierung als biographische Konstruktion', in A. Diezinger, H. Kitzer, I. Anker, I. Bingel, E. Haas and S. Odierna (eds) *Erfahrung mit Methode. Wege sozialwissenschaftlicher Frauenforschung*, Freiburg im Breisgau: Kore, pp 269-99.

Wohlrab-Sahr, M. (ed) (1995) *Biographie und Religion: Zwischen Ritual und Selbstsuche*, Frankfurt-am-Main: Campus.

Historicising the 'socio', theory, and the constant comparative method

Tom Wengraf

Overview

This methodological appendix is divided into two sections, which consider:

- some consequences of a profoundly historicising approach to the 'socio' of sociobiography;
- some underplayed implications of the constant comparative method beyond Glaser and Strauss' classic emphasis on grounded theorising (1967).

It emerges from a struggle to understand how Sostris related its research questions and its methodology.

- Sostris' *sociological and social policy* research can be seen as an attempt to improve and change social meta-narratives of societal description and thus of consequent social policy recommendation;
- Sostris' *research methodology* is based on the case narratives of individuals processed in a Grounded Theory (GT) way.

How is the connection to be made between emergent case theory and discussion characteristic of most of the chapters in this volume on the one hand, and the general questions arising from prior theorising about grand historical transformations (for example, from pre-risk to risk society, from the welfare societies of the third quarter of the 20th century to the World Trade Organisation [WTO] society currently emerging from the last decade) on the other?

This appendix starts by arguing that, in the sociobiographical approach that characterises Sostris, 'socio' should be profoundly historicised. It identifies the problematic nature of *type*, as in the notion of searching for 'typical' cases in 'typical' contexts.

It addresses one particular feature of the 'classic' GT methodological programme: the drive towards the higher and more abstract transhistorical generalisations of formal theory, the type of theorisation whose construction is the primary desired output from Glaser and Strauss' GT research programme (1967). With Burawoy (1991, 2000), we argue that our primary task is not to develop transhistorical generalities but rather *to enrich the understanding of the focal cases* partly by undertaking the reconstruction of theory.

Another methodological issue that is addressed is the direction of implied causality between the 'parts' and the 'whole', between 'micro' and 'macro'. There exist *interactionists* and *structuralists*. Interactionists typically argue for something close to 'methodological individualism' – it is the interaction of individuals that sustains and modifies the produced product that appears as a dominant social order. Like Marx in his (1844) *Economic and Philosophic Manuscripts*, they find it most productive to start from the micro-realities and derive the macro-order. This is attractive because of the strong place this provides for apparently irreducible human agency. The structuralist counter-argument suggests that the main line of causality starts with the macro-order (currently the new world global [dis]ordering process), which constrains and shapes the micro-(dis)orders that proliferate under its aegis. The whole (mutating global society) is more than the sum of its parts and constrains them.

Sostris, we argue, takes a position of weak structuralism, remaining sensitive both to the large constraints but also to the often less visible freedoms of even the very vulnerable and constrained individuals with which our research has been concerned.

Sostris is something of a hybrid. More concerned than GT with general concepts that, by way of mediating typologies, yield understanding of the *unique* nature of the historical configuration of each particular case, it is case-focused rather than theorising-focused. It promotes a 'differential social science', not one that attempts to find a multitude of different cases that are only to be subsumed under generic transhistorical types and mechanisms. Out of the comparison of cases, we seek new understandings of cases that are historically and culturally specific and differentiated – a 'clinical' understanding, not a GT generality (or formal theory) that transcends all of them.

Although it predominantly operates with a weak structuralism, Sostris could certainly allow for an interactionist research programme that was (and some are) also concerned with historical differentiation. Its weak structuralism is negotiable; its desire for historical specificity is not.

Unlike most structuralisms, however, Sostris is less determinist about the future because it treats models of the present as less well-known. It is structuralist, but attempts to explore – as insufficiently known – the macro-structures and meta-narratives into which it wishes to insert its cases, and uses the case material as evidence for the rectification of provisional models of such theorised structures and tendencies. In the sequence of research practice, it is the moment of the constant comparison of cases that allows both for the improvement of general concepts and for the improvement of our case understanding.

Let us now begin with method.

Breckner and Rupp's Appendix A provides an overview of the development of a relatively systematic biographical–narrative interpretive method (BNIM) in social research and its use in Sostris. They show how stories of action and inaction enable the researcher to consider both the conscious and the unconscious *meanings*, *contexts* and *conditions* of action as well as the observed and the less observed *consequences* of action. They also stress that a still-living individual's biography is always unfinished, if only because the very fact of telling and spelling out a biography within the person's current perspective may in itself lead to a change in that perspective, either through the actual process of telling or through a reflection on the transcript of the told (for an example of individual change through successive rebiographising, see Wiersma, 1992). In addition, the impacts of further events in the person's life (and the restructuring and mutation of perspectives that this can give rise to) also tends to produce further rebiographising.

A strong aspect of the methodological imperatives of BNIM used in Sostris is that the interview attempts to minimise the external concerns and theories of the researcher and to maximise the free associative flow of the interviewee. Similarly, in the analysis of the interview material, the hypothesising about its significance and meaning comes from, and is always corrected by, the flow of new data (see Wengraf, 2001, pp 231-300, for details and examples). The wilful introduction of prior generalising theory is resisted. The theory about the particular case – answering 'What is this case a case *of*?' (Ragin and Becker, 1992) – is seen as emerging internally from within the case.

This GT methodology does not mesh with the generalising concern of Sostris and the emphasis of Chapter One in an obvious way. Chapter One situated Sostris in the context of changes in the social-scientific understanding of contemporary mutations in global society and in West European societies. It discussed some of the changes in social-scientific mega-models (theories) and meta-narratives of the contemporary world market and world disorder that have occurred, partly accepting and partly reinterpreting models of postmodernity, global fluidity, neoliberal and global restructuring and the like.

How to handle this apparent contradiction between external general theorising and a method starting from an internalist theorising from the case will be considered later in this chapter. First we consider why the concept of the 'socio' in socio-biography must be profoundly historicised.

Historicising the 'socio'

The 'socio' as the research focus of Sostris

What is meant by saying that Sostris is a *socio*biographical research project? The research inquiry methodology used in Sostris was that of individual, personally narrated biographies, analysed case by case. In addition, in this volume, our method of presentation has also been biographical, comparing the psychosocial dynamics of the lives of individual people. However, to avoid confusion, the method of inquiry and the method of presentation in Sostris should be seen as *different* from the Sostris research focus.

We formulated our research focus as being on social strategies in risk society (hence 'Sostris'). We wanted the strategies of persons struggling to deal with 'the social as difficulty' to illuminate that social with which they were being obliged to deal. We also wanted to illuminate how a societal transition, starting in the final quarter of the 20th century and leading to a new type of risky society for more people, might then lead to makers of social policy (understood very broadly) being obliged to develop a new type of *social policy strategy*. The accounts of individual lives were the indispensable method. However, the focus – the goal – was to understand the social, and convey that understanding of the social[1].

We wanted to develop a better model of this new world (dis)order, to understand its current biography so far, but not just to improve our understanding. As Chapters Fourteen and Fifteen spell out, we wanted this research to help; we wanted to enable appropriate new social policies to be developed[2].

What was the best way to characterise and understand the dynamics of this (dis)order (the mutating matrix and context for past, present and hopefully future generations of individual people)? What criteria did we have for developing a good enough biography of the birth and development of such a new type of society, provisionally entitled 'risk society'?

We should stress that the notion of the 'biography' of a society may, perhaps, only be an analogy, a metaphorical use of a concept originally restricted to individual people. A society is not a person, and thinking of societies as being 'like people' can lead to ignoring the way that they are not. However, when people write 'our island story', for example, when they construct a meta-narrative of the 'history of world society and its recent globalisation', when they distinguish between deceptive and less deceptive histories of some or all of the human race, or of long-standing organisations such as the Christian Church, or the English State, they can find it productive to think of this being a sort of 'biography'. Likewise, historically minded sociologists and societally minded historians construct explicit or implicit 'biographies'. In Chapter Fourteen, we extended the notion of a biographising object of study to that of organisations (agencies); for this chapter, we shall – with all due reserve and caution – extend it still further to the biography of a society or type of society[3].

We think one part of the answer is now clear. Just in the same way as for individuals, as regards a society we also want to stress the *constantly unfinished* nature of such a biography. One key reason for taking such a standpoint is this: the very fact of telling a biography within the currently dominant perspective may in itself lead to a change in that society's biography – rebiographising – either through the actual process of the telling or through a reflection on the transcript of the told. (Sociologists talk of self-fulfilling prophecies; more creative are prophecies of societal futures designed to make such dystopian futures *less* likely.)

By researching the meanings for persons of current arrangements and strategies, we want *to change* the self-biographising of our auto-destructive society and societies. We want the real lived lives of the people we study[4] to be part of the *collectively* told story of our society, a society much fuller of planetary risk and of risk to the physical planet than the blander concept of 'risk society' might wish to acknowledge. Were this to happen, it would be part of a mutation in that socially told story and part of a mutation in societally held perspectives on the adequacy of social (policy) strategies[5].

As I have said before, we are gradually working out that such a biography-of-society approach to our understanding of the whole society (complex of societies) requires a profound historicisation (McDonald, 1996) of our understanding of the social. (This is more difficult for sociologists than we think, a fact I will discuss later in this chapter.) Not just any historicisation will do. Our models of historical possibilities in this historicisation must be no less open-ended in its concept of collective historical possibility than our model is at the level of the individual's historical possibilities – probably even more so[6].

The mutating 'structure and culture' of a society also requires historicisation. Being concerned with clarifying the interaction between subjects and their own contexts of activity, decision and social survival and success, we initially used Giddens's approach. However, we eventually found Archer's formulation (1995) more than adequate for our purposes.

The essential idea of structuration theory – a blander, more individualist version of Bourdieu and Passeron's reproduction theory – is that social structures and cultures are continually reproduced through the social action of subjects. Archer's historicising rectification stressed the 'iterative and mutative dimension' of this incessant activity, the way in which *previous* structuration provides the context for, and the constitution of, the 'subjects about to act', and the way in which the effects of their consequent action *in that moment* (t1) are likely to partially confirm, but may also partially modify, the *new structuration* of the social field and the subjects within it, in which (now at t2) further consequent action *in a new moment* takes place.

What are the implications? What became most important for us in Sostris, and difficult for sociologists and social policy experts to do, is to assume that we *do not already know*, for a given moment, what the overall social structure or social policy context *really is*.

Since we do not know what the structural context is of the subjects (or agents) whose lives we are studying, we therefore cannot fit their unknown lives into a known structure or into an existing classification of an existing social policy regime. At the level of the individual case, we do not know how the general social structure or the overall policy regime actually works[7]. We are *waiting for the case – for several cases – to tell us* (see Chamberlayne and King, 2001).

If the underdetermined and changeable life course of the individual develops *within* and *as part of* the under-determined and changeable life course of the social, what are the implications for the concept of transition as we try to 'do' the biography of the social?

We like to think – politicians, social scientists and policy makers alike – that 'in a transition' we know what we are in transition *to*. We like to think we know where we are headed, even if we admit to not knowing the details of the life journey involved. Gellner argued (1965) that this is a device to conceal an unwelcome truth. We know we are no longer capable of staying who we were; but we do not want to think that we *do not know* who – or what – we might become (what our world might be like) once this transition is complete.

The real truth about historical transitions is that there is no end to transiting and, for any transition, there is *no final stable-state guaranteed outcome*. The absence of a guaranteed meta-narrative is the absence of this guarantee, or of end of history, or of end of agency[8].

However, this also means that we can always continue to imagine alternative possibilities; no reason ever to believe the Blatcher-Brown neoliberal mantra of TINA ('there is no alternative'), no reason to consider that dystopia is unavoidable, no reason to stop hoping (Bloch, 1986). The narrative direction we hope our fought-for transition will take and the provisional outcome we hope it will have is not guaranteed; however, neither can our opponents guarantee the success of what (from our point of view) is their anti-narrative, the story that guides their counter-policy. Although we do not know where this transition will take us (and them), we do know we can fight for the direction we want it to take.

To return to our original question. The 'socio' we are trying to think with in our sociobiographical approach may be relatively determined for its past, up to and including the moment of writing. However, it can never be determined, indeed it is always underdetermined, for the future of who we are, and the 'biographies' of the social we are trying to understand and inflect.

What are the practical implications for methodology?

Such a historicisation of the 'socio' helps us avoid, or at least recognise faster, two mistakes of method that can be seen as profoundly linked: insufficiently critical notions of the typical model and of the known model.

Mistake I: hoping to discover the *typicality* of cases[9]

The original Sostris approach was formulated in a paper by Mike Rustin (1998). It argued that the way in which the individual life history would contribute to sociological understanding is to be by way of identifying the typical.

> The aim of the project is to investigate the realities of exclusion, and responses made to it, as social as well as individual phenomena. We are concerned to investigate the meanings of social exclusion *for typical subjects in specified typical contexts of social structure.* We are interested in the individual lives of our subjects, but especially in as much as we can identify their socially-typical features.... Perhaps our key methodological problem is how to identify in individual life-stories those features which are representative or typical of their societal context. (Rustin, 1998, p 112, emphasis added)

Intensive qualitative research never achieves a large enough extensive sample for statistical generalisation. Even if all our cases from across all seven countries had come from one country only, they could not have achieved statistical 'representativeness'. Demonstrating or proving 'typicality' or 'representativeness' was consequently impossible in Sostris for this reason alone. We were well aware of this feature of intensive study of relatively few cases (Scheff [1997] makes a completely convincing case for comparisons between a small number [low-N] of cases), and never attempted nor required 'statistical' typicality.

However, a question might be raised. Could the aim have been revised to become that of putting forward ideas – through Sostris acting as an exploratory qualitative study – of 'possibly typical cases', *hypotheses* to be proved or disproved by later survey research on a large enough large-N sample?

> Our problem as researchers is to clarify how the social contexts which frame our subjects' life-histories are constituted, what are their most causally significant features, and in what ways they are typical of an historical moment or of a distinctive social space [or 'field'; see Appendix A of this volume]. (Rustin, 1998, p 113)

Unfortunately, such a superficially plausible rewrite of the aims would fall foul of a much greater problem. What were these 'typical social contexts' in terms of which we would explore the cases to be notionally found 'in' them?

The trouble was that we had no given list of distinctive historical moments – or 'social spaces' – let alone social contexts, and consequently hypotheses about the typicality or otherwise of any one of them could not be tested.

The search for 'typical subjects in specified typical contexts of (a known and fixed) social structure' – or 'typical subjects at specified typical moments of a (known) historical process' (and they are not that different) – therefore turned out to be a problematic aim for Sostris.

Since we began with life stories structured by the subjects themselves, we could not *anticipate* the social contexts that were going to turn out to be relevant to an individual's biography. Each narration led us on a journey into a different and specific life world, social structure and culture. Given restructuration theory (Archer, 1995), each moment of the individual's life had to be thought of as being in a mutating life world, structure and culture. Sometimes this mutation of world and context was abrupt and obvious (see Chapter Two of this volume), at other times subtle and barely perceptible.

Perhaps the best way of characterising what we found ourselves doing is that we were no longer attempting to hypothesise the typical; rather, we were 'learning about the possibilities of the present from the variety of the actual' in ways that could not be pinned down to, and exhausted by, a finite set of theoretical propositions[10]. (We hope this may, to some extent, have happened also to you in the reading of this book.)

Mistake 2: expecting to start from, or achieve, a common meta-narrative or macro-model

Implicit in the previous account is a second problem. More often without realising it than being very conscious of it, we tried to develop a common macro-narrative, a narrative of macro-change – or a common meta-model construed in more static terms but implying such a meta-narrative nonetheless – into which all the case histories of our individuals would fit.

This took the form of imagined departure points, terminus points, or one-word process descriptions of a sociological sort. Departure points were those inherent in all words with the prefix 'post-', such as postmodern, or post-industrial, or post-Fordist. Terminus points were those inherent in *characterisations of the process* as a transition: exclusion, military and monetary global restructuring, modernisation, individualisation, fluidisation, retreat of state welfare, and so on; or those identified by a *putative end state*, or *now state:* risk society, network society, world domination by multinational corporations, privatised welfare society, and so on.

Our mistake was not that we considered such a number of these models and meta-narratives of possibilities and tendencies. It was right and productive to do so. Our mistake, rather, was that we tended to think, and found it very hard not to assume, that, either as a starting point for understanding cases or as a Sostris finding emergent *after* our study of all the cases, we should:

- be able to fix on one;
- know what the end of history actually was;
- be clear what epoch we are passing through;
- know the end of the transition and therefore agree on what the transition was[11].

Unfortunately, the transition is ongoing. The battles have not yet been settled, and so the future is not yet known. Our sketches of the 'whole society and its historical movement' are necessarily no more than suggestive. We can suggest some of the contradictions of the macro-order as it appears in the contradictory-movement of history and histories, but only as *glimpses.*

The more we studied the complexity of cases, and the more we took account of the psychosocial dynamics of lives, the less plausible became any attempt to decide on a master narrative (or main model) to the exclusion of the tendencies and counter-tendencies identified by all the others. The chapters of this volume do typically consider cases in relation to arguments about a variety of contradictory processes (both macro and micro, let alone meso). However, we think the suggestive power of such arguments is strengthened rather than weakened by the fact that *no single model or meta-narrative* constrains the discussions that they generate together (nor the chapters of this book that they inform).

The nature of the future at any point (the present) is open, where a retrospective biographising of an individual or of a world society occurs, and after which a different perspective occurs from which a different biographising would emerge. Therefore, a non-chaotic *multiplication* of such perspectives for existing or possible biographies of actual existing societies seems the most robust way of preparing for observing – and inflecting –the future.

So far we have argued that historicising the 'socio' in sociobiography means multiplying the number of available meta-narratives and models of the 'biography of (world) society' that might illuminate the cases being considered (rather than foreclosing prematurely on any one). This also means learning about the possibilities of the present from the varieties of the actual.

However, we must now go beyond the notion of illumination or being suggestive. Illumination suggests passivity; we need a guide to an active research practice. We return again to a question posed before: how do we relate a case (or cases) to such a multiplicity of meta-models and meta-narratives? Just saying 'Multiply them!' is not enough.

The 'actual' as an anomaly for previous (grand or grounded) theory

Do we use cases to confirm, disprove, or rectify theory? There are different ways of relating a 'case' to a 'generalisation' of which it might be an instance. One way is to ask if it is a confirming instance of the theory in question. Another way – which is perhaps more 'creative' as a response to existing theory – is to play the case against the theory, to show it as flatly disproving the theory, a 'disconfirming instance'. Simply treating the case as illustrative or 'confirming instance' fails to advance the theory. Simply finding a theory that the case 'disproves' eliminates the theory, and thereby fails to advance it also. However, treating the case as an opportunity to rectify an existing theory is much more creative. What might this mean? Burawoy (1991) argues strongly that his 'extended case method' (each particular historical situation is a case) works to reconstruct existing social theory "by constituting the social situation as anomalous with regard to some pre-existing theory":

> The extended case method derives generalisations by constituting the social
> situation as anomalous with regard to some preexisting theory (that is, an
> existing body of generalizations), which then is reconstructed. (Burawoy,
> 1991, pp 280-1)

We agree. In addition, thinking comparatively, and reconstructing (rectifying) theory that previously could not account for the cases that were anomalous for it, also leads to enriching our understanding of the case. The accumulation of cases analysed in their own terms leads to the moment of constant inter-case comparison and the rectification of theories, but this moment of inter-case comparison should have a double output:

(a) the 'reconstruction' of existing theory(ies); but also
(b) the reconsideration of the significance and even the description of the already-analysed cases[12].

The classic formulations of GT only concern themselves with the generation of theory, not with any return to the cases, and the theory they are concerned with is a formal, dehistoricised one. We shall try to show that the constant comparative method is richer than their use of it.

The dominant drive for Glaser and Strauss's GT approach is to start from within the particularity of the particular case but then to drive towards higher and more abstract and more general theorisation. The classical goal of GT research tends to be the elaboration of some (grounded) general theoretical propositions. Breckner and Rupp put this well:

> On the next step of comparison, the similarities and differences between the different fields of problems under investigation (such as lone parenthood and long-term unemployment) could be approached with the aim of constructing hypotheses about the general and specific mechanisms operating in different social fields and the challenges. This step can be extended to an unlimited variety of social phenomena and social fields, aiming at gaining more and more wide-ranging and abstract theoretical concepts that can explain common mechanisms of social action and perception while remaining empirically based at the same time.... In Sostris, the question of how the analysed responses formed part of general biographical and socio-structural patterns developing as a response to risk situations and social exclusion in Western European societies (in comparison with East Germany as representing an Eastern European society in transition). Sostris also examined the way in which these patterns were bound to national and local conditions and how they could have been approached by a comparison *across* different categories and *across* different countries. This was the most general level that the Sostris research was designed to attain. (Appendix A, p 301)

This drive towards the most "wide-ranging and abstract theoretical concepts" is definitely one line of development of grounded theorists ambitious for theory. In our Sostris work, we were certainly concerned to do this, moving inductively from particular cases to generalising theory. However, in retrospect, we found our relation to GT more complicated and conflictual than we at first realised.

Grounded Theory in many of its uses has been solely preoccupied with establishing a strongly generalising theory in which the first case of (say) nursing care is explored for its relatively general features. This generalising model is rectified and developed by each of the succeeding cases until saturation is reached, where each new case adds nothing to the grounded generalisations (about nursing care) that have been developed so far. The grounded theory achievement is then the generalisations that have been generated, a generic theory of nursing care, for example.

These generalisations often take the form of typologies, 'typified' kinds of social role and social process. Glaser and Strauss (1967) used the idea of 'status passage'; in this volume a distinction has been between blocked and non-blocked life journeys, and between inadequate and sufficient levels of reflexivity, among others. Our conclusions (presented in Chapter Fifteen of this volume) support such relatively abstract typologies and, and Appendix A provides a rationale for such work.

What is the problem, then? Two aspects can be considered: one has to do with the abstraction of micro-interaction from their contexts; the other with the loss of historical specificity of cases. The two points are not necessarily related, but empirically often are.

The abstraction of micro-interactions from their contexts

One main weakness of Glaser's and Strauss's use of their own methodology has been its social structural 'thinness' – the focus on micro-interaction. One might say that in their reaction to the previous dominant paradigm of functionalist systems theory, and in their symbolic interactionist commitment to recognising the subjective perspective of the actor, Glaser and Strauss were averse to broader social structural approaches, regarding them perhaps as sociologically determinist. In other words, in their American interactionist way, Glaser and Strauss were more sensitive to their subjects' own capacity to generate social meaning than to the structures and cultures that constrain and form this process. Their preferred method of generating social theory inductively is synchronous here with their implicit theory of how social reality is generated from interactive experience, a constructivist perspective which was taken to a more extreme point by the ethno-methodological approach of Harold Garfinkel and his followers.

Layder (1993, pp 51-70) is helpful here in suggesting the ways in which issues of power and other macro-structural and macro-institutional features can be obscured or denied by inductive research refusing to go beyond the phenomenological discourse and immediate behaviour of the face-to-face interviewee.

> What seems to be missing from the interactionist's analytical scenario is a parallel concern with the wider, structural or macro aspects of social life, as they are implicated in the ... phenomena which are their characteristic focus .... Situated activity possesses its own partly independent properties, but it is a mistake to imagine that the micro-world is self-contained and self-sufficient. Everyday behaviour takes place against the backdrop of wider social, economic and political circumstances which impress themselves upon this behaviour just as much as these circumstances may be seen as the eventual product or outcome of this type of behaviour.... The very fixity of this concentration [of grounded theory on micro phenomena] is a factor which prevents grounded theory from attending to historical matters of macro-structure as a means of

enriching contemporary or, as we shall call them, present-centred forms of research on micro-phenomena. It should be possible to augment the processual and dynamic analyses of interactional phenomena by a parallel focus on the historically antecedent forms that provide their institutional backdrop. (Layder, 1993, pp 67-8)

Our more 'European' concern for the structural and for the macro (not just the interactional and the micro) is one definite difference. There is, however, a further difference – a concern for historical specificity (of both macro *and* micro).

Our concern for the historical specificity of particular cases

A further problem with the classic GT approach, from our point of view, is the way that the specificity of particular cases is *lost* in its subsumption by a generic and generalising theory. To take the earlier nursing hypothesis as an example, a GT search to discover the universals of nursing care involves not a concern for different specific configurations of such care but for stripping away the particularities in order to discover the universal. Differences are the trivia: the concern is for the *general*, the most abstract and wide-ranging theoretical concepts.

While a concern for the general is certainly one part of Sostris' programme, it is not the only one. We were also concerned to develop and protect our news of difference. A consequence of our assumptions concerning constant mutation in a truly historicised understanding of the 'socio' is that our grounded theory has to use very general concepts. Yes, indeed, but it must be above all a grounded theory using such general concepts *to grasp and convey historical differences, and unique configurations.*

From our point of view, therefore, classic Grounded Theorising subsumes particular cases too quickly under transhistorical generalities, and this is true even at the level of the micro-interactions that it favours (for example, different cases of nursing care in the US). At the level of the macro-structural features (different organisations of health regimes and hospitals for the elite and for the residuum in Nazi Germany, Soviet Russia, Sweden, the US and the UK), it tends to have little to say. Classic GT neglects such a macro-structural level, yes, but even if it did not, it would try to find common features rather than explain historically the historical differences between regimes.

We follow the methodology of inductive inference from particulars established within the GT protocols but, in contrast to the eagerly generalising and interaction-focused approach of Glaser and Strauss, in our Sostris approach we make more 'European' assumptions of structural and cultural constraints and have, we think, in the first place, a stronger orientation to the specificity and uniqueness of cases. *We do not want the richness of cases to be lost by being simply displaced by and being hidden behind formal transhistorical generalities* (universal theoretical propositions).

Burawoy (1991; and see also Ragin, 1987) provides a useful summary of this point: and that of the historical (genetic, biographical) focus of research that historicises the 'socio':

> The extended case method constructs *genetic* explanations, that is, explanations of particular outcomes. An example would be Weber's analysis of the historically specific constellation of forces, including the motivational component provided by the Protestant ethic, which gave rise to Western bourgeois capitalism. A generic strategy looks for similarity among disparate cases, whereas the genetic strategy focuses on differences between similar cases. The goal of the first is to seek abstract laws or formal theory, whereas the goal of the second is historically specific causality. (Burawoy, 1991, p 281)

One of the goals of our research is to be able to return to the particular historical cases, and the particular historicised social from which we began, but a return enriched by the experience of the constant comparative method intrinsic to GT. There is generalising from case comparisons, yes, and the 'reconstruction' of theory that occurs there, yes; but there is also what might be called *reparticularising* as well. The development of higher-order and more general arguments that does not take the understanding of other particular cases any further – or makes them less intelligible – fails the value-added test (in this discourse, 'value' is the degree of case understanding of several cases).

The constant comparative method, which Glaser and Strauss identified as the key component in their approach, points both to the generalising and universalising project of formal grounded theories (which, perhaps unfortunately, is the name by which their approach became known) but also to the return to the concrete case (that variety of an actualised historical possibility) in which they were less interested but in which we are more interested.

Burawoy remarks, in respect of the Chicago School, that "the search for transhistorical laws obscured real history, the seismic shifts in the political and social landscape of the 1920s and 1930s" (2000, p 12). We could say that, where the danger for historians is that they are so keen to return to their particular case that they only leave it for thinking more conceptually and generally for too short a time, the danger for sociologists is that they are so keen to rise to the level of generalities and universalities that they are too quick to leave the concrete historical cases, and too reluctant to return to them.

The constant comparative method

Constant comparison of cases with each other, and with theory: an oscillating practice

However, we think there is more common ground than Burawoy suggests between a generalising and historicising approach. The locus of such common ground between Sostris historising sociobiography (and perhaps Burawoy's approach, but perhaps not) and GT generalising lies in the zone of the constant comparative method.

After the case summary is completed and presented, the workshops generalise from a particular case, yes, but also test any more general concepts by reparticularising for other cases. They attempt to show the way the new theorising arising from case B adds value to the understanding of each of the other particular cases, A and potentially C. However, after any given comparative session, some were more concerned with elaborating the more general concepts that the constant comparison workshop had thrown up, while others were more concerned with reanalysing the cases in the light of the new insights and conceptualisations achieved. After the next session, different people might follow these paths of further development of understanding.

Re-equilibrating between externalist and internalist modes of comparing

How does this comparison happen? We can distinguish two impulses in this process of case comparison, each of which can lose its way or become excessive. One is an 'external-aspect rotation model'; the other is an 'internal case-dynamic/ configuration model'.

- External-aspect rotation cases can be compared by any analytic or descriptive category available within a discipline or discourse prior to and external to the case being considered, for looking at life courses or social situations. The danger of the external-aspect approach is that (a) there are no limits to the number of such definable aspects; (b) there is no necessity from within the cases for any one or any other aspect to be selected or ignored. Most qualitative researchers have had some experience of developing matrices of analytical aspects that, in a search for an impossible completeness, got so complicated they had to be abandoned. The mind's capacity to hold aspects in mind, let alone use them, is strictly limited.
- Internal case-dynamic/configuration models stick very closely to the grounded and often case-specific categories and accounts of the case as developed by the researcher plunged into all the detail of their case. Such internal saturation in the psychosocial dynamics of the case in context, as resumed in the case history and in the case structure, means more of a case-to-case free association method of thinking, rather than an external aspect-by-aspect rotation. The danger here is that there is no way of ensuring that whole-case to whole-case free-associative thinking will be systematic or produce thinking that will be productive of general concepts or theories relating to any disciplinary field, or even to the Sostris research questions!

My sense is that the Sostris team often moved between such externalist and internalist practices of constant comparison in a rather under-conscious way. We were struggling for systematic thinking and for the elaboration/rectification of appropriate theory concerning social strategies in risk society. However, sometimes there were revolts against a system that seemed to stultify intuitions, and sometimes a revolt against too much intuitive work that was starting to lose its way. There is probably no equilibrium position in the messy practice: only, like bicycle riding, constant corrections of successive disequlibria!

Conclusion

A final point about the (re)presentation of our work in this volume. If, as is argued elsewhere, general concepts are always imbricated in any case description whatsoever (Wengraf, 2001, pp 302-10), and if all general mega-models and meta-narratives only have real meanings if they are spelled out in the imaginary and the reality of particular historical cases and stories, then constant comparison always points in both directions. Therefore, it should improve, and be tested by, better articulations of our general concepts and by better articulations of the variety of the actual that our empirical work permits.

The interaction between the conceptual and the empirical that good use of the constant comparative method can do so much to enhance can be stultified by either:

- generic concepts and theorising that are not interested in reilluminating the particularity of individual case histories;
- case-history descriptions that turn a blind eye to discussing and improving the conceptual bases of their own descriptions and to the theories implicit in those case descriptions.

Hopefully, the methodology of the presentation of cases/theorising in this book maintains an overall 'corrected disequilibrium' and a fruitful interaction between case description and conceptual discussion[13].

Notes

[1] A first formulation of this was in Rustin (1998, p 112): "This research programme elicits its primary data from individual life-histories ... but the aim of the project is *to investigate the reality of exclusion, and responses to it as social* as well as individual *phenomena*" (emphasis added).

[2] We wanted inappropriate social policy to be seen for what it was — destructive, or at least a wasteful alibi. Of course, our research was orientated towards distinguishing which of the two.

[3] In an influential publication, Benedict Anderson (1983) drew attention to the cultural construction of collective identities as inseparable from the phenomenon of nationalism. One could say, that collective folk biography contributes to the 'social being' of all societies.

[4] And, of course, those researched by hundreds of other researchers. See, for the 'risky' First World, Bourdieu (1999) and Davies (1997). For many in the Third World, the new world order of the Washington-dominated North already means the drain of resources to the North, military devastation by the North or its client states, the designed economic correlate of malnutrition and impoverishment, and migrations of populations fleeing death by war or famine or a thousand WTO/IMF-imposed cuts.

[5] The truth of the deregulation of the labour markets of the North can be seen in the more advanced deregulation of the South and some of the East with its liquidation first of a living wage and then of formerly living labour.

[6] At both collective and individual levels, biographies of 'agency' are to some extent incoherent and strain after consistency and strategy. Therefore, they are open to greater and more adequate reflexivity, contain at any given moment a variety of different courses of action that could be taken, and always contain the possibility of conscious agency for seeing and doing differently.

[7] If we do not know how it works, then we do not know what it is. This is an operational definition of *knowing*. There is a weaker sense of knowing – for example, knowing the welfare legislation and rhetoric of a given regime or society – but it is one that keeps us blind to our own ignorance and reduces the impulse to explore the social as a still-too-unknown country.

[8] The valuable contribution of the struggle against the dominance of meta-narratives that preoccupied a lot of Western social theory some time ago was that it has built such an awareness into much social thinking. On the other hand, this meta-meta-narrative (that meta-narratives should not be accepted) can have its own pernicious consequences – a postmodernist denial of reality, for example, or a denial of any value in trying to understand it.

[9] The discussion of the 'typical' is a critique of Rustin (1998). Rustin (personal communication) argues that this case against the notion of the 'typical' is overstated. He argues that "we do undoubtedly seek inferences from particular cases to the 'typical', in the senses for example in which we interpret phenomena which are due to gender differences, to Southern as opposed to Northern social patterns, to the crisis of corporatism, etc. Another way of putting this is that we move from the particular to the general…. Without this 'inductive generalisation' and 'part–whole analysis', we don't think we would be doing socio-biographical analysis at all, but just describing lots of unique cases in the manner of much largely descriptive oral history". Although I agree with the practice of Sostris, I remain unhappy about the implications of the term 'typical'. However, I agree with Rustin's argument that, in sections of this chapter, I "go a bit overboard on contingency".

[10] This relates to a key feature of the BNIM approach we used. At different moments in analysing the data of the lived life and of the told story, there is a constant stress on

imagining possible alternative life decisions, alternative outcomes and the significance of the choices actually made (Wengraf, 2000, pp 149-59; 2001, pp 302-9).

[11] The very title of the project – *Social strategies in risk societies* (Sostris) – might be taken that we knew that the society was to be best characterised as a 'risk society', and made a promise to emerge with a list of (typical or exhaustive) social strategies pursued in such a society, or at least in the transition to such a society.

[12] Other forms of knowledge generation from individual cases adopt similar heuristic procedures. Rustin (2001) has argued that psychoanalytic theory has developed since its origins through a continuing interaction between received theories and anomalous case experiences, each being subject to reinterpretation in the light of the other. This, he argues, has been the driving force of development of psychoanalytic ideas, at least within the British object-relations tradition that has been notable for its clinical case-oriented approach.

[13] For a discussion of the relation between theorising and narrative presentation, see Wengraf (2001, pp 347-54, 362-5).

References

Allport, G. (1962) 'The general and the unique in psychological science', *Journal of Personality*, vol 30, pp 405-22, (reprinted in P. Reason and J. Rowan (eds) (1981) *Human inquiry: A sourcebook of new paradigm research*, Chichester: John Wiley & Sons, pp 63-76).

Anderson, B. (1983) *Imagined communities: Reflections on the origin and spread of nationalism*, London: Verso.

Archer, M.S. (1995) *Realist social theory: The morphogenetic approach*, Cambridge: Cambridge University Press.

Ragin, C. and Becker, E. (1992) *What is a case? Exploring the foundations of social inquiry*, Cambridge: Cambridge University Press.

Bloch, E. (1986) *The principle of hope*, Oxford: Basil Blackwell.

Bourdieu, P. et al (1999) *The weight of the world: Social suffering in contemporary society*, Cambridge: Polity Press (shortened version of their *La misère du monde*, Paris: Editions du Seuil, 1993).

Breckner, R. (1998) 'The biographical–interpretive method: principles and procedures', in *Sostris Working Paper 2: Case study materials – the early retired*, London: Centre for Biography in Social Policy, University of East London, pp 99-104.

Burawoy, M., Burton, A., Ferguson, A., Fox, K., Gamson, J., Gartrell, N., Hurst, L., Kurzman, C., Salzinger, L., Schiffman, J. and Shiori, U. (1991) *Ethnography unbound: Power and resistance in the modern metropolis*, Berkeley, CA: University of California Press.

Burawoy, M. (2000) 'Introduction: reaching for the global', in M. Burawoy, J. Blum, S. George, Z. Gille, T. Gowan, L. Haney, M. Klawiter, S. Lopez, S. O'Riain, M. Thayer *Global ethnography: Forces connections and imaginations in a postmodern world,* Berkeley: University of California Press, pp 1-40.

Chamberlayne, P., Cooper, A., Freeman, R. and Rustin, M. (eds) (1999) *Welfare and culture in Europe: Towards a new paradigm in social policy*, London: Jessica Kingsley.

Chamberlayne, P. (2000) *Cultures of care: Biographers of carers in Britain and the two Germanies*, Bristol: The Policy Press.

Chamberlayne, P., Bornat, J. and Wengraf, T. (2000a) 'Introduction: the biographical turn' in P. Chamberlayne, J. Bornat and T. Wengraf (eds) *The turn to biographical methods in social science: Comparative issues and examples*, London: Routledge, pp 1-30.

Chamberlayne, P., Bornat, J. and Wengraf, T. (eds) (2000b) *The turn to biographical methods in social science: Comparative issues and examples*, London: Routledge.

Davies, N. (1997) *Dark heart: The shocking truth about hidden Britain*, London: Chatto and Windus.

Gellner, E. (1965) *Thought and change*, Chicago, IL: University of Chicago.

Glaser, N. and Strauss, A. (1967) *The discovery of grounded theory*, Chicago, IL: Aldine.

Layder, D. (1998) *Sociological practice: Linking theory and social research*, London: Sage Publications.

McDonald, T.J. (ed) (1996) *The historic turn in the human sciences* Ann Arbor, MI: University of Michigan Press.

Polkinghorne, D.E. (1995) 'Narrative configuration in qualitative analysis', in J. Hatch and R. Wisniewski (eds) *Life history and narrative*, London: Falmer, pp 5-23.

Ragin, C. (1987) *The comparative method: Moving beyond qualitative and quantitative strategies*, Berkeley, CA: University of California.

Ragin, C. and Becker, H. (1992) *What is the case? Exploring the foundations of social enquiry,* Cambridge: Cambridge University Press.

Rustin, M.J. (1998) 'From individual life histories to sociological understanding', in *Sostris Working Paper 3: Case study materials – lone parents*, London: Centre for Biography in Social Policy, University of East London, pp 112-19.

Rustin, M.J. (2001) 'Give me a consulting room: the generation of psychoanalytic knowledge', in *Reason and unreason: Psychoanalysis, science and politics*, London: Continuum Books, pp 30-51.

Scheff, T. (1997) 'Part-whole morphology: unifying single case and comparative methods', in *Emotions, the social bond and human reality: Part-whole analysis*, Cambridge: Cambridge University Press, pp 19-52.

Sostris (1998) *Sostris Working Paper 2: Case study materials – the early retired*, London: Centre for Biography in Social Policy, University of East London.

Wengraf, T. (1998) 'Sostris at the level of the comparative study of cases', in *Sostris Working Paper 3: Case study materials – lone parents*, London: Centre for Biography in Social Policy, University of East London, pp 120-7.

Wengraf, T. (2000) 'Uncovering the general from within the particular: from contingencies to typologies in the understanding of cases', in P. Chamberlayne, J. Bornat and T. Wengraf (eds) *The turn to biographical methods in social science: Comparative issues and examples*, London: Routledge, pp 140-64.

Wengraf, T. (2001) *Qualitative research interviewing: Biographic narrative and semi-structured method*, London: Sage Publications.

Wiersma, J. (1992) 'Karen: the transforming story', in G.C. Rosenwald and R.L. Ochberg (eds) *Storied lives: The cultural politics of self-understanding*, New Haven, CT: Yale University Press.

Index

Entries for case studies are in *italics*
Page references for notes are followed by n
A separate index for cited references is provided at the end

A

absenteeism 208
active welfare policies 74
Afro-Caribbeans 242-3
  see also Steven
agencies *see* social agencies
agency 4, 324n
Ahmet 181
alcoholism 90, 92, 123
Ali 181
Alice 200, 201
Ana 217-19, 223, 224-5, 274, 277
Andreas 182, 184
Anna 180
Aphrodite 179-80, 189
Apollo 134, 147n
ascription 152
auto-constraints and hetero-constraints
  56

B

Barcelona 209n, 258, 263-4n
Bauhof youth training programmes
  (Halle) 254, 257, 258, 263n
Berlin Wall 36-7, 65, 66, 219
Bernard 58n, 115, 116, 121-3, 125-6, 275
biographical blockage 23-4, 26, 274, 277,
  319
  see also Heike; Nicolás
biographical dynamics 23, 26, 31, 72,
  214, 217, 224, 247, 262, 277, 280, 285,
  285n
biographical method 18n, 289-90, 291
biographical resources 16, 37-8, 52, 73,
  116-18, 126, 239, 276, 278, 280-1, 284
  see also Harold; Zenon
Biographical Narrative Interpretive
  Method (BNIM) 2-5, 284-5, 310-11,
  324-5n
  analysis 295-9
  generalisation 299-302
  interviews 293-5

and migration 216-25, 226
and mobile societies 8-10
and social agencies 247-8, 249, 260-1,
  262
and social change 271, 276-7
and social policy 78-9, 278, 283-4,
  302-3
and society 312-14
texts as strategies 292-3
biographical work 12, 146, 243, 247-62,
  276-8, 284
see also Steven
blocked journeys *see* biographical
  blockage
Bosnia 217-18, 272
Britain *see* United Kingdom
Broca, La (Barcelona) 258, 263n
Bromley-by-Bow Centre 249-53, 254,
  257, 258, 264n, 281

C

Caisse d'allocations familiales 54-5, 283
Camden Refugee Education Project
  254-5, 264n
case dynamics *see* internal case-dynamic/
  configuration models
case studies 16-17, 323
  biographical analysis 295-9
  comparing 300-2, 318-9
  constant comparison of 321-3
  generalisation 299-302
  historical specificity 320-1
  and theory 317-18
  typicality 314-15
case (re)construction 23, 36, 53, 64, 243,
  248, 292-3, 302-3
Chicago School 290, 321
Chile 202, 205, 206-7
Christina 188-9
Christopher 196-7, 198-9
Christos 180
civil society 14, 283, 285
class 77-8, 167, 181

Index to references